D0934745

THE ARABIAN PENINSULA

THE ARABIAN PENINSULA
Society and Politics

EDITED BY

DEREK HOPWOOD

St Antony's College, Oxford

ROWMAN AND LITTLEFIELD
TOTOWA, NEW JERSEY

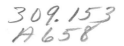

First published in 1972

This book is copyright under the Berne Convention. All rights are reserved. Apart from any fair dealing for the purpose of private study, research, criticism or review, as permitted under the Copyright Act, 1956, no part of this publication may be reproduced, stored in a retrieval system, or transmitted, in any form or by any means, electronic, electrical, chemical, mechanical, optical, photocopying recording or otherwise, without the prior permission of the copyright owner. Enquiries should be addressed to the publishers.

© George Allen & Unwin Ltd, 1972

First published in the United States 1972
by Rowman and Littlefield, Totowa, New Jersey

ISBN 0-87471-122-3

Printed in Great Britain

FOREWORD

In the Lent Term of the academic year 1968–69, the Centre of Middle Eastern Studies at the School of Oriental and African Studies, University of London and the Middle East Centre of St Antony's College, Oxford, held a joint Seminar on the Arabian Peninsula. Staff and students from both institutions attended the meetings of the Seminar, which was followed by a three-day conference held at the School in London in March 1969. In addition to members of the staff of both institutions, other invited scholars from Middle Eastern countries, the United States of America and the United Kingdom participated in the conference. The papers which were presented were subsequently prepared for the press by Dr Derek Hopwood of St Antony's College. They represent the opinions of their individual authors. It is our hope that their publication will not only provide students of the Middle East with an introduction to the social economic and political problems of Arabia and the Persian Gulf, but also generate wider interest in further research and study of the area. During the last few years a happy and fruitful academic co-operation has been established between the staff and students of the School's Centre of Middle Eastern Studies and the Middle East Centre at Oxford. We are grateful to both institutions for their financial and administrative support in holding this Seminar and Conference. We also wish to thank the Kuwait Oil Company and the Shell Company for their generous grants in aid. Finally, we should like to thank the Publications Committee of the School for its help towards the publication of this volume and Diana Grimwood-Jones for having prepared the index.

August 1970

A. H. HOURANI, *Oxford*
P. J. VATIKIOTIS, *London*

NOTE ON TRANSLITERATION

The transliteration has been made uniform throughout. Diacritical marks, apart from 'ain (ᶜ) and hamza ('), have not been used. The only exceptions are slight variations in Omani place names and in the note on sources in J. C. Wilkinson's paper where diacritical marks have been used. The maps to this paper also use a slightly different system of transliteration.

CONTENTS

NOTES ON THE CONTRIBUTORS

ABU-HAKIMA, A. M.   Professor in the University of Jordan.

BATHURST, R. D.   Engaged for several years in political liaison with tribes and governments in the Gulf and Oman.

BURRELL, R. M.   Lecturer in the Contemporary History of the Near and Middle East at the School of Oriental and African Studies, University of London.

HOPWOOD, DEREK   Middle Eastern Bibliographer, Oxford University and St Antony's College, Oxford.

KELIDAR, ABBAS   Lecturer in the Politics of the Near and Middle East at the School of Oriental and African Studies, University of London.

KELLY, J. B.   Professor of British Imperial History, University of Wisconsin.

LIENHARDT, PETER   Faculty Lecturer in Middle Eastern Sociology in the University of Oxford, and College Lecturer, St Antony's College, Oxford.

LUQMAN, ALI M.   Journalist and poet from Aden.

PENROSE, EDITH   Professor of Economics with reference to Asia, University of London.

RENTZ, GEORGE   Curator, Middle Eastern Collection, Hoover Institution, Stanford University, Stanford, California.

SAYIGH, YUSIF   Professor of Economics at the American University of Beirut.

†SHEA, THOMAS W.   Senior Economist, Arabian American Oil Co. (previously Assistant Professor of Economics and Statistics, Villanova University).

STOAKES, FRANK   Lecturer in Government, University of Manchester.

WILKINSON, J. C.   Lecturer in the Geography of the Middle East, University of Oxford.

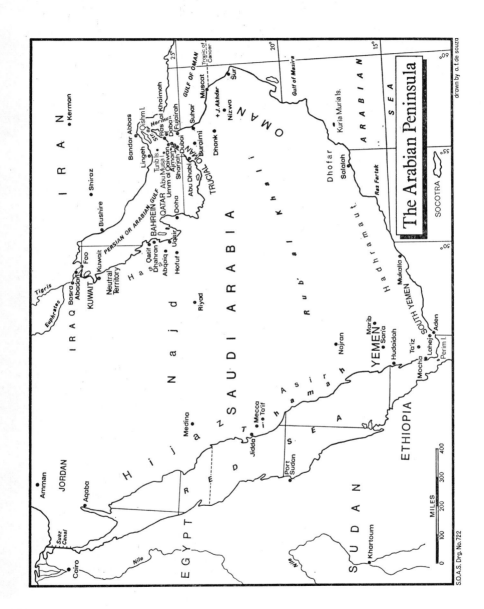

The Arabian Peninsula

drawn by o. f. de souza

S.O.A.S. Drg. No.722

BIBLIOGRAPHICAL SURVEY

I

SOME WESTERN STUDIES OF SAUDI ARABIA, YEMEN AND ADEN

DEREK HOPWOOD

Most Westerners writing on the Arab world fall into one of two categories. There are those for whom the 'reality' lies in the great cities of the Middle East. They contend that it is amid the throbbing life of these cities that political, economic and cultural history is made, that patterns of Arab history must be sought amongst the rulers, the ᶜ*ulama'*, the *harafīsh* of Cairo, the great families and notables of Damascus, or the merchants of Aleppo. Others approach the Arab world from the desert and feel at home with the 'pure' inhabitant of the desert or tribal world. To understand and write profoundly about this world almost always implies a first-hand and intimate knowledge of its inhabitants and its society. To isolate either of these two approaches implies a less than complete approach to the totality of the Arab world, but the writers of the papers in this volume have concentrated on one of them and it has been my task to look at studies written in the latter category.

The Arabian peninsula has attracted to itself a large number of devotees and almost all the works under consideration have been written as a result of first-hand experience, a situation which has begun to change only in very recent years when works based on documentary research have begun to appear. What has been written previously has been largely impressionistic travel literature (but often of a more than transitory value), professional journalism or political memoirs. Historians are only now starting to work in the field – by a historian I mean one who searches for and then investigates the patterns of past human life and by choosing those patterns which seem significant writes his history. The lack of historical works of this nature on nineteenth-century and twentieth-century Arabia is clear (although some of the papers in this volume now demonstrate this approach). A competent journalist or other personal observer can trace the story of contemporary or near contemporary events and often has the advantage of close acquaintance with local factors, but what he writes is not history.

The title originally assigned to this paper, 'Published Sources for the

Study of the Arabian Peninsula', was too wide to have much meaning and could presumably include anything from India Office records on the Persian Gulf and Aden, an incomparably dull subject to write about, to the wealth of descriptive and travel literature that has appeared on Arabia. Once government documents had been rejected the field was still extensive. The writings of the nineteenth century and earlier represented something perhaps strictly outside the scope of the conference, something approaching creative literature or the history of exploration. Moreover, writers such as Hogarth, Kiernan and Jacqueline Pirenne had all written the history of Arabian exploration and most of us have read (at least in part) Burton, Palgrave, Niebuhr, Burckhardt and Doughty. Nor would I want to dispute Lawrence's verdict that *Arabia Deserta* 'is the first and indispensable work upon the Arabs of the desert'. With a number of notable exceptions, the literature of the twentieth century on Arabia is more humdrum, less suitable to be classed as 'literature' but growing in volume especially in recent years. I have noted at least 150 books published since the Second World War. Clearly not all of these can be covered in a paper as short as this and some criteria of selection had to be established. I have omitted studies of the oil industry which, although of great relevance to the Arabian peninsula, are often of some technicality. The lighter books of memoirs have likewise been omitted, these with great reluctance as several of them display those peculiar and attractive qualities of affection, humour and tolerance shown by British servicemen overseas. What remains is a substantial number of studies of the peninsula, the Gulf states apart, and travel literature published by Western writers since the end of the Second World War which deal largely with contemporary or near contemporary affairs. I have divided these works geographically as nearly as possible.

A theme common to many of these works is, and has to be, the impact of modernity on traditional societies (using both those over-used terms without any value judgements attached). This conflict (explicit even in some of the titles, *Farewell to Arabia*, *Yemen on the Threshold*) is seen more sharply in the Arabian peninsula because resistance to change has been more prolonged than in other parts of the Arab world and because change has come only recently and swiftly. The changes have been described by different authors with impartiality, with regret for the fading of the 'immortal image of mystery that Arabia represented', with self-justification for systems and governments imposed and left behind, or together with an expression of that deep feeling aroused by solitude and the desert.

If we take the end of the Second World War as the starting point of this survey (and wars are taken as milestones in history even if they are not directly relevant to the area concerned) one of the first books to appear was Philby's *A Pilgrim in Arabia*,[1] his sixth book on Arabia. Although not all would agree with the inscription on his grave 'Greatest of Arabian Explorers', he was one of the most prolific. His biography remains to be written, but this I hope will soon be remedied. *A Pilgrim in Arabia* had first appeared three years earlier but in only a limited edition. His perceptive introduction showed clearly the state of mind of the Middle East during the war and he boldly stated of the Arabs: 'One and all . . . demand complete independence for all the Arab peoples' – a statement little heeded at the time. He also demolished the concept once popular among certain Britons that all Arabs instinctively liked them – 10 per cent he regarded as pro-British. In the first part of the book he described the pilgrimage in chapters of intrinsic interest to the student of Islam and worthy to stand beside those of Burton. Philby then moved on to politics and a certain pessimism crept in, a likely result of his differences with Ibn Saᶜud. The King was 'still the great man of Arabia . . . indispensable to its progress' but the guiding of the state into the modern world could no longer be the work of one man. The Wahhabis could govern a primitive, largely tribal society, but would find it increasingly difficult to deal with the economic and other pressures of the modern world.

Philby's autobiography, *Arabian Days*,[2] appeared in 1948 but somewhat belied its title since a substantial part of the work was devoted to the period of his life before he settled in Arabia. Once there his friendship with Ibn Saᶜud flowered until he became, as described by the king, 'leader of the opposition'. His earlier first steps in Arabia were taken when Sir Percy Cox, Chief Political Officer in Mesopotamia, sent him in an attempt to divert Ibn Saᶜud from his growing hostility towards Husain. It was to Philby's later satisfaction that he had reported then that the future of Arabia lay with Ibn Saᶜud and not Husain. On other occasions, notably in the introduction to *A Pilgrim in Arabia*, his predictions and the policies he advocated have proved to be correct, but his was often a lone voice.

Arabian Highlands[3] was one of Philby's authoritative travel books, but more than that it provided in great detail topographical, anthropological and much other information on the lands of ᶜAsir and Najran. It completed Philby's description of Arabia south of a line from ᶜUqair on the Persian Gulf to Jiddah. Of particular interest was the journey he made at the request of Ibn Saᶜud to inspect and map the Saudi Arabian-Yemen frontier. Dotted about the narrative there were also snippets of information on the functioning of Wahhabi rule in the south under those officials met in remote areas.

No Middle Eastern monarch has had a Boswell more assiduous than Philby, nor is a family history better known than that of Al Saᶜud. On the anniversary of fifty years of Ibn Saᶜud's absolute rule in Arabia Philby published *Arabian Jubilee*.[4] It was a record of unparalleled change under 'a great Wahhabi monarch', but one tempered with anxiety for the future. The portrait was one of a king disturbed by the currents he had set free and bewildered by the inroads of a world he did not fully welcome. The old man lost his fire towards the end of his reign and, in Philby's eyes, only occasionally regained it when back in familiar situations, settling desert disputes in conclave with his Bedouin sheikhs. In its auto-biographical aspect, *Arabian Jubilee* traced a relationship unique in Middle Eastern history, a meeting of east and west which ended in a clash of disparate views. The publication of the book was the occasion for bringing into the open Philby's dispute with the king's family, in which, as he wrote later, he 'opened his campaign against the increasingly prevalent laxity, extravagance and corruption'.

Philby's next work, *Saudi Arabia*,[5] chronicled the rise of Saudi power, an event in the history of Arabia 'second in importance only' to the rise of Islam. It was a detailed compilation of local history based on unrivalled access to local traditions and sources, written in the only possible way – with a deep understanding of Bedouin life and society. The outstanding theme was once more the development of the Wahhabi state through to its apogee under Ibn Saᶜud, but the reader throughout has to keep in mind the poignancy of the final tragedy – the confrontation between a puritan Islamic state and the secular world. Ibn Saᶜud could have done nothing to prepare his people for this. 'He came to the problems of the modern world as an amateur' and continued to the last the traditions of personal autocratic rule. The book was published after the death of Ibn Saᶜud and in a foreword Philby recognized that the material and spiritual climate of Arabia had undergone a permanent change, but despite grave problems he was not without hope for the future. The appointment of Faisal as President of the Council of Ministers was especially welcome.

Land of Midian[6] was a record of travels in north-west Arabia during the years 1950 to 1953. Philby had chosen to visit this area after Ibn Saᶜud had forbidden him to travel to Buraimi and Oman because of possible British suspicion of political motives. Midian was the land of the pre-Islamic kings of ᶜAd and Thamud and was on the spice route from the south. Philby was following in the footsteps of other Arabian explorers, Doughty, Burton, Musil and others (including Lawrence). His especial search was for ancient inscriptions. This was the last published account of Philby's journeys during which he had covered more of Arabia than any other western traveller. His accounts of travels, recorded in great detail, constitute a unique source of information but are written in a curiously flat and matter-of-fact style which bars them from the ranks of the greatest travel literature.

Forty Years in the Wilderness[7] was the perhaps ironic title of Philby's last work (apart from the posthumously published *Arabian Oil Ventures*),[8] but it was rather to John the Baptist, a voice crying in the wilderness, than to Moses who led the children of Israel out of the wilderness, that one must look for similarities (although Philby denied that he modelled his life on that of his namesake). For the beginning and end of this apologia were exile from Arabia for having raised his voice against contemporary corruption. Philby outstayed his welcome at the Saudi court, not because of his personal failings, but because both the nature of society and Britain's position in the world had changed. Philby had abandoned the western world to identify himself with a desert king's regime and felt betrayed when that regime began to betray its own ideals. In addition, the advice of a former official of the strongest power in the area became less valuable as that power lost its strength. He had also to bear the resentment felt against the close confidant of a former ruler by his heirs. He was not content to remain a silently discontented survivor of the *ancien régime* and the publication of works critical of the Saudis caused his exile. But it was quickly realized that in exile his freedom to criticize was greater and at the end of the book Philby was back in the wilderness. His tragedy was that of every man who lives to see his own familiar world crumble away and his return to a changed Arabia was a sadder fate than his exile.

Colonel Gerald de Gaury devoted much of his writing to Arabia, on a more superficial level than Philby but in a more immediately attractive style. Less committed to the Saudis, he nevertheless wrote in engaging detail and with obvious sympathy for a country in the process of change. The title of his book published in 1946, *Arabia Phoenix*,[9] was the clue to his approach. He accompanied Sir Andrew Ryan who in 1935 presented his credentials in Riyad as the first British minister to the court of Ibn Saᶜud. It was a land largely untouched at that time by modern civilization that attracted de Gaury, but evidence that the phoenix was about to reappear was everywhere. The postscript to the book was a question: how would the country face her dilemma? De Gaury was not certain, but he went a little way in his next work, *Arabian Journey and Other Desert Travels*,[10] to answer the question. It was a collection of travel narratives, not an attempt at political analysis, but contained comments on social and economic problems. He saw the chief hope for the orderly development of the country to lie in Ibn Saᶜud's character. Despite the speed of modern travel and progress de Gaury still had an eye for the past, certainly his real affection was for the Arabia of the past, and he regretted those changes which were, implicitly, for the worse.

Philby and de Gaury were travellers and historians who did not attempt to write a general survey of Saudi Arabia. The first of this genre to appear after the war was Twitchell's *Saudi Arabia*.[11] The author was an engineer who had been responsible for reopening the gold mines of the Hijaz, for negotiating the first oil concessions in 1933 and for surveying water and agricultural resources. His book was of great value as a primary source for the economic history of the country, and further included sections on geography and social and political development. Much of his material was not original but his text was enlivened with first-hand experiences, particularly his friendship with Ibn Saᶜud. He had a deep admiration for the late king, as had most Europeans who met him. Perhaps this admiration led him a little too easily into optimism for the future of the country. Writing in the third edition in 1958 he believed that King Saᶜud and Aramco would 'progress together to their mutual advantage' and Faisal would co-operate with the king to establish 'efficiency in government administration'. The second and third editions of the book contained only piecemeal additions and consequently lost their value as the text became more out of date.

The last notable work to appear in the forties, although it was written in 1936, was Colonel Dickson's *The Arab of the Desert*.[12] The book's sub-title, *A Glimpse into Badawin Life in Kuwait and Saudi Arabia*, was a misnomer, for into his work Dickson poured in great detail the observations of a long life among the Arabs. It is a book that cannot be repeated as the material for it was gathered during a period that has now passed. It is a record of the 'charming and unspoiled' Bedouin. The author largely ignored modern developments yet he had played a leading part in bringing the oil era to the region. His book contained a wealth of material on every aspect of the personal, social and material life of the Bedouin, but little on the problems facing a traditional society in a period of change. Nevertheless, it is a work which can justly stand comparison with other great works on the Arabs, proof that an Englishman could and did love the desert and its inhabitants. One criticism would be that the author overloaded his book and that selective pruning would have been an advantage.

Of the 1950s four or five studies merit some attention. Sanger's *The Arabian Peninsula*[13] was the second comprehensive work on the area by an American. The author was a diplomat who had worked in Arabia. His study covered most of the Arabian Peninsula and included material on Aden, Yemen and the Gulf States. Again his theme was 'the impact of western civilization' and America's role in this. For him, on the material side at least, there was no doubt that the change was for the better. His survey was not systematic, but rather a personal and digressive approach which brought immediacy to his text. His treatment of areas outside Saudi Arabia was of particular interest, notably his description of the negotiation of the treaty with Imam Yahya. His chapters on Saudi Arabia covered what was by then largely familiar territory, but his work probably served its purpose of introducing Arabia to America. Its chief drawback was the lack of a really critical assessment of the path the states of Arabia were following. It was not clear whether he realized the depth of the changes America had helped to bring about or how great was her responsibility for them.

It is useful to follow Sanger's work with a consideration of Lipsky's *Saudi Arabia*[14] which appeared five years later and was one of the American series, Surveys of World Cultures, produced by the Human Relations Area Files Press. Books in this series are produced by 'interdisciplinary teams' and systematic files on the country concerned are utilized. The resultant books are compendia of information, 'area handbooks', which have a curiously lifeless quality. It is difficult to rid one's mind of the image of endless card indexes. Opinions appeared as statements of fact and should be challenged. Saudi Arabia was described as a 'backwater' – in whose eyes? 'Slander, mendacity, and treachery are commonplace' and 'bribery and assassination are *almost* recognized weapons' in the foreign policy of Arab countries. Terms such as 'commonplace' and 'recognized' (even if qualified) need considerable substantiation. The weight given to different topics was presumably determined in a previously agreed formula for the whole series. This practice led to certain oddities. For example, only four pages were devoted to Islam in Saudi Arabia (in a work of some 350 pages) while the diffusion and control of information, a subject of lesser import, was given eight. This necessitated the collection of non-facts – 'The government of Saudi Arabia has not engaged in systematic or large-scale information and propaganda activities', 'there are no public cinemas in the country', and so on. Despite the drawbacks of producing studies according to this system, notably the lack of any personality in the writing, undue repetition and the tendency for the material to become out of date, the series does provide useful, if not easily readable information.

To return to a more personal, perhaps more romantic view of Arabia, van der Meulen, former Dutch consul in Jiddah, was a man in Philby's mould who wrote about Arabia in some ways with even greater authority since as an Arabist he had studied under Snouck Hurgronje. His book on Hadhramaut appeared in 1932 and in 1957 *The Wells of Ibn Saᶜud*[15] was published. It was both a euology and a lament. It was in praise of Ibn Saᶜud, the hero of the book and the author's 'personal hero', but was a lament for the fact that heroes do not always make wise rulers especially when confronted with sudden and enormous wealth. The author had sought spiritual integrity in the Islam of the Wahhabis but found that the revenues from oil had opened the doors of the kingdom so that the materialism of the 'so-called Christian west' had come flooding in. Aramco efficiency tempted the Arab away from his familiar life and put nothing of real value in its place. Van der Meulen blamed the Americans not so much for a process which was largely inevitable but for not having given greater assistance and advice to an inexperienced government. The consequence was that they had continued to pay 'their gold into the hands of an inexperienced child!'. The hero had not become a wise ruler. To the author, Husain of Mecca was not a hero but as a ruler he would not have led his country into the 'chaos' of which Ibn Saᶜud was guilty. Although the tone of the book's conclusion was pessimistic the text was full of glimpses of life in Saudi Arabia and contained telling portraits of Ibn Saᶜud and Philby.

Van der Meulen's next work, *Faces in Shem*,[16] was a collection of sketches of 'Arabians', both Europeans and others, whom the author met in the Hijaz, Yemen and the Hadhramaut. His concern for the subjects of the sketches and his deep knowledge of the area were both equally obvious in his vivid writing.

The last great travel book to appear on Arabia was Thesiger's *Arabian Sands*,[17] published in 1959 but describing an earlier period. His Arabia was not a remote image. It was something he lived with in great intimacy and hardship – 'a bitter desiccated land'. The sands were both villain and hero of his book and like Captain Ahab's whale a challenge to be overcome. As Thesiger wrote, 'no man could live there and emerge unchanged'. But the desert was peopled and his friendships with individual Bedouins emerged as one of the strongest features of a book packed with comment on their code of conduct, religious observances and social customs. As with all great travel books, however, there was something more than mere description. The whole was seen, perhaps with a tinge of romanticism, through the affectionate eye of a sympathetic man under the spell of the desert. The memories of hardship and squalor were transmuted into 'the yearning to return'.

Eleven years after his death Ibn Saᶜud still attracted biographers. David Howarth's *The Desert King*[18] appeared in 1964, admittedly the work of an outsider and non-specialist, fortunately not following too closely in the path of Armstrong's *Lord of Arabia*. It was written without hyperbole and although it naturally lacked the intimate touches of a writer who had spent many years in the company of Ibn Saᶜud, the author was able to draw on the reminiscences of contemporaries and on unpublished documents. While adding little new material, Howarth was able to give an overall picture of Ibn Saᶜud's reign unaffected by personal considerations. The early years were an oft-recounted story but the last section dealt skilfully with the great period of change following the discovery of oil.

The familiar picture emerged of the ageing ruler surrounded by the wealth and corruption which he did not comprehend. More than most he had lived to see his ambitions achieved yet lived longer to see them crumble away. Those who knew him testified that he was unhappy and bewildered in his final years although never expressing remorse. After so many years as ruler self-criticism was perhaps impossible.

The most impressive recent general survey of the Arabian peninsula was David Holden's *Farewell to Arabia*.[19] It was not the work of a historian but of a journalist of long experience in the area with an ability to combine sensitive description with political reporting. His study was the sum of post-war works on Arabia, a farewell to the old but a more than lukewarm welcome to the new. The old Arabia was passing (in some places had already passed) and on the whole the change was welcomed by the author. Welcome or no the process is irreversible despite the fierce rearguard action that the 'old Arabia' is maintaining. The author saw his book as a study of 'the process of change in action'. It was also a study of the ending of the particular relationship that Britain maintained with the fringes of the Peninsula, of conflict with Yemen and Saudi Arabia, of the beginning of the end in Aden and of the imponderables of the Gulf. The British era in Arabia will soon come to an end, but what will take its place? Holden offered no easy solution and believed that further change would not come peacefully.

Soulié and Champenois in their brief study *Le royaume d'Arabie saoudite face à l'Islam révolutionnaire*[20] drew the contrast between '*l'Islam révolutionnaire*' of President Nasser's Egypt and '*l'Islam traditionaliste*' of King Faisal's Arabia. The contrast in religious terms has little meaning as Nasser has not set out to 'revolutionize' Islam, and in fact the authors underlined that the conflict was rather between a state whose constitution was the Koran and one which had chosen to follow the path of secular socialism. They modified the religious contrast by adding that the differences between Egypt and Saudi Arabia were not only (perhaps one should say not even) doctrinal but part of '*un antagonisme séculaire*' between the sedentary and the nomadic. But while this antagonism may be at the root of the conflict the struggle has long since developed into one for power and influence in which the label 'reactionary' is given to others by those who claim to be progressive, and 'secular' by those who claim to follow the true path. The authors brought out clearly in their book the gradualist course chosen by Faisal, Saudi Arabia's '*réponse originale*' to the problem of progress without loss of one's '*arrière – plan de spiritualité*', but the very facts of modernization demanded the introduction of alien ideas and techniques which were brought in by those anxious to build their new world on the ruins of traditionalist Islam.

Gerald de Gaury's biography[21] of Faisal did not add very much new material to the history of the Al Sa'ud, but was a useful, if at times perfunctory, study of Faisal's periods of office under King Sa'ud and later as king himself. Much space was devoted to the war in Yemen and in the appendix were printed Faisal's restrained replies to Egyptian propaganda. They were a clear demonstration of the conflict outlined in the previous book, but Faisal was at pains to point out that his dispute was with the Egyptian leaders and not with the people whom God had 'afflicted . . . with their present rulers'. Saudi Arabia's modernization had to come about within the ambit of Islam, not of socialism or communism, and the country needed to avoid the introduction of 'malicious and dangerous trends' which were turning people away from Islam.

Coverage of works relating to other areas of Arabia – Yemen and South Arabia – will have to be given in less detail. There has been a recent upsurge of interest in Yemen, for little of note was published in the forties and fifties. Professor Faroughy's *Introducing Yemen*[22] was an introductory handbook to the country containing basic information on its geography, economy, social conditions and history. Unfortunately the book was badly produced and contained certain inaccuracies. The historical sections, especially those dealing with the later years, were the most useful. Heyworth-Dunne's *Al-Yemen*[23] was a similar handbook and included a fairly detailed account of the 1948 'revolution'. It was a by no means comprehensive survey of Yemen but contained much obviously first-hand information.

Although Wendell Phillips' *Qataban and Sheba*[24] should perhaps not be mentioned as a serious study of Yemen, his lavishly equipped American Foundation Arabian Expedition did achieve considerable archeological success in the Wadi Beihan in the Aden Protectorate and in Ma'rib in Yemen. The expedition's stay in Yemen was an indication of how not to succeed by trying too hard and ended in the infamous escape from the Imam's soldiers. Moreover, Phillips' explanation of the reasons for their flight would not be one acceptable to Yemeni officials.

Because of the paucity of material, Claudie Fayein's *A French Doctor in the Yemen*[25] was a timely and charming addition to the literature on Yemen. It was a clear and intimate record of eighteen months spent in San'a and elsewhere. Dr Fayein without pretension to scholarship made a sympathetic yet clear-eyed record of life amongst those Yemenis she met during her travels and on duty. Gunther Pawelke's *Jemen: das verbotene Land*[26] was written after his diplomatic mission to the Imam in 1953. The account of his journey through Yemen was supplemented by information on the history, institutions and economy of the country.

Erich Bethmann, a former missionary in the Middle East, added only a booklet – an introductory chapter – about the country, *Yemen on the Threshold*.[27] Too short to contribute much to our understanding of the country, it did contain perceptive remarks especially on Zaidism. It was in the religious field that the author was able to meet Yemenis on a deep level of understanding. The most valuable section of his book dealt with the Yemeni attitude towards religion and towards its future accommodation with the contemporary world. Another French view was given by François Balsan in *Inquiétant Yémen*,[28] a light-hearted and non-too-profound view. His experiences were as a contractor working for the Yemeni government and after many frustrating encounters with an antique bureaucracy any balanced view of the country was to his credit. He obtained relief from interminable negotiations in travel and archeological excursions.

The 1960s dragged Yemen again into the world headlines and a number of new studies appeared although we are still awaiting a definitive work. Harold Ingrams, the famous bringer of comparative peace to the hadhramaut, wrote his study *The Yemen: Imams, Rulers and Revolutions*,[29] as a historical background to the republican revolution. His Yemen was the greater geographical area and he included material on Aden and the Protectorate. He forecast that when Egyptians and the British had finally disappeared from the area the state of Yemen would remain divided as in the past. A modern version of the shifting pattern of alliances – a republic and an imamate – might continue to exist. His old-fashioned though understandable conclusion was that the area would never be as happy as it was in the days when Britain was regarded as a 'beneficial presence'. The Arabs had now to deal with a 'false' modernity for which they were ill prepared.

Manfred Wenner's *Modern Yemen*[30] covered the same ground as Ingrams, not of course from the same background, and treated the history of the period 1918–66 in greater detail. His style was straightforward, his narrative concise and based on an impressive number of Arabic sources. It was history free from the sound of the grinding of personal axes. Consistent with the theme of this paper, the crisis laid bare by the author was that of a medieval autocrat facing the demands of the twentieth century. The Imams' policy of attempting to stem the impact of modernization had led to great changes accompanied by violence. The rulers of Yemen trying to balance the opposing forces calling for or rejecting reform had not succeeded. Nor in Wenner's opinion had the republican regime solved these problems and it had failed to recognize the historic role of the imamate. He, like Ingrams, foresaw the continuation of a divided Yemen in the immediate future.

Eric Macro traced in his work *Yemen and the Western World*[31] the course of outside interest in the country. This had changed from commercial activity in the earlier years to political and military rivalry in the later period. Great attention was given to the various frontier disputes between Britain and the Ottomans in the first place and then with the Yemenis. These were aggravated in the 1950s as the British laid their plans for the Aden Federation. Tension increased as Egypt helped to stir the brew. The author followed through in some detail the development of Egyptian and Russian involvement in Yemen and the disintegration of the British present in Southern Arabia. He offered no forecast, pessimistic or optimistic, of future developments.

The works by Ingrams, Wenner and Macro were historical, leading up to the war between republicans and royalists – a war which attracted foreign correspondents to the area. The well-known American correspondent, Dana Adams Schmidt, gave a deeply-felt survey[32] of the 'unknown war' based on the reports of eye-witnesses and on his own investigations, from the flight of the Imam Muhammad al-Badr until the Egyptian agreement to withdraw in 1967. He visited both republican and royalist camps. The resultant account was both vivid reporting and admirable journalism possessing the advantages and drawbacks of this genre. It had the immediacy and political insight of good reporting but naturally lacked the precision of the specialist. The Yemen, for Schmidt, was the battleground on which the quarrel between two incompatible Arab systems was being fought out – 'The Yemen war has been fought . . . only partly because of Yemen.' The disastrous course of the Egyptian intervention was clearly drawn, culminating finally in withdrawal and stalemate, and for the author the future would surely be filled with strife. The Yemenis were victorious only in the sense that they had obliged the foreigner to withdraw.

It is logical to move from a survey of recent books on Yemen into a consideration of those dealing with 'natural' Yemen – Aden and South Arabia. Although many of the problems of the two areas were similar, the essential difference was the direct involvement of Great Britain for well over a century, from the pioneering of Captain Haines through the heyday of empire to ignominious scuttling. Several of the works concerned had the urgency of apologias for recent actions, but there was still evidence of the more 'classical' interest in Arabia for its own sake. Van der Meulen had published in 1947 a second study of South Arabia, *Aden to the Hadhramaut*,[33] a record of a journey made in the Aden Protectorate in 1939. In his account, as a Dutch colonial civil servant, he made a point of observing British colonial methods. He travelled when Hadhrami prosperity was at a peak and paid tribute to the efforts of Ingrams to bring security to the area. He believed, however, that the Hadhramis themselves would be able to continue without British assistance. Colonel Hamilton (The Master of Belhaven) in *The Kingdom of Melchior*[34] described his own part between the two world wars in bringing the Pax Britannica to the Western Aden Protectorate in the area of the Yemen frontier. The book was both a record of achievement and a criticism of an inconsistent British policy which failed to profit from the Anglo-Yemen treaty of 1934. It was complementary to Ingrams' account of British policy in the Hadhramaut and was a good insight into the social and political conditions of an area for which the author, despite his disclaimer at the end, developed considerable affection. He was one of the small group of Britons who not always willingly but usually with considerable devotion spent their lives in the remoter areas of the Arab world. (It is perhaps interesting to note here that a third edition of Ingrams' record of his achievements, *Arabia and the Isles*,[35] was issued in 1966. The author added a preface in which he criticized the establishment of the Federation of South Arabia because it destroyed the independence of the Protectorate states. He looked sadly on the fading of the British Empire and the loss of 'will . . . to show power'.)

Three ex-governors and/or High Commissioners of Aden produced their apologias soon after leaving office. Sir Tom Hickinbotham published his study, *Aden*,[36] after many years' service there as a colonial official and finally as governor. It was during his period of office that the proposals for federation were approved by Whitehall. Despite the opposition it provoked the author believed that it was not ill-timed but that British reaction to Yemeni attacks should have been stronger and more positive. Sir Charles Johnston presided over and was an architect of the merger which brought Aden into the Federation of South Arabia in 1963. *The View from Steamer Point*[37] was a good-natured account of the delicate processes leading to the merger which he favoured despite opposition from several leading Adenis. Federation was the only way to save the Protectorate states from falling under the influence of Yemen – 'a gloomy enough prospect under the Imam, and a desperate one under the distraught Republic'. Sir Kennedy Trevaskis' *Shades of Amber*[38] was the most recent personal account of life at the top in Aden. He it was who had to bear the brunt of opposition against the Federation of which he was considered the chief architect. He was also known to be a supporter of the tribal rulers against the Adeni nationalists. He himself believed that the grenade thrown at him in December 1963 came indirectly from the hand of ᶜAbdallah al-Asnag whom he had antagonized by refusing to regard him as a responsible leader. Trevaskis claimed that Asnag had been a terrorist from the beginning – a belief fostered by his earlier deep involvement with the tribal rulers in the Protectorate which had led him to ignore other forces in the area. Trevaskis was retired at the moment when, as Tom Little pointed out in his book *South Arabia*,[39] there was in the Federation some unity of feeling between the politicians of Aden and the Federal ministers.

Little covered the whole story of British involvement in Aden but especially the later years from the merger until the disastrous exit. As another journalist writing about the area he doubted that British policy would ever have been successful. Commitment to the shaikhs was too deeply ingrained and realization that other forces were at work came too late. The painful route to final abnegation of responsibility was made only too clear. The end of the British era in Aden is a satisfactory point at which to end this survey of western writings on Arabia, satisfactory chronologically speaking but far from satisfactory for those who seek a creditable end to empire.

REFERENCES

1	H. St J. B. Philby	*A Pilgrim in Arabia* (London, 1946).
2	H. St J. B. Philby	*Arabian Days* (London, 1948).
3	H. St J. B. Philby	*Arabian Highlands* (Ithaca, N.Y., 1952).
4	H. St J. B. Philby	*Arabian Jubilee* (New York, 1953).
5	H. St J. B. Philby	*Sa'udi Arabia* (London, 1955).
6	H. St J. B. Philby	*Land of Midian* (London, 1957).
7	H. St J. B. Philby	*Forty Years in the Wilderness* (London, 1957).
8	H. St J. B. Philby	*Arabian Oil Ventures* (Washington, 1964).
9	G. de Gaury	*Arabia Phoenix* (London, 1946).
10	G. de Gaury	*Arabian Journey and Other Desert Travels* (London, 1950).
11	K. S. Twitchell	*Saudi Arabia*, 3rd edn (Princeton, N.J., 1958).
12	H. R. P. Dickson	*The Arab of the Desert* (London, 1949).
13	R. H. Sanger	*The Arabian Peninsula* (Ithaca, N.Y., 1954).
14	G. A. Lipsky and others	*Saudi Arabia* (H.R.A.F., New Haven, 1959).
15	D. van der Meulen	*The Wells of Ibn Saᶜud* (London, 1957).
16	D. van der Meulen	*Faces in Shem* (London, 1961).
17	W. Thesiger	*Arabian Sands* (London, 1959).
18	D. Howarth	*The Desert King* (London, 1964).
19	D. Holden	*Farewell to Arabia* (London, 1966).
20	G. J.-L. Soulié and L. Champenois	*Le royaume d'Arabie Saoudite face à l'Islam révolutionnaire 1953–64* (Paris, 1966).
21	G. de Gaury	*Faisal: King of Saudi Arabia* (London, 1966).
22	A. Faroughy	*Introducing Yemen* (New York, 1947).
23	J. Heyworth-Dunne	*Al-Yemen* (Cairo, 1952).
24	W. Phillips	*Qataban and Sheba* (London, 1955).
25	C. Fayein	*A French Doctor in the Yemen* (London, 1957).

Also in this genre one should mention Eva Hoeck's

		Doctor amongst the Bedouins (London, 1963).
26	G. Pawelke	*Jemen: das verbotene Land* (Düsseldorf, 1959).
27	E. W. Bethmann	*Yemen on the Threshold* (Washington, 1960).
28	F. Balsan	*Inquiétant Yémen* (Paris, 1961).
29	H. Ingrams	*The Yemen, Imams, Rulers and Revolutions* (London, 1963).
30	M. W. Wenner	*Modern Yemen* (Baltimore, 1967).
31	E. Macro	*Yemen and the Western World* (London, 1968).
32	D. A. Schmidt	*Yemen: the Unknown War* (London etc., 1968).
33	D. van der Meulen	*Aden to the Hadhramaut* (London, 1947).
34	Master of Belhaven (A. Hamilton)	*Kingdom of Melchior* (London, 1949).
35	H. Ingrams	*Arabia and the Isles*, 3rd edn (London, 1966).
36	T. Hickinbotham	*Aden* (London 1958).
37	C. Johnston	*The View from Steamer Point* (London, 1964).
38	K. Trevaskis	*Shades of Amber* (London, 1968).
39	T. Little	*South Arabia* (London, 1968).

PART I

HISTORY

2

THE DEVELOPMENT OF THE
GULF STATES

AHMAD MUSTAFA ABU-HAKIMA

In writing on this subject it will be necessary to limit oneself to certain states and certain aspects of development, otherwise the subject will be too wide to tackle in the present survey. The eastern and northern shores of the Gulf, i.e. Persia and Iraq, al-Ihsa' province of Saudi Arabia, and Oman will therefore be excluded. The countries which will be studied are: Kuwait, Bahrain, Qatar and the Trucial States, with special emphasis on the first. As far as the nature of development is concerned, the present chapter will endeavour to survey the political aspect, together with other auxiliary factors which usually lead to development.

From the first glance at those states, therefore, one can see that one is confronted with two types of political unit. The first is an independent state and the second a group of amirates or shaikhdoms which fell under British protection as a result of special treaty relations. But Kuwait, the independent state of today, was until 1961 more or less a British protectorate too. It might be worth our while to notice that these states stretch on the western shore of the Arabian Gulf from its northernmost edge to its southernmost end with only one intermission, namely that of al-Ihsa', a territory that lies between Kuwait in the north and Qatar in the south. In spite of the fact that these states vary widely in their systems of government, it should be noted that there is a common factor among them. They are all Arabian territories, inhabited in the main by Arabian tribes who mostly belong to the ᶜAdnani or northern division of Arabs, the southern being called Qahtani by Arab historians and traditionalists.

For the sake of convenience and because most of the shaikhdoms will be studied in other chapters, Kuwait will first be studied in detail, and the other protectorates, the shaikhdoms of Bahrain, Qatar and the seven Trucial States: Abu Dhabi, Dubai, Sharjah, ᶜAjman, Umm al-Qaiwain, Ras al-Khaimah and Fujairah, will be dealt with at a later stage.

THE SHAIKHDOM OF KUWAIT[1]

To appreciate the political development of Kuwait one has to look very briefly at the early history of the place. The state of Kuwait is named after

31

its capital Kuwait which was originally a very small fishing centre on the north-western corner of the Arabian Gulf. The name 'Kuwait' is a diminutive of '*kut*', meaning a small fortress. This town was also known to the eighteenth-century European travellers as Grane (sometimes spelled 'Grain' or 'Graen') which is in turn a diminutive of the Arabic '*qarn*', meaning a small hill.[2] The town's earliest history might date back to the mid-seventeenth century. Yet Kazimah, in the neighbourhood of Kuwait, was famous in the seventh century AD and is alluded to in various Arabic verses.[3]

The ᶜUtub[4]

The earliest settlers of Kuwait of whom we have record in the seventeenth century are the Bani Khalid tribes, who ruled eastern Arabia in the sixteenth, seventeenth and eighteenth centuries. It was their Amir Barrak who is said to have established Kuwait. But late in the seventeenth century a number of Arabian tribes, united under the name of ᶜUtub, travelled from the southern part of central Arabia, because of severe drought, to the coasts of the Gulf near Qatar. They dispersed along the shores of the Gulf and finally met again at Kuwait where towards the middle of the eighteenth century they gradually established their independence of the Bani Khalid.

Famous among the ᶜUtub confederacy were Al Sabah, Al Khalifah and Al Jalahimah clans. It might be useful to note here that these ᶜUtub (singular ᶜUtbi) were the cousins of Al Saᶜud, and they all claim to be descended from Jamilah, a branch of the Great ᶜAnazah tribe, now inhabiting northern Arabia.

Rise and Development of Kuwait in the Eighteenth Century

Al Sabah became the rulers of Kuwait in about 1750. By the end of the eighteenth century, Kuwait became an established shaikhdom as far as politics, economics and government are concerned. Its fleet was said, with Muscat's, to have monopolized the conveyance of trade in the Persian Gulf.[5] Its Arab ruler was independent of all foreign control including Ottoman. Shaikh ᶜAbd Allah ibn Sabah was its second and most efficient ruler to whom Kuwait owed not only its independence but also its prosperity. He rose to power in about 1762 after the death of his father Shaikh Sabah ibn Jabir, who gave the present ruling family its name. Shaikh ᶜAbd Allah ruled until his death in February 1815.[6] This long reign of Shaikh ᶜAbd Allah was destined to go through certain difficulties of a political and economic nature. But before going into the details of these difficulties, it is necessary to examine the structure of Kuwaiti society during his reign. It might be interesting to notice at this early phase of Kuwaiti society that it continued almost unchanged until the early 1950s, i.e. until the time when oil began to change the face of the land and its inhabitants.

Kuwait was the meeting point of the ᶜUtub who, as previously mentioned, by the 1780s must have flocked together from the various islands and shores of the Gulf to Kuwait on its northwestern corner. Local traditions and the records of the time both speak of influential Arabian families among the new settlers which play an important part in forming the government in a tribal society. As a matter of fact Kuwait was from the start a tribal society, but with a difference.

ᶜAbd Allah ibn Sabah

As the rule of Shaikh ᶜAbd Allah was to influence government and statesmanship in Kuwait for a long time to come, an examination of Kuwait under his rule would be very useful. Local tradition in Kuwait states that Shaikh ᶜAbd Allah was chosen as a ruler from among other brothers although he was the youngest.[7] The choice was made by the townspeople, who were mainly merchants, for his qualities of courage and wisdom, which an Arab usually likes to see in his chief.[8] It is important to note that he was chosen by his townsmen in the manner his father was chosen before him. In other words he was given the right to rule by his people – he did not simply inherit that right.

From the start the merchants played a great role in running the daily affairs of Kuwait, so there was no danger of its ruler, in this case the Shaikh, becoming a despot. Indeed Shaikh ᶜAbd Allah was very far from becoming one.

It is also important to remember that much of Kuwait's internal policy has been dictated by the external situation, i.e. the state of affairs in neighbouring countries. Two factors, activity on the waters of the Gulf and the policies of the countries surrounding those waters, have always had their influence on Kuwait and the other Gulf States. The shaikhs of Kuwait knew how to handle these factors and make them work for their benefit.

During Shaikh ᶜAbd Allah ibn Sabah's rule in the eighteenth and early nineteenth centuries one can see how those two factors were to affect the policies of Kuwait. First there was the growing British interest in the Gulf waters, after the British had eliminated other European maritime powers, namely the Portuguese, Dutch and French; and secondly there were the other land forces, comprising the Wahhabis, on the eastern Arabian shores, the Ottomans in Iraq and the Persians on the eastern shores of the Gulf. Though it is beyond the scope of this paper to go into the details of how each of these two factors helped mould the policies of Kuwait, it can be briefly stated that Shaikh ᶜAbd Allah managed to build a fleet which was able to defy the local fleets in the Gulf; and he followed a friendly policy towards the British from 1775, bringing them to Kuwait in 1793 to shelter their Basra factory for over two years, with the result that the factory workers took ᶜAbd Allah's side in repelling the Wahhabi attacks on Kuwait in 1795.[9] Both Ottoman Iraq and Persia were too weak to disrupt the rapid growth of Kuwait in the eighteenth and the early nineteenth centuries. It might be worth our while to turn briefly to Kuwait's internal political structure during this period, a structure which remained mainly unchanged until Kuwait became an independent state in 1961.

Paternal Rule

Both local traditions and contemporary European sources[10] speak of an early paternal system of government in Kuwait. Al Sabah became rulers of the town by local tribal choice – that is, the ᶜUtbi families of Kuwait chose Sabah, the ancestor of the present ruling family, to look after the administration of their town. He therefore became an Arabian sedentary amir who was a resident of an Arab town. But Kuwait was a community where merchants had the upper hand because of the wealth which they accumulated in the early days of the rise of their town, and so their influence on the political attitudes of their ruler was important. And members of the ruling family of Al Sabah might also be called merchants, in the sense that they have always had their own business.[11] Though the ruler had it in his hands to settle the disputes among the town's people, local traditions speak of a *qadi* or judge who used to settle matters relating to Islamic (*shariᶜah*) Law. The names of these judges are given in the books written by local historians.[12] It could be therefore safely assumed that the policies of Kuwait, until quite recently, were decided by its rulers, the Shaikh, who sought advice from the merchants and from a *qadi*.

Shaikh Mubarak the Great and the Exclusive Agreement of 1899

As far as the running of the shaikhdom's foreign policy is concerned no major change took place until the first few years of the rule of Shaikh Mubarak Al Sabah (1896–1915). For in 1898 Shaikh Mubarak of Kuwait, anxious to avoid any extension of Ottoman control from Iraq, turned to Great Britain and in 1899 signed a comprehensive treaty which contained most of the provisions included in the various agreements with Bahrain and the Trucial States, whereby the ruler undertook not to have direct relations with any other foreign power, and not to sell, lease or cede land to any such power.[13] Great Britain thus became responsible for conducting the foreign relations of Kuwait and, incidentally, for its protection against foreign aggression. Shaikh Mubarak entered readily into this agreement because he realized that Kuwait's continued independence could only be insured by British protection.[14]

After the signing of this treaty of 1899, and until 1946 when the golden oil tap was turned by Shaikh Ahmad al-Jabir Al Sabah, there were no radical changes in the policies of Kuwait. Yet the First World War and the Berlin-Baghdad Railway project at the beginning of the twentieth century were major factors in giving Anglo-Kuwaiti relations the intimacy which continued until the days of independence. The Second World War had of course its effects on Kuwait's internal as well as external political development. The huge improvement in human communications through the media of air transport and radio accelerated social, political and economic change. Yet the role of oil was paramount.

Oil and Development

It is not possible to include in this brief survey of Kuwait the history of oil discovery, but it might be useful to mention that because of the cordial Anglo-Kuwaiti relations, and following the lines of 1899's 'exclusive' agreement, Shaikh Mubarak the Great offered the British another 'exclusive' agreement regarding the search for oil in Kuwait in 1913.[15] It is true that the oil concession to the Kuwait Oil Company came later than that date, and it is true too that oil was struck during the year 1938, but the golden tap was not turned on until 30 June 1946, during the rule of Shaikh Ahmad al-Jabir Al Sabah.[16]

Oil, Government and Politics

The discovery of oil in Kuwait was bound to have its effects on society. Thus the changes which were to come could be measured by the amount of oil and money earned *per capita* and how the ruler made use of this fabulous wealth.

Until the reign of Shaikh Ahmad al-Jabir Al Sabah (1921–50), Kuwait remained a paternal shaikhdom with the ruler at the head of the administration, running a country of about 15,000 square kilometres with only one big town of about 50,000 people and a considerable nomadic population – the boundaries of the shaikhdom were fixed at the ᶜUqair Conference held in Saudi Arabia in 1922.[17] Shaikh Ahmad al-Jabir continued to administer the shaikhdom in the traditional manner though in the 1920s he tried to form a Consultative Assembly to help him in his administration. The Assembly was doomed to die soon after its birth,[18] though its death should in no way minimize the importance of the traditional role of Kuwaiti merchants, who continued to help the Shaikh run the administration of their country until the time became ripe for the recent birth of democratic rule.

It has been pointed out that although oil was found in Kuwait in 1938 production was not started until 1946. With the growth of the industry came a great human influx into Kuwait. Together with their cousins, the people of Kuwait, the new arrivals who came from the Arab countries of the Middle East and Arabia began to transform traditional Kuwaiti society. Their right arm was the newly discovered wealth drilled from under the earth which was helping not only to develop the face of the earth, but also to bring prosperity to those who formed the traditional society of Kuwait.

Shaikh Ahmad al-Jabir did not live long enough to witness the great changes; this lot fell to his successor Shaikh ᶜAbd Allah al-Salim Al Sabah (1950–65). Thanks to ᶜAbd Allah's apprehension of internal and external affairs, Kuwait reached its present state of development as a modern state. But before discussing development in government and politics during ᶜAbd Allah's rule, it is important to give some relevant statistical information on his shaikhdom with reference to population and oil.

The census of 1958 put the population of the shaikhdom at about 300,000,[19] the majority of whom lived in Kuwait town. The census carried out in 1965 put the number of the population at 467,789.[20] It might be useful to state here again that more than half of the population come from neighbouring and distant Arab countries, and that among the foreign population there are a few thousand Persians, the majority of whom come from the opposite littoral of the Gulf and have Arab ancestry.[21]

Kuwait earns most of its income, if not all of it, from oil. During the last five years of Shaikh Ahmad al-Jabir's life (1946–50) oil revenue rose from £280,000 in 1946 to more than £4 million per annum. By 1952 Shaikh ᶜAbd Allah's share soared to some £50 million. The London *Times* of 18 May, 1961, estimated Kuwait's annual oil revenue at about £150 million and by 1963 the £200 million mark was reached. Then in 1966 the official *Year Book* published by the Ministry of Information and Guidance gives the figure of 248,127,432 Kuwaiti dinars for oil revenue.[22] These figures put Kuwait in a unique position among the nations of the world as far as income *per capita* is concerned. Kuwait Oil Co., which is half owned by British Petroleum and half owned by Gulf Oil, is said to have enjoyed an overall income of 1,700 million US dollars during the twelve years 1946–58.[23] The *New Statesman* has estimated that Britain benefits to the tune of 600 million US dollars a year from Kuwait, a figure which includes British Petroleum profits, the sterling income from the sale of oil and the Shaikh's investments. There are also considerable private Kuwaiti investments in England.[24]

Oil and Democracy in Kuwait

Sudden and unexpected wealth can be either a blessing or a curse depending on how it is used. For Kuwait it came as a blessing because it has been a shaikhdom with a democratic rule ever since it was established in the mid-eighteenth century. When Shaikh Ahmad al-Jabir died in 1950, Shaikh ᶜAbd Allah al-Salim was the nominated successor, and it was he who laid down the solid foundations of modernization in Kuwait. This does not mean that Kuwait had been cut off from modern influences prior to the oil age – before the 1940s the wealth of certain Kuwait merchants was estimated at millions of Indian rupees.[25] Shaikh ᶜAbd Allah's role in the transformation of his society cannot be underestimated.

This period of change extending from 1950 to 1968 can be divided into two periods: (1) 1950–61, and (2) 1961–8. During the first eleven years, thanks to the wise judgement and sound administration of Shaikh ᶜAbd Allah, the main lines of the democratic progress of Kuwait were demarcated. Examples are the fields of education and health. Money was allotted to make education at all levels free to all those who lived in Kuwait and the British system of a national health service was embraced by the Department of Health. Free medical treatment, hospitalization and medicine have since been extended to all who made Kuwait their home, i.e. Kuwaitis and foreigners alike.

Private enterprise was given ample chance to help develop the country and was generously compensated by the government.[26] Schools, each of whose costs exceeded the million pounds sterling mark, were built in large numbers. Roads were paved, at first in and around Kuwait town, and by 1961 there were dual carriage roads connecting almost all parts of the country. And the social pattern was keeping pace with this rapid development in buildings and road construction. Free education was extended to scholarships for studies abroad, where Kuwaiti boys and girls were sent to obtain university degrees. These boys and girls came back to run the various government departments, bringing with them western ways of thinking and behaviour which were modified by local traditions to suit the Kuwait Arab environment. Changes in society and urbanization which took place in the 1950s were astounding to the present author who spent the period 1953–8 in Kuwait and returned to a very different place in 1964. By 1961 Kuwait was ready for the new phase of its history, namely its transformation into the modern state that it is today.

The State of Kuwait 1961–8

It was now clear that the treaty of 1899 with Great Britain could not continue to serve relations between Kuwait and Britain in the 1960s, and so its replacement by the Treaty of 1961 was very welcome. Thus Kuwait became on 19 June 1961, completely independent of Great Britain. On 16 July of the same year Kuwait joined the League of Arab States and was accepted, two years later, on 14 May 1963, as a member of the United Nations.

Directly the 1961 Treaty was signed, Shaikh ᶜAbd Allah announced a provisional system of government, a Constituent Assembly, which was established to carry out two duties. The first was to draft a constitution for the country within a year or not later than January 1963; the other was to fulfil the duties of a chamber of deputies. Having prepared the draft of the Constitution a few months previously, the Assembly finished its work in January 1963. The draft was approved by Shaikh ᶜAbd Allah as submitted on 11 November 1962.[27]

The National Assembly

The first elections to fill the fifty seats of the Assembly were held on 23 January 1963. The Assembly was given considerable power. First, though the Amir of Kuwait appoints the ministers, they are responsible to the Assembly which can force them to resign on a vote of no confidence. Secondly, it has power in respect of the Prime Minister, for if the deputies find that they cannot co-operate with him their House will notify the Amir who will either dismiss the Prime Minister or dissolve the Assembly. One could briefly say that a new democratic state was born in Kuwait.

The Constitution

The Constitution, which was drafted by an elected committee of five members of the Assembly at twice-weekly meetings over many months, is an impressive document. Professor ᶜUthman Khalil ᶜUthman, the Egyptian legislative authority, was the brains behind it. It is divided into five sections and contains 183 Articles, which contain a great deal of useful information. As this information might help us to understand developments and changes in the state, some of them are given below:

Article One: Kuwait is an Arab, independent, fully sovereign State. Neither its sovereignty nor any part of its territory may be relinquished. The people of Kuwait form a part of the Arab nation.

Article Two: The religion of the State is Islam, and Islamic Law shall be a main source of legislation.

Article Three: Arabic is the official language of the State.

Article Four: Kuwait is a hereditary Amirate, the succession of which is confined to the descendants of the late Mubarak Al Sabah. The heir apparent shall be named within one year of the accession of the Amir.

His appointment shall be effected by an amiri decree upon the nomination of the Amir and the approval of the National Assembly which shall be passed by a majority of its members in a special sitting. If the appointment is not made in the way shown above, the Amir shall nominate for the position of heir apparent at least three descendants of the late Mubarak Al Sabah and the National Assembly shall pledge allegiance to one of them as heir apparent.

The heir apparent must have attained his majority and be of sound mind and the legitimate son of Muslim parents.[28]

A special law issued within one year of the date on which the Constitution comes into effect, shall lay down the other rules concerning the succession of the amirate.

Article Six: The system of government in Kuwait shall be democratic, under which sovereignty is vested in the nation, the source of all powers. This sovereignty shall be exercised in accordance with the rules prescribed in this Constitution.

Other articles deal with guarantees for personal liberty, public rights and duties. The Kuwait Constitution, in brief, reflects modern trends in a traditional society preparing to meet those trends. At the same time Kuwait was getting ready to meet its external obligations both to the Arab countries and the rest of the world.

Current Political Trends in Kuwait

A sense of pan-Arabism, expressed on the one hand in generous brotherly help[29] and on the other in Arab nationalist feelings, is the dominating factor in Kuwait's foreign policy. Other factors, none the less, play their part in moulding the relationships which Kuwait now enjoys with neighbouring and other states. Although Kuwait's enormous wealth from oil revenues has enabled her to boost her importance in the Arab world, even before the discovery of oil, she followed a policy which enabled her to get along very well with her neighbours. To her Arab sister countries Kuwait extended financial aid, after creating in 1961 the Kuwait Fund for Arab Economic Development with an initial capital of 50 million dinars to be covered from Kuwait Government reserves. The capital reached by 1966–7 the 200 million dinars mark,[30] and by 1967 ten Arab countries had been given long-term credits from this fund. The total amount of loans to those countries was 56,550,000 dinars.[31]

Help was also extended to the poor shaikhdoms of the Trucial Coast, Sharjah, Dubai, ᶜAjman, Fujairah, Umm al-Qaiwain and Ras al-Khaimah. As early as 1953, Kuwait was supplying those shaikhdoms freely with teachers and medical aid, and by 1958 schools and clinics had been built there by Kuwait.[32] The Minister for External Affairs had likened this aid to the Trucial States to brothers sharing a loaf.[33]

Again for the sake of convenience and geographical order, of the other shaikhdoms of the eastern Arabian coast, Bahrain will be studied first. But the present paper will not go beyond the study of certain developments in Bahrain which conform to the general pattern of development in Kuwait and the remaining shaikhdoms.

Historical Background
One does not need here to go into the ancient and medieval history of Bahrain, but it is useful to keep in mind that its earliest recorded medieval history indicates that it was ruled by ᶜAbd al-Qais Arabs centuries before the advent of Islam to eastern Arabia. It is also important to remember that during the Middle Ages and until about the early sixteenth century the name Bahrain included not only the present archipelago but the entire eastern Arabian coast from near Basra in the north to the Trucial coast in the south. Under the ᶜAbbasid caliphate, and even earlier under the Umaiyads, Bahrain formed one of the caliphate's provinces (*wilayat*). Then when the Portuguese came to the Gulf early in the sixteenth century Bahrain became one of their strongholds in the Gulf area, their advent bringing possibly the first contact between Bahrain and the European nations who followed the Portuguese, not only to the East Indies but also to the Gulf – namely the Dutch, the French and the English.

It was during the ascendancy of British influence in the Gulf in the late eighteenth century that the rule of Al Khalifah, which has continued up to the present day, began.

Al Khalifah, Rulers of Bahrain, 1782
It has already been said that Al Khalifah, the cousins of Al Sabah, were living in Kuwait together with Al Sabah and other ᶜUtbi families early in the eighteenth century. Al Khalifah remained in Kuwait until 1766, when they migrated to Qatar in the south where they established themselves at Zubarah on the Peninsula's north-western coast. Bahrain was at that time under the rule of an Omani Arab tribe under Shaikh Nasr Al Madhkur whose residence was at Bushire on the Persian coast of the Gulf. Hostilities between the ᶜUtub, (of both Kuwait and Zubarah), and Bushire, caused Shaikh Nasr to attack Zubarah in 1778 and later, unsuccessfully, in 1782. The result of this was that the ᶜUtub of both Kuwait and Zubarah attacked and occupied Bahrain in November 1782.[34] For the

first few years after the capture of Bahrain, Al Khalifah used to run its affairs from their headquarters in Zubarah, but later in the century Al Khalifah moved to Bahrain and, especially after the Wahhabi attacks of 1796–8, Zubarah became a deserted town.

Early Government and Involvements

The nineteenth century in eastern Arabian politics was perhaps one of the most disturbed periods of its history. Bahrain was, naturally, involved in that turmoil, although a lot of her involvement was forced upon her because of Muscat's previous claims to her. The first half of the century was also the time when piracy in the Gulf was most widespread.[35] Bahrain, under the Al Khalifah rule, was involved in piratical incidents, and it was under the pretext of subduing piracy in the Gulf that Britain's political relations with Bahrain and other shaikhdoms of eastern Arabia were begun. It should be remembered at this juncture too, that, in Bahrain and the remaining shaikhdoms of eastern Arabia, political sway was in the hands of one man, the shaikh, and Bahrain had been ruled by Al Khalifah through almost all of the nineteenth century.

Britain and Bahrain

After the third British expedition of 1819[36] against Ras al-Khaimah, the shaikhs of Bahrain signed the 1820 general Treaty of Peace with the British government, undertaking to abstain from all plunder and piracy by land and sea except by way of acknowledged war. This treaty with Britain was followed by others in a matter that was unique in the history of eastern Arabia. Not only did Bahrain sign, but all the other shaikhdoms of what, after one of those treaties, came to be called the Trucial coast, also signed. Among other treaties between Bahrain and Britain was the 1861 Perpetual Treaty of Peace and Friendship concerning such matters as slavery, maritime aggression and Britons trading with Bahrain.

Although the Ottoman presence in eastern Arabia was nominal in the eighteenth century, it became a force to be reckoned with in the nineteenth when the Ottoman Sultan in Constantinople sent first his Viceroy, Muhammad ᶜAli Pasha of Egypt[37] and later Midhat Pasha against the Wahhabis. The British were becoming alarmed lest the revival of Ottoman influence in eastern Arabia would endanger their position in the Gulf.[38]

From time to time, as in the years 1870 and 1874, the British government rejected Ottoman claims to sovereignty over Bahrain, while at the same time taking the opportunity to consolidate British power there. Two treaties were signed for this purpose with Shaikh ᶜIsa Al Khalifah in December 1880 and in March 1892. By these the shaikh bound himself not to enter into any relationship with a foreign government other than the British without the latter's consent, and there were also stipulations about the disposal of Bahrain territories.[39]

In 1902 a British political agent was posted to Bahrain, and in July 1913 a Convention was signed by the British and Ottoman governments which included the recognition of Bahrain's independence and her control over a number of neighbouring islands. Three years later Ibn Saᶜud signed a treaty with the British Government in which he also agreed to refrain from aggression against Bahrain.

Modern Bahrain 1935–68

In April and May of 1923 there were internal troubles in Bahrain which led to the abdication of Shaikh ᶜIsa after a reign of fifty-four years, and the succession of his son Hamad, first as deputy ruler for twelve years, and on the death of Shaikh ᶜIsa in 1935 as Shaikh of Bahrain.

With the accession of Shaikh Hamad the story of modern Bahrain begins, because during the nineteen years of his rule Bahrain was transformed into a modern state. As Bahrain was traditionally a great pearl-fishing centre conditions in the pearl industry were reformed, the position of the divers was bettered, and municipalities, education and other public services were developed. To this development reference will be made later.[40]

Oil and Development

In 1930 Shaikh Hamad signed a Concession Agreement with the Bahrain Petroleum Company, and three years later the first tanker-load of oil left Bahrain. On 20 February 1942, Shaikh Hamad died and was succeeded by his son Shaikh Salman Al Khalifah. Under the new ruler the march of progress continued in all fields, especially external affairs. In 1958 Shaikh Salman visited Saudi Arabia for a meeting with King Saᶜud ibn ᶜAbd al-ᶜAziz. As a result of this visit an agreement was signed between the two rulers providing for the sharing of the profits derived from an oil found in an area of sea that had hitherto been the subject of a dispute between the two countries. The importance of this political step lies in the fact that Shaikh Salman by negotiating with King Saᶜud not only solved that problem but also took Bahrain forward in the field of international politics. It was also during the later part of Shaikh Salman's reign that the British government transferred to Bahrain a number of responsibilities that had been until then undertaken by Britain, including such matters as legal jurisdiction over Muslim foreigners and other matters.

In 1961 on Shaikh Salman's death his eldest son Shaikh ᶜIsa ibn Salman who was then twenty-eight, succeeded him. In spite of his youth the new ruler had gained a lot of experience in administration during his father's life – he understood the running of the various councils or committees on which Bahraini democracy is run.

Councils and Committees in Bahrain

In Bahrain as in Kuwait the shaikh had the ultimate power in administration, but unlike Kuwait, which after obtaining complete independence in 1961 is now run by the Assembly and various ministries, Bahrain, which has not yet gained full independence, is still under the shaikh, who is helped by departments run by councils and committees. Usually a member of the ruling family, i.e. a shaikh, is to be found at the head of the administration of each department. This also applies to the six municipal councils of the six big towns of Bahrain, the presidents of which are all members of the Al Khalifah family.

To go back to the departments, the president from the Al Khalifah family is assisted by a director who could be either British or a native of Bahrain. According to the last census carried out in 1959, about 143,213 people live in the six said towns with the municipal councils, which gives them the right to vote to select the members of their municipal council. Women are not excluded from voting; as a matter of fact they were given this right long before some of their sisters in larger Arab countries.[41]

It should be remembered that the story of the administrative system in Bahrain does not go much further back than thirty years. The first committee to be established was that of education in 1931, and since then a stable and efficient administration has been built up with numerous departments to deal with public health, public works, education, labour affairs and minors' estates. In addition to these departments, a number of committees were established to deal with matters affecting the public interest. They included the Committee of Trade Disputes and Diving Matters, the Religious Endowment Committee (*Auqaf*), etc. The members of some of these committees were nominated, while the members of others were either elected or nominated.[42]

There is no doubt that the creation of the committees and departments came as a result of pressure from the people of Bahrain on the ruler. By participating in these committees the people of Bahrain began to take an increasing part in the administration of their country and were in fact the first people of the Gulf to do so. However, by examining the various political establishments in Bahrain, one can easily observe that the ruling family is very well represented in the various councils and committees. Bahrain is no exception to the rule governing this political aspect of government in the shaikhdoms of the Gulf. For the same phenomenon can be seen spreading in each shaikhdom.

Bahrain in Arabian Gulf Politics

Because of its wealth in pearls, Bahrain used to be the most contested bone in the Arabian Gulf area before the discovery of oil in other parts of the Gulf. But after the 1930s Bahrain was not contested for its rich pearl fisheries. There was the Persian (Iranian) claim still standing together with claims from Bahrain herself to territories in the neighbouring Qatar Peninsula. Saudi Arabia, during the zenith of Wahhabi power in the nineteenth century, had practised some sort of control for short intervals over Bahrain. The Sultan of Muscat did not, in the nineteenth century, drop his ancestors' claim to Bahrain made in an earlier period.

To go into the details of any of the four above-mentioned claims would need a lengthy study and are therefore beyond the scope of this paper. However, perhaps claims and counter-claims might have been a major factor in Bahrain's decision to join the projected Union of the Arabian Gulf States.[43]

THE SHAIKHDOM OF QATAR

The Peninsula of Qatar which is now the Shaikhdom of Qatar gained importance in the area only recently after oil was struck there. The Al Thani rule of the Peninsula is not as old as the rule of Al Sabah or Al Khalifah in eastern Arabia. Until oil was found in Qatar in the 1940s the country was inhabited mainly by nomadic tribes.

The Population

After the discovery of oil in Qatar the population of the Peninsula was almost doubled. The twenty thousand people or so became more than 40,000.[44] The early inhabitants of Qatar belong to various Arabian tribes who are mainly of Najdi (central Arabian) origin.[45] Al Thani themselves moved to Qatar from Najd early in the eighteenth century.

Historical Background

It has already been stated that in 1766, Al Khalifah departed from Kuwait and settled at Zubarah in Qatar. And until the occupation of Bahrain by Al Khalifah in 1782, Zubarah was the centre of their trade which was mainly the collecting and marketing of pearls. As a result of the occupation of Bahrain, Al Khalifah's trade multiplied because of their trade with India.[46] Zubarah, however, shared in that flourishing trade, but the Wahhabi attacks[47] towards the end of the eighteenth century forced Al Khalifah to withdraw for sometime from Zubarah to their new settlement in Bahrain. Though Al Khalifah returned partially to Zubarah early in the nineteenth century and showed a great interest in keeping that place as one of their domains on the main land, Qatar was slowly drifting from them, and other tribes were rising to power.

Perhaps the most important event in the history of Qatar in the nineteenth century was the return in the 1870s of Ottoman rule to eastern Arabia. Qatar was incorporated in the Ottoman province there and its shaikh of Al Thani was made a *Qa'im-Maqam* or an Ottoman provincial ruler of the Peninsula.[48]

Al Thani, Rulers of Qatar

Al Thani claim their descent from Thani ibn Muhammad ibn Thamir ibn ᶜAli of the Bani Tamim, one of the largest subdivisions of Mudar or Nizar, the Northern Arabs or ᶜAdnan. According to Al Thani's local tradition their ancestors left al-Washm in Najd and settled at Jibrin oasis in eastern Qatar late in the seventeenth century. They soon moved to the north and inhabited Zubarah, where they stayed for some time; but later they departed to live at Doha, the present capital of Qatar which was then a very small town. The Qatar local tradition goes on to say that Al Thani ruled Doha as vassals of Al Khalifah, rulers of Zubarah. This point is interesting for those who will go into the details of claims and counter claims to Zubarah by both Al Khalifah and Al Thani. However, it was Muhammad ibn Thani, ruler of Doha, who was the first among Al Thani shaikhs to seek independence for his tribe from Al Khalifah's dominance. Yet Muhammad does not seem to have been successful in achieving independence on his own. It was not until 1872, and with Ottoman help, that he became independent of Al Khalifah, because it was at that juncture in the history of Qatar that the Peninsula became a part of the Ottoman province of al-Ihsa'.[49]

It should be recalled in this connection that under Ottoman rule of eastern Arabia, the Ottoman Pasha would only ask the various shaikhs for nominal allegiance. Thus under the Ottomans the shaikhs of Qatar were virtually independent. This becomes very clear under Muhammad's successor, Shaikh Qasim ibn Muhammad (1878–1913), who was a great fighter and who managed to spread his influence all over the Peninsula.

ᶜAbd Allah ibn Qasim Al Thani

But this real zest for a free hand in the running of Qatar affairs did not outlive Shaikh Qasim, for during the reign of his son ᶜAbd Allah (1915–49) Qatar became a British-protected shaikhdom. The Ottomans continued to recognize the Shaikh of Qatar as their local deputy ruler until 1914, i.e. until the beginning of the First World War. However, on the eclipse of Ottoman rule in Arabia, the Shaikh of Qatar signed in 1916 a treaty with Britain embodying the provisions contained in what was called the 'exclusive' treaties already signed by the Trucial States, Bahrain and Kuwait. It should also be remembered that it was under ᶜAbd Allah that Zubarah was annexed in 1937 by Qatar. After the death of ᶜAbd Allah, he was succeeded by his son ᶜAli (1949–60). ᶜAli abdicated in 1960 and was succeeded by his son Ahmad.

Oil and State

Shaikh Ahmad Al Thani and his predecessors ruled Qatar as tribal chiefs. No major changes took place in Qatar in the field of government even after the exploitation of oil. The shaikhdom is headed by the shaikh who, since the Treaty of 1916 with the British, has to be chosen from among Al Thani family with the formal blessing of the British political agent who usually resides at Doha, the capital.

In accordance with the provisions of the 1916 Treaty, the Political Agent runs the external affairs of the shaikhdom, and, though not officially, he is consulted on important decisions affecting the internal affairs as well.[50] But the enormous wealth which oil brought to Qatar has had its effect on the internal administration of the shaikhdom. As a result of the spread of education and the rapid growth of towns, roads, etc. a great deal of the administration of the various departments passed into the hands of the civil servants, both Qataris and foreigners. However, this should not indicate that a radical change in the tribal system of government is taking place. The Shaikh of Qatar is still the sole ruler. It is true that oil brought along with it some changes in the patterns of human life, but it has not yet effected radical changes in government.

Qatar, Bahrain and the Trucial States

In the field of politics in the area, however, Qatar has always been on bad terms with Bahrain. This resulted from the previously-alluded-to Zubarah affair.[51] Bahrain did not accept Qatar's annexation of Zubarah in 1937. But Bahrain seems helpless, for the time being, to do anything to reassert her rights there. Another political problem is the demarcation of the southern boundaries with Abu Dhabi. A similar problem arises with Saudi Arabia. Will Qatar, through the newly proposed Union of the Arabian Gulf Shaikhdoms, find a solution to those border disputes? If so, what can Qatar offer Bahrain in compensation for Zubarah, for example?

Qatar and the Persian Gulf States

Since the British Government has indicated its willingness to withdraw from the Gulf area in 1971, it becomes quite apparent that Qatar's 1916 Treaty with Britain will have to be replaced by another, not necessarily with Great Britain. Here again there is the possibility of the Union of the Arabian Gulf shaikhdoms taking over from Great Britain certain responsibilities. But the Union might be unable to work on its own, when other powers in the area are taken into consideration, since Persia, Saudi Arabia and Iraq each have by far a larger population than that of all the shaikhdoms put together.

THE TRUCIAL STATES (SHAIKHDOMS)

Finally a few pages on the Trucial States exploring possible fields of development in that area will, it is hoped, clarify the new prospects of change, political, economic, social and so forth.

The Trucial Coast[52] of today comprises seven shaikhdoms which were once fewer in number. Al Qawasim[53] were the masters of the Trucial Coast for the second half of the eighteenth and the early years of the nineteenth centuries.

It might be worth while noticing in this context that among the population of the Trucial shaikhdoms, which is about 120,000, the great majority are settled Arabs. These are mainly Sunni Muslims too. There are a few Persians, Baluchis, Pakistanis and Indians. The following table[54] might also be useful for this study:

TABLE I – *Estimates of Area and Population*

Trucial State	Area square miles	Capital town	Population of Whole country	Persons per square mile
Abu Dhabi	26,000	8,000	25,000	1.0
Dubai	1,500	40,000	60,000	40.0
Sharjah	1,000	9,000	15,000	15.0
Ras al-Khaimah	650	5,000	12,000	18.0
Fujairah	450	2,000	3,500	7.8
Umm al-Qaiwain	300	2,500	33,000	10.0
ᶜAjman	100	2,000	2,500	25.0
Total	30,000	68,500	121,000	4.0

There are many expatriates from other parts of the Arab world, especially Palestinians and Iraqis. From a glance at this table, one can see that Abu Dhabi is the largest in area, Dubai is the most densely populated while Ajman is the smallest.

It might also be useful to produce here another table[55] of the neighbouring countries for the sake of comparison with the previous one.

TABLE II – *Countries Bordering the Persian Gulf*

Country	Area square miles	Population in thousands	Persons per square mile
Saudi Arabia	927,000	6,000	6
Persia (Iran)	628,000	21,000	33
Iraq	172,000	6,539	38
Muscat and Oman	82,000	550	7
Trucial Coast	30,000	121	4
Kuwait	6,200	468	75
Qatar	4,000	45	11
Bahrain	213	143	761

Britain and the Trucial Shaikhdoms

Early in the eighteenth century, Britain, represented by the English East India Company, began its monopoly of the trade and politics of the Gulf area. Ras al-Khaimah together with other Qasimi ports were attacked in 1819 by the Indian Navy. A series of treaties were signed by the various shaikhs of the Trucial Coast during the nineteenth century. But one must stress a major fact, namely that the once united coast under the Qawasim became divided into separate small shaikhdoms or political entities, the last of which to come into existence as a shaikhdom was Fujairah in 1952. It should also be stated here that, out of seven Trucial shaikhdoms, five originally were under Qasimi control or belonged to the Qasimi tribe. These are Sharjah, ᶜAjman, Umm al-Qaiwain, Ras al-Khaimah and Fujairah.

Administration of the Trucial Shaikhdoms

Change that swept the old administration in Kuwait, Bahrain and Qatar, as a result of the discovery of oil, will soon be reaching the Trucial shaikhdoms. Indeed it has reached Abu Dhabi which has recently become a rich oil-producing shaikhdom. But until a noticeable change in administration becomes clear one has to study the present system, which is run by the British Government, and try to see the prospects for development in government, the economy and so forth.

The seven shaikhdoms have been dealt with collectively by the British Government ever since treaty relations with them were established. For many years relations with them were conducted through an Arab Residency Agent with his headquarters at Sharjah.[56] At the beginning of the Second World War a British Political Officer was appointed to Sharjah. In 1953 his status was raised to that of Political Agent and in 1954 his headquarters were transferred to Dubai, where a new Agency has been built for him. In 1951 a Council of Trucial States Rulers was formed with the object of inducing them to adopt a common policy in administrative matters, such as regulations for motor traffic, the issue of nationality and passport laws and so on. The Council meets two or three times a year and Education and Health Committees have been established, and one hopes, as a result of the discovery of oil in Abu Dhabi, and the prospects of its discovery in the other shaikhdoms, to see the newly born Union of the Gulf States gaining momentum.

In 1951 the British Government, with the co-operation of the rulers, raised a force called the Trucial Oman Levies for the maintenance of law and order and the protection of the shaikhdoms against external aggression. Its strength was originally 500 men, but soon it was raised to 1,000 men. These forces, who came to be called the Trucial Oman Scouts, are recruited locally but are officered and trained by British personnel. Recently police forces coming under the authority of the states themselves have been established in Abu Dhabi and Dubai. The headquarters of the Trucial Scouts, however, is Sharjah.

The rulers mostly administer 'palm-tree justice' personally in cases which are not referred to a *qadi* for settlement according to *shari°ah* (Muslim) Law, and exercise jurisdiction only over their own or each other's subjects.[57] All foreigners, whether Muslims or non-Muslims, are subject to the jurisdiction of the Political Agent. Some cases of a mixed nature are settled by a Joint Court presided over by the Political Agent and the Ruler concerned. In the British House of Commons on 15 May 1963, the Lord Privy Seal stated that the British Government would relinquish jurisdiction when the development of satisfactory legal and judicial systems justified such action. Already steps are being taken in this direction in Abu Dhabi.[58]

When one looks into British relations with the Trucial shaikhdoms one can say that though Britain was ultimately responsible, the actual handling of affairs was delegated. Until 1858, all contacts of a diplomatic or administrative nature were conducted through the East India Company; from 1858 by the Government of Bombay acting for the British Crown and from 1873 to 1947 by the Government of British India. Since 1947, when India attained independence, negotiations and contacts have been effected through the Foreign Office in London.[59]

By virtue of the 1892 'Exclusive' Treaty, the British Government became responsible for the external affairs of the shaikhdoms. These affairs were entrusted to the Political Resident for the Gulf at first. But later this became the responsibility of the Political Officers on the Trucial Coast in Sharjah who later became Political Agents in Dubai and Abu Dhabi.

Internal Affairs

Having discussed the British role in the external affairs of the shaikhdoms, it might be useful to underline some unseen acts of British interference in their domestic affairs. 'The close personal contact maintained between the Political Agents and the Rulers,' says a Political Resident,[60] 'is an outstanding feature of the British position in the Arabian Gulf. They meet each other frequently, and more often socially than for official talks. Possibly the social meetings are more important than the official ones as a hint dropped here and there in the course of casual conversation is often more effective than formal advice, and the rulers, being Arabs, are quick to resent any attempt to teach them their business.' Another Briton[61] writes, 'The British Government does not interfere in the internal affairs of the various states except that jurisdiction over certain classes of foreigners is in the hands of the Political Agents.' This neutrality of the agents could be questioned in two events when two rulers were deposed: the first is that of Shaikh Saqr ibn Sultan al-Qasimi of Sharjah who was deposed in 1965, and the second of Shaikh Shakhbut ibn Sultan of Abu Dhabi who was deposed in August 1966 and replaced by his younger brother Shaikh Zayid.

THE UNION OF THE ARABIAN GULF SHAIKHDOMS

Before concluding this paper, a few lines on the Union of the Arabian Gulf shaikhdoms will not be out of place. This Union was proposed in February 1968 as a response from the Shaikhdoms of Bahrain, Qatar and the Trucial Coast to the British decision to withdraw from the Gulf by the end of 1971.

To appreciate the idea behind establishing a union of this nature, the student of Gulf politics must keep in mind the Persian claims to Bahrain, the Saudi interests in the lands of the shaikhdoms forming the union, Iraq's presence in the area and last but not least the position of Kuwait.

It was very difficult for most of the experts on the Gulf area to visualize the idea of a union of this nature among the shaikhdoms concerned. Yet the news of February 1968 must not come as a surprise to those experts, for if the British decide to withdraw it is only natural for these shaikhdoms to look for the means to protect their interests, especially their petroleum wealth. They could not possible invite any of the three major states bordering on the Gulf to protect them and perhaps to please those powers, it might be more helpful to keep them away. Since each of these shaikhdoms has one problem or more with one if its neighbours, the surrounding big power will think twice before taking any hostile step towards a member of the proposed union. The Shah's state visit to Saudi Arabia in

November 1968 could be seen in this perspective. Among questions discussed during the visit were most probably those relating to the new union.

It should not be assumed that the union has passed the test of establishment. Certain questions such as those relating to border and other disputes, previously discussed, are facing the rulers in their meetings which are held in the capitals of the shaikhdoms. Will the union be, therefore, a success? This is the question. There are certain factors which indicate the chances of success. The tribes of the shaikhdoms are related in the main to Mudar. The danger of being swallowed by a more powerful neighbour will certainly tell the rulers that 'in unity there is strength'. Some of the rulers in whose territories oil was found first started helping the poorer shaikhdoms in a fraternal manner. Indeed, Shaikh Zayid of Abu Dhabi made it clear that Abu Dhabi's oil is not her own but it should be shared by the neighbouring shaikhdoms, in whose territories oil had not yet been found. Kuwait, though not yet a member of the suggested union, has been giving aid to the Trucial States in the fields of health and education since 1955. Nevertheless, it would be difficult for Kuwait, if the union materializes, to keep out of it. It could, on the contrary, become an active member.

In conclusion, it can be safely said that the Gulf States are heading towards modernization in their governmental machinery, and in the economic and in the social fields. That development is following, more or less, the Kuwaiti pattern. One will soon be missing the good old days when life was simple and void of the sophistication of the developed countries.

REFERENCES

1 For a detailed study on the rise and development of Kuwait see Abu-Hakima, A. M., *History of Eastern Arabia* (Beirut, 1965), chapters 2 and 3.
2 An examination of any good map of Eastern Arabia will show many places with the name *qarn*.
3 Yaqut mentions Kazimah about twenty times in his *Mu^cjam al-Buldan*. See vols i, ii, iii and iv.
4 Arabic *^cataba* meaning 'moved very frequently'. See Ibn Manzur, *Lisan al-^cArab* (Beirut, 1347/1955), p. 597.
5 See Saldanha, J. A., *Selections from State Papers, Bombay, Regarding the East India Company's Connections with the Persian Gulf (1600–1800)* (Calcutta, 1908), p. 409 *et seq.*
6 See Abu-Hakima, Ahmad Mustafa, *Ta'rikh al-Kuwait* (Kuwait, 1387/1967), vol i, part One, p. 328. This date is given by Ibn Bishr in his *^cUnwan al-Majd fi ta'rikh Najd* (Mecca, 1349/1930), vol i, pp. 165, 176.
7 See al-Quina^ci, Yusuf ibn ^cIsa, *Safahat min ta'rikh al-Kuwait* (Damascus, 1374/1954), p. 10.

8 *Ibid.*

9 See Seetzen, Dr, 'Letters to Baron von Zach' in *Monatliche Correspondentz*, xi and xii, July–December 1805, pp. 234–5.

10 As clearly stated by Sir Harford Jones Brydges in his *Brief History of the Wahauby* (London, 1834), pp. 12–14, in his portrait of Shaikh Abd Allah ibn Sabah.

11 This tradition is still followed until the present day.

12 See al-Qina ᶜi, *op cit.*, pp. 33–7.

13 *Treaties and Undertakings in Force between the British Govt. and the Rulers of Kuwait* (Calcutta, 1919), p. 2.

14 *Ibid.*

15 *Ibid.*, p. 14.

16 Cf. Dickson, H. R. P., *Kuwait and her Neighbours* (London, 1956), p. 597, *et seq.*

17 Cf. Wahba, Hafiz, *Jazirat al-ᶜarab fi al-qarn al-ᶜishrin*, (Cairo, 1935), p. 88, and *Kuwait and her Neighbours*, pp. 270–8.

18 Cf. al-Rashid, ᶜAbd al-ᶜAziz, *Ta'rikh al-Kuwait* (Baghdad, 1344/1926), vol ii, pp. 213–14.

19 This was a rough estimation of the population as it was very difficult to include exact figures of the Bedouins in it.

20 *Al-Kitab al-sanawi* (Ministry of Information and Guidance, Kuwait, 1967), p. 7.

21 Those are the descendants of early Arabian emigration. Niebuhr, the Danish traveller, made a famous remark about the name 'Persian Gulf', when he noticed those Arabs living along its eastern shores.

22 See *Al-Kitab al-sanawi*, p. 16.

23 Hewins, R., *A Golden Dream* (London, 1963), p. 241.

24 *Ibid.*

25 For example al-Ghanim and al-Hamad families.

26 Examples can be easily traced in *Kuwait al-yaum*, the official weekly gazette, 1954–.

27 *Kuwait al-yaum*, a special issue 15 Jumada II 1382/12 November 1962, pp. 1–24.

28 This article shows how Al Sabah managed to preserve their right to continue their rule over the country which began in the 1750s. This makes it constitutional rule rather than paternal.

29 Rendered to other Gulf States and distant Arab countries in the Middle East and North Africa.

30 *Kuwait al-yaum*, no. 360, 7 January 1962, p. 1.

31. *Al-Kitab al-sanawi*, 1967, p. 82.

32 *Ibid.*, pp. 170–1.

33 The writer believes that many Kuwaits share the same opinion with the Minister of External Affairs.

34 The document relating to this affair is among the papers of the *Factory Records, Persia and the Persian Gulf*, India Office Library, London, see vol 17 dispatch no. 1230, dated 4 November 1782.

35 For an analytical study of piracy in the Gulf see Kelly, J. B., *Britain and the Persian Gulf 1795–1880* (Oxford, 1968), chapters 3 and 4.

36 The first took place in 1806 and the second in 1809.

37 A study of the Egyptian archives (in Cairo) relating to this period is essen-

tial to supplement the papers in the Public Records Office (in London). The Egyptian papers are in both Arabic and Turkish, and they are very well preserved.

38 See Lorimer, J. G., *Gazetteer of the Persian Gulf* (Calcutta, 1915), vol i, I, p. 967, *et seq.*

39 *Gazetteer*, vol i, I, p. 922.

40 See Belgrave, J., *Welcome to Bahrain* (London, 1965), p. 103 for a detailed discussion of this development.

41 See Belgrave, *op. cit.*, pp. 12–21, for government, and pp. 24–7 for development in Bahrain.

42 *Ibid.*

43 See above.

44 Al-Dabbagh, Mustafa, *Al-Jazira al-ᶜArabiya mautin al-ᶜArab wa-mahd al-Islam* two vols (Beirut, 1963?), vol ii, p. 198.

45 *Lamᶜ al-shihab fi sirat Muhammad ibn ᶜAbd al-Wahhab*, ed. A. M. Abu-Hakima (Beirut, 1967), p. 169.

46 *History of Eastern Arabia*, pp. 177–80.

47 See above.

48 *Al-Dabbagh, op. cit.*, vol. ii, p. 212, and see also below.

49 See *Gazetteer*, i, I, p. 802, *et seq.*

50 See Hay, R., *The Persian Gulf States* (Washington, 1959), pp. 15 and 30.

51 See above.

52 Named after the 'Perpetual Treaty of Peace' which was signed by the various Arab shaikhs of the coast in 1853.

53 They are said to have emigrated to Eastern Arabia from Samarra in Iraq in the seventeenth century, and they belong to Mudar or ᶜAdnan. See al-Dabbagh, *op. cit.*, vol ii, p. 150.

54 Fenelon, K. G., *The Trucial States: A Brief Economic Survey* (Beirut, 1967), p. 79.

55 *Ibid.*, p. 83.

56 See *The Persian Gulf States*, pp. 19–27.

57 *The Trucial States*, pp. 12–13.

58 *Ibid.*

59 *Ibid.*

60 See Hay, *op. cit.*, p. 20.

61 Fenelon, *op. cit.*, p. 12.

3

WAHHABISM AND SAUDI ARABIA

GEORGE RENTZ

Wahhabism as the name of a modern Islamic reform movement in Arabia is shunned by the participants in the movement, who consider it a term coined by their enemies to suggest that they are a new sect outside the pale of orthodox Islam. They hold that their movement is *al-daᶜwah ila al tauhid* ('the call to the doctrine of the Oneness of God'), a return to the original principles of Islam and a repudiation of all innovations contrary to the practices of the Prophet Muhammad and the early generations of pious Muslims. The name Wahhabism is, however, so common in the West that it is used here for the sake of convenience without any implication of heresy.

The Wahhabite state did not officially adopt the name Saudi Arabia until 1932, but, as this paper will show, a state that was both Wahhabite and Saudi existed, with brief interruptions, from 1744 on.

Arabia at the Beginning of the Eighteenth Century
At the beginning of the eighteenth century, one foreign power had a foothold in the Arabian Peninsula, the Ottoman Empire in the Hijaz. The Ottoman Sultan proudly styled himself the Servant of the Holy Cities, Mecca and Medina, where his delegates held office. At the same time, the Ottoman government recognized as the local authority in Mecca and much of the Hijaz the Hashimite Sharif, a descendant of the Prophet, whose line had been established in Mecca since the tenth century.

The Makramid dynasty of the Ismaili or extremist Shiᶜite persuasion was strong in the remarkable valley of Najran near the northern border of the Yemen. In the Yemen itself the Ottomans, who had first occupied the country in the sixteenth century, were gone, and the Imam of the Zaidi or moderate Shiᶜite persuasion held sway in the highlands. Oman was the home of the Ibadis, the spiritual heirs of the first Islamic sect, the Khawarij, but their line of Yaᶜrubi imams was declining and soon to disappear. The chief of the tribe of Bani Khalid dominated the oases west of Qatar on the Arabian side of the Persian Gulf, whence his tribe had driven out the Ottomans.

Not only was Arabia rent by sectarianism, but an old and deep division also set the nomads against the town dwellers. Scores of Bedouin tribes and scores of little towns all sought to maintain themselves as independent, and they were often at war with each other.

Islam in Arabia was a far cry from the Islam of the Prophet. Reverence for sacred stones and trees and the cult of saints, both living and dead, were common everywhere. In the eyes of orthodox Muslims, many of the practices prevailing were examples of the cardinal sin of syntheism, the association of anything or anyone with God, Who alone is deserving of worship.

The grand accomplishment of Wahhabism was that it brought unity to the larger part of this fragmented land, and within its domains it restored Islam to its early undefiled form.

The Founder of Wahhabism

In 1703 or 1704 Muhammad ibn ᶜAbd al-Wahhab was born in the town of al-ᶜUyainah in Najd. His father and grandfather were both Hanbali judges. Receiving from his father instruction in religious subjects and the Arabic language, the youth memorized the Koran before he was ten and not long after made his first pilgrimage to Mecca and first visit to Medina. Wherever he went he found manifestations of heathen syntheism. To further his studies he returned to Mecca and Medina. One of his teachers in Medina, a native of Najd, showed him the 'weapons' he had prepared for the redemption of the Arabian heartland: a house full of books.

From the Holy Cities Ibn ᶜAbd al-Wahhab in his search for knowledge went on to Basra. There for the first time he openly condemned syntheism and innovations, for which his reward was to be roughly handled and driven out of town. Staggering along barefoot in the summer heat on the way back to Arabia, he was rescued by a good Samaritan, a donkey-master of the town of al-Zubair.

Ibn ᶜAbd al-Wahhab wished to go to Damascus, an old centre of Hanbali scholarship, but he lacked the means. Instead he steered a home-ward course, pausing in al-Hasa to sit for a while at the feet of a Shafiᶜi divine.

When Ibn ᶜAbd al-Wahhab returned to Najd, he found that his father had moved to the nearby town of Huraimila. As the father apparently disapproved of his son's reforming zeal, Ibn ᶜAbd al-Wahhab bided his time and did not begin his public preaching in Najd until after his father's death in 1741. When the first few adherents came in, the reformer took heart from the Koranic verse, 'How many a small band has vanquished a great band by God's will'.[1]

In Huraimila, Ibn ᶜAbd al-Wahhab composed his most important

[1] Koran, ii (al-Baqarah) 249.

work on the doctrine of God's Oneness, in which he vigorously attacked syntheism and stressed the need for a return to the uncorrupted religion of the seventh century. He maintained that there was nothing new in what he advocated and that he was reaffirming the views of Hanbali scholars of earlier times.

As Ibn ᶜAbd al-Wahhab's doctrines spread, his position grew precarious in Huraimila, where a plot was laid to kill him. He decided to move back to his native town of al-ᶜUyainah, whose ruler was one of the most influential figures in Najd. Under the ruler's protection he carried out a series of acts dramatizing his demand for reform: cutting down sacred trees, razing the revered tomb of Zaid ibn al-Khattab, who had fallen in the battle against Musailimah the False Prophet, and stoning an adulterous woman, thereby reviving an ancient sentence in abeyance for many years.

Ibn ᶜAbd al-Wahhab's onslaught against the existing state of affairs disturbed the chief of Bani Khalid to the east, who pressed the lord of al-ᶜUyainah to rid himself of the reformer. Ibn ᶜAbd al-Wahhab assured the lord that no earthly power could prevail over those who had God's support and promised him that if he held fast he would one day rule the land of Bani Khalid and territories beyond it – but the lord reluctantly told him that he had to go.

The Alliance with the House of Saᶜud and the Spread of Wahhabism 1744–92

In the summer of 1744 Ibn ᶜAbd al-Wahhab chose as his new home the town of al-Dirᶜiyah, which lies between al-ᶜUyainah and al-Riyad. He came without an invitation from the ruler of the town, Muhammad ibn Saᶜud, but the ruler's wife and brothers persuaded him to receive the reformer with honour. These two, Muhammad ibn Saᶜud and Muhammad ibn ᶜAbd al-Wahhab, entered into a compact sealed by the same oath the Prophet and the men of Medina had sworn to cement their alliance. The reformer promised the ruler that if he held fast to the doctrine of God's Oneness, he would win dominion over lands and men. The ruler swore allegiance to the reformer in the cause of Islam and declared his readiness to undertake the jihad. This compact has endured for well over two centuries. Today the destinies of the House of Saᶜud and the House of the Shaikh[1] remain indissolubly linked. The reigning King of Saudi Arabia, Faisal Al Saᶜud, is a descendant on the male side of Muhammad ibn Saᶜud and on the distaff side of Muhammad ibn ᶜAbd al-Wahhab. Members of both houses hold key posts in the Council of Ministers of the kingdom.

Once the shaikh settled in al-Dirᶜiyah, converts came flocking in. Some

---

[1] In Saudi Arabia Muhammad ibn ᶜAbd al-Wahhab is *the* Shaikh, and his progeny bear the name of Al al-Shaikh.

men did their work at night so that they could sit with the shaikh by day and hear him recite traditions of the Prophet. Inspired by the teacher in Medina for whom books were weapons, the Shaikh sent letters to rulers and religious scholars in other towns to win them to his views. Before long, however, he realized that other weapons must also be used. The first military expedition out of al-Dir°iyah was a puny affair: riders on seven camels, some of whom fell off their mounts. But they found their quarry, a company of Bedouins, and they brought home booty. From then on booty taken from the iniquitous became one of the main sources of revenue of the Wahhabite state.

The shaikh's campaign against syntheism brought al-Dir°iyah into conflict with a number of towns in central Najd. Early on, the staunchest opponent was the neighbouring town of al-Riyad, whose ruler was a disciple of a blind saint and whose religious people attacked the shaikh in insulting terms.

Muhammad ibn Sa°ud died in 1765 with much of Najd under Wahhabite control, though al-Riyad still held out. His son °Abd al-°Aziz took his place by the side of the shaikh. As for the shaikh, it was said that no camels were mounted and no opinions were voiced by Muhammad or his son °Abd al-°Aziz without his approval. The shaikh was the supreme judge in questions of religion, and religion ruled the state.

In 1773 al-Riyad finally gave up its struggle against Wahhabism, which had lasted more than a quarter of a century. The shaikh decided that he should now retire from active participation in public affairs. Although he continued until his death in 1792 to be the intimate adviser of °Abd al-°Aziz in religion, war, and politics, he gave most of his time to a regime of worship and to the instruction of his wide circle of students.

Beginning in the late 1750s the expansion of Wahhabism embroiled al-Dir°iyah with powers beyond the confines of Najd. The chief of Bani Khalid invaded Najd, and the Wahhabites retaliated by raiding into his territory. The Ismaili lord of Najran, whom the Wahhabites called Qarin Iblis ('Satan's Accomplice'), marched in 1764 to a point not far south of al-Dir°iyah, where he inflicted a severe defeat on the Wahhabites which he failed to follow up. In the mid-1770s the puritans of Najd repulsed a second Ismaili invasion from Najran, and the Ismaili chieftain died on the way home.

The power of the reformers soon began thrusting beyond the Arabian peninsula. A British observer in Basra reported:

'. . . when I arrived at Bassora in the year 1784, his [the Wahhabite commander's] proceedings and marauding marches caused great anxiety and alarm to the paçha of Bagdad, to his governor at Bassora, as well as to the best informed Turks. For these last were aware that his doctrines, when examined by the simple text of the Koran, were perfectly orthodox, and consonant to the purest and best interpretations of that volume.'[1]

The head of the strong tribe of the Muntafiq in southern Mesopotamia advanced into Najd with cannon in his train, but in the end he came to al-Dirᶜiyah with a request to be accepted as a believer in the tenets of Wahhabism. By the later 1780s the writ of the reformers ran north to the southern edge of the Syrian Desert and south into the Valley of the Dawasir, the last peopled stretch before the Empty Quarter. Two expeditions from Najd reached Qatar on the Persian Gulf and the coast facing it to the west. Another expedition won a signal victory over the forces of Bani Khalid near the present town of Abqaiq (Buqaiq). In 1792 the iconoclasts of Najd descended on the oasis of al-Qatif, the principal Shiᶜite centre on the Arabian side of the Persian Gulf, and destroyed the Shiᶜite places of worship there.

Only four or five years after the compact between Ibn ᶜAbd al-Wahhab and Ibn Saᶜud the Wahhabites began having difficulties with the Sharif of Mecca. When Wahhabite pilgrims preached their doctrines during the rites of the pilgrimage, the Sharif arrested them and held some in confinement until they died. The historical sources contain no mention of Wahhabite pilgrims for a period of about twenty years ending in 1770, when the reigning sharif allowed a number to come. A Wahhabite divine visited Mecca and held a disputation with three of the ᶜulama' there which seemed to prepare the way for better relations, but shortly thereafter the ban on Wahhabite pilgrims was reimposed. In 1788, Ghalib ibn Musaᶜid became the Sharif of Mecca. Soon after his accession he invited a Wahhabite mission to his court, but the ᶜulama' of Mecca refused to join in a debate. Turning hostile, Ghalib began attacking the Wahhabites in the western reaches of Najd and inciting against them the nomad tribes under such leaders as Hisan Iblis ('Satan's Charger'). This was the start of a bitter war that lasted until the Wahhabites entered Mecca in 1803.

In 1792 the Shaikh Muhammad ibn ᶜAbd al-Wahhab died at the age of nearly ninety. Buried with no elaborate ceremonies and no memorial in stone or clay, he left behind four sons who were eminent religious scholars as well as many other students dedicated to the propagation of Wahhabism.

[1] Sir Harford Jones Brydges, *An Account of the Transactions of His Majesty's Mission to the Court of Persia, in the Years 1807–11, to Which is Appended a Brief History of the Wahauby* (London, 1834), vol. ii, p. 9.

Wahhabism Ascendant 1792–1814

Muhammad ibn ᶜAbd al-Wahhab and his associates, Muhammad ibn Saᶜud and his son ᶜAbd al-ᶜAziz, laid the foundations for Wahhabism as a religious and political force in Arabia, extending its mandate over the whole of Najd and beginning the progress towards the Persian Gulf and the Red Sea. ᶜAbd al-ᶜAziz outlived the shaikh by eleven years, and his son Saᶜud reigned from 1803 to 1814. These two kept the early momentum going, carrying the doctrines of Wahhabism farther afield to the four points of the compass.

ᶜAbd al-ᶜAziz annexed al-Qatif and the inland oasis of al-Hasa, perhaps half of whose inhabitants were Shiᶜites. For a time the island of Bahrain and its rulers, the House of Khalifah, became subject to al-Dirᶜiyah. The presence of many Hanbalis along the southeastern coast of the Gulf (what is now called the Trucial Coast) facilitated the acceptance of Wahhabism there. Near the end of the eighteenth century the first Wahhabite governor went to the oasis of al-Buraimi, the gateway to inner Oman, at the request of the residents. Early in the nineteenth century the men of Najd set foot on the shores of the Arabian Sea at the eastern end of the peninsula. Among the tribes they won over was Bani Bu ᶜAli, whose members have cleaved to the faith ever since. The chief of this tribe journeyed to al-Dirᶜiyah for further instruction, and on returning home he proved a persuasive missionary.

The one ruler of consequence in eastern Arabia who doggedly opposed the Wahhabite advance was the Sultan of Muscat, an Ibadi but not the head of the Ibadi community, his regime having become secular. To stave off the Wahhabites, the Sultan often paid them tribute; he also sought and at times received the help of allies – the British, the Sharif of Mecca, and the Persians.

The long war with the Sharif Ghalib of Mecca found the Wahhabites steadily driving the sharif back towards his capital as more and more of the tribesmen of the borderlands joined their ranks. In 1803 the shaven-pated soldiers of Allah came crowding into the Holy City and proceeded to destroy the domed shrines where people offered prayers to saints rather than to God. The puritans burned all the hookahs and stringed instruments they could lay hands on. Two years later they performed the same cleansing operation in Medina. The Sharif Ghalib was allowed to retain his office, but for a decade al-Dirᶜiyah controlled the Hijaz. Wahhabism has always contained a strain of the old Arab nationalism, which has roots going back far beyond the type of nationalism inspired by the French Revolution. The truth of this was demonstrated by the way in which the Wahhabites set about obliterating all traces of Ottoman influence in the Hijaz.

In the mountains of ᶜAsir, south of the Hijaz, Wahhabism enjoyed the staunch support of able leaders. From this base the movement spilled over into the lowland of Tihamah along the Red Sea, reaching as far south as ports in the Yemen. In the highlands of the Yemen the Zaidis preserved their independence. Wahhabites made quick descents on Hadhramaut on the far side of the Empty Quarter, where they are remembered as 'the men in the camel's-hair cloaks', but they did not succeed in attaching the region to their state.

In the north the Wahhabites advanced into Mesopotamia and Syria. In 1802 they broke into Karbala', the resting place of the Prophet's martyred grandson al-Husain, and demolished many objects sacred to the Shiᶜites. Sweeping across the desert, they harassed the settled areas and cities of the Twin Rivers. On the side of Syria their arms threatened Damascus.

ᶜAbd al-ᶜAziz and his son Saᶜud refined and developed the administration of the state. For all the important towns they appointed governors and judges responsible for the implementation of the basic principles of Islam, including the regular collection of the religious tax, the *ẓakah*, which is designed to be a sort of redistribution of wealth. A scholar of Baghdad characterizes ᶜAbd al-ᶜAziz's reign as follows:

'Through him the wars which used to take place among the tribes of Najd came to an end. Peace and security existed among the Bedouins and the settled people. Camels, horses, sheep, and goats used to graze in the desert and give birth to their young, guarded by no more than a single man.'[1]

A British historian of Arabia says that ᶜAbd al-ᶜAziz 'secured by summons or armed force the more or less sincere adhesion of all the peninsula, except the south-west', and then he affirms that the power of the state 'rested less on military compulsion than on spiritual influence'.[2]

Another British historian, in discussion Saᶜud's rule, says:

'The tendency of the Wahhābi government in Najd . . . was essentially civilizing. Among the principal objects kept in view were the establishment of law and order, the suppression of local wars and private feuds, and the substitution for the latter of state-inflicted punishments and state-awarded compensation. . . .'[3]

[1] Ibrahim Fasih ibn Sibghat Allah al-Haidari, *Unwan al-majd fi bayan ahwal Baghdad wa-Basrah* [*sic*] *wa-Najd*, MS 1286/1869–1870, f. 112v.

[2] D. G. Hogarth, *Arabia* (Oxford, 1922), pp. 103–104.

[3] J. G. Lorimer, *Gazetteer of the Persian Gulf, 'Oman and Central Arabia* (Bombay, 1915), vol. i, p. 1064.

Even before the end of the eighteenth century the swelling strength of Wahhabism aroused the apprehension of the Ottoman government, and an Ottoman expeditionary force made a futile attempt to drive the Najders away from the Arabian seaboard of the Persian Gulf. The later years of the reign of Sultan Salim III, whom the Janissaries overthrew in 1807, were troubled by Bonaparte's invasion of Egypt and the rising of the Serbs in the Balkans. Losing the Holy Cities, the Sultan perforce turned to his new Viceroy of Egypt, Muhammad ᶜAli, to stem the Wahhabite tide.

The Intervention of Muhammad ᶜAli and the Fall of al-Dirᶜiyah, 1811–18
Muhammad ᶜAli, an officer commanding Albanian troops of the Ottoman army who had become the Pasha or Viceroy of Egypt, did not heed immediately the Sultan's injunction to strike against the Wahhabites; he held back for some years while tightening his control over Egypt. In 1811 he made that control absolute by massacring several hundred of his Mameluke rivals at a ceremony celebrating the departure at long last of the expedition to Arabia. The initial plan called for the converging of three armies on Arabia from Egypt, Syria, and Mesopotamia, but in the end only the army from Egypt advanced, under the command of Muhammad ᶜAli's son Tusun.

In the first encounter in the Hijaz the Wahhabites, despite their inferior equipment, routed the invaders. New levies from Egypt enabled Tusun to take Medina and Mecca, but the Wahhabite ruler, Saᶜud, kept his main forces intact until his death in 1814. The wisdom of the strategy of inducing the enemy to overextend his lines of communication was shown when a valiant woman, Ghaliyah of the tribe of the Buqum, at the head of Wahhabite soldiers won a victory in the mountains east of Mecca.

The death of Saᶜud deprived the Wahhabite state of the leader who might have preserved it. His son and successor, ᶜAbd Allah, lacked Saᶜud's skill as a commander. Muhammad ᶜAli himself had come to Arabia to direct operations from 1813 to 1815. When he returned to Egypt, he put his son Ibrahim Pasha in his place. Slowly and methodically Ibrahim moved his siege artillery and ammunition train eastwards. ᶜAbd Allah, instead of harrassing the enemy in open country, shut himself up in al-Dirᶜiyah. The Wahhabite capital was strongly fortified, but Ibrahim was persistent, and after a siege of about six months. he forced ᶜAbd Allah to surrender in September 1818, bringing to an end the first Wahhabite state, nearly three-quarters of a century after its founding.

The Revival of the Wahhabite State, 1819–38
By order of Ibrahim Pasha, al-Dirᶜiyah was razed in 1819. Many members of the House of Saᶜud had fallen during the siege, and others had been

carried off to Cairo. The future looked bleak for the reform movement, but the Wahhabite faith was ingrained in the people of Najd and the House of Saʿud had not lost its capacity for producing talented rulers. In this chaotic time the line of succession was not fixed, but a cousin of the great Saʿud, Turki ibn ʿAbd Allah, soon came to the forefront. Driven out of the partially rebuilt town of al-Dirʿiyah by the occupying forces, Turki in 1824 established himself in al-Riyad, which has since remained the capital of the state. Muhammad ʿAli's troops withdrew from Najd to the Hijaz.

The character of Turki's rule is revealed by a speech he made to his provincial governors after he had heard complaints against one or more of them. He severely condemned the sin of oppressing the subjects of the state and warned that the penalty would be deposition from office and exile. He told the governors that they were mistaken if they thought that they had conquered lands with their swords; the power of Islam had brought these lands under the sovereignty of the state.

An aspirant to the rule arranged the assassination of Turki in 1834, but Turki's oldest son Faisal succeeded him at once and followed in his father's footsteps. In 1838 Muhammad ʿAli again sent troops into Najd, where they defeated Faisal and took him as a prisoner to Cairo. On this occasion the occupation lasted two years.

The Second Revival of the Wahhabite State, 1840–91

In 1840 Muhammad ʿAli of Egypt forsook Arabia after nearly three decades of largely fruitless ventures there. Two members of the House of Saʿud began in succession to rebuild the Wahhabite state, but in 1843 the second of them gave way to Faisal ibn Turki, who escaped from captivity in Egypt and came home to inaugurate his second reign. Faisal, according to a British historian, was

'. . . distinguished by his dignity and self-possession and was respected for the justice of his decisions, but he was greatly feared, especially by the Bedouins, on account of his merciless severity. . . .

'In his dominions Faisal seems to have maintained perfect order, and from the very first year of his reign he showed great energy in protecting the yearly pilgrimages to the Holy Cities against marauding Bedouins.'[1]

Lieutenant Colonel Lewis Pelly, the British Political Resident in the Persian Gulf, who visited Faisal in al-Riyad in 1865, described him as

'. . . a just and stern ruler who had been unprecedently successful in

[1] Lorimer, *Gazetteer*, i, p. 1109.

curbing the predatory habits of his tribes; and who was desirous of inculcating among them more settled habits, and of turning their minds towards agriculture and trade.'[1]

Faisal spoke to Pelly about his rule:

'... be Arabia what it may, it is ours. We dare say you wonder how we can remain here thus cut off from the rest of the world. Yet we are content. We are princes according to our degree. "We feel ourselves a king every inch."'[2]

Faisal died in 1865, only a few months after Pelly's visit. He was in a sense the refounder of Saudi Arabia, where the ruling family today calls itself the House of Faisal, a branch of the House of Saᶜud. The realm, however, slipped into a decline not long after his death. A civil war between two of his sons undermined the authority of the state, which came to be hemmed in on three sides by powers inimical to the House of Saᶜud. The opening of the Suez Canal brought the Ottomans back into western Arabia in strength, and in 1871 they seized the northern part of the Arabian coast of the Persian Gulf. In Najd the House of Rashid expanded at the expense of the House of Saᶜud.

The Uncontested Rule of the House of Rashid, 1891–1902
Since the first half of the eighteenth century the House of Saᶜud had re-pelled challenges for supremacy by other dynasties in Arabia. Late in the nineteenth century the tables were turned. The House of Rashid of the tribe of Shammar, originally established by the House of Saᶜud in the town of Ha'il for the governing of the northern province of Jabal Shammar, extended its influence southwards, profiting by dissension in the House of Saᶜud. By 1884 the House of Rashid became the dominant power in Najd, and in 1887 it posted a garrison in al-Riyad. ᶜAbd al-Rahman, the youngest son of Faisal ibn Turki, held out in al-Riyad, largely on suffer-ance by the House of Rashid. A great military victory by the House of Rashid over its opponents in Najd in 1891 made ᶜAbd al-Rahman's position in al-Riyad untenable, and he went into exile, taking with him his son ᶜAbd al-ᶜAziz, then about eleven years of age. Ultimately the father and son settled in Kuwait on the Persian Gulf. The occupation of Najd by the House of Rashid was much less onerous than the earlier occupation by the hosts of Muhammad ᶜAli, as the members of the nor-thern house were themselves Wahhabites, though somewhat milder in their views than many men of central Najd.

[1] Lewis Pelly, *Report on a Journey to the Wahabee Capital of Riyadh in Central Arabia* (Bombay, 1866), p. 7.
[2] Pelly, *op. cit.*, p. 55.

Wahhabism in the Twentieth Century[1]

ᶜAbd al-ᶜAziz ibn ᶜAbd al-Rahman Al Faisal Al Saᶜud was the architect of the Kingdom of Saudi Arabia and the man who did most to determine the course of Wahhabism in the twentieth century. In 1902 ᶜAbd al-ᶜAziz left his place of exile in Kuwait and in a bold exploit captured al-Riyad from the forces of the House of Rashid. He rebuilt the base of Wahhabite power in Najd and thwarted Ottoman attempts to conquer the region. Early he set his sights beyond the borders of Najd; he was fond of saying that his aim was to regain the lands his forefathers had held. Although he was a deeply religious man, his policy could often properly be described as secular. In 1913 he threw the Ottomans out of al-Hasa and al-Qatif.

The unruly Bedouins, even though many were fervid Wahhabites, had always been hard to manage. ᶜAbd al-ᶜAziz's grandfather Faisal had been concerned with settling some of them in towns,[2] but ᶜAbd al-ᶜAziz himself adopted a more ambitious programme. Starting in about 1912, he encouraged the Bedouins to found perhaps two hundred *hijrahs*, new towns which were a combination of military cantonment, agricultural colony, and missionary centre for the propagation of Wahhabism. The settlers called themselves Ikhwan (Brothers).[3] Devotees of the jihad against unbelievers, that is, all non-Wahhabites, the Ikhwan rendered valuable service to ᶜAbd al-ᶜAziz in building up Saudi Arabia. During the years just after the First World War the Ikhwan were the backbone of the armies that annexed first ᶜAsir, then Jabal Shammar, where the House of Rashid was overcome, and finally the Hijaz, where King al-Husain, the former Sharif of Mecca who pretended to sovereignty over all the Arabs, was forced to abdicate. In 1921 ᶜAbd al-ᶜAziz took the secular title of Sultan in place of the religious title of Imam borne by all his predecessors, and after the conquest of the Hijaz he took in 1926 the even more secular title of King.

In the 1920s the Ikhwan became a source of embarrassment for ᶜAbd al-ᶜAziz rather than a support. Without his concurrence they carried their raids against unbelievers into the new states of Transjordan and Iraq, where they came to blows with the mandatory power, Great Britain. The chiefs of the Ikhwan lodged protests against ᶜAbd al-ᶜAziz for introducing such innovations as motor vehicles, aircraft, telephones, and wireless telegraphy. ᶜAbd al-ᶜAziz maintained that these devices had nothing to do with religion. On this question the Wahhabite ᶜ*ulama*' temporized,

---

[1] This section and the following one are in part condensed from my chapter on Wahhabism in A. J. Arberry, *ed.*, *Religion in the Middle East*, (Cambridge, 1969), vol. ii, pp. 170–84.

[2] See pp. 62–3 above.

[3] For a longer account of the Ikhwan, see my article on the subject in the new edition of *The Encyclopaedia of Islam*.

but at least they did not strongly side with the extremists among the Ikhwan.

In the late 1920s many of the Ikhwan joined in an open revolt against ᶜAbd al-ᶜAziz, only to be brought to heel early in 1930. Thus the course was set for Saudi Arabia: a moderate form of Wahhabism would rule the state, and changes that did not conflict with the fundamental principles of Islam would be accepted in Wahhabite society.

In 1933 the grant of an oil concession to an American company proved to be the first step on the way to providing a tremendous impetus to the process of change. The company discovered oil in 1938 and began production on a large scale in 1946. The revenue of the state, estimated at about £50,000 during the early years of ᶜAbd al-ᶜAziz's reign, rose to about two thousand times this amount before he died. The new wealth posed threats to the moral standards of Wahhabism, but after a certain amount of stumbling during the early stages, the Wahhabite society is showing greater maturity in the management of its financial affairs.

The oil industry and other businesses have brought foreign men and women into Saudi Arabia in considerable numbers. The traditions of Arab hospitality have triumphed over the xenophobia of extreme Wahhabism, and the newcomers are welcomed in a way that would have shocked the chiefs of the Ikhwan in the 1920s.

Wahhabism has also of late shown more tolerance towards other Islamic sects. When British-led forces expelled the Ibadi Imam from Oman in the 1950s, he found a sanctuary in Saudi Arabia. When a republican revolution unseated the Zaidi Imam of the Yemen in 1962, Saudi Arabia came to the aid of his resistance movement in the northern mountains.

With the greatly expanded revenue in Saudi Arabia, development there is bringing about a revolution in such fields as communications and education. Regular flights by the government airline, paved roads, and trains link once isolated areas with the main centres. The press is vigorous, and television and radio are widely watched and listened to. The school system supplements the traditional Islamic curriculum with many courses in the Western sciences and humanities leading up to and including the university level. Girls' schools are becoming increasingly popular.

Saudi Arabia, until not long ago largely an Islamic island, has taken a plunge into the international community with membership in the United Nations and various other international organizations. Many Saudi Arabs go abroad for business, study, or pleasure. The exposure to new ideas, customs, and practices goes on apace. Some of the people, particularly the youth, demand a faster pace of change. At the same time, a strong conservative Wahhabite strain endures in government and society. Progressives calling for a constitution are told that the Koran is the kingdom's

constitution. The future of the Wahhabite state depends on the harmoniz-
ing of the views of the impatient progressives and the conservatives who
cherish the proven values of two centuries of history.

Wahhabism and the Islamic World

No study of Wahhabism in Saudi Arabia can be complete without giving
some consideration to its possible connection with similar reform movements in other parts of the Islamic world in the nineteenth and twentieth
centuries. The precise nature of the connection is often difficult to determine. Early in the career of Ibn ᶜAbd al-Wahhab he and his disciples were
active in sending books and epistles to prospective converts. Once Mecca
and Medina were occupied, the Wahhabites secured a better forum for
the dissemination of their doctrines. The exposition of their creed reached
as far west as North Africa in the first years of the nineteenth century.
Recent research has indicated that the so-called Wahhabites of India
borrowed little from the Wahhabites of Arabia, but it is likely that other
movements in India, such as the Faraidi and Ahl-i Hadith, were more
closely associated. The Sanusism of Libya, which had its origins in Arabia
in the nineteenth century, and the Mirghanism and Mahdism of the Sudan
have a definite affinity with Wahhabism. Modernist reformers such as
Muhammad ᶜAbduh, Muhammad Rashid Rida, and other adherents of
Salafism have acknowledged their debt to the writings of Ibn ᶜAbd al-
Wahhab and his Wahhabite colleagues.

4

THE ORIGINS OF THE OMANI STATE

J. C. WILKINSON

The history of Oman as a state is dominated by three recurrent themes, the tribal picture, the story of the imamate and the struggle between Omanis and foreigners for control of her coastal provinces. The very title of the modern state, 'The Sultanate of Muscat and Oman', highlights these three themes. If this chapter concentrates on the early history of the country it is not entirely due to the author's personal interests but rather because he believes it is only through a study of the origins of the tribal pattern and its relationship to the Ibadi imamate that the fundamental issues effecting 'national' unity can be understood.

Oman (correctly ᶜUmān) early evolved as the name for the geographical region centred on the mountain range which extends from the Musandam Peninsula at the mouth of the Persian Gulf to Jaᶜlan. Farther up the Gulf the oases of the modern Hasa province form the central point of what the Arab geographers know as 'al-Bahrain' whilst 'al-Shihr' formed the easterly extension of Hadhramaut, Oman's neighbour, in south Arabia. The landward extension of these three geographical regions is clearly defined by the great sand barrier of the Empty Quarter but their respective influences on the few peoples who inhabit the wastelands which separate them defines the respective outer limit of each region. The recent importance of drawing frontiers between the states of modern Trucial Oman and Saudi Arabia, that is between 'ᶜUman' and 'al-Bahrain', has been matched by a longer history concerning control of 'Mahraland' on the south coast at present reflected in the ownership of the Dhofar province by the Sultan of Muscat and Oman. But whilst these mountains of Oman have formed a focal point in the settlement of the peoples of the Arabian Peninsula they also command the point where the commerce of the Indian Ocean is channelled into the historic trade route of the Persian Gulf. Oman has therefore been profoundly influenced by both its desert and maritime environment, by its situation as part of the Arabian mainland and by its position as an integral part of a major maritime commercial complex. From the earliest times the peoples of these two quite different cultural environments have met in the mountain core of the country and evolved a society that is unique. It is the nature of this society that has, in part,

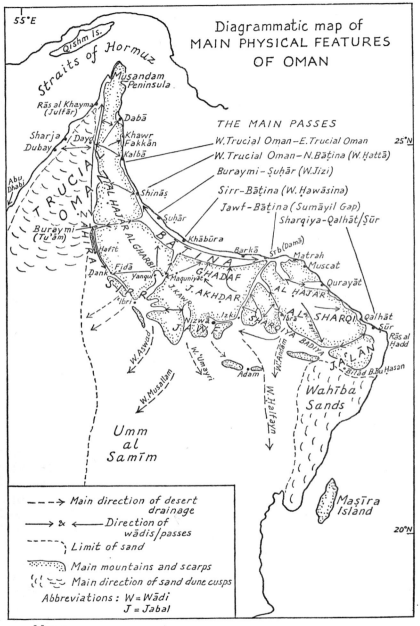

Map 1

determined the form of an Omani political unity, but it is physical rather than cultural factors which have allowed an independent Omani state to survive in some form for nearly 1,200 years.

A glance at Map 1 will show that the node of the mountains is the central massif of the Jabal al-Akhdar. The uneroded limestone plateau of the Jabal itself may be considered as the ultimate bastion of the Omani fortress, as the events of the 1950s only too well demonstrated, but it is the villages of the Ghadaf, Jauf and 'Suma'il Gap' which are the real heartland of Oman (cf. Map 2) and the specific area to which the name Oman tends to apply. Entrenched in the stupendous valleys in the eastern side of the Jabal, protected by an outer ring of foothills and the two arms of the Rub‘ al-Khali which extend towards the mountains in the Dhahirah (al-Zahirah) and the Sharqiyah on the west, these villages enjoy a perfect natural defence. The physical configuration of the Omani mountains are also partly responsible for certain characteristics of Omani society. The interdependence of the enclaves of settled territory are offset by the isolation of the valleys, and isolation is perhaps the key word in Omani 'national' development. Not only is the Jabal al-Akhdar isolated, but within it every valley is defensively and economically independent, whilst even the village is often a fully viable unit, a fortified settlement watered by its individual qanat. It is only when these inherent individualistic trends are subordinated to a higher interest that the peoples of the mountains can unite and it is only then that the Omanis can become masters of their own land and enjoy the fruits of their maritime situation.

With this brief sketch of the physical factors influencing Oman's development as a state we can try to isolate some of the historical factors which have determined its nature. From the beginnings of history it is possible to trace settlement in Oman from the desert fringes and from the Persian mainland; until the coming of Islam it was the latter which determined the cultural environment of the landscape. The basic economy of interior Oman today has been determined by pre-Islamic Persian influences. By the technique of subterranean galleries (qanat), a major step forward from the simple techniques of ghail and well irrigation was achieved. This appears to have taken place in two main stages; the earlier development (Achaemenid?) was along the western side of the mountains from northern Oman as far, perhaps, as the borders of the Jauf and Sharqiyah whilst the latter (Sasanid), using new techniques, developed the mountain valleys, particularly those of the Ghadaf. It was probably during Sasanid times also that the settlement potential of the Batinah coast was fully exploited. Although there has been some subsequent development of ghail irrigation, wells and the simplest forms of qanat, all the large villages of interior Oman rely for their main water supply on the

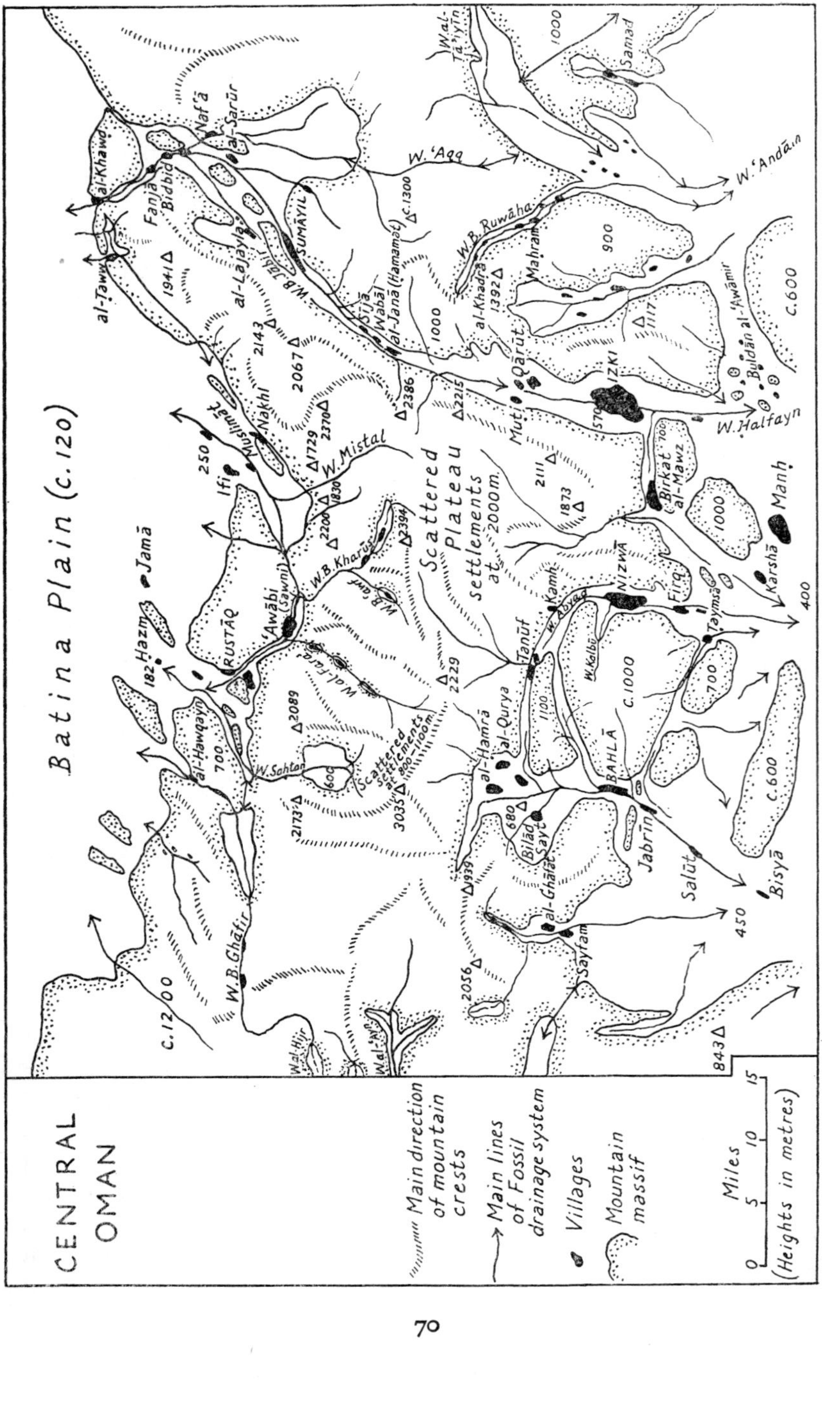
CENTRAL OMAN
Main direction of mountain crests
Main lines of Fossil drainage system
Villages
Mountain massif
Miles
0 5 10 15
(Heights in metres)
Batina Plain (c.120)
Scattered Plateau settlements at 2000m.
Scattered settlements at 800–1100m.
RUSTĀQ
'Awābi (Sawni)
NIZWĀ
BAHLĀ
IZKI
SUMĀYIL
Nakhl
Ifi
Jamā
Hazm
al-Hawqayn
W.B. Ghāfir
W. Mistal
W.B. Kharūs
W.B. Ruwāha
W. 'Aqq
W. 'Andām
W. Halfayn
Fanjā
Bidbid
Naf'ā
al-Sarūr
al-Khawd
al-Taww
al-Lajayla
Tanūf
Kamh
Firq
Taymsā
Karshā
Manh
Birkat al-Mawz
Mutī
Qārūt
Mahram
al-Khadrā
Jabrīn
Salūt
Bisyā
Sayfam
al-Ghāfāt
Bilād Sayt
al-Hamrā
al-Qurya
Samad
Buldān al-'Awāmir
W. Kalbū
W. Sahtan
W.B. Jābir
Sijā
Wabāl
al-Janā (Hamamat)
3035
2089
2173
2229
2143
2067
2370
1729
1830
2200
2394
2386
2215
2111
1873
1941
1392
1117
1939
2056
843
c.1300
c.1200
c.1000
c.600
1000
900
700
600
570
450
400
250
182
1100

Map 2

original Persian *qanat*. The permanent settlement pattern of Oman was thus largely determined in pre-Islamic times by non-Arabs and the areas under cultivation were considerably greater than they are at present. The concomitant of this economic exploitation of the terrain was the Persian social organization; until the time of Islam the structure of village society was fundamentally feudal.

The first stories concerning the arrival of the Arabs in Oman (and here we must distinguish between Arabs and what might be termed 'proto-Arabs') relate the history of the migration of an Azd group, the Malik ibn Fahm, who were accompanied by Rasib and Mahrah groups of the Qudaᵉah. These groups spread along the southern coast of Arabia and elements started reaching the borderlands of Oman where they began to settle in the Jaᵉlan. Here they were outside the settled region under Persian control but their further movement northwards into the confines of the Jauf brought them into direct conflict with the Persians. The stories concerning this migration are, of course, semi-legendary but the corpus of evidence points to it having taken place in pre-Sasanid times, probably in the second century A D. The degree of success the stories claim for these first Arabs in the battles with the Persians is probably exaggerated, but that they were successful in obtaining a foothold in the settled lands along the western side of the mountains is fairly clear. This migration was followed by that of many other groups from western Arabia. Long before the majority of the major groups (see Map 3 and note on sources, pp. 86–88) had arrived in Oman the Persians had regained control of much of the settled area. Perhaps because of the pressure of the new Arab settlers in north-west Oman, perhaps because new sailing techniques had placed the maritime emphasis on the Batinah ports, the evidence indicates that it was eastern Oman that became the centre of Persian interests and the Sasanids appear to have made no attempt to rule directly in most of northern Oman. Suhar became their commercial capital whilst Rustaq, as its name implies, became their chief town in the interior. Their control of the hinterland was exercised through an Arab chieftain, who bore the title of Julanda, and their direct physical control there appears to have been limited to the central core of Oman. This territory which they directly controlled went under the name of Mazun.

The relationship between the Arabs and the Persians is symbolized in a so-called treaty between the Sasanid monarchs and the Arabs. It is fairly clear that this treaty refers to the period of the development of new Persian interests in the Arabian Peninsula in the sixth century. By this time the Arab presence in Oman must have developed beyond the stage whereby it could be controlled by military tactics alone. The Malik ibn Fahm settlement in Oman and their spread beyond into al-Bahrain (used always in its original geographic sense) was but the first manifestation of the Arabs as an active power in eastern Arabia. The arrival of Arab tribes in Oman came from two directions, along the borderlands of the settled regions of south Arabia and through the northern gateway of Tuwam (Buraimi) where a major migration route through central Arabia to al-Bahrain brought tribes to all the settled lands bordering the Persian Gulf. This route also completed a major system of tribal migration routes linking north, south, west, east and central Arabia; an understanding of this 'circulation' pattern is a prerequisite if any sense is to be made of the relationship of Arab groups in pre-Islamic times. Although the southern route continued to bring in Malik ibn Fahm and Qudaᶜah groups until early Islamic times it seems probable that it was the Taiy who were the only other major group to arrive in Oman by this route. All the other groups shown on the map appear to have arrived in Oman from the north and the first to arrive from this direction were the ᶜImran Azd, possibly in pre-Sasanid times. Bahrain came to be dominated by the ᶜAbd al-Qais and the good relations which prevailed between them and the Azd is symbolized by the right to settle granted by 'Malik ibn Fahm', king of the Azd. The amicable relationship between the Azd and the ᶜAbd al-Qais and their spectrum of relations with other tribal groups of eastern Arabia, notably their enmity with the Bani Saᶜd (Tamim), was later to play an important part in the history of the Omanis in Basra. The presence of a large Kindah element in Oman was also to play a role in the establishment of the Ibadi state throughout much of southern Arabia for the Azd and Kindah appear to have established good relations both in Oman and in Basra where some of their clans shared the same *Khums*. The saying that although the Kharus (Yahmad, Azd) are the source of the *imamah* the Kunud are the source of *fiqh* not only refers to the scholarly attainment of the Kindah clan in Nizwa from the eleventh to fourteenth centuries but also symbolizes the relationship of the two tribal groupings in Oman. A special word must also be said about the Bani Samah for the arrival of this powerful group (other Qurashi groups deny their genealogy) in northern Oman via al-Bahrain posed a threat to the Azd and ᶜAbd al-Qais tribes already settled there. An understanding was reached with the leading Azd group of northern Oman, the As(a)d ᶜImran, and the Bani Samah settled peacefully. They remained, however, a highly independent group with no particularly close tribal links with other groups in Oman whilst in Basra they were not associated with the other Gulf tribes but formed part of the ᶜAliyah *Khums*.

The last major tribal group that must be touched on are the most important in Oman's history, the clans of the so-called Azd Shanu'ah grouping. The last of the major Azd genealogical groupings to arrive in Oman, its

Omani clans left their kinsmen in western Arabia and, migrating through Yamamah and al-Bahrain where they appear to have established something of a tribal ascendancy, entered Oman. It seems likely that their arrival coincided with a period of weak Persian rule, perhaps at the end of the fifth century for they penetrated and settled in the very heartland of Mazun, the Huddan with their capital at Yanqul in the 'Jabal Huddan' and the Ma^{c}awil and Yahmad in the Ghadaf. They appear quickly and amicably to have gained the leadership over the other Azd tribes of south-east Arabia and established particularly good relations with the powerful Bani Hina, the leading Malik ibn Fahm clan who, in their turn, were closely allied to the ^{c}Atik, the shaikhly clan of the ^{c}Imran, and the Bani Salimah, a highly powerful and individual clan of the Malik ibn Fahm in south-east Oman and the then leading Arab tribe of south-west Persia. Their ascendancy over the tribes of Oman in general however was due to their relationship with the Persians. Settled in the Persian controlled area of interior Oman the Ma^{c}awil and Yahmad were directly subject to them but in return their shaikhly section was recognized as the kings of the Arabs. With the support of the Persians their tribal links were reinforced and the Ma^{c}wali Julanda not only exercised control over the Arabs, with their own *suq* at the port of Daba outside Mazun, but also had a loose control of the majority of Arab groups from Mahrah territory to Bahrain, that is the whole territory of 'Greater Oman'.

The use of the word 'settle' in connection with the Arabs of Oman in pre-Islamic times should not be taken literally. Although they lived in the mountains and foot-hills they were not villagers. In bedu fashion they divided the mountain terrain into tribal *dars* and this is the origin of the primary settlement pattern shown in Map 3. Their way of life must have been much the same as the mountain bedu, the *shawawi*, of Oman today. On the other hand they formed associations with the villages in the valleys and this is reflected in the frequency of the name of wadis bearing a tribal name (W. Bani Kharus, W. Bani Ma^{c}awil, W. Sahtan, W. Bani Ghafir, W. Ta'iyin, etc.) but, perhaps with the exception of some of the Azd groups in central Oman, few of the Arabs actually cultivated the land themselves. However, even in pre-Islamic times there had been some dispersal of groups from the primary tribal *dars* and this, in the course of time, was to build up new relations and help integrate Arab society above the tribal level. Whilst the majority of Arabs had not become cultivators, large numbers, notably Azd groups, had begun to settle on the coasts and become fisherfolk, sailors and minor traders. The tribesmen had spread to the Persian side of the Gulf and many had become assimilated into the indigenous population. A kind of maritime kingdom under the leadership of a clan of the Bani Salimah controlled the entrance of the Gulf under the aegis of the Sasanids: this Julanda (ibn Karkar) family continued to control it into Buyid times. Their way of life and their subjection to the Persians was a frequent taunt thrown at the Omani and other Gulf tribes in early Islamic times.

The immediate impact of the call to Islam was the eviction of the Persian ruling class from Oman and the transfer of power to the Arabs. Within a few years the caliphs abandoned direct administration of Oman and for the greater part of the following 150 years the country was left entirely in the hands of the Julanda and subject to a form of tribal regime that differed little from that of the bedu of the desert. The villages now became the property of the tribal groups in whose *dar* they lay and whilst the peasants were probably little worse off, as individuals, than they had been under Persian rule the former organization of the village life, which at least ensured the continued prosperity of their community, must have virtually collapsed.

Whilst interior Oman was lapsing into tribal anarchy the real foundations of a 'national' concept were developing elsewhere. It was the Islamic *misr* of al-Basrah which became the focal point for the Arabs of the Persian Gulf in the dynamic development of the new Islamic Empire of the East. The favour the first Azd settlers from central Oman (the last of the major tribal groupings to come to the *misr*) somewhat fortuitously found with its future governor, Ziyad ibn Abihi, the organization of Basra into *Akhmas* giving the Omani Azd the leadership of a number of tribal groups in their own *khums*, the influx of new Azd bedu groups towards the end of Mu'awiyah's reign, the subsequent coup of AH 64, which gave them the ascendancy in Basra as a whole, the brilliant part they played under the generalship of al-Muhallab ibn Abi Sufrah and his sons in the campaigns against the Khawarij fanatics and in extending Muslim power in Khurasan mark the stages in the spectacular rise of the Azd as one of the most formidable groups in the eastern caliphate. The death of al-Muhallab, the machinations of al-Hajjaj ibn Yusuf and the collapse of Yazid ibn al-Muhallab's revolt in AD 720 mark the equally precipitate collapse of their power: 'The fires of al-Mazun [a sneering reference to the "Persianized" Omanis] and its peoples are extinguished, they sought to kindle a revolt but you have left no standard for them to follow nor any soldier of al-Muhallab's people' sang their victorious enemies.

Thus the Azd and other Omani and south-Arabian tribes joined the growing opposition to the Umaiyad caliphs and the overbearing Hijazis. Many of the discontents started drifting back to their home country; they were a very different people from the simple tribesmen who had left it a few decades before. It is almost impossible in a paper like this to express the political aspects of the Ibadi movement which now took root amongst the Omanis, for a detailed study of its origins is essential to any real understanding of its ideology. All that can be done is to point to certain features. Originally Ibadism represented a version of Kharijism that was suited to the milieu of the Basran community. It took its roots amongst the 'quietists' (qaʿadah), the leaders of the community who had too much responsibility to act as the Khariji fanatics had done in AH 64 or those who had too much wealth and position to lose, for it counted amongst its adherents many rich and powerful merchants. Whilst the early Ibadis sought their first martyrs amongst the Khawarij of Nahrawan and Nukhailah it strongly disapproved of fanaticism and developed from the very groups who were absent from those battles. The quietists were continuously torn between the desire to act on their beliefs and a cautious, pragmatic approach to the political situation. The example of the enormously rich Abu Bilal who seceded (61/680–1) from Basra and tried to induce the quietists to join him, as he planned, in going to Oman and from there to march on the Holy Cities represented their dilemma; had he set the example and the quietists failed him or had he dissipated his potential in an ill-considered, if magnificent, gesture? Many merchants were later to satisfy their consciences by secretly financing the new Ibadi states whilst the political and religious leaders served the cause by missionary activity amongst potential revolutionary groups and then directing and guiding the Ibadi states as they were formed. The Ibadis' militancy dates from the first years of the second century AH; although they knew persecution under al-Hajjaj the last fifty years of the first century marked what can perhaps be termed the intellectual, rather than the political development of the movement. The fact that they carried on an open dialogue with two of the caliphs and continued to hark on the fundamental issues of the original Khariji secession indicates that they were not considered a serious threat by the early Umaiyads.

The nub of their argument, common to all Khawarij movements, was that ʿUthman had betrayed the Muslim Community with whose welfare he had been entrusted and that he had consequently been deposed (and incidentally killed) at the will of the community. (It is significant to note that one of the crimes of which Ibn Ibad accused ʿUthman in his letter to the Caliph ʿAbd al-Malik was that the merchants of al-Bahrain and Oman could not sell their goods except through his state monopoly.) From this fundamental issue stems the idea that the powers and duties of the leader of the community (Imam al-Muslimin) are prescribed by the Prophet through the Koran and the Sunnah (to which can be added, later, Ijmaʿ in Oman). If the leader breaks this Islamic constitution then it is the duty of the Islamic community actively to disassociate itself from him (bara'ah) and he looses their support (wilayah). In the later Ibadi development of this theme the imam is not automatically deposed (nor for that matter may he refuse or resign the imamate for it is a religious obligation); rather the *ulama*' suspend judgement (*wuquf*) until such time as the two parties meet together and, if it is adjudged that the imam is at fault, he is called on to make a formal repentance (*taubah*). Provided he shows himself in earnest his *wilayah* is restored to him. It is only when these conditions are not fulfilled that either party may proceed to more drastic action. The parallels of these concepts of leadership of the community with that of the tribe need no stressing here, nor the fact that they are diametrically opposed to any form of dynastic rule.

The Ibadi ideal was to restore the pure Islamic state as it had existed before it started to be corrupted by ᶜUthman. In their early days the leading Ibadis were concerned primarily with the nature of that state: the traditions transmitted from Abu Shaᶜtha' Jabir ibn Zaid al-Yahmadi al-ᶜUmani (AH 23–c. 103) and other of their early *ulama*' provide the corpus of Ibadi law and would seem to justify their claim that they developed a true legal system that was earlier and more authentic than that of the four orthodox schools. This clearly is debatable ground, but from a practical point of view it cannot be overemphasised that for considerable periods of Oman's history its system of government has rigidly adhered to a literal interpretation of the *shariᶜah*, with which few purists would argue, from the level of the individual to the administrative and financial organization of the state. Time and again one finds that when the needs of the state would have justified a temporary waiving of these principles this has not been done. The rigid adherence to the *shariᶜah* along with the somewhat egalitarian principles of the Khawarij in general has largely determined the social and economic organization of the country.

Space does not allow for any development of the historical stages by which the Ibadi state was set up in Oman. We must pass over the short-lived but spectacular imamate of ᶜAbd Allah ibn Yahya al-Kindi who, with a joint force of 'Yamani' tribesmen from Oman and southern Arabia captured Sanᶜa, Mecca and Medina at the end of Umaiyad times, of the brief imamate of al-Julanda ibn Masᶜud to which the Ibadis date their *wilayah* in Oman, of the establishment of Ibadi states elsewhere and also the events leading up to the battle of Majazah (177 AH) by which Julanda rule was overthrown and the Ibadi state finally established, and merely spare the briefest glance at what has been termed the First Imamate in this paper. This imamate, whose heyday may be considered the ninth century AD, was in many ways Oman's golden age. Whilst the period of rule by the Yaᶜaribah imams in the seventeenth century rivals, if not surpasses, it in political power and wealth the First Imamate, even allowing for idealizing through the passing of time, represents the nearest a true Ibadi community has ever been established in Oman. The modern revival of fundamental Ibadism, which gathered momentum in the eighteenth century under Abu Nabhan Ja'id ibn Khamis al-Kharusi (1734/5–1822) and eventually found fruition in the imamates of Salim ibn Rashid al-Kharusi (1913–20) and Muhammad ibn ᶜAbd Allah al-Khalili (al-Kharusi, al-Yahmadi al-Azdi; 1920–54), was profoundly influenced by the model of the First Imamate and drew its inspiration from its personalities.

The First Imamate represented the unification of Oman as a state into which, more or less, was incorporated the Hadhrami Ibadi state. It represented the triumph of Ibadi ideology over the fissiparous tribal structure and illustrates to this day the basis of Oman as a state. The tribal situation was the fundamental problem the Ibadis in Basra had to tackle in order to set up their state and it is no coincidence that the four missionaries (according to one account) were non-Azd – one Kindah, two Bani Samah and a Riyami. The Ibadis themselves gained power in Oman by exploiting the tribal situation which had flared up in the mid-second century AH and even the leading Ibadi figures tended to behave as Khariji fanatics pursuing tribal vendettas in the guise of piety. Certain groups like the powerful Bani Hina were not reconciled until well on into the First Imamate whilst their behaviour in eastern Oman left certain resentments that were never completely overcome. Nevertheless as the old generation Ibadis died a new spirit of moderation made itself evident in the imamate and this resulted in the breakdown of many old tribal attitudes. The early imams showed an extraordinary awareness of the value of a sound commercial atmosphere and the problems of the basic agricultural economy, and it is from this time that the differences between the Arabs and the indigenous village population were largely eliminated. The Arabs became villagers and the villagers were incorporated into the tribal structure of the Arabs. Exactly what this meant to Oman can be judged by comparing its social structure with that which developed in the Hadhramaut after the final collapse of the Ibadi Imamate there in the late eleventh century AD.

Despite these changes the Ibadi state represented a highly delicate balance in the tribal situation. The imamate became the prerogative of the Yahmad, the most powerful Azd clan, whilst the Bani Samah families of the Jauf may be considered the imam-makers. The choice of Nizwa as the seat of the imamate reflects this balance. The port of Suhar, the largest and wealthiest town, was precluded if for no other reason than that the leader of the Omani state must reside in the interior in order to control directly the tribal situation. (Despite the fact that Yaᶜaribah interests were increasingly directed towards their overseas empire they never lost sight of this fundamental principle: the alienation of the Al Bu Saᶜid from the peoples of the interior is in no small measure due to the fact that from the early nineteenth century onwards they made Muscat, Zanzibar and then Salalah, in far away Dhofar, their capitals.) The old Sasanid centre of Rustaq, although the main stronghold of Oman at that time, was ruled out as the seat of the First Imamate for it lay in the heart of the Ghadaf, the territory of the imams' own tribal group, the Yahmad. In the Jauf, however, there was a nice balance of tribal power. The majority of tribesmen were of Qudaᶜah (Qamr-Riyam) origin and although they were strongly under Yahmad influence were sufficiently independent to be able to break with them, (as happened upon the break-up of the First Imamate), whilst nearly all the important tribal groupings were represented by important clans in the villages there. The geographic advantages of Nizwa made it the natural choice.

The term capital must, however, be used with discretion. The whole structure of imamate government, deriving in large measure from the structure of bedu society, militates against a sophisticated government machinery or any court society. Whilst the imam's residence represents the focal point in the Ibadi community physical power remains vested in the hands of the leaders of the community. The danger of leaving military power in the hands of a single individual was recognized from the start as the most important single factor which could lead to the degeneration of Ibadi government. The missionary Musa ibn Abi Jabir al-Sami placed control of the original Ibadi troops (*al-shurat*) into the hands of his local governors appointed from the Basran-trained Ibadis before he was prepared to select an imam; once security had been established this formal organization of the *shurat* began to disappear. Beyond a small garrison of troops controlled by the imam and his *walis* in the key fortresses, military force has always been raised, under imamate government, from the local tribes whose absolute duty it is to provide help by reason of their oath of obedience to the imam. This decentralization of physical power has been one of the important factors which has led to the continuation of an active tribal structure in the sedentary community of Oman and why its leaders have tended to remain in their villages in direct contact with the source of their power. The structure of this society has militated against the development of feudal power within the villages.

It is easy to see that the Ibadi politico-religious ideology is an impractical basis for the permanent development of a state. It automatically develops a cycle which encompasses its own downfall. As the country is united so does its wealth and prosperity increase and the religious ideal weaken; the leadership becomes the prerogative of a single group and degenerates into temporal power (*saltanah*). There ensues a struggle for power in which tribal ᶜ*asabiyah* is brought into play and every potential weakness in the country exploited until full-scale civil war is the outcome.

The situation is usually resolved by one or more of the parties calling in an outside power, normally with disastrous results for the Omanis in general. This is the story of the First Imamate, of the Nabahinah, of the Yaᶜaribah and of the Al Bu Saᶜid.

To conclude this paper one such cycle covering the period from the collapse of the First Imamate to the rise of the Yaᶜaribah will be taken not simply to illustrate these generalizations, but to show how the collapse of the first real Omani state also developed certain regional trends in Oman which have permanently weakened the unity of the state throughout its subsequent history.

The immediate cause of the events which led to the collapse of the First Imamate was the deposing of the Yahmadi Imam, al-Salt ibn Malik al-Kharusi, by the leading Sami ᶜalim, Musa ibn Musa, in 272/886 on the grounds of his senility. The background to this act and ensuing events are of extraordinary interest and became the theoretical point for party strife for five hundred years. To elucidate the actual historical events, deliberately distorted by the accounts of interested parties, is beyond the scope of this paper, and only certain political repercussions can be touched on. The main effect of the first incidents was an alignment of the tribes deriving from their primary settlement pattern. The alliance of certain Azd clans, the Yahmad, ᶜAtik, Hina and Salimah, reflected their control of the richest territories of Oman including the rapidly developing Batinah Coast ports. The Huddan (Azd) Bani Harith (Azd) and Bani Samah primary tribal *dars* were largely excluded from this rich territory but so long as their shaikhly clans were represented in the balance of power in the imamate they had been able to look after the interests of their tribal kinsmen and elements of the tribes lived in and benefited from the favoured territory. The immediate impact of the first tribal skirmishes was that the Yahmad alliance revenged its initial defeat at the battle of Raudah by killing Musa ibn Musa and plundering the property of the Bani Samah and Huddan in the Jauf. Thereupon many elements of the northern tribes living in central Oman and the Batinah withdrew to their main tribal *dars*, raised a force of their tribesmen and bedu elements of the ᶜAbd al-Qais from the Dhahirah and marched on Suhar where they declared the Huddani leader imam. They were completely routed by the Yahmad alliance under the military leadership of the Bani Hina shaikh. It will be noted that there was nothing of Nizar-Yaman in the tribal alliance of the two parties, but when the Samah, determined to avenge their defeat, called on the help of the ᶜAbbasids, this was exactly how they presented the issue. It will further be noted that all religious interests had been abandoned by the tribal leaders whilst most of the ᶜulama' instead of trying to moderate the issue, exacerbated it in theoretical squabbles and a remarkable display of religious bigotry. The combination of an appeal to Nizar ʿasabīyah, the chance to crush the hated *shurat* and of gaining control over the rapidly developing commercial potential of the Omani ports left the ʿAbbasids in little doubt over their course of action. The results of their invasion were disastrous to the Yahmad alliance and the ensuing reign of terror of the ʿAbbasid general, nicknamed al-Bur, became a byword in Omani history. Perhaps the most permanent effect of the actions of the ʿAbbasid troops and their Sami allies was the massive destruction of the *qanat* system of central Oman.

The stages in the recovery of imamate power need not concern us but it was not until the middle of the eleventh century AD that the Omanis once again gained control of their coastal provinces, and then only for the briefest of periods. Once again a new era of unity appeared to have dawned and with the help of Omani troops the Hadhramaut was also restored to Ibadi control; an expedition sent to Yemen was only forestalled by Fatimid help for the Sulaihid ruler. It was the Yahmad who once again provided the driving force in this recovery, but all their efforts were nullified by the declaration of Imam Rashid ibn Saʿid, in 443/1052, that the supporters of Musa ibn Musa in deposing al-Salt had been heretics. The issue of this *fatwa* resulted in a profound spiritual and political division in Oman and was reflected in the development of the so-called Nizwa and Rustaq parties. Gradually the Yahmad alienated the tribes of the Jauf and many of the leading ʿulama', reacting to the Yahmad claims to the spiritual leadership, subscribed to Sunni legal schools. The Yahmad finally dropped their pretensions to the imamate in their attempts to retain power and it was their '*muluks*' who finally succumbed to the Nabahinah (ʿAtik Azd). Despite subsequent invective against the Nabahinah there is little doubt that the early Nabahinah *muluks* ruled in a way that was closer to the Ibadi ideal than had the later, so-called imams of the Kharus, but without the unified support of the ʿulama' their power was inadequate to weld Oman together as a single unit and they in their turn declined into local dynastic rulers.

It should be clear from this historical outline that the tribal structure of Oman had undergone some fairly deep changes. The gradual sedentarization of the tribes led to the dispersal of many clans from their original primary *dars* thereby weakening the original tribal structure whilst the historical events brought to an end many of the original alliances. The civil war and its aftermath saw the collapse of what may be considered the primitive tribal political heritage of the desert and its partial replacement by locality alliances, that is of alliances based on the interests of village *wadi* or 'lateral' tribal relationships of the region. The modern tribal confederations of Oman are the direct product of the primary settlement

pattern modified by the development of 'vertical' locality ties of seden-
terization.

The Nabahinah period may perhaps be considered a gestation period
when these new tribal groupings were forming and the impact of the
sedentary environment became stronger than it ever has been, before or
since. The regional tendencies had, however, as we have seen been developing since the tenth century. In central Oman, Yahmad power became
confined to the Ghadaf and was further isolated due to the complete
destruction of the Batinah coastal settlements (they were redeveloped by
the Yaᵉaribah) and the shift of the maritime commercial centres to south-
east Oman. The centre of gravity in central Oman shifted to the Jauf
where the natural defences of the region saved the last remnants of a
'national' consciousness. The penalty paid for this survival was complete
isolation, spiritual and physical. From the end of the ninth century to the
seventeenth century its people were almost entirely cut off from the wealth
of the coast. During this period the Omanis of central Oman developed
an introspection that has marked the history of their country ever since.
In contrast south-east Oman became increasingly orientated towards the
economy of the Indian Ocean as Qalhat, under the influence of the Hormuzi dynasty who originated there, replaced Suhar as the major port of
Oman. Although Muscat gradually replaced Qalhat in this role the
regional ports of the south-east, Qurayat and then Sur, continued to
retain important links with the East African trade until the present century. This maritime influence extended as far inland as the villages of the
Sharqiyah where the modern history of its leading family, the shaikhs of
the Harith (or Hirth) reflects the opposing pulls of the politics of central
Oman and those of East Africa. The ties of the people of south-east Oman
to the central node were further weakened by the fact that their conversion
to Ibadism had been largely superficial and they were not closely connected with the power structure of central Oman even at the height of the
First Imamate. It is only a really strong central government that can keep
the semi-bedu fringe of the south-east under its control as the modern
history of the Bani Bu ᵉAli amply illustrates.

The alienation of northern Oman has, however, proved the most endur-
ing factor in isolating central Oman. The political independence of the
Trucial States and the northern limits of the twentieth century imamate
stem from early history. We have already seen the origins of this alienation; the civil war which brought to an end the first imamate was followed
by a deliberate policy of converting the tribesmen in the north to Sunni
Islam by the Bani Samah leaders. But although an antagonistic northern
region is a permanent threat to the safety of central Oman and removes
one of its outer defences, northern Oman itself is incapable of preserving

its independence without the support of central Oman. Its ports fell into the hands of the maritime powers in the Gulf whilst its inland regions increasingly fell under the domination of 'Bahraini' dynasties. The Wahhabis are but the most recent manifestation of a 'Bahraini' presence in Oman and illustrate the same processes which brought northern Oman under the successive influence of the Qaramitah, ᶜUyunids (?) and Jubur (the Portuguese Benjabar) in the Middle Ages. This 'Bahraini' influence was accompanied by the migration of large numbers of ᶜAmir (ᶜAmir ibn Saᶜsaᶜah and ᶜAmir Rabiᶜah) tribes who began to dominate in western Trucial Oman and the Dhahirah (the Al Bu Falah of Abu Dhabi are from the Hilal, one of the shaikhly groups, while the Naᶜim (Nuᶜaim) and Al Bu Shamis form a large confederation of various ᶜAmir tribes). Elements of these ᶜAmir tribes began to penetrate into central Oman and formed the last of the major genealogical groupings to settle in the country. (It should be noted that during the Dark Ages many of the older bedu groups, notably the ᶜAbd al-Qais and Wa'il tribes began to sedentarize.)

These broad regional trends were matched by a tendency to fragmentation within the regions themselves. Not only was central Oman divided into its component parts but, even within a small region like the Jauf, Bahla, Nizwa and Manh developed a growing rivalry. After evicting the Nabahinah the attempts by the Jauf leaders to set up imamates in the fifteenth and sixteenth centuries foundered in mutual jealousies until finally the last Nabahinah *muluk* dynasty, by allying itself with the Jubur, Hilal and other semi-bedu ᶜAmir groups, once again regained control of their original homeland of the Jauf from which they had been ousted. But this power finally collapsed under the onslaught of the ᶜUmairi *malik* of Suma'il who allied himself both with the Portuguese and the dissident Bani Hina shaikhs in whose tribal affairs the Nabahinah had unwisely meddled; in the end it was the leaders of the semi-bedu ᶜAmir groups who won the day and took possession of nearly all the main forts on the western side of the mountains, from the Sharqiyah to the Dhahirah. With a new tribal power from the desert in control of much of the Jauf, with the unifying spirit of Ibadism so weak that it was not even possible to find *qadis* for the villages of the Ghadaf, with the Portuguese fortifying the coastal villages and ports of Oman for their last stand in Arabia, and with the few remaining Omani groups who retained control of their heritage at loggerheads with each other who would have believed that within the space of twenty-five years the Omanis would once again be reunified under the rule of an Azdi imam and the foreigner driven from their land? The maritime empire the Yaᶜaribah were to build was to rival that of the European powers and from its wealth Oman, for a century or so, once again became a 'land abounding in fields and groves, with pastures and unfailing springs', ruled by its own imamate government. Another major imamate cycle had begun.

There are many factors explaining this rebirth, but let us leave the last word with one of the Omani chroniclers (*Kashf*, tr. Ross, pp 154–5):

'Now the people of ᶜOmān are endowed with certain qualities, which it is my hope that they may never lose. They are a people of soaring ambition, and of haughty spirit; they brook not the control of any Sultān, and are quick to resent affront; they yield only to irresistible force, and without ever abandoning their purpose. A man of comparatively poor spirit, judged by their standard, is on a par as regards magnanimity with an Amīr of any other people. Each individual aims at having the power in his own hands . . . and his neighbour has the same ambition. Unfortunately none are worthy of such things, but those whom God elects, pious, chaste, and blessed persons, who are not swayed by their desires, nor prone to be led away by blind passions. . . . There were none to be found, whether dwellers in houses or dwellers in tents, whether "Bedū" or "Hadhr", whether on the mountain heights or in the sandy level, but had quaffed the draught of terror, and suffered from the general destruction which encompassed religion, property, and life, except those for whom God tempered their troubles . . . in this manner they (the people of Oman) ceased not to struggle in the abyss of desolation, walking in evil ways, until God vouchsafed for them the appearance of his wise servant, the Imām of the Musalmāns, Nāsir-bin Murshid-bin Mālik. . . .'

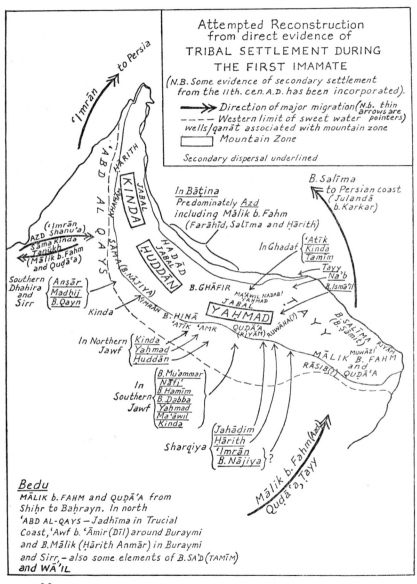

Map 3

NOTE TO TRIBAL MAP

1. *Genealogical Affiliations of Groups shown*

AZD

1. *Mālik ibn Fahm:* Ḥārith, Farāhīd/Muwāziᶜ Hamīm, Hinā, Khamām (Shubābah), ᶜAmr and Salīmah.
2. *Shanu'ah:* Yaḥmad, Maᶜāwil (Julandā) and Nadab
3. *ᶜImrān:* (a) Asd (shaikhly clan ᶜAtīk)
   (b) Ḥajr (the Hadād group probably represents a confederation of Ḥajr clans and possibly included a number of the
   other main Azd branches, sections of which were to be
   found in Oman)

QUḌĀᶜA *(closely affiliated to Aẓd)*

1. *Mahrah* groups: Riyām, Bani Ismāᶜīl, Naᶜb, Bani Mu'ammar(?)
2. *Others:* Rāsib

KINDA- *and* ṬAIY: no sub-groups shown. Nearly all the secondary dispersal of Kindah were (shaikhly ?) clans of the Ḥārith al-Aṣghar but there were also some Thābit ibn Rafd and Sakūn. All Ṭaiy groups are sub-sections of the Nabhān ibn Ghauth.

SĀMAH *(ibn LUᶜAY):* Nājiyah (probably the main mass of tribesmen) Bani Ghāfir, Bani Ḍabbah and Nāfiᶜ

Miscellaneous: Madhij, Bani Qain, Anṣār (Azd), Ruwāhah (ᶜAbs) and Tamīm were probably all comparatively small elements of these tribal groups who settled in Oman in early Islamic times.

2. *Primary and Secondary Settlement*

The primary settlement pattern (predominantly pre-Islamic) has been shown in block capitals. The secondary dispersal of clans in villages outside their main tribal areas has been shown by underlining. It is impossible to draw a neat distinction between this primary and secondary dispersal. The leading groups migrated to Oman over a period of three or four centuries in pre-Islamic times and huge groups like the Mālik ibn Fahm and ᶜImrān (in so far as such genealogical groupings ever existed) were widely dispersed throughout southern Arabia, Oman (outside Mazūn), Persia and at Baḥrain before the arrival of other tribes. Thus whilst a group like the Ḥārith are shown in Ibrā as a secondary dispersal (we know they were there in AH 145) their presence there probably represents the settlement of a clan in the general dissemination of the Mālik ibn Fahm groups from their main tribal *dār* in the S.E. (where groups settled from southern Arabia from perhaps the second century to at least the eighth century AD) towards the north, where the region around Dabā became the Ḥārith's own primary *dār* (we know that they were the leading clan of the area at the time of the apostasy war). Their settlement on the Bāṭinah coast, on the other hand, probably meant little more than the presence of some shaikhly families during the First Imamate: their position there became untenable during the civil war which brought to an end the First Imamate (end of the ninth century AD) and they retired to their primary *dār* in the Dabā area. The problems of portraying the tribal settlement pattern as it existed in early Islamic times in map form are so great that the result should be treated as only the most general guide of what was a highly complex situation.

NOTE ON SOURCES

The writer of this paper has been faced with a considerable problem over quoting sources. He has merely attempted to sketch certain aspects of a much larger study he is preparing on Oman, primarily based on the extensive local and Ibadi source material. Many of these works are virtually unknown to Europeans and themselves represent compilations; little point is served in stating the sources without an extensive bibliographical note and a reconstruction of the primary sources from which they have been drawn.

As a result he has decided to omit all references and footnotes with the exception of the following note on a major work which is the most important source for reconstructing the early tribal situation in Oman, the *Kitāb Ansāb al-ᶜArab* by (Abū al-Mundhir) Sal(a)mah ibn Muslim (Musallim?) al-ᶜAutabī. From internal evidence this book appears to have been written in the late fifth/eleventh century. ᶜAutabī, who also wrote a work called *Kitāb al-Imāmah*, appears, from a slightly dubious passage in a short work by al-Sālimī called *al-Lamᶜah al-Murḍīyah min Ashiᶜᶜah al-Ibāḍīyah* (Tunis, no date, pp. 78 and 84), to have been the grandson or great-grandson of the author of the 24 volume work known as *al-Ḍiyāʾ* (*fī al-Fiqh wa-al-Sharᶜīah*) famed in Omani and Maghribi Ibadi circles alike. Both were called Salmah ibn Muslim al-ᶜAutabī and there is evidence which indicates that these names ran in the family as far back as the ninth century. If the two ᶜAutabī's are in fact to be distinguished then the *kunyah* of Abū Ibrāhīm has been confused with that of his grandson and their respective works attributed to one man, Abū al-Mundhir Salmah ibn Muslim: for example Abū Isḥāq Ibrāhīm Aṭfayish writing on the copy of the *Ansāb* in Cairo (Dār al-Kutub MS. 2461; cf. footnote in vol. i, p. 52 of his edition of al-Sālimī's *Tuḥfat al-Aᶜyān*, Cairo, 1380/1961, and in his introduction to Ibn Duraid's *al-Malāḥin*, Cairo, 1347 AH.) and C. Guillain (*Documents . . . de l'Afrique orientale*, vol. i, pp. 476 ff.) describing the copy which he brought to Europe where it lay incorrectly catalogued until rediscovered by R. D. Bathurst in the Bibliothèque Nationale. Furthermore this error, if error it be, appears to reach back, at least, until the beginning of the seventeenth century for it occurs in the lists of *ʿulamā'* in the *Kashf al-Ghummah*, (Damascus MS., *Ta'rīkh* 347, p. 528) and the *Qāmūs al-Sharīʿah* (vol. viii, p. 307) both of which, in fact, derive from the *Minhaj al-Ṭālibīn* of Khamīs ibn Saʿīd al-Shaqṣī, the chief elector of the first Yaʿrabi Imam, Nāṣir ibn Murshid. Thus Z. Smogorzewski's statement in *Essai de Bio-bibliographie Ibadite-Wahbite. Avant-propos*, (R.O. v. 1927, p. 51 fn. 4) that Abū al-Mundhir Salmah ibn Muslim, the author of the *Ḍiyā'*, was of the first half of the fifth/eleventh century is of limited value, particularly as he gives no supporting evidence, but it does generally help confirm the dating which the present writer ascribes to the *Ansāb*.

We know very little indeed about ʿAutabī, but from evidence within the work itself there is reason to believe that he was a member of the Azdi Ṭāḥiyah clan and that his *nisbah* probably derived from a quarter of Suhar called ʿAutab, the site of a famous battle fought in Shaw. 278/892, in the civil war which brought to an end the First Imamate and in the events of which his forebears were deeply involved.

The writer has used two manuscripts; the Paris MS. Arabe 5019 of 291 folios (abbreviated A.) and a second one (abbreviated AB.) of 219 folios originally from the library of the great ʿālim, Abū Nabhān, Jā'id ibn Khamīs al-Kharūṣī (*c.* 1734/5–1822) which is now in the possession of Dr T. M. Johnstone. AB (which is titleless) was copied in Jum. I 1089/ May 1678 and is the earliest of all the copies traced; the writer is fairly certain that the various copies in existence stem from a highly defective and very incomplete transcript that must have been rediscovered about the end of the seventeenth century. In passing it is worth noting that the first four books of the *Ṣaḥīfat al-Qaḥṭānīyah* (Rhodes House, Oxford. MSS. Afr. S.3) turn out, on closer examination, to be a poor and unacknowledged recension of ʿAutabī by the prolific and unreliable mid-nineteenth-century author, Ibn Ruzaiq.

Much of the content of ʿAutabī's voluminous work has nothing to do with Oman. It represents a hotch-potch of history and biography strung around the framework of Arab genealogy and no attempt has been made to evaluate its potential value as a new source from studies other than Oman. From the point of view of the latter it contains much that is not found in other local sources, although virtually all the historical material has been picked up by al-Sālimī in his *Tuḥfah* (*op. cit.*) but as a contribution to studies on the tribal situation there the *Ansāb* contains much valuable information that has not been found elsewhere. It is also important for throwing light on the main source previously used, a highly confusing and incomplete account of early tribal migrations to Oman, that feature in the 'standard *sīrahs*' (the compilation of standardized early history common to many works of the eighteenth century, most famous of which is the *Kashf al-Ghummah*).

Elucidation of ᶜAutabī's original contribution (whether his own or the recording of Omani traditions) takes one into the whole vexed field of Arab genealogy. It is made doubly difficult by both the highly defective nature of the extant texts and of ᶜAutabī's habit of giving contradictory information in different parts of the work without references or comment. It is not always a simple matter to determine which is the local and which the non-Omani contribution. Whilst there is some original material in most of the sections on each of the major tribal groupings (his treatment of these is highly uneven and in the extant form of the work is largely concerned with the Qaḥṭāni groups) the concentration of Omani material is found, not unexpectedly, in the final part of the work dealing with the Azd. Most unfortunately, it is missing its end pages and is full of lacunae.

Whilst the *Ansāb* contains much original information it is highly fragmentary and is only really of value when used in conjunction with a number of other original sources, notably those preserved in the *Tuḥfah* (*op. cit.*), the biographical sections in the *Kashf* (*op. cit.*) and volumes viii and ix of the massive ninety-volume *Qāmūs al-Sharīᶜah* by Jumaiyil ibn Khamīs ibn Lāfi Al Saᶜdī (N.B. this work was started in 1206/1791–2 and not in Yaᶜāribah times as stated in B.M. Sup. Cat 1894, p. 122 – whence errors in Brocklemann, Schacht and others). These sources often provide us with incidental information concerning the relative importance and locations of different groups which is often absent in the *Ansāb*. Further important clues are sometimes to be found in 'classical' writers of both Omani (e.g. Ibn Duraid and al-Mubarrad) and non-Omani origin.

5

MARITIME TRADE AND IMAMATE GOVERNMENT: TWO PRINCIPAL THEMES IN THE HISTORY OF OMAN TO 1728

R. D. BATHURST

Pre-Islamic Period

Only archeological investigations will decide who the original inhabitants of Oman were. Fragmentary evidence available so far suggests a people in Oman at the middle of the third millennium B C who had trade connections with India and Baluchistan and who may have been the first to domesticate the camel. If it can be accepted that Oman was 'Magan', as some archeologists claim, then there is proof that its harbours were in use during the Sumerian period. Other evidence suggests that copper from Jabal al-Maᶜadin near Wadi ᶜAhin is of the type used by the Sumerians at Ur and Kish, and inscriptions on the statues of Gudea of Lagash indicate sea voyages around the Arabian Peninsula in the first half of the third millennium. Certainly there was a seafaring people occupying the western shore of the Persian Gulf in the Assyrian era and, in view of the prosperity of South Arabia during the first millennium, it is possible that the inhabitants of Oman were involved in maritime trade many centuries before Alexander the Great.[1]

Trading by land and sea would have brought Arab merchants and sailors to Oman from the south-west, perhaps as early as the Achaemenid period, and such contacts probably increased during the prosperity enjoyed up to, at least, the advent of the Himyarite kingdom (115 B C). In Seleucid times the most active merchants in the Persian Gulf were at Gerrha (modern al-ᶜUqair), and were renowned for their pearl-fishing and for their caravan trade to south Arabia, perhaps via Oman. Moreover,

---

[1] Knud Thorvildsen, 'Burial Cairns on Umm an-Nar' in *Kuml-Arbog for Kysk Arkaeologisk Selskab* (1962), p. 219; T. G. Bibby, 'A Forgotten Civilisation of Abu Dhabi' in *BP Magazine*, xiii (1964), pp. 29–33; H. Peake, 'The Copper Mountain of Magan' in *Antiquity*, ii (1928), pp. 456–7; cf. W. F. Leemans, *Foreign Trade in the Old Babylonian Period* (Leiden, 1960), p. 121 *et seq*; S. A. Pallis, *The Antiquity of Iraq* (Copenhagen, 1956), p. 661. Also *Cambridge Ancient History*, i (1924), pp. 262, 415–6, 427, 430–1, 544; cf. revised edition (1963), Ch. 19, pp. 8, 24–6; G. F. Hourani, *Arab Seafaring in the Indian Ocean in Ancient and Early Medieval Times* (Princeton, 1951), pp. 10–11.

a trade based on Oman ports during the first centuries of the Christian era is suggested in *The Periplus of the Erythrean Sea*.[2]

Popular Arab tradition relates that it was probably in the early Sasanid period that substantial numbers of Arabs, reputedly the Azd, first settled in Oman. Considerable migration from Yemen is linked with the bursting of the Maᶜrib dam. Archeological evidence indicates that there were no less than six ruptures of the dam, the last of which occurred before AD 570.[3] According to tradition, after battles with the Persians in Oman the first wave of migratory Azd were followed by compatriot tribes from Yemen. Other tribes are said to have entered from the north and settled in the villages of Tauwam (now called al-Buraimi) and of al-Zahirah. These arrivals claimed descent from ᶜAdnan, the legendary ancestor of the northern Arabs, and thus precipitated a confrontation with the earlier migrants who, according to accepted genealogical tradition, were descended from Qahtan, the legendary ancestor of the southern Arabs. Modern research gives rise to doubts about the validity of delineating tribal alliances so simply but such distinctions were an important factor during attempts by the caliphate to subjugate Oman. The designations in use then were 'Nizari' and 'Yamani', terms expressing political rather than ancestral groupings.[4]

From Islam to the Arrival of the Portuguese

At the time of Islam Oman is said to have been ruled by the Al al-Julanda ibn al-Mustatir from whom the Bani Julanda of Oman are believed to be descended. Most of the early authorities place ᶜAmr ibn al-ᶜAs' proselytizing mission to Oman in the year 8 (629/30), the death of Muhammad occasioning his return to Medina. According to the native chronicles, after the people's acceptance of Islam, the Persians resident in Oman were told to submit also, and on their refusal were expelled from the country. They had occupied the coast whilst the Azd had held the mountains and the desert.[5]

It is not clear at what time the Ibadis became the dominant sect of the Khawarij in Oman. There may have been Khariji imams before the first Ibadi one was elected, but it was not until the fall of the Umaiyads

[2] *C.A.H.* vii (1954), p. 172; *The Periplus of the Erythrean Sea*, trans. W. H. Schoff (London, 1912), pp. 33–7; Hourani, *op. cit.*, pp. 13–44.

[3] H. von Wissman, 'Himyar, Ancient History' in *Le Muséon*, lxxvii (1964), pp. 493–4.

[4] See *Encyclopaedia of Islam*, n.s., i, p. 73, article 'Abd al-Kays', and pp. 811–13, article 'Azd'; Al-ᶜAutabi, Salamah ibn Muslim, *Ansab al-ᶜArab*, Bibliothèque Nationale Paris MS. (arabe 5019), fol. 221b.

[5] See Hedwig Klein, *Kashf al-Ghummah, Kapitel XXXIII der anonymen arabischen Chronik*, dissertation, (Hamburg, 1938), p. 22; Al-Azkawi, Sirhan ibn Saᶜid, *Kashf al-Ghummah*, British Museum MS. Or. 8076, fol. 325; Sir William Muir, *Annals of the Early Caliphate* (London, 1883), p. 50; Al-ᶜAutabi, *op. cit.*, fols 271a–272a.

that the Ibadis were able to set up their own government. They then elected al-Julanda ibn Mas°ud as their first imam, c. 750. No details are available of how he was elected. The electoral procedure which subsequently became practice, and which, by reason of its derivation from early Islamic custom, may have been followed, was the *bai°ah* or public acclamation of allegiance. Such an election by the Ibadi community was, *ipso facto*, an attempt to set up its own spiritual and temporal ruler in place of government by caliphs chosen by unacceptable methods. Ibadis stipulate that the imam shall be elected by the community of believers from among those suitably qualified, the choice not being dictated by patrilineage or tribal origin. They also reserve the right to depose imams.[6]

For four centuries from the election of al-Julanda the Islamic kingdom was never settled enough to permit continuous autonomous, or continuous caliphal rule in Oman. Al-Julanda's imamate was terminated by a caliphal expedition under Khazim ibn Khuzaimah, c. 753, no other imam being elected until about 791. There were five subsequent imams before 887, during which time attacks by caliphal troops and maritime pirates were successfully repulsed. Severe civil disturbances caused the deposition of the last of these imams, al-Salt ibn Malik, and had the effect of increasing polarization into Yamani and Nizari political factions. As a result of the Nizaris appealing to the caliphal governor of Bahrain the country was overrun by caliphal troops in 893. But the occupation was only temporary and, after the governor had been overthrown, a total of eight imams were elected in quick succession before the first successful Carmathian invasion in 930/1. A degree of autonomy enabled three imams to serve before a caliphal force reconquered this dissident extremity in 943. New, Buwaihid, conquerors came c. 965, briefly losing control to the Carmathians, but regaining it and releasing it to the separist Buwaihid Prince of Fars in 972–3. Successive Buwaihid governors brought benevolent rule and by 999–1000 this permitted the election of an imam. Buwaihid control was temporarily lost during 1050/1–3 but was recovered by recapture from Fars whence also the Seljuk conquest of Oman was launched in 1063. Oman remained in Seljuk hands for a continuous period of about eighty years. The date of death of the last Seljuk governor seems to have preceded the election of the Imam Muhammad ibn Khanbash, c. 1150–60. An important phase of the Ibadi imamate ended with his death in 1162–3 as there was an interregnum until the next election in 1406–7.[7]

Despite these numerous invasions by °Abbasid, Carmathian, Buwaihid

[6] *Kashf al-Ghummah*, fol. 266a; Hedwig Klein, *op. cit.*, pp. 36–7; Elie Adib Salem, *Political Theory and Institutions of the Khawarij*, The Johns Hopkins University Studies in Historical and Political Science, Series lxxiv, no. 2 (1956), p. 53.

[7] *Kashf al-Ghummah*, fols 328a–328b, 329b–333a, 334a; Al-Tabari, *Annales*, ed. M. J. de Goeje (Leiden, 1879–80), iii, pp. 78–9; cf. Hedwig Klein, *op. cit.*, pp. 35–6, 46. Ibn Hauqal,

and Seljuk forces Oman's trade increased, and at times brought great prosperity. Indeed, it was the size of the potential tribute that motivated some of the invasions. Before Islam Persians had dominated the trade of the Arabian Sea and had controlled the ports on the coast of Oman. After the conquest the Arabs took over the Persian shores of the Gulf and increasingly controlled the trade. When Baghdad became the commercial metropolis of the Middle East in early ʿAbbasid Abbasid times, the ports of al-Ubullah and Siraf, and to a lesser extent the ports of Oman, became entrepots for trade with the East.[8]

There were two routes to the Indies. The first was via Suhar and Muscat, and then straight across the sea to southern Malabar, a route normally followed by ships on the China run. The second route was a coasting voyage down the Makran and Indian coasts. Omani traders and sailors took a large part in this expansion of trade. One source records the voyage of an Omani merchant to China in about the middle of the eighth century, while another, al-Masʿudi, writing before 947, speaks of Killah (probably Kedah in Malaya) as a place where Muslim ships of the Sirafis and the Omanis met the ships that came from China. Direct trading between the Gulf and China more or less stopped in 878 when Canton was sacked, though there is a report of a direct voyage by a Jewish merchant of Oman early in the tenth century.[9]

Information on early Muslim contacts between the Persian Gulf and East Africa is vague. It is suggested that Omanis migrated there in flight from al-Hajjaj in 690 and that Persians followed from Shiraz and Siraf in the ninth and tenth centuries. By the tenth century ships from Siraf and Oman were trading there regularly, seeking ivory and ambergris as well as slaves, and al-Masʿudi, sailing to Oman, described the sailors of the Indian Ocean as 'the people of Oman Arabs of the Azd'. Other writers mention voyages from Oman going as far south as Sofala.[10]

Suhar became a depot for goods from China and a centre for trade in all directions. From the mountains and coastal plantations came the fruits which gave the ports an importance independent of their use as entrepots for Eastern and African trade. Muscat shared in the trade. Ibn al-Faqih

---

[8] G. F. Hourani, *op. cit.*, p. 64, *et passim*.

[9] Al-Masʿudi, *Muruj al-Dhahab*, ed. C. Barbier de Meynard and Pavet de Courteille (Paris, 1861–77), i, pp. 307–8.

[10] *Ibid.*, p. 232; Hourani, *op. cit.*, pp. 79–81.

Surat al-Ard, ed. J. H. Kramers (Leiden 1938), fasc. i, pp. 38–9; S. B. Miles, *The Countries and Tribes of the Persian Gulf* (London, 1919), i, pp. 90–2, 104, 108, 114, 125, 128–9; M. J. de Goeje, *Mémoire sur les Carmathes du Bahrain* (Leiden 1862), pp. 13, 17, 29; Ibn Hauqal, *Kitab al-Masalik wa al-Mamalik*, ed. M. J. de Goeje, Bibliotheca Geographorum Arabicorum ii (Leiden, 1873), p. 22; Ibn al-Athir, *Al-Kamil*, ed. C. J. Tornberg (Leiden, 1867–76), viii, pp. 298–9, 372–3, 417–8, IX, p. 28.

al-Hamdani, writing in the late ninth century, described it as the starting point for ships sailing to India and Kulum Mali (Quilon), and al-Muqaddasi, writing in the late tenth century, as a fine town, rich in fruits, the first place which the ships from Yemen reach. Suhar was prosperous by the tenth century and was reckoned by Ibn Hauqal to be more important than Zabid or Sanᶜa, while, in the late thirteenth century, Muscat was deemed to be a considerable centre of trade with Africa and the East coast of the Persian Gulf.[11]

The commerce of the ports was not uninterrupted. Suhar, especially, suffered invading forces. It was destroyed during Carmathian times and, after being rebuilt, was occupied by the Buwaihids in 972-3 and 1041-2. Under the late Buwaihids, when Siraf declined, control of the Gulf trade passed to the Bani Qaisar of the island of Qais. By the first half of the eleventh century they dominated the Gulf and ruled the shores of Oman. The Arabs of Oman and the Gulf continued to voyage to India, the East Indies and Africa though trade between Suhar and the Far East ended about the middle of the twelfth century. According to Ibn al-Mujawir Suhar was already destroyed by about 1225 and its trade had passed to Qalhat and Hormuz.[12]

During the earliest period of the interregnum in the interior of Oman, from 1162-3, Qais undoubtedly held control of the Oman ports. When the commercial rise of Hormuz brought about the decline of Qais and its subsequent capture in 1229, it is unlikely that the Hormuzis immediately took over the Omani ports. It is not known at what date Hormuzi control came. Given their tremendous commercial supremacy during the fourteenth and fifteenth centuries and evidence of their suzerainty over Oman ports up to the arrival of the Portuguese it would seem that Hormuzi control of Omani sea trading lasted for almost three centuries.[13]

The interregnum in the imamate may have been a result of the rise to power of the Nabhani tribe whose *muluk* took to ruling the interior. Details of these are not available but the names of some are mentioned in connection with external events in 1261-3, 1275, 1277 and c. 1329. The interregnum appears to have ended with the election of Malik ibn

[11] Ibn Hauqal, *Surat al-Ard*, p. 38; Al-Muqaddasi, *Kitab Ahsan al-taqasim fi maᶜrifat al-aqalim*, ed. M. J. de Goeje, B.G.A. iii (Leiden, 1877), pp. 93 and 105; Ibn al-Mujawir, in A. Sprenger 'Die Post- und Reiserouten des Orients', *Abhandlungen für die Kunde des Morgenlandes*, iii (1864), 3, pp. 145-6, Ibn al-Faqih al-Hamdani, *Kitab al-buldan*, ed. M. J. de Goeje (Leiden, 1885), pp. 11-12. Cf. *E. of I.*, iii, pp. 391-4, article 'Maskat', iv, pp. 504-6, article 'Suhar'.

[12] J. Aubin, 'Les Princes d'Ormuz du XIIIe au XVe siècle' in *Journal Asiatique*, ccxli (1953), p. 81; Ibn al-Mujawir, *Ta'rikh al-Mustabsir*, ed. Oscar Löfgren (Leiden, 1951, 1954), p. 287; *E. of I.*, ii, pp. 649-50, article 'Kays'.

[13] *Kashf al-Ghummah*, fol. 352a; cf. H. A. R. Gibb, *The Travels of Ibn Battuta A.D. 1325-1354*, Hakluyt Society, 2nd series, nos 110, 153 (Cambridge, 1958), ii, p. 397.

al-Hawari in 1406–7. From his death in 1428–9 for the rest of the century election to the imamate was not continuous, successive imams being unable to retain control. But these spells of imamate rule may have progressively weakened Nabhani influence as there is record of an order in 1482 providing for the return of property expropriated by them. Stability in Oman only came with the election in 1500–1 of Muhammad ibn Ismaᶜil who held office until his death in April 1536.[14] It was during his reign that the first European sea-traders reached the Persian Gulf and changed the whole pattern of maritime trading and power in the East.

The Portuguese Period 1507–1650

In 1507 Albuquerque passed up the Oman coast sacking or forcing the submission of Ras al-Hadd, Qalhat, Quryat, Muscat, Suhar and Khur Fakkan. Qalhat was then the chief Hormuzi port in Oman. Unable to conquer Hormuz, the principal objective, as planned, Albuquerque had to be content with a treaty, tribute and a customs arrangement. Portuguese paramountcy was finally established in 1515 when Albuquerque returned with twenty-six ships and 2,200 men. For the next thirty-two years until the Turks entered the scene, the Portuguese theoretically had control of Hormuz and its Arabian littoral dependencies, but in fact suffered revolts at Hormuz, Bahrain, Muscat, Quryat and Suhar in 1522, at Muscat and Qalhat in 1526 and at Bahrain in 1529. The Turks came into conflict with the Portuguese in the Gulf from 1546 capturing the forts of Basrah and al-Qatif, and sacking and capturing Muscat in 1551. Attempts were made to gain control of the Arab ports by capturing Bahrain but were unsuccessful. Thirty years later a Turkish naval expedition sent from Mocha surprised the Portuguese in Muscat and sacked the town, evident Portuguese weakness being exploited by the ruler of Fars with a siege of Hormuz during the following year. The loss of Suhar to Omani tribes shortly before 1600 was a further example.[15]

In the interior of Oman the Imam Muhammad, whose reign had seen the Portuguese domination of the Gulf trade network, had died in 1536. The reigns of his successor, his son Barakat, and of those who immediately followed – of whom details are unclear – were terminated by a resurgence in power of the Nabahinah and by the activities of other tribes who sought to emulate them. But from about 1561 to the rise of the Yaᶜrubi imamate in 1624 the chronicles make no mention of other elections. Reasons are not given, though much is made of a dispute over

---

[14] *Kashf al-Ghummah*, fols 352a–353b; H. A. R. Gibb, *op. cit.*, p. 398; cf. Aubin, *op. cit.*, p. 85.
[15] F. C. Danvers, *The Portuguese in India* (London, 1894), i, pp. 152–78 *et passim.*, pp. 492 *et passim.*

the validity of the imamates of Muhammad and his son, such theological controversy perhaps preventing elections. Neither is the resurgence of the Nabahinah explained. Until 1624 power in Oman was divided and disputed between the Nabahinah and petty princes only able to exert influence around their immediate tribal areas.[16]

At the end of 1624 the election of a member of the Yaᶜrubi tribe as imam introduced an era in which the country was united under a strong imamate, the Portuguese were expelled and a large part of the trade of the Arabian Sea was captured. But the election of an imam is not sufficient in itself to guarantee a return to law and order. Nasir ibn Murshid, the first Yaᶜrubi imam, elected in al-Rustaq, had first to gain control of one of the traditional seats of imamate rule in Oman proper, the forts of Nizwa or Bahla. Thenceforth the success of his campaigns would depend on raising forces strong enough to defeat the powerful provincial *muluk*. There was little advantage in exploiting the traditional Yamani/Nizari dichotomy as the tribal wars of the Nabhani period had shown there was too much flexibility in that. He could only persuade the tribal leaders by appealing to their piety, by offering them governorships of provincial towns captured, or by holding out opportunity of plundering territory overrun. By these methods, in approximately eight years, the entire country was subdued. During the first stage Nasir's authority was extended over almost the whole of the Eastern Hajar, domination of Wadi Samayil, Samad al-Shaᶜan and Wadi al-ᶜAqq securing the route of access to the Sharqiyah and Jaᶜalan, and his holding of Ibra giving him control of the numerous villages in that area. To the north the Portuguese had enclaves at Muscat, Muttrah, Sur and Quryat but could not claim authority elsewhere. In the Western Hajar, Nasir controlled the entire mountain range as far as Wadi Dhank except for the area of ᶜIbri, Maquniyat and Bahla, only the last of which had he attempted to take. On the coastal side of the mountains he held al-Rustaq and Nakhl while the Portuguese held the ports.[17]

Portugal's position in the Persian Gulf and Arabian Sea was now being challenged by other European nations anxious to participate in the trade. In 1616, for example, a permit was granted to the English to build a factory at Jask from which overland trade with the Persian capital could be conducted. Such activities were anathema to the Portuguese who were strangely unable to offer resistance. In 1602 the Shah expelled their puppet Hormuzi *malik* from Bahrain and in 1610 and 1615 their fleets

---

[16] *Kashf al-Ghummah*, fol. 357b; cf. fol. 352b.

[17] Ibn Qaisar, ᶜAbd Allah ibn Khalfan, *Sirat al-Imam al-ᶜadil Nasir ibn Murshid*, British Museum MS. Add. 23, 343, i, fols 4a–8a; cf. Al-Maᶜwali, Abu Sulaiman ibn ᶜAmir, *Qisas wa-akhbar jarat bi-ᶜUman*, BM. MS. Or. 6568, fol. 113b *et seq.*

were defeated by the English off Surat. Although they seized Gombroon from the Persians in 1612 they were expelled from it in 1615. Their only success at this time was the recapture of Suhar, a display of opportunism rather than aggression. About 1620 they were dislodged from a fortified position near Julfar and at the end of 1620 their Gulf squadron suffered another defeat by the English. Thus the pressure built up, and in 1621 Shah ᶜAbbas claimed the island of Hormuz. The Portuguese repudiated this, but by January 1622 the Persians and English had seen they had a common cause and joined forces to besiege the Portuguese there. Its celebrated loss, by surrender, occurred towards the end of April.[18]

The loss of Hormuz was an important stage in the decline of Portuguese power in the Gulf, and if the English had fallen in with the Persian desire to take Muscat, their banishment from the Gulf would have been complete. In the event, the Persians took further advantage of Portuguese confusion by adding Suhar and Khur Fakkan to their holdings on the Oman coast. The return of Ruy Freire de Andrade from English captivity provided a temporary reversal of this trend. For a period of seven years the verve and military skills of Andrade and Botelho made it seem possible that Portuguese pre-eminence could be restored. Suhar was recovered from the Persians, a fort and monasteries were built at Basrah, Gombroon was blockaded and the fort at Hormuz besieged. Kung and Bombarreca on the Persian coast were sacked but when Anglo–Persian agreement had been reached to attack the Portuguese in Muscat, their military base, it had to be abandoned because of Portuguese successes at sea. Fortifications at Muscat were improved and in July 1627 Portuguese assistance was given to the Shaikh of al-Qatif, who was being pressed by Persian forces, as well as an attack being made on Bahrain fort. The Persian coast was ravaged. Some relief came only when Botelho was obliged to return with his fleet to Goa where he took charge in July 1629. Ruy Freire, nevertheless, continued to harrass the Persians to such an extent that early in 1630 they sued for peace. The Portuguese were then allowed to trade at the Persian port of Kung, on the same conditions as the English at Gombroon, and were granted permission to found a garrison – adjoining that of the Persians – at Julfar.[19]

[18] Manuel de Faria y Sousa, *The Portuguese Asia*, trans. Captain John Stevens (London, 1695), iii, p. 303; C. R. Boxer, 'Anglo-Portuguese Rivalry in the Persian Gulf, 1615–1635', in *Chapters in Anglo-Portuguese Relations*, ed. Edgar Prestage (Watford, 1935), pp. 74–83; Sir Arnold Wilson, *The Persian Gulf* (London, 1954), p. 150.

[19] *Documentos Remettidos da India*, India Office Portuguese Records, vol. 94, bk 19, fol. 41, bk 22, fol. 117, Viceroy to King 27 February 1626, bk 28, fol. 172, King to Viceroy 31 March 1631; Boxer, *op. cit.*, pp. 89, 103, 106–14; India Office Records, *Original Correspondence (O.C.) 1159*. Isfahan to Company 30 May 1624, *O.C. 1192*, Captain Weddell to Company 27 April, 1625, *O.C. 1173*, Consultations at Gombroon 1 January—10 February 1625, *Factory Records Persia – Persian Gulf (F.R.P.G.)*, i, p. 175, Surat to Factors in Persia

In the interior of Oman, although Ibadism was a strong rallying point, from the ninth century until the emergence of the Yaᶜrubi dynasty elected imams had been unable to gain control of the whole of the country or to establish a tradition of rule by central imamate government. In the second stage of his reinstatement of the imamate, Nasir ibn Murshid changed this. He undertook a series of campaigns in the Western Hajar as a result of which ᶜIbri, al-Ghabbi and Bat were wrested from the Al Hilal and Jibur, Bahla from the Bani Hinaᶜah, Samayil from the Al ᶜUmair, Yanqul and Tauwam from the Al Hilal and, finally, Liwa Fort near Suhar, a gathering point for his enemies from the interior, was captured after a siege of six months. With his imamate extended to cover the whole of the mountain range of Oman, Nasir was able to turn his attention to the Portuguese enclaves.[20]

On the coast the Omanis had had little opportunity for independent trading. When the Portuguese lost Hormuz they preserved the facade of the treaty with Hormuz by bringing to Muscat Muhammad Shah, nephew and namesake of the former ruler of Hormuz, and had set him up as titular prince of Arabia (Oman). Despite this, it was the Portuguese who had firm control over nearly all the ports from Ras al-Hadd to the tip of the Musandum Peninsula, as well as Julfar and Khasab on the other side. These included Sur, Quryat, Muscat, Muttrah, Sib, Suhar, Khur Fakkan, Dabba and Liwa. Only three other coastal villages, Khur al-Jaramah, Tiwi and Qalhat, could be reckoned as trading ports, but were of little importance. The principal ports were Sur, Muscat with Muttrah, and Suhar, while Julfar and Muscat were of considerable importance for Portuguese control of shipping.[21]

The high-handed behaviour of the Portuguese towards the Hormuzis and the Persians had been responsible, as much as anything else, for their expulsion from Hormuz. Their behaviour towards the Omani Arabs had been no less oppressive. For the Imam Nasir real stability in the imamate could only be achieved by recapturing the ports. The early 1630s, when Ruy Freire's resources in soldiers and shipping were severely limited by the Portuguese–Dutch conflict in India, were particularly opportune. In a series of campaigns, an attack on Muscat was terminated by a truce providing for the return of property expropriated at Suhar; an attack on Julfar resulted in the capture of both the Persian and Portuguese forts,

[20] Ibn Qaisar, *op. cit.*, fols 9a–23a.

[21] Pietro della Valle, *The Travels of Sig. Pietro della Valle* (London, 1665), p. 233; *Carmelites, op. cit.*, p. 331, Antonio Bocarro, *Livro do Estado da India Oriental*, BM. MS. Sloane 197, pts ii and iii.

18 November, 1625. Anon., *A Chronicle of the Carmelites in Persia* (London, 1939), p. 283; cf. Paul Craesbeeck, *Commentaries of Ruy Freyre de Andrada*, ed. C. R. Boxer (London, 1930), p. 207; cf. Faria y Sousa, *op. cit.*, iii, p. 325.

and an attack on Dabba was concluded by a truce. The Persians' loss at Julfar encouraged them once again to make common cause with the English over capturing Muscat, but plans fell through in March 1633 when the Governor of Shiraz was executed by Shah Safi. Ruy Freire's death in December 1632 now had a profound effect on Portuguese military capabilities and encouraged the imam to try for Suhar. A siege begun in August 1633 was lifted only when a truce had been concluded, by which the Portuguese agreed to abstain from war, to surrender their fortified posts at Muttrah, and to permit Omanis to trade freely at Muscat. Further campaigns were conducted in 1634 against Portuguese positions in Sur and Quryat, where at Sur, at least, the imam's troops gained control of the fort.[22]

Some of the pressure the Portuguese had felt at sea was relieved in 1635 when a peace treaty was signed at Goa with the English, but preoccupation with the Dutch prevented any attempts to regain ports from the imam. The next recorded Omani attack on the ports was on Muscat in 1640 but it was repulsed with considerable loss. Suhar was attacked in November 1643 and taken, and this gave the imam his first opportunity to develop normal trading contacts with other European nations. Campaigns continued, but details are available of only a few of the engagements. It is known that fighting broke out around Muscat during the winter of 1643 and that in early 1647 'Muscat has been the objective of a terrible war, and attacked and besieged by the neighbouring Arabs'. On 16 August 1648 a major campaign was launched against Muscat and by 11 September the Portuguese had been obliged to withdraw from the approaches. Truce discussions and fighting were intermittent until 30 October when a treaty of peace was signed by Sultan ibn Saif al-Ya'rubi, General of the imam's forces, and the Portuguese Captain-General. The terms included the surrender by the Portuguese of the forts at Quryat and Dabba, freedom for the imam's ships to navigate to any port, and freedom from dues in Muscat.[23]

Six months later the Imam Nasir died, on 23 April 1649, his cousin and general, Sultan ibn Saif, being elected imam on the same day. The final siege of Muscat began almost immediately. It was well underway by

[22] Carmelites, *op. cit.*, p. 102 *et seq.*, pp. 329–31; Della Valle, *op. cit.*, pp. 235–7; Ibn Qaisar, *op. cit.*, fols 24a–33b; Boxer, *op. cit.*, p. 118; I.O. Records, *F. R. Surat*, i, p. 171, Consultations at Surat 18 December 1632, p. 196, Commission to Captain Weddell, 24 January 1633 *O.C. 1492* Swally to Company 27 January 1633, *O.C. 1499* Ship *Mary* to Surat 15 March 1633, *O.C. 1504*, Gombroon to Company 24 March, 1633.

[23] Philippus, Sanctissima Trinitate, *Voyage D'Orient du R. P. Philippe de La très-Saincte Trinité Carme Deschaussé* (Lyon 1669), p. 82; *Documentos Remettidos*, Vol. 103, bk. 48, fol. 290, Viceroy to King 15 February 1644, Vol. 104, bk. 59, fols 68, 70, 74, 88; Danvers, *op. cit.*, ii, p. 273; Carmelites, *op. cit.*, p. 358; *O.C. 2089*, Gombroon to Surat 4 December 1648.

25 October when terms were broken off, and in mid-December Sultan's army entered the town. The Portuguese sought refuge in the factory and in Fort Jalali. But so many entered the Fort that, on 23 January 1650 the Captain-General, Francisco de Tavota, had to surrender for lack of supplies. Three days later the factory surrendered also.[24]

When Nasir ibn Murshid came to power the coastal occupations of the Omanis – trading, sea-going and fishing – were all subject to Portuguese and Hormuzi control, and indirectly this affected the livelihood of the tribes who bartered at the coast. Without control of the ports, and the benefit of the income they produced, the imamate could not claim to be the overall authority. The capture of the Julfar forts and the town of Dabba paved the way for the siege of Suhar in 1633, but it was the capture of Suhar Fort ten years later which presaged the exclusion of the Portuguese from Omani waters. The imam's subjects were then free to trade unrestrictedly with other European nations and it only remained for them to drive the Portuguese out of Muscat. The campaign of 1648, though unsuccessful, did reduce the Portuguese to accepting humiliating terms, and their expulsion thereafterwards was only a matter of time.

Maritime Power and Imamate Government 1650–1719
The expulsion of the Portuguese from the coast of Oman was the prelude to a war which the two adversaries waged for a century or more. Portuguese vessels which the Omanis had taken over at the fall of Muscat provided the nucleus of a warlike fleet. The skills to operate and fight with large vessels were already available as many Omani Arabs had served in Portuguese ships. The first thirty years of Omani maritime freedom, until the death of the Imam Sultan ibn Saif I in December 1679, saw a transformation of maritime power in the Arabian Sea. War was taken to the Portuguese in India and East Africa, numerous battles were fought at sea and the Omanis steadily increased the size and quality of their fleet. The Portuguese had opportunities – off Muscat in March 1652 and February 1653 and off Suhar in 1672 – to recover key bases on the Oman coast but they went by default for reasons of cowardice or pride. In East Africa, from 1652 onwards, they successively lost their ports until only the stronghold of Mombasa was held, and in 1665 that also capitulated. Even their settlement at Mozambique was threatened by an Omani attack in 1669. Portuguese settlements in India were subjected to attack and plunder; Bombay in 1661 or 1662, Diu in November 1668 and January 1676, Bassein in 1674 and Kung in Persia in 1670. And when an

[24] Ibn Qaisar, *op. cit.*, fol. 50a; *Kashf al-Ghummah*, fol. 373a; Carmelites, *op. cit.*, pp. 358–9; *Documentos Remettidos*, Vol. 105, bk. 60, fol. 331, Viceroy to King 18 December 1650.

attempt was made to regain control in East Africa at the end of 1678, an expedition headed by the Viceroy himself was scattered by the arrival of Omani ships.[25]

What were the reasons for the Omani successes? Principally, the demoralization of the Portuguese, aggravated by lack of resources and conflict with their European rivals and the rulers of the various Indian states; the hostility of the native peoples of East Africa and the natural abilities of the Omanis as sailors. The acquisition of ships by capture, or purchase, the engagement of European mariners – and Portuguese captives – to serve in the imam's ships, and assistance from the Dutch and English with navigators, gunners and ammunition, all combined to make the Omani fleet at times the most powerful in the Arabian Sea.

The Arabian Sea and the Persian Gulf offer no finer trading base than the harbours of Oman, situated strategically between the Gulf and the coasts of India and Africa. The Portuguese, and before them the Persians and Hormuzis, had realized that the arbiter of Persian Gulf trade must hold the Omani ports. The part that the Arab inhabitants of Oman played in the coastal and sea-going trade in pre-Yaᶜrubi times is obscure. Banian or Indian merchants had resided in Oman ports from the commencement of trading contacts with India and the control of trade by Portuguese primarily based in India encouraged the placing of agencies in their hands. Portuguese control of shipping was exercised by the pass system and the levy of customs dues. All Indian or Muslim ships passing through the Gulf of Oman or the straits of Hormuz not only had to carry Portuguese passes but also had to touch at Muscat, or later Kung, and pay customs duties of not less than 10 per cent on their cargoes. This enormous revenue had fully justified maintaining a fleet at Muscat as well as fortified posts all along the coast.[26]

When all these posts had fallen to the Omanis, the Imam Sultan

[25] Carmelites, *op. cit.*, pp. 359, 1247; Faria y Sousa, *op. cit.*, p. 472; *O.C. 2119* Account by Robert Cocks of voyage in *Friendship*, *O.C. 2270* Gombroon to Company 15 May 1652, *O.C. 2296* Isfahan to Company 10 December 1652, *O.C. 2317* Gombroon to Company 28 February 1652, *O.C. 3213* Surat to Company 26 March 1667, *O.C. 3910* Aungier to Company 15 December 1673, *O.C. 4175*, fol. 2, Surat to Company 2 February 1676, *O.C. 3906*, fol. 1, Bombay occurrences 4 February 1674; *F. R. Bombay*, VI, pp. 64, 70, Bombay to Company 7 and 17 February 1674, VII, p. 12, Bombay to Company 17 January 1676; *E. R. Surat*, CV, pp. 66, 76, Flower to Surat 14 August 1668, Gombroon to Surat, 26 November 1668; *F.R.Misc.*, II, p. 48, Gombroon to Company 2 March 1669; *Documentos Remettidos*, Vol. 104, bk 56, fol. 466, Viceroy to King 28 January 1653; Anon., *Relacao da Iorna da que fes o Governador Antonio de Sousa Coutinho ao estreito de Ormus* (Lisbon, 1653), pp. 1–10; Justus Strandes, *The Portuguese Period in East Africa*, ed. J. S. Kirkman (Nairobi, 1961), pp. 227, 229–32; Carré, *The Travels of The Abbé Carré*, ed. Sir Charles Fawcett (London, 1947–8), i, pp. 115–28; J. Fryer, *A New Account of East India and Persia*, ed. W. Crooke (London, 1909–15), ii, p. 192; Robert Orme, *Historical Fragments of the Mogul Empire* (London, 1782), p. 64.

[26] *O.C. 1764*, Swally to Company 29 December 1640.

immediately employed captured Portuguese ships on trading runs, and in some measure trading routes were taken over by the Omanis. From East Africa slaves, ivory and gold could be brought to Mocha and the Persian Gulf. From the Canara and Malabar coasts of India, rice and spices could be brought to Oman and the north, and from Surat all kinds of cloth and piece goods. Coffee from Mocha and dates and coconuts from Dhofar could be transported to the Persian Gulf whence the market towns could be supplied with goods emanating from the Indian Ocean, and the dates, pearls, fish and horses from the Arab shore and the Oman coastline could be taken to Surat and other ports in western India. Indian commodities could be sent to Mocha by sea or, via al-Qatif, by land across the peninsula. Drugs from southern Arabia could also be brought to Muscat for sale to European traders.[27]

But the difficulties of competition for the international trade were great. Five European nations were competing for the trade as well as the native peoples of Arabia, Persia and India and – through their Arab or Portuguese intermediaries – East Africa. The situation was complicated further by native boats being required to carry a pass from the authority or European company controlling the port traded to or from thus exposing themselves to seizure by the enemies of those who had issued the pass.[28] As France, England and Holland were intermittently at war with each other, in various combinations, and the Omanis were permanently at war with the Portuguese and, at times, with the Danes, the question of what pass should be carried or what flag flown was a matter of diplomacy rather than alliance or allegiance.

The Imam Sultan's relationship to Nasir ibn Murshid, the first Ya'rubi imam, raises some doubts about the validity of his election. The Ibadis reject any claims of patrilineage or heredity in the election of imams, the office being offered to the best qualified member of the community. Sultan may have been this, but there is no doubt that the election of the person who had been responsible overall for the most successful attack on Muscat in October 1648 was particularly appropriate for the Omani–Portuguese contest. But despite his successes in expelling the Portuguese and following up the maritime advantages gained, Sultan had to suffer criticism for the worldliness of his imamate. His involvement in commerce would have drawn the court away from the influence of the centres of puritanical Ibadism in the mountains and, as one native writer puts it, 'he had agents who were known to buy and sell on his account'. Another

---

[27] Philippus, *op. cit.*, p. 80; Jean de Thévenot, *The Travels of Monsieur de Thévenot into the Levant* (London, 1687), ii, pp. 160–82; Charles Lockyer, *An Account of the Trade in India* (London, 1711), pp. 205–8.

[28] Cf. Fryer, *op. cit.*, i, p. 267; Dr J. F. Gemelli Careri, 'A Voyage Round the World' in *Churchill's Voyages*, iv (1744–6), p. 180.

writer mentions his sending merchants to India, Persia, Sanᶜa, Basrah and Iraq.[29] Moreover, when Sultan died there were no longer any Christians occupying the coastal ports, the war with them had been taken successfully to India and East Africa and the imamate was relatively stable. Such conditions did not demand any compromise with Ibadi principles and the fittest man – regardless of tribe or station – could be elected as Sultan's successor. In fact the imamate passed to Sultan's son Bilᶜurub and there can be no doubt that with his election a custom of patrilineage was established and a ruling dynasty created, a custom which was to drive a wedge between the Ibadi pietists and the tribal leaders who had come to favour the Yaᶜrubi dynasty.

At sea the systems of monopolies and passes, the frequent inter-European wars and the use of the Omanis as allies in those wars had led to the development of piracy. Extensive piracy pure and simple does not seem to have appeared much before the end of Sultan ibn Saif I's reign (1649–79), but the Omanis were well prepared to participate in it. Maritime hazards obliged merchant ships to be well armed or escorted. The Omanis heeded this and their fleet became noted for the size of its ships and weight of armament. It was this strength, untrammelled by governmental authority or even at times encouraged by it, and coupled with the raiding instincts of the Arab tribesman, which made them so formidable. They reacted to the European-controlled trading system and European and native piracy by resorting to buccaneering themselves.

Inevitably, both maritime trading and piracy by Omanis became somewhat independent of imamate government in the interior. During the rule of Saif ibn Sultan I (c. 1692–1711) the imam's dominions stretched not only along the immediate shore to embrace the pearl fisheries of the Persian Gulf to the north and to Ras Fartak to the south-west but also as far as East Africa.[30] There the expulsion of the Portuguese had permitted imamate authority to be extended over Omani settlers, native Muslims and African coastal tribes. Even if the imams had so wished, it would have been difficult for them to exercise control over Omani ships which, each year, were journeying farther south on the Indian and African coasts. Piratical activities came to a head during the reign of Saif ibn Sultan I, a most active one in terms of foreign adventure. They represented a breakaway from 'war' on flimsy pretexts to blatant aggression having no other purpose than plunder. Attacks on settlements on

[29] *Kashf al-Ghummah*, fol. 373a; Ibn Ruzaiq, Humaid ibn Muhammad, *Al-fath al-mubin al-mubarhin sirat al-sadat albu sa'idiyin*, Cambridge University Library MS. Add. 2892, fol. 127b.

[30] Careri, *op. cit.*, iv, p. 185; Lockyer, *op. cit.*, p. 210; A. Hamilton, *A New Account of the East Indies*, ed. Sir W. Foster (London, 1930), i, p. 49; H. Cornwall, *Observations on Several Voyages to India* (London, 1720), p. 42.

the Indian coast, campaigns in East Africa and the seizure of trading fleets off Mocha and in the Persian Gulf characterized Saif's reign.[31] Muscat virtually controlled the passage into the Persian Gulf and customs duties levied and plunder gained combined to make the country prosperous. Muscat became a major mart town. It was resorted to for drugs such as Socotra aloes, asafoetida, olibanum (frankincense), putchock and myrrh, minerals such as alum and sulphur, ivory from East Africa, coffee from Mocha, pearls from the Gulf, and horses, dates, fish, livestock, fruits and vegetables as produce of Oman.[32] Its role as an entrepot as well as a provisioning place for water, livestock and cereals made it one of the most important ports in the Arabian Sea.[33]

The prosperity this brought is evident from the fortunes of the fourth Ya'rubi imam, Saif ibn Sultan I. He is given the credit for the construction of seventeen *aflaj* and the planting of 20,000 date and 6,000 coconut palms. He occupied himself entirely with trading and external affairs, his personal ownership of 24 large ships, 28 barques and 1,700 slaves being clear evidence of the extent to which his attitude diverged from the asceticism advocated by the puristic *'ulama'*.[34]

His successor Sultan ibn Saif II (1711–19) showed, in his short reign, a continuation of the aggression and piracy of the Omani fleets, particularly in the Persian Gulf where attacks on Persian islands and coast were to bring severe retribution in later years. Unlike his father, Sultan was a spendthrift and within a few years had spent all he had inherited, as well as what he could borrow from the *auqaf*.[35] By the end of his reign the strain between the Ibadi *'ulama'* and the tribal supporters of the Ya'rubi dynasty was too great. Sultan's death brought about an intense struggle between the tribal leaders who, feeling that patrilineal succession was unquestionable, favoured the election of Sultan's son Saif, although he was a minor, and the *'ulama'* who supported the candidature of Muhanna

---

[31] Cf. N. Manucci, *Storia Do Mogor or Mogul India 1653–1708*, ed. W. Irvine (London, 1907–08), iii, p. 491, iv, p. 180; G. W. Forrest (ed.), *Selections from the Letters, Despatches, and Other State Papers Preserved in the Bombay Secretariat* (Bombay, 1887), i, p. 266; J. Biddulph, *The Pirates of Malabar* (London, 1907), p. 75.

[32] Bodleian MS., Eng. Misc. b, 7, fols 1–4; Bodleian MS., Rawlinson A334, fol. 72a; Hamilton, *op. cit.*, i, pp. 45, 47, 159; Lockyer, *op. cit.*, pp. 208–10; Cornwall, *op. cit.*, p.42.

[33] Goods for which European ships found a ready market at Muscat were tutanag (coarse tin), copper, lead, steel, iron, guns, arms, nails, anchors, fir-masts – all these reflected the needs of the aggressive Omani seafarers – as well as glassware, china and Indian goods (V. Lockyer, *op. cit.*, pp. 209 and 217, and Bodleian MS., Engl. Misc. b, 7, *loc. cit.*). The latter source, which is the account book for trade done at Muscat by an English ship during the period July-September 1704, gives a good idea of the dominance of the imam's *wakil* at the port.

[34] Al-Ma'wali, Abu Sulaiman Muhammad ibn 'Amir, *Nabdhah fi ansab al-Ma'awil*, Zahiriyah (Damascus) Library MS., Tarikh 385, p. 431; Al-Salimi, 'Abd Allah ibn Humaid, *Tuhfat al-A'yan bi-sirat ahl 'Uman* (Cairo, 1380/1961), ii, p. 100.

[35] *Kashf al-Ghummah*, fol. 374a.

ibn Sultan al-Yaᶜrubi. It was the civil war which followed that ensured the downfall of the dynasty.

Civil War 1719–1728

Saif ibn Sultan II was the direct descendant of three famous imams, and represented a direct continuation of the dynasty which had made Oman powerful. But as a minor (of perhaps twelve years of age) he was not acceptable to the ᶜulama', who favoured the appointment of Muhanna. However, at the election the tribal leaders were deceived into thinking that Saif had been elected and only later, privately in the fort at Nizwa, was Muhanna proclaimed imam, in May 1719.

The deception brought about a rebellion led by Yaᶜrub ibn Bilᶜurub (son of former Imam Bilᶜurub) which resulted in Muhanna being besieged in the fort of al-Rustaq. Deficient of tribal support, he was obliged to surrender and was killed shortly afterwards, c. 1720–1. Yaᶜrub acted as regent for Saif, but after a year was able to persuade the ᶜulama' to grant the imamate to him, in June 1722. But other Yaᶜaribah were dissatisfied with this and a rebellion was now launched by Bilᶜurub ibn Nasir al-Ya-ᶜrubi. He captured a series of key forts before isolating and besieging Yaᶜrub at Nizwa, whereupon Yaᶜrub had to yield his imamate. Saif was now formally proclaimed imam, with Bilᶜurub as regent.

This may have settled the internal squabbles of the Yaᶜaribah but was not acceptable to other tribes. Their dissatisfaction came to a head when swearing fealty to Saif in Nizwa, and took the form of a dispute between Bilᶜurub and the Bani Ghafir. Their leader, Muhammad ibn Nasir al-Ghafiri, persuaded Yaᶜrub to come out of retirement and lead a rebellion. Yaᶜrub and his supporters attacked Izki but had to fall back on Nizwa where they in turn were besieged by Bilᶜurub's forces. Muhammad ibn Nasir had been raising an army and scattered the besiegers on arrival at Nizwa. The fight was then taken to Bilᶜurub in al-Rustaq where he was compelled to surrender. Muhammad proclaimed Saif imam, again, in about June 1723, and in the same month Yaᶜrub died.[36]

The involvement of Muhammad ibn Nasir, and his Bani Ghafir and northern tribe supporters, in imamate affairs in Oman proper seems to have been the cause of the next development. The Bani Hinaᶜah, under the leadership of Khalaf ibn Mubarak, started a rebellion against the imamate. They captured Muscat and Barkah but were then defeated in a short battle at Barkah. Muhammad ibn Nasir himself turned to attacking allies of the Bani Hinaᶜah, the Bani ᶜAli of Yanqul, whilst Khalaf's tribesmen attacked the villages of al-Sirr. On the coastal side of the mountains

---

[36] *Ibid.*, fols 374a–378b.

Khalaf then took al-Rustaq and Nakhl and an ally of his took Suhar. An unsuccessful attempt by Khalaf on al-Hazm ended the first phase of the contest.[37] There was a six months' lull, Khalaf's forces controlling the coast and Muhammad's controlling the interior. Although Khalaf held the more important passes, thus denying Muhammad a route to the coast, and received the revenue of the ports, Muhammad had a considerable advantage in troops. He was able to draw on several tribes of the *bedu*, the better fighters, and particularly those of the north who can be regarded as mercenaries (in terms of loot and plunder) rather than as tribes who had a definite stake in the imamate. It may have been Muhammad's introduction of large numbers of unruly Sunni tribesmen which encouraged the Omanis to split into those who supported the Bani Hinaᶜah, the 'Hinawis', and those who supported Muhammad ibn Nasir al-Ghafiri, the 'Ghafiris'.

Hostilities resumed when Muhammad set out to defeat the remaining Hinawi opposition in the interior, the ᶜAwamir villages and the Sharqiyah. A force brought from Muscat by Khalaf was defeated near Ibra and this was followed by a successful siege of al-Rustaq. Then, abruptly, Muhammad summoned the tribes to Nizwa and asked to be replaced as regent for Saif. A not unexpected result, given the circumstances, was that he was elected Imam, on 27 September 1724. His election had no apparent effect on the opposition of the Hinawi faction. Geographical factors, as well as random distribution of opposed tribes, had determined the approximate areas of Muhammad's and Khalaf's spheres of influence. However, a successful attack against Samayil now upset this, and gave Muhammad control of a route to the coast. A further campaign against Bani Hinaᶜah and Bani ᶜAli territory finally gave him control of the whole of the interior. With more troops from the north he moved on to Suhar. Khalaf's army met him there and, ironically, the two principal antagonists of five years of civil war were killed in the same battle. The leaderless situation resulting enabled Saif to take the initiative and after first taking the fort of al-Rustaq, he proceeded to Nizwa where he was proclaimed Imam in the latter half of March 1728.[38]

Conclusion

Lack of information prevents us from examining the conditions under which Ibadi imams were elected in Oman, the stipulations attaching to their appointment, and the grounds on which some were deposed. Details of the way in which they governed are also not available but, for the Yaᶜrubi period, enough is known of their involvement in maritime trade

[37] *Ibid.*, fols 378b–380a.
[38] *Ibid.*, fols 380a–386a.

for it to be possible to examine the effect of this on the character of the imamate.

Clearly, during the Ya°rubi dynasty, control of succession to the imamate passed out of the hands of the °ulama'; for once full involvement in maritime trade had become possible, patronage dispensed by successive imams far exceeded anything experienced before. The rise of the dynasty coincided with a period of intense European competition for port facilities and trading agreements, with countries bordering the Arabian Sea and Persian Gulf, and the advantages offered by such agreements behoved the existence of a self-perpetuating form of government.[39]

The prosperity from trade gave the Ya°rubi family, and their principal tribal supporters, a considerable proprietary interest in the accession to the imamate.[40] It is not clear to what extent the °ulama' condoned this but the final break came in 1719 at the death of the most profligate of the Ya°rubi imams, Sultan ibn Saif II. Characteristically, but necessarily, the candidate of the °ulama' held a totally different view about the functions of the imam.[41] If the Ya°aribah had been able to agree amongst themselves they might have been able to preserve their power, despite the opposition of the °ulama'.[42] But their squabbles led to the civil war, and the Ghafiri/Hinawi conflict which came out of it transformed the structure of tribal allegiances, leaving the Ya°aribah deficient of substantial support. The emergence subsequently, at the time of the Persian invasion, of a strong man of another tribe, Ahmad ibn Sa°id Al Bu Sa°idi, led to an eclipse of Ya°rubi power. The new dynasty also involved itself in maritime trade and foreign adventure but, within a few decades, abandoned the title of imam and made no further pretence of spiritual leadership.

[39] Indeed, the Ibadis do not regard it as religiously imperative to have an imam at all (see Salem, *op. cit.*, p. 52).

[40] Cf. E. Tyan (*Institutions du Droit Public Musulman*, Paris, 1954–6) . . . 'but it is a fact that as soon as a Kharijite group comes out of anarchy and comes to organize itself in a regular political form, the electoral procedure is abandoned . . . to make place for the hereditary and dynastic principle' (ii, p. 559).

[41] In fact Muhanna abolished customs duties at Muscat and did not appoint an agent there (see *Kashf al-Ghummah*, fols 374b–375a).

[42] Al-Salimi comments, . . . 'when the Ya°aribah changed the way of life of their venerable forefathers and in their foolishness deemed the country to be their heritage and attacked each other to possess it God took it away and placed it in others' (*op. cit.*, ii, p. 168).

6

A PREVALENCE OF FURIES:
TRIBES, POLITICS, AND RELIGION IN OMAN AND
TRUCIAL OMAN

J. B. KELLY

Since the early decades of the eighteenth century two forces have shaped
and directed Oman's political life. One is the schism between its Ibadi
and Sunni inhabitants, which has divided Oman since the second century
AH; the other is the Hinawi–Ghafiri factionalism among the tribes. How
far these factors continue to affect its politics today it is not easy to
decide with any certainty; but since they have had such a marked effect
upon Omani life up to our day they would seem to merit examination
and attention. As the religious question has found its prime expression
in the role and function of the Ibadi imamate as the ruling institution of
the country, it would seem to be a valid subject for enquiry whether the
imamate is to be regarded now simply as an archaic survival which has
no constructive role to play in the evolution of Oman as a modern state,
or whether it still retains sufficient vitality to make it a force to be
reckoned with in the political future of Oman.

The alignment of the tribes of Oman into the Hinawi and Ghafiri
factions dates from a series of civil wars in the first half of the eighteenth
century, fought over the succession to the Ibadi imamate. Two tribes,
the Bani Hina and the Bani Ghafir, were in the forefront of the fighting
in its early stages, and as the contest wore on and drew in most of the
tribes of Oman, they tended to range themselves on either the Hinawi or
the Ghafiri side. To some extent, however, this alignment merely re-
affirmed a disunity in Omani society which had existed since pre-Islamic
times, between the tribes of Yemeni or Qahtani origin and those of Nizari
or ᶜAdnani origin; for as a rule the Yemeni tribes embraced the Hinawi
cause, and the Nizari, the Ghafiri. It also emphasized the religious particularism which divided the population, for most of the Yemeni tribes
were Ibadi by profession, and most of the Ghafiri, Sunni. There were,
however, important exceptions to both rules, as was indicated by the
fact that the Bani Hina and Bani Ghafir were both Ibadi tribes.[1]

[1] It should be explained here that there is some uncertainty about the validity of the
identification of the Yemeni tribes as being Ibadi by religious persuasion and Hinawi in
politics, and the Nizari tribes as Sunni and Ghafiri, particularly in our present state of know-

The Al Bu Saᶜid Imamate and Sultanate

The civil wars raged on for a quarter of a century, long after the leaders of the Bani Hina and Bani Ghafir had been killed fighting each other. The duration of the conflict, as well as its character, profoundly altered the place and role of the imamate in the life of Oman. It debased the office by making it a trophy to be won by force of arms, and it brought into contempt the theological qualifications normally required of a successful candidate. What was of equal moment, because it terminated in the accession to power of the Al Bu Saᶜid dynasty the war completed the transformation of the traditional basis of ruling authority in Oman which had begun under the later Yaᶜaribah imams. Like them, Ahmad ibn Saᶜid, who was elected imam with both Hinawi and Ghafiri support in 1749, drew much of his strength from his mercantile and maritime resources and less from his position as a territorial lord. His successors in the Al Bu Saᶜid line were essentially merchant princes, whose interests and energies were primarily directed to enterprises outside Oman, and who relied for the maintenance of their rule in the country upon the fruits of these enterprises.

When Ahmad ibn Saᶜid died in 1783 his second son, Saᶜid, was elected imam. Within three years of his accession Saᶜid ibn Ahmad had so antagonized his subjects that his son, Hamad, was able to wrest control of much of the country from him. Hamad made his capital, not in the interior at Nizwa, the traditional seat of the imamate, or at Rastaq, its seat in Yaᶜaribah times, but at Muscat, on the coast. It was a change which symbolized the shift in the basis of ruling power in Oman from the land to the sea. It also underlined the secular nature of Hamad ibn Saᶜid's regime and his disdain for any religious sanction for his rule; for he left his father to reside at Rastaq in his capacity as imam, and made no attempt to depose him or to have himself elected imam in his place. On Hamad's death in 1792 his uncle, Sultan ibn Ahmad, seized Muscat, and a year later he entered into a compact at Barqa, on the Batinah coast, with his brothers, Saᶜid and Qais, by the terms of which he retained Muscat while Saᶜid continued to live at Rastaq as imam and Qais remained in possession of Sauhar. The compact of Barqa was not only a practical acknowledgement of the existing distribution of power in Oman at the time but it was also a further stage in the decentralization of authority, which had been from the start, and was to remain, the abiding principle of Al Bu Saᶜid rule. Ahmad ibn Saᶜid had begun the process by adopting the custom initiated by the imams of the Yaᶜaribah dynasty a century earlier, of providing

---

ledge of Omani society and in the face of the several exceptions to this proposition which are known to exist. On the other hand, the generalization does not wholly lack grounds, and it has a use in describing and accounting for tribal alliances and antipathies.

for the sons of the reigning imam by appointing them to the governorships of the more important towns. Ahmad ibn Saᶜid's sons had rewarded
his trust by rebelling against him and declaring their independence when-
ever opportunity afforded, thereby forcing him to devote much of his
time and energy to reducing them to obedience. Their example was to be
emulated time and again in the history of Al Bu Saᶜid rule.

Sultan ibn Ahmad, like Hamad ibn Saᶜid before him, made no effort
during his reign at Muscat (1792–1804) to deprive his brother Saᶜid of
the imamate. Instead, he was content to rule, as Hamad had, with the
title of 'Saiyid', in its meaning of 'lord'. According to Percy Badger,

'... the title so applied, was an innovation; it tended, moreover, to
distinguish the ruling family, and to give them a corporate dignity
and pre-eminence over all other native chiefs and grandees. The
"House of the Seyyids", like the reigning "Houses" of Europe, has
become a recognized dynasty, having the first claim to the succession'.[2]

Badr ibn Saif, Saiyid Sultan's nephew and immediate successor, also
made no attempt to depose his uncle, the Imam Saᶜid ibn Ahmad, or to
assume his title. Nor did Sultan's son, Saᶜid, who murdered Badr and
took his place on the *masnad* at Muscat in 1806, interfere with the imam.
Saᶜid ibn Ahmad lived on undisturbed at Rastaq until his death, c. 1821,
when the Ibadiya of Oman were left, for the first time in many generations, not only without an imam but even without a candidate in sight.

The presence of an imam, of course, was not held by the Ibadiya to be
an unconditional necessity. Like the early *Khawarij* from whom they
sprang, the Ibadiya rejected the convention that Islam required a permanent and visible head, just as they denied the right of succession to the
imamate to be inherent in any one family, even in that of the Prophet.
Yet not only had the Omani Ibadiya been accustomed for lengthy periods
of their history to have an imam, but they had also been introduced by
the Yaᶜaribah imams to the principle of hereditary succession (though
not of primogeniture); and the election of Saᶜid ibn Ahmad on the death
of his father in 1783 seemed to indicate that the Al Bu Saᶜid were following
the Yaᶜaribah's lead. It might well be asked, therefore, why it was that
Saiyid Saᶜid ibn Sultan, who was to prove the greatest of the Al Bu Saᶜid
princes, did not at any time in his life seek the dignity of the title. One
answer is that he simply did not want it, in view of the duties and responsibilities which it entailed. Like his father and grandfather before
him, he was primarily interested in affairs and adventures abroad – in
Bahrain, in Bandar ᶜAbbas, and, above all, in East Africa – and he did
not care to be under the obligation to keep his court at Nizwa, Rastaq

[2] *History of the Imâms and Seyyids of Omân* (London: Hakluyt Society, 1871), Appendix A.

or Sauhar, the three towns in which, by custom, the imam could properly lead the Friday prayer. Saiyid Saᶜid preferred Muscat, with its view upon the open sea, to the narrow confines of the inland towns, and from the middle of his life onwards he passed the greater part of his time amid the soporific delights of Zanzibar. Another conjecture, which is that favoured by Percy Badger (although, as he himself admits, he could find no fully satisfactory explanation), is that even if Saᶜid had aspired to the imamate the tribes would not have accepted him. He was already suspected, like his father, of having succumbed to 'the contagion of the world's slow stain' through his traffickings with Christians and Hindus, his penchant for innovations, and his consortings with Abyssinians and Baluchis. What was perhaps more to the point was that he had failed to afford his subjects effective protection against the Wahhabis of Najd, who since the turn of the century had been ravaging Oman. The Wahhabi incursions, and, even more, the militancy of Wahhabi proselytism, had aroused in the more devout Ibadiya a corresponding militancy, with the paradoxical result that they were, at once, more exacting in their assessment of the qualities required in a candidate for the imamate, and less convinced of a pressing need to find a successor to the Imam Saᶜid ibn Ahmad. For prudence dictated that they should avoid provoking the fierce sectarians of Najd by such a gesture of defiance as the election of a new Ibadi Imam would constitute. The upshot was that for nearly half a century after the death of the Imam Saᶜid the Ibadi community of Oman was without an imam, that is to say, the community was in a condition of *kitman*, or concealment.

An abortive attempt to restore the imamate as the ruling institution of the country was made in 1846, when Saiyid Hamud ibn ᶜAzzan of Sauhar, a grandson of Qais ibn Ahmad and head of the cadet branch of the Al Bu Saᶜid, made a bid for the leadership of Oman which Saiyid Saᶜid ibn Sultan had virtually forsaken. The stimulus for the move was the renewal of Wahhabi depredations in northern Oman the previous year, to which Saiyid Saᶜid had reacted by buying off the invaders with presents and promises of tribute. He further disgusted the upland tribes by concluding a convention with the British Government in October 1845, which imposed a total ban upon the exportation of slaves from his East African possessions. The Yal Saᶜad, an Ibadi tribe which dwelt in the Batinah and on the eastern slopes of the Hajar Mountains to the west of Sauhar, and which had successfully defied the Wahhabis' attempts to subdue them, approached Hamud ibn ᶜAzzan with the suggestion that he should organize a confederacy of northern tribes against the Wahhabis. Hamud was, to all intents and purposes, ruler of Sauhar in his own right. Although the principality had been annexed to Muscat by Saiyid Saᶜid on the death of Hamud's father in 1814, it was regarded by the Al Qais branch of the Al Bu Saᶜid as their hereditary fief. Hamud had seized control of it in 1830, when Saiyid Saᶜid was away in East Africa, and Saᶜid had reluctantly concluded an agreement with him nine years later, conceding to him *de facto* autonomy. There was little coyness in Hamud's response to the advances of the Yal Saᶜad shaikhs in 1845. At the beginning of 1846 he made over to them the fort at Sauhar and his inland strongholds, and he wrote to the *tamimahs*, or paramount chiefs, of several other tribes deploring the lax government of Saiyid Saᶜid and urging them to repudiate it. He also began cultivating, or refurbishing, his reputation for piety and abstinence, so as to win the approval of the *mutawiᶜah* elements among the Yal Saᶜad and of the *mutauwaᶜ* class in general among the Ibadi tribes.[3]

Whatever ambitions Hamud may have nurtured for the imamate, they were never gratified. His son, Saif, sensing the threat to his patrimony which his father's transactions were creating, decided to wrest control of Sauhar from him. His first step was to take the field against the Wahhabis, and in the summer of 1848, in conjunction with the ruler of Abu Dhabi, Saᶜid ibn Tahnun, he expelled their garrison from the Buraimi Oasis. He then turned on the *mutawiᶜah*, who were by this time in practical command of the government of Sauhar. At the turn of 1849, with scant ceremony, he drove them from the town, and his father along with them. Hamud found refuge at Rastaq with his brother, Qais ibn ᶜAzzan, and with his help he contrived the murder of his son in March 1850. *Mutauwaᶜ* intolerance may also have stoked the fires of filicide; for in addition to his expulsion of the zealots from Sauhar, Saif ibn Hamud had earned their enmity by concluding an agreement with the British Political Resident in the Gulf in May 1849, which prohibited the importation of slaves into the principality. Hamud ibn ᶜAzzan did not live long to profit from his crime. A month after the murder he was captured by the regent of Muscat, Thuwaini ibn Saᶜid, imprisoned in Fort Jalali, and tortured to death. The following year Sauhar was incorporated in the Muscat dominions.

On this note of Grand Guignol the curtain was rung down on the attempted revival of the imamate. It was not to be raised again for a decade and a half. In the interval, however, there was a certain amount of scurrying about in the wings, particularly at Rastaq, as efforts were made to assemble a new cast. Realizing that what the sacred drama needed

---

[3] *Mutauwaᶜ* (*mutawi ᶜah* in the plural) literally means 'one who submits or obeys'. Among the Ibadiya of Oman the term refers to the more conspicuously devout believers who regarded it as their God-given duty both to inspire their co-religionists to a strict observance of the proscriptive tenets of their faith and to castigate potential backsliders. One suspects, to judge from the record of their activities over the past century and a half, that their zeal was prompted less by theological abstractions than by simple bigotry.

was a powerful backer, Qais ibn ᶜAzzan sent one of his nephews off to Riyad to solicit the support of the Amir Faisal ibn Turki Al Saᶜud. Faisal responded by sending an army of 5,000 men to Oman, under the command of his son, ᶜAbd Allah, at the beginning of 1853. ᶜAbd Allah ibn Faisal rode into the Buraimi Oasis in February of that year, voicing all manner of threats and demands on behalf of 'his children, the shaikhs of Oman', including one for the transfer of Sauhar to Qais ibn ᶜAzzan. The Wahhabi commander, as was the custom, was bought off by the Muscat authorities with gifts and tribute, and he returned to Najd before the beginning of the summer, leaving Qais to ponder on the inconstancy of new-found friends. Three years later, in 1856, Saiyid Saᶜid ibn Sultan died. On his death his eldest surviving son, Thuwaini, succeeded to his dominions in Oman, and another son, Majid, to Zanzibar and the East African possessions. The *de facto* division of the Sultanate was made permanent five years later by the Canning Award. A few months after the announcement of the award Qais ibn ᶜAzzan tried to overthrow Thuwaini. He failed, and he paid for his failure with his life. Thuwaini gained nothing from his death except the implacable hostility of Qais's son, ᶜAzzan, who now took his father's place as head of the collateral branch of the Al Bu Saᶜid. Thuwaini moved against Rastaq towards the close of 1864 in an endeavour to crush ᶜAzzan, as he had crushed his father. ᶜAzzan was saved by the intervention of the Wahhabi *na'ib* at the Buraimi Oasis, who threatened a descent upon Muscat if Thuwaini did not desist.

A curious alliance now developed between the Wahhabi Amir, Faisal ibn Turki, and ᶜAzzan ibn Qais, backed by the Ibadi *mutawiᶜah*. The common bond which united these otherwise ill-matched partners was their detestation of the ruling Al Bu Saᶜid line and their resentment at the curbing of the slave trade from East Africa, a resentment sharpened in the case of the *mutawiᶜah* by their anger at the loss of Zanzibar, which they attributed both to Thuwaini's feebleness and to the machinations of his British allies. Several dozen dhows, laden with hundreds of slaves, had been seized in African and Arabian waters during the 1861, 1862 and 1863 trading seasons, and in the 1864 season the Sultan of Zanzibar had made it more difficult for Arabs from Oman and the Gulf to smuggle slaves out of his dominions, as they had been accustomed to, by forbidding the coastwise shipment of slaves from any of his mainland ports during the fair season. When Colonel Lewis Pelly, the Political Resident in the Gulf, visited Faisal at Riyad in March 1865, the Wahhabi ruler made no secret of his hatred of Thuwaini or his irritation over the slave trade question. There is little doubt that, if he had lived, Faisal would have sought to destroy the ruler of Muscat. As it was, he died before the year was out, and it was left to his son and successor, ᶜAbd Allah, to bring about the destruction of Thuwaini ibn Saᶜid.

If the testimony of Abu ᶜIsa, Palgrave's travelling companion in Arabia, is to be believed, ᶜAbd Allah had begun plotting the assassination of Thuwaini early in 1865. The instrument of assassination was to be Thuwaini's own son, Salim, and he was to be supported by some discontented members of the Al Bu Saᶜid, by ᶜAzzan ibn Qais, and by certain of the Ibadi *mutawiᶜah*, led by Saᶜid ibn Khalfan al-Khalili of the Bani Ruwaihah, who had been active in the campaign to elect ᶜAzzan's uncle, Hamud ibn ᶜAzzan, to the imamate twenty years earlier. The opportunity and the occasion for the murder of Thuwaini occurred at the beginning of 1866, when Thuwaini, encouraged by Colonel Pelly, was getting together an expedition to expel the Wahhabi garrison from the Buraimi Oasis. On the night of 13 February 1866, with the aid of a Wahhabi accomplice, Salim ibn Thuwaini stabbed his father to death in the citadel at Sauhar. The parricide now became nominal ruler of Oman, but his survival in that role depended upon his unceasing conciliation of the combination which had brought him to power – the *mutawiᶜah*, ᶜAzzan ibn Qais, and the Wahhabis – and upon their calculations of his usefulness to their further plans. Trapped in a situation from which he could not escape unscathed, Salim sought desperately to ingratiate himself with the *mutawiᶜah* by instituting a strict religious regime at Muscat. However much this might ease his situation in the capital, it did nothing for his standing in the interior, where the Ibadi tribes regarded him with loathing as the creature of the Wahhabis.

Three of the more powerful of these tribes, the Hirth, the Hajariyin, and the Bani Bu Hasan, which normally professed loyalty to the main Al Bu Saᶜid line, joined Salim's uncle, Turki ibn Saᶜid, in an attempt to overthrow him in the summer of 1867. Salim survived the attempt – largely through the intervention of the Political Resident, Colonel Pelly – and Turki was forced to retire into exile in India. Deprived of his leadership, the three tribes, headed by Salih ibn ᶜAli, the *tamimah* of the Hirth, and joined by another prominent Hinawi tribe, the Habus, turned to ᶜAzzan ibn Qais as representing the best chance of getting rid of Salim. Religious enthusiasm for the campaign was manufactured by the *mutawiᶜah* under the guidance of the two principal Ibadi divines, Saᶜid ibn Khalfan al-Khalili of the Bani Ruwaihah and Muhammad ibn Sulaiman al-Gharibi of the Yal Saᶜad, and at the beginning of October 1868 a horde of tribesmen, with ᶜAzzan ibn Qais at their head, descended upon Muscat and drove Salim out. Later that month ᶜAzzan was elected imam by an assembly of tribal and religious shaikhs at Muscat. According to the testimony of the Political Agent at Muscat, the election was conducted along traditional lines and in conformity with Ibadi prescription. It seems clear that Sa⁣ᶜid ibn Khalfan al-Khalili initially coveted the imamate for himself, but, finding that he was unable to drum up the support necessary for election, he contented himself with the role of chief minister to ᶜAzzan.

For the first two years of his reign ᶜAzzan was very much under al-Khalili's thumb, with the consequence that he allowed full scope to the *mutawiᶜah*'s intolerance in Muscat, and embarked upon a policy of expropriating much of the property of the main Al Bu Saᶜid line to serve the purposes of the new regime. This double oppression, coupled with other considerations, caused the British Government to withhold formal recognition from him and to deny him the subsidy due to Muscat from Zanzibar under the Canning Award, a deprivation which helped contribute to his eventual downfall. Within Oman, ᶜAzzan was forced to engage in an almost constant series of punitive expeditions to maintain or extend his grip upon the country. In these expeditions he displayed a capacity for military command which had not been seen in the Al Bu Saᶜid line since Ahmad ibn Saᶜid's day. Within months of his accession he had also to face a more potentially dangerous threat than that from refractory tribesmen. His election had not only marked his break with his former allies, the Wahhabis, but it was in itself an act of defiance towards the Amir ᶜAbd Allah ibn Faisal. ᶜAzzan went even further in his rejection of his former patron in the summer of 1869, when he drove the Wahhabi garrison from the Buraimi Oasis. Highly angered though he was by this act, ᶜAbd Allah ibn Faisal was incapable of avenging it because of the distractions of more urgent problems nearer home.

ᶜAzzan turned next to deal with his internal enemies among the Ghafiri tribes, most of which had held aloof from his election and the most powerful of which, the Bani Bu ᶜAli of Jaᶜalan, the Bani Riyam of Oman proper, and the Janabah of eastern Oman, were actively opposed to him. He had mixed success in his campaigns against them. Although he managed to capture the *tamimah* of the Bani Riyam, who was traditionally regarded as the head of the Ghafiri faction, the tribe continued to defy him from its strongholds in the Jabal Akhdar. The Bani Bu ᶜAli, who had been converted to the Wahhabi practice of Islam sixty years earlier, at first submitted to him but later revoked their allegiance when it seemed that it might involve them in conflict with ᶜAbd Allah ibn Faisal. The Janabah, which was the principal seafaring tribe of eastern Oman and whose nomadic sections ranged the country from the Sharqiyah to Dhofar, eluded his grasp, and in the summer of 1870 their shaikhs, together with those of the Bani Bu ᶜAli, took the lead in approaching Turki ibn Saᶜid – lately returned from Bombay where he had escaped the loose surveillance kept over him – with an offer of support if he were to take the field against ᶜAzzan.

The Janabah and Bani Bu ᶜAli shaikhs were doubtless helped in reaching their decision by a warning from Majid ibn Saᶜid, the Sultan of Zanzibar, who was already aiding Turki with money, that they would not be permitted to visit Zanzibar while ᶜAzzan remained imam. Since the Bani Bu ᶜAli were the principal smugglers of slaves from Zanzibar to Oman the warning carried with it a not very subtle threat to cut off their source of supply. Some of the Ghafiri tribes of northern and Trucial Oman also threw in their lot with Turki, notably the Naᶜim, two of whose shaikhs ᶜAzzan had recently imprisoned. With their aid, Turki defeated ᶜAzzan in battle near Dhank, in the Dhahirah, in October 1870. The imam escaped with his life but three of his principal Hinawi supporters, the *tamimahs* of the Hajariyin, Habus and Yal Saᶜad, were slain. Turki was now joined not only by the Bani Riyam under their *tamimah*, Saif ibn Sulaiman, and his other Ghafiri allies, the Bani Bu ᶜAli and the Janabah, but, more significantly, by disaffected elements of the Hajariyin, Habus, and Bani Bu Hasan, and by the Wahibah and Duruᶜ. The Bani Bu Hasan and the Wahibah were both Hinawi tribes, the latter being a powerful nomadic tribe of eastern Oman, like the Janabah. The Duruᶜ, the third of the great nomadic tribes of Oman, which frequented the central Omani steppes between the Hajar and the Rubᶜ al-Khali, normally did not align itself with either the Hinawi or the Ghafiri faction.

Dividing his force into two contingents, Turki moved on Muscat in January 1871. He was blocked at Samad by Salih ibn ᶜAli of the Hirth but the second contingent, under Saif ibn Sulaiman, stormed and took Matrah, just to the north of Muscat, at the end of the month. ᶜAzzan ibn Qais, who had been directing the defence of the town, and Saif ibn Sulaiman were both killed in the fighting. Muscat was occupied shortly afterwards but Saᶜid ibn Khalfan al-Khalili continued to hold out in the main forts. He was induced to surrender to Turki through the intervention of the Political Resident, Pelly, acting in somewhat naïve good faith. No sooner had Pelly left Muscat than al-Khalili and his son were put to death.

It was perhaps fitting, in an unhappy sense, that the final act in the dismantlement of ᶜAzzan ibn Qais's imamate should have been accomplished with British help, however, unwitting; for it was the British Government's failure to accord recognition to him which largely brought about his fall. Recognition had been withheld, partly because of disagreement between London and Calcutta over policy towards Muscat and Zanzibar in these years, but mainly because of the severity of his regime, which bore heavily upon Indian traders in Muscat and Matrah. Yet by the

latter months of his reign ᶜAzzan was shaking himself from the constrict-
ing influence of al-Khalili and the other *mutawiᶜah*, and he was ruling
with greater moderation though with no less firmness. The political
difficulties with which he had had to contend were great. He had to
endure the enmity of the Ghafiri tribes, the reason for which is largely
self-explanatory (he had been elected mainly with Hinawi support),
although it also owed something, as did the dissatisfaction which arose
among the Hinawi tribes in the last few months of his rule, to his failure
to keep up his subsidies to them, and to redeem his promises to remove
al-Khalili and Salih ibn ᶜAli from his government. ᶜAzzan erred griev-
ously in neglecting to conciliate the leading Ghafiri tribes, for no ruler of
Oman could expect to survive long on the support of one faction to the
exclusion of the other. ᶜAzzan's omission was Turki ibn Saᶜid's opportunity, and Turki played skilfully upon the Ghafiri tribes' discontent
over the Imam's treatment of them. Again, ᶜAzzan's efforts to centralize
the government of Oman were more ambitious than those of any Al Bu
Saᶜid ruler before him, and they aroused, as they were bound to, the
hostility of the great territorial chieftains. Although Salih ibn ᶜAli
remained loyal to him to the last, there is little doubt that, had ᶜAzzan
lived, Salih would inevitably have clashed with him. It was ᶜAzzan's
tragedy that the British authorities of the day never grasped the significance of his election and of his administration of Oman between
1868 and 1871, and it was the fault primarily of Lewis Pelly that they
failed to do so; for Pelly never understood the essential nature of ᶜAzzan's
regime (he long believed, from its puritanical attributes, that it was a
Wahhabi off-shoot), and he was a blatant partisan of Turki ibn Saᶜid.
Almost alone among British observers of events in Oman in these years,
Percy Badger realized their true import and appreciated the singular
qualities of ᶜAzzan ibn Qais. But by the time that Badger made his
views known, ᶜAzzan was dead.

With his passing, the heart went out of the imamate movement for
many years to come. Although Saiyid Turki ibn Saᶜid was plagued
throughout his reign by tribal unrest and rebellion, the fractiousness of
the tribes was not directed towards the re-establishment of an Ibadi
theocracy. Turki, and his son, Faisal, who succeeded him in 1888, ruled
with the fluctuating support of a shifting coalition of Hinawi and Ghafiri
tribes, whose loyalty the Sultan secured by the customary Al Bu Saᶜid
policy of alternating bribery with coercion. Salih ibn ᶜAli was never
reconciled to the restoration of Al Bu Saᶜid rule in the direct line, and he
remained an implacable foe of the ruling house for the remainder of his
life. What sentiment for the Imamate endured was kept alive by the
mutauwaᶜ class, and it had its heart at Rastaq, where ᶜAzzan's brother,

Ibrahim ibn Qais, ruled as a virtually autonomous prince, though nomin-
ally as the *wali* of the *saiyid* of Muscat. The lessons of 1868–71 were not
entirely lost upon the house of Saiyid Saᶜid, for two of Turki's brothers,
Barghash, the Sultan of Zanzibar, and ᶜAbd al-ᶜAziz, at different times
began to affect *mutauwaᶜ* ways and to suggest modestly that they might
be suitable candidates for the imamate. Their murmurings fell upon deaf
ears. Saiyid Faisal ibn Turki began to hint at a similar ambition in the
first few years of his reign, but he received no encouragement from the
mutauwaᶜ establishment, despite his attempts to curry favour with them
by turning a blind eye to infractions of the ban on the importation of
slaves, and by shirking his treaty obligations to suppress the traffic.

Discontent with Faisal's rule, particularly among the Hinawi tribes,
degenerated into open rebellion in 1895 and culminated in the capture
and sack of Muscat by the rebels later that year. As with past rebellions,
the uprising had mixed and even conflicting origins. It was fomented
largely by the veteran Salih ibn ᶜAli, who suspected the Sultan of plotting to unseat him in the chieftainship of the Hirth. Other tribal leaders
were incensed by Faisal's recent defaulting on their subsidies. The Sultan
of Zanzibar, who dreamt of resurrecting the old unified sultanate, encouraged the malcontents with arms and money. The *mutawiᶜah*, who were
for ever anathematizing the ruling house for its laxity, debauchery, and
besottedness with foreign gewgaws, needed no urging to join the revolt.
Faisal ibn Turki survived the rebellion by inducing some of the Ghafiri
tribes, with promises of substantial subsidies, to come to his aid, and by
buying off Salih ibn ᶜAli with whatever funds he could scrape together
from his threadbare treasury. What saved him as much as anything was
the lack of unity and want of definite purpose in the rebel ranks. Although
the white *mutauwaᶜ* banner was raised over Faisal's palace during the
occupation of Muscat, and reports were put about that the rebellion had
been declared in the name of Saᶜud ibn ᶜAzzan, the son of ᶜAzzan ibn
Qais, the sense of mission present in 1868 was lacking. Saᶜud ibn ᶜAzzan
had been Salih ibn ᶜAli's nominee in a short-lived attempt to revive the
Imamate in 1875, but the Hirth chief showed little enthusiasm for a
similar attempt twenty years later.

The idea, however, did not entirely disappear with the end of the
rebellion of 1895. Three years afterwards, Saᶜud ibn ᶜAzzan shadowed
it forth to an assembly of tribal and religious shaikhs which he had con-
vened at Rastaq. Salih ibn ᶜAli had been slain in a tribal skirmish in 1896,
his son ᶜIsa succeeding him as *tamimah* of the Hirth, and Ibrahim ibn
Qais had died in 1898. Saᶜud ibn ᶜAzzan had followed him as *wali* of
Rastaq, and it was shortly after his appointment that he summoned the
meeting to discuss the possible revival of the imamate. The meeting

failed to reach any decision upon his candidature, and a year later the matter became a dead issue when Sa°ud was murdered at prayer.

The Restoration of the Ibadi Imamate

The two major attempts in the nineteenth century to revive the imamate – unsuccessful in the case of Hamud ibn °Azzan in 1846, fleetingly successful in that of °Azzan ibn Qais in 1868 – had revolved around the personalities and characters of the candidates for the office. What the promoters of the movement had wanted were men cast in the mould of the heroic imams of tradition, who would afford Oman the stern and militant leadership of which it was deemed to stand in need, and which the Al Bu Sa°id sultans had increasingly failed to provide since the fourth decade of the century. The imams whose names resounded throughout Ibadi history had been in their day powerful chieftains, more noted for their political sagacity and military prowess than for their piety and skill in scriptural disputation. Hamud ibn °Azzan and °Azzan ibn Qais, however much their resources and power might differ, were essentially men of such metal. The turn of the present century brought a change both in the direction of the imamate movement and in what was held to constitute the beau-ideal of an imam. Theological attainments now became the prime qualification for the office, political capacity merely of secondary importance.

In part, this shift in emphasis was due to the movement's having fallen much more under the control of the *mutawi°ah*; in part, it was a reflexion of the calculations of the tribal chieftains who supported it. *Mutauwa°* sentiment, which had grown even more rigid and intolerant over the years, as their cause languished, was honed to a fine edge of fanaticism in the first decade of this century by the preaching of one of their number, °Abd Allah ibn Humaiyad al-Salimi, a blind scholar who was later to produce a history of the imamate (*Tuhfat al-a°yan fi-sirat ahl °Uman*). Al-Salimi first appeared on the political scene as one of the instigators of the 1895 revolt, and his influence became even more pronounced after the turn of the century. To him, as to the other *mutawi°ah*, the restoration of the imamate was absolutely essential if Oman was to be saved from the pernicious foreign influences which seemed – at least to their overheated imaginations – to be seeping through every crack and crevice in the ramshackle administrative edifice of Al Bu Sa°id rule. To these contentious ecclesiastics the reigning Sultan, Faisal ibn Turki, was little better than a *kafir*. Although an Ibadi like themselves, he had failed in his dispensation of justice to apply the *Shari°ah* in strict conformity with the Ibadi interpretation. He could not speak, read, or write literary Arabic, and indeed the language in which he appeared to converse most easily was Gujerati. He and his dynasty had so intermingled their blood with that of Africans, Abyssinians, Baluchis and Indians that they could scarce be looked upon any longer as Arabs. Faisal ibn Turki not only tolerated Hindus, Jews and Christians at Muscat, but he also permitted the importation of liquor and tobacco into the capital. He relied upon the British for his continuance in power, and he looked to India, not Arabia, for cultural inspiration. He had flouted the wishes of his subjects by yielding to British demands to curb the slave trade and the arms traffic, and he had been notoriously fickle in his apportionment of subsidies to the tribes, while at the same time he had increased the duties on goods passing to and from the interior.

Whether or not this was a fair estimation of the character and government of Faisal ibn Turki, it was the view taken of that hapless ruler by the *mutawicah* and several of the upland tribes in the early years of the century. It required only a miscalculation of a major order on his part to translate their contempt into active hostility, and Faisal made that miscalculation in 1912 when, as a means of more effectively controlling the flow of arms into Oman, he set up a central warehouse for their distribution at Muscat. cIsa ibn Salih al-Harithi expostulated strongly with the Sultan about his action, but a far more significant and dangerous expression of protest was made by the *tamimah* of the Bani Riyam of the Jabal Akhdar, Himyar ibn Nasir al-Nabahini, the acknowledged leader of the Ghafiri faction. Spurred on by cAbd Allah ibn Humaiyad al-Salimi and a number of Ibadi *culama'* and *mutawicah*, Himyar ibn Nasir called an assembly of tribal chieftains at Tanuf, his seat of power, in May 1913, when he proceeded to secure the election to the imamate of Salim ibn Rashid of the Bani Kharus. Salim ibn Rashid's principal distinction seems to have been that he was the nephew or the son-in-law of al-Salimi (the accounts of his relationship differ), that he was descended from a line of imams in the early Middle Ages, and that a forebear, the *mutauwac* shaikh, Zacad ibn Khamis al-Kharusi, had helped to unite the four sub-sects of the Ibadiya during the reign of the Imam Ahmad ibn Sacid, after the Ibadi community had been torn apart by the conflicts of the first half of the eighteenth century.

A month after al-Kharusi's election the forces of the Ghafiri confederation moved against Nizwa, expelled the Sultan's *wali* and garrison, and made the town the seat of the imamate, as it had been in the past. Izki fell in July, and the following month, Samail, commanding the road to Muscat, was taken. cIsa ibn Salih, who had so far exhibited a distant attitude towards al-Kharusi's election. mainly out of jealousy of Himyar ibn Nasir, joined the rebellion after the capture of Izki and acknowledged the new imam. The new Hinawi-Ghafiri coalition was probably the most formidable ever effected against an Al Bu Sacid ruler, and the fact of its formation and the weight of tribal support which it attracted testified to the yawning gulf which had opened between the Al Bu Saᶜid and their subjects. Had it not been for British intervention in the years after 1913 the Sultanate would surely have been destroyed as an institution, and the line of Ahmad ibn Saᶜid overthrown. As it was, the partisans of the imamate were eventually forced to accept that, so long as the Al Bu Saᶜid ruler enjoyed British backing, he could not be deposed, while on his side the Sultan was driven to concede formally that his authority over his turbulent subjects in the mountains had been reduced to little more than a fiction.

The Sultan Taimur ibn Faisal, who succeeded his father on his death in October 1913, made various attempts from the close of that year onwards, usually at British urging, to open negotiations with the leaders of the imamate confederacy. Although these attempts foundered on the shaikhs' granitic contempt for him, they served to reveal clearly the causes of that contempt, which were essentially those which had lain behind their antipathy to his father, viz., the suppression of the slave trade and the arms traffic, the Sultan's laxity in applying the strict letter of the *Shariᶜah* in civil and criminal cases, his toleration of the importation of liquor and tobacco at Muscat, his association with infidels, and particularly the British, and his interference with the flow of goods between the interior and the coast. What also emerged from the spasmodic attempts at negotiation, undertaken during breaks in the fighting, was that Himyar ibn Nasir had been replaced as the dominant figure in the coalition by ᶜIsa ibn Salih. The Harithi chief's ascendancy was made doubly plain by the events of 1920 which brought the civil war to a close. In July 1920 the Imam al-Kharusi was murdered by a Wahibah tribesman. The candidate chosen to succeed him was Muhammad ibn ᶜAbd Allah al-Khalili of the Bani Ruwaihah, a grandson of the *mutauwaᶜ* leader, Saᶜid ibn Khalfan al-Khalili. He was the nominee of ᶜIsa ibn Salih, and it was largely through the efforts of the *tamimah* of the Hirth that al-Khalili's election was procured. The disquiet engendered in the confederate ranks by the assassination of the old imam and the election of the new, coming on top of the discomfort caused by the imposition by the Sultan the previous year of penal taxes upon goods coming from the interior to the coast for sale, had put the imamate leaders in a readier frame of mind to respond to the Sultan's overtures for a peace settlement. Through the mediation of the British political agent at Muscat a delegation of tribal and religious shaikhs, led by ᶜIsa ibn Salih, met representatives of the Sultan at Sib, on the coast north of Muscat, and worked out an adjustment of their differences which was incorporated in a written agreement signed by both sides on 25 September.

A number of differing interpretations have subsequently been placed upon this agreement, particularly during and since the uprising of 1957, by various individuals and agencies interested, for one reason or another, in the affairs of Oman. Most of the large constructions placed upon the agreement, where they do not simply derive from partisan calculation, depend more upon Western concepts of political and territorial sovereignty than they do upon the actual instrument itself and its contents. It has been called a treaty, which it certainly is not, either in a legal sense or by the more liberal standards of the *Oxford English Dictionary*; and even the author of a recent, unremittingly partial study of legal questions in the Persian Gulf has been forced to this conclusion.[4] It has also been asserted that the 'treaty' of Sib recognized the legal existence and independence of an imamate state of Oman, separate and distinct from the Sultanate of Muscat and Oman. Again, to cite the same author, who is clearly sympathetic to the Imamate cause,

'. . . there is nothing in the treaty which shows that the Sultan by signing it had in fact intended to relinquish his sovereignty over Oman, although he did not expressly assert it. There does not seem any reference in the treaty to the independence of Oman or to the government of the Imam'.[5]

Commonsense alone, apart from the actual conditions of its signing, compels rejection of the claim that the agreement recognized the independence of the imam. In September 1920 Muhammad ibn ᶜAbd Allah al-Khalili had been in office barely two months. He had been selected for his piety and his knowledge of Ibadi theology, his election had been obtained by ᶜIsa ibn Salih, and he had no power and little authority which did not derive from his association with his patron. In short, he was not independent. Taimur ibn Faisal refused to accept him as a signatory of the agreement of Sib, and the Sultan was supported in his refusal by the British political agent and mediator, R. E. L. Wingate. Perhaps most significant of all, ᶜIsa ibn Salih did not hold out for al-Khalili's participation in the agreement.

It is only by looking at the agreement itself, in the light of the circumstances attending its conclusion and of those which brought it to pass, that its real nature can be discerned. The parties to the agreement are described in the preamble: 'This is the peace agreed upon between the Government of the Sultan, Taimur ibn Faisal, and Shaikh ᶜIsa ibn Salih ibn ᶜAli on behalf of the people of Oman whose names are signed hereto

---

[4] See Husain M. Albaharna, *The Legal Status of the Arabian Gulf States* (Manchester, 1968), p. 243.
[5] Albaharna, *op. cit.*, p. 242.

. . .' The body of the agreement consists of eight articles or provisions, four applying to 'the people of Oman', four to 'the Government of the Sultan'. The first four stipulate that duties of not more than five per cent shall be paid on goods brought from the interior to Muscat and the other coastal towns; that 'the people of Oman' shall enjoy security and freedom in the coastal towns, and that no restrictions shall be placed upon persons entering and leaving Muscat and these towns; and, finally, that 'the Government of the Sultan shall not grant asylum to any criminal fleeing from the justice of the people of Oman. It shall return him to them if they request it to do so. It shall not interfere in their internal affairs'. The second group of stipulations requires 'all the tribes and Shaikhs' to be at peace with the Sultan, not to attack the coastal towns, and not to interfere in his government. They provide also for freedom of movement and security for persons going into Oman on lawful business or for commercial purposes, and for freedom of commerce. No asylum was to be granted to any wrongdoer who fled to the tribes and shaikhs for refuge. Finally, claims against 'the people of Oman' by merchants and others were to be decided according to the law of Islam.

It has been contended that, in theory, according to Ibadi doctrine and Omani tradition, the very presence of an imam renders any other government for the Ibadi community illegitimate, and that the existence of the imamate since its revival in 1913 automatically conferred the imprimatur of illegitimacy upon the Sultan's government. It is a doubtful proposition at best, and one which will certainly not stand the test of application to the course of Omani history. Applied to the agreement of Sib, it is even less tenable. Nowhere in the agreement is there any reference to the imam al-Khalili or to his government. Still less is there any denial of the legitimacy of the Sultan's government. On the contrary, as his is the only government mentioned in the agreement, the signing of it by ᶜIsa ibn Salih and the associated chiefs can be taken as an explicit acknowledgment of that government, and, by extension, of its legitimacy. Since the imam is not alluded to in the agreement, he can hardly be said to be a party to it. It follows, therefore, that the argument put forward of late years that the agreement recognized, albeit implicitly, not only his independence but also that of a state of inner Oman, separate and distinct from the coastal sultanate, is unsound. In fact, to argue thus is to read back into the agreement a concept which was only developed thirty years afterwards. What was implicit in the agreement of Sib was a recognition by the Sultan of his loss of authority over a number of the tribes in the interior, and, conversely, an acknowledgment of the power and authority of the great territorial chieftains, and of ᶜIsa ibn Salih above all. As such, the agreement can hardly be called a startling departure in the history of

Al Bu Saᶜid's rule in Oman. Rather was it the latest in a long and melancholy series of expedients and compromises by which the Al Bu Saᶜid Sultans sought to accommodate their incapacity for effective government to the fierce and inveterate autonomy of the upland tribes.

For thirty years after the conclusion of the *modus vivendi* at Sib relations between the Al Bu Saᶜid Sultan at Muscat and the tribes of the interior would appear to have been harmonious, if somewhat distant. So long as he did not attempt to interfere in their territories, the chiefs of the imamate confederacy did not challenge his government elsewhere in the country or his right to conduct its external relations. In 1921 the Sultan acceded to the International Arms Convention, in 1923 he gave an undertaking to the British Government regarding the grant of oil concessions in Oman, in 1925 he granted the D'Arcy Exploration Company the right to undertake a geological expedition to the interior, and in 1937 he granted an oil concession for the country to Petroleum Concessions Limited. The concession was granted by Taimur's eldest son, Saᶜid, who had replaced his father as Sultan in February 1932, when Taimur, who had retired to India late in 1931, voluntarily abdicated. A young man of twenty-one years of age at his accession, Saᶜid ibn Taimur was content to carry on the government in an unspectacular fashion, his principal accomplishments in the early years of his reign being to set its finances in order, and to secure a slackening of the reins of British supervision. He also began quietly but steadily to exert more personal control over the administration of his territories, being assisted in this task by Ahmad ibn Ibrahim, the former *wali* of Rastaq and nephew of ᶜAzzan ibn Qais, who had been expelled from his family seat by the imam's forces in 1917.

Real power in the interior of Oman in the nineteen-twenties and thirties was wielded by ᶜIsa ibn Salih, at the head of what was essentially a Hinawi confederation, the alliance with the Ghafiri tribal faction having gradually been attenuated, if not completely dissolved, by the fortunes of war, the election of ᶜIsa ibn Salih's nominee as imam, and the death of the Ghafiri leader, Himyar ibn Nasir al-Nabahini, whose place as *tamimah* of the Bani Riyam had been taken by his son, Sulaiman, a young man of morose disposition and dissolute habits. The Imam al-Khalili in his early years in office was little more than the creature of ᶜIsa ibn Salih, to whose efforts he owed the consolidation of his spiritual authority in central Oman. Late in 1925, on learning that Ibn Jiluwi, Ibn Saᶜud's governor in Hasa, had sent a tax-collecting party to the Buraimi Oasis, ᶜIsa ibn Salih led a strong force northwards into the Dhahirah with the intention of bringing the entire district, up to and including the oasis, under his control. He took Dariz, ᶜIbri and Dhank, and then, at the beginning of December, a severe attack of dropsy and a quarrel with one of the confederate tribes forced him to abandon Dhank and retreat homewards. The Imam al-Khalili was said to have been so humiliated by this ignominous outcome that he offered to resign the imamate early in 1926. He was prevailed upon not to do so, and during the next twenty years his influence and authority steadily grew, as age overtook ᶜIsa bin Salih and the Ghafiri tribes of inner Oman made their accommodation with the regime at Nizwa.

ᶜIbri constituted the westernmost outpost of the districts under the authority of the Imam al-Khalili and his coadjutive tribal leaders up to 1954. From ᶜIbri the northern bounds of their territory ran through Dariz and over the crest of the western Hajar to Rastaq. Its heart was the towns and villages of the upper reaches of the Wadi Halfain and adjacent *wadi*-systems – Nizwa, Izki, Firq, Bahlah, Yabrin, and other ancient Ibadi centres – and the plateaux and high valleys of the Jabal Akhdar, the central massif of the Hajar. The tribal composition of the region was such that neither faction, Hinawi or Ghafiri, wholly predominated, though the balance of strength between Hinawi tribes like the Bani Ruwaihah (the Imam's tribe), Bani Hina, Al Bu Saᶜid, and ᶜAwamir, and Ghafiri tribes like the Bani Riyam, Bani Rashid, ᶜIbriyin, and Kunud seemed to be tilted in favour of the latter. The main bastion of Hinawi strength lay in the Sharqiyah, to the eastward, where the three principal tribes, the Habus, Hajariyin and Hirth, were all Hinawi. The Habus occupied the villages and valleys at the head of the Wadi Ithli and Wadi Andam, while the Hajariyin shared the Bathaᶜ Badiya, or upper reaches of the Wadi Bathaᶜ, with the Hirth, whose *tamimah* resided at Qabil. In its lower course, the Wadi Bathaᶜ runs through the province of Jaᶜalan, where the only Hinawi tribe, the Bani Bu Hasan, also acknowledged the Imam al-Khalili. The dominant tribes of Jaᶜalan, the Bani Bu ᶜAli and Janabah, both Ghafiri, not only rejected the Imam's authority but the Bani Bu ᶜAli also followed the Hanbali rite as a consequence of their previous association with the Wahhabis. Their *tamimah*, who resided at Sur, was also acknowledged as chief by the Janabah sections settled in that port, though not, it would appear, by the Bedouin sections of the tribe. He had somewhat enlarged ideas of his importance, and in the 1920s he had endeavoured to secure British recognition of himself as autonomous 'Amir of Jaᶜalan'. The western branch of the Janabah, whose paramount shaikh resided at ᶜIzz, to the south of Nizwa, followed the Imam. So also did the nomadic Wahibah, the powerful Hinawi tribe which roamed the sands from the Sharqiyah to the Arabian Sea, and the Duruᶜ, the third great nomadic tribe, which frequented the stony steppes to the south and east of the rocky wilderness of the Hamra Duruᶜ. The factional allegiance of the Duruᶜ has shifted from time to time, and even from section to section:

in the nineteen-forties, for instance, one of the tribe's three sections is said to have been aligned with the Hinawis while the other two inclined to the Ghafiris.

ᶜIsa ibn Salih died in 1946, and he was succeeded in the chieftainship of the Hirth and the leadership of the Hinawi faction, first by Muhammad and then by Salih ibn ᶜIsa, who was about twenty-seven years of age. ᶜIsa's death produced two immediate changes in the balance of Omani politics. One was an accession of power to the Imam al-Khalili, who despite his reputation for sanctity, learning, and severity in the dispensation of justice, had always lived in the shadow of his patron. The other was the emergence of Sulaiman ibn Himyar, the *tamimah* of the Bani Riyam, now grown more stable if scarcely more congenial or less profligate, as one of the principal arbiters of the politics of inner Oman. Two further developments in this period, which were to confound those politics and to arouse the interior from its placid introspection, were the resumption of oil exploration and the resurgence of Saudi activity in the region after a long lapse.

No attempt had so far been made by the concessionary companies to search for oil in central Oman. Neither the D'Arcy Exploration Company's expedition in 1925 nor the expedition sent into the interior by Petroleum Concessions Limited in the winter of 1938–9 had ventured into the Imamate domains. Instead, they had skirted their northern edge, and the Petroleum Concessions expedition had largely followed the D'Arcy expedition's route, travelling by way of Yanqul, ᶜIbri and Dhank to the Buraimi Oasis. When, two or three years after the end of the Second World War, exploration parties began surveying the area around Buraimi, the imam let it be known that he would tolerate no prospecting in the region where his writ ran. Nor would he grant permission to Christians even to traverse his territory, as Wilfred Thesiger discovered early in 1949, when he travelled from the Buraimi Oasis, along the northern edge of the sands and the Umm al-Samim, to the Wahibah country. Although on this occasion the imam relented and allowed Thesiger to return to Buraimi by way of the Oman steppes, he was greatly displeased when Thesiger returned a year later and made his way through the Duruᶜ country with the aim of reaching the Jabal Akhdar. Determined that Thesiger should not make contact with Sulaiman ibn Himyar, the imam sent a party of a hundred armed men to Thesiger's camp at Ma'mur, where the *dirah*, or range, of the Duruᶜ meets that of the western Janabah, with orders to kill the explorer if he advanced any farther. Sulaiman ibn Himyar, however, was so anxious to make contact with Thesiger that he journeyed to the latter's camp, although, as he told Thesiger when he arrived, he was not prepared to defy the imam further by taking him up into the Jabal Akhdar. This duality of feeling was an interesting reflexion of his relationship with the imam, and Sulaiman cast further light upon its nature when he revealed to Thesiger the reason for his anxiety to meet him. He wanted him to convey a request to the Political Resident in the Gulf, roughly similar to that made to the Government of India twenty-five years earlier by the *tamimah* of the Bani Bu ᶜAli of Jaᶜalan, for recognition by the British Government as *amir* of the Jabal Akhdar, with a treaty status equivalent to that of the Trucial shaikhs. Thesiger, who was struck by the forcefulness though not the amiability of Sulaiman's personality, and who thought that the imam's suspicion of the Bani Riyam chief was easily accounted for by his ambition and worldliness, delivered the request in due course. It was not granted.

It is highly doubtful whether Sulaiman ever thought it would be, and in any case developments then going on to the north-westwards made it likely that in due course he would be able to resort to an expedient which Omani chieftains before him had occasionally employed to achieve their ambitions, viz., call in the Wahhabis. Saudi Arabia in October 1949 had put forward a claim to the frontier with Abu Dhabi which extended up to the Buraimi Oasis, and the Saudi Government had subsequently let it be known that it considered the lands beyond Buraimi to be populated by Saudi Arabian tribes. It was presumably out of solicitude for the welfare of these tribes that visits to Saudi Arabia were arranged for some of their shaikhs in 1950 and 1951, and that an intense interest in the history, politics, and tribal structure of Oman was taken in these years at Riyad, Dammam, and Dhahran. The same concern led the Saudi Government in August 1952 to send an armed party under an *amir* to occupy part of the Buraimi Oasis, and to resume the benevolent supervision of the tribes of the Dhahirah which it had been forced to relinquish some eighty years earlier. Sultan Saᶜid ibn Taimur, who regarded the tribes in question as coming under his authority, appreciated the return of the Saudis no more than his forebears had done, and he proceeded to assemble a force of several thousand men at Sauhar with the intention of sending the Saudis packing, back along the road to Najd. The Imam al-Khalili was, if anything even more enraged by the pretensions of the foreign sectarians, and he reacted to their presence much as he had done twenty-seven years earlier. He proclaimed *jihad* against them, ordered several hundred tribesmen to assemble at Dariz, forbade the tribal leaders loyal to him to have anything to do with the Saudis, and wrote to Saᶜid ibn Taimur swearing friendship and asking to be told what further measures he should take. Thanks to the intervention of the United States ambassador at Jiddah, to whom the Saudi Government had turned to extricate it from its difficulties, the British Government agreed to dissuade Saᶜid ibn Taimur from launching his attack upon the Saudi position at Buraimi. It was an unhappy decision from the point of view of the Sultan's interests: not only did he suffer a loss of reputation as a consequence of the breaking-up of the expedition, but the success of the Saudi Arabian razzia was responsible for many of his subsequent troubles.

Sulaiman ibn Himyar, who had been in touch with the Saudis since 1951 at least, naturally took a different view of their incursion, and in November 1952 he travelled to Riyad through the agency of the Saudi *amir* at Buraimi, Turki ibn ᶜAbd Allah ibn ᶜUtaishan. There was little, however, that his new-found friends could do to advance his ambitions while the old Imam al-Khalili lived. Sulaiman had, therefore, to cultivate patience, unfamiliar though the exercise might be to him. In May 1954 the Imam Muhammad ibn ᶜAbd Allah al-Khalili died, at about the age of sixty-eight, During his tenure of the imamate he had been the very embodiment of the spirit of Ibadism – austere, stern, exclusive – and the impression which he had conveyed to the world outside was that of a dour intolerance and a rigid xenophobia. It was unlikely, as the taint of the twentieth-century spread to Oman that his successor would, or could, be in the same mould. Two candidates for the office had been spoken of in the years immediately preceding his death, ᶜAbd Allah ibn Salim al-Kharusi, the son of the Imam Salim ibn Rashid al-Kharusi, and Muhammad ibn ᶜAbd Allah al-Salimi, the son of the blind *mutauwaᶜ* chronicler, ᶜAbd Allah ibn Humaiyad al-Salimi. Al-Kharusi was said to be the candidate of Sulaiman ibn Himyar, as his father had been the candidate of Sulaiman's father in 1913, and for that reason perhaps, he was probably unacceptable to the Hinawi faction. Whether he was or not, he was either not put forward at the election of 1954 or he was passed over in it. Muhammad al-Salimi would appear to have been the choice of Salih ibn ᶜIsa, the *tamimah* of the Hirth, for after the election, in which he was unsuccessful, he was reported to be living in one of the Harithi villages in the Sharqiyah.

Information concerning the actual election is sparse to the point of inexistence. No light is shed upon it by two recent books on the history of Oman, R. G. Landen's *Oman since 1856* (Princeton, 1967) and Wendell Phillips's *Oman: a History* (London, 1967), or by the legal work already referred to, Husain M. Albaharna's *The Legal Status of the Arabian Gulf States* (Manchester, 1968). Landen states, without citing any authority for it, that the Sultan Saᶜid ibn Taimur stood for election and lost. Albaharna says the same, relying upon a pamphlet put out by the Arab Information Centre in New York in 1957. Phillips has nothing to say about the Sultan's candidature. On the surface it seems improbable that Saᶜid ibn Taimur should have put himself forward. He was reported in the spring of 1950 to have expressed the hope that no new imam would be elected on al-Khalili's death. He had no wish, it was said, to submit himself as a candidate because to do so would be to introduce an elective principle into his right of succession as ruler, and into the basis of his authority.

The new imam elected in May 1954 was Ghalib ibn ᶜAli, a thirty-five year old shaikh of the Bani Hina, who was serving at the time as the Imam al-Khalili's *qadi* at Rastaq. Ghalib ibn ᶜAli is variously reported to have been the death-bed choice of al-Khalili, and to have been forced upon the old imam by Sulaiman ibn Himyar, and, perhaps, by Salih ibn ᶜIsa. The mode of his election is uncertain. Wendell Phillips in his book says it was not according to Ibadi tradition, but he gives no evidence or reason for his statement. Ghalib ibn ᶜAli was presumably selected more for his religious qualities than for his secular accomplishments, for subsequent events soon made it clear that he was very much under the thumb of Sulaiman ibn Himyar and his brother, Talib, the *wali* of Rastaq, who by some reports was the prime mover in his brother's election.

Talib ibn ᶜAli lost little time in availing himself of the opportunities for personal and political aggrandizement afforded him by his brother's elevation to the imamate, opportunities made all the rosier by Saudi Arabia's activities in the northern corner of the Dhahirah, and by the appearance of an exploration party of Petroleum Development (Oman) Limited in the central Oman steppes in the summer of 1954. The exploration party had landed at al-Daqm, on the southern coast of Oman, in February 1954, and it spent the next few months in surveying the country to the southwestward. Its main object, however, was to move into the interior and to prospect in the *dirah* of the Duruᶜ. On the death of the Imam al-Khalili contact was made with the shaikhs of the Duruᶜ, who agreed to allow the party into their territory. Getting wind of these exchanges, Talib decided to intervene, for he was determined that if oil were to be found under the steppes and sands of inner Oman it should be exploited, not by PDO for the benefit of Saᶜid ibn Taimur, but only under an arrangement which would secure the payment of all revenues to his brother and his comitatus. To this end, Talib put it abroad that the Imam Ghalib regarded the concession under which PDO was operating as invalid, since it was granted by the Sultan in 1937 without the consent, or even the knowledge, of his predecessor. To bring the Duruᶜs to heel, Talib sent an armed force to seize the tribe's date plantations at ᶜIbri, on which they largely relied for their livelihood. The Duruᶜ shaikhs responded by journeying to al-Daqm and leading the PDO surveying party, and its protesting escort of Muscat troops, back to their *dirah*. In October the surveying party set up camp at Jabal Fahud, where it soon became apparent that neither its operations in the steppes would be safe nor the situation of the Duruᶜ improved while Talib's force remained at ᶜIbri. Late in October, therefore, the Muscat troops and the Duruᶜ moved on ᶜIbri and expelled Talib's men from the town.

Naturally, Talib reacted irately to this setback, and he was provoked still further in November by the Sultan's appointment of a *wali* to ᶜIbri and by the reinforcement of the Muscat garrison there. The consolidation of Al Bu Saᶜid authority in the interior, at this particular place and at this particular time, threatened to play havoc with Talib's plans for the immediate future; for the occupation of ᶜIbri not only drove a wedge between him and the rest of the coterie backing the Imam Ghalib, on the one side, and the Saudi outpost at Buraimi, upon which they were relying for material and tactical support, on the other, but it also interfered with the activities which Talib was engaged in abroad. Towards the close of November 1954 he submitted an application from his brother for the admission of the imamate of Oman, described in the application as an independent, Islamic state, to membership of the Arab League. At the same time a counter-move was initiated, in concert with the Saudis, against the newly established Al Bu Saᶜid position at ᶜIbri. While Ghalib ibn ᶜAli tried to rally a tribal force around his flag at Bahlah to march against ᶜIbri, the Saudis set out to suborn the shaikhs of the Bani Kalban and the Al Yaᶜaqil, the principal tribes inhabiting the ᶜIbri district, and to win over the Duruᶜ shaikhs to the southward. Neither effort met with much success. Sulaiman ibn Himyar, who preferred at this stage in the proceedings to play a waiting game, failed to produce the tribesmen he had apparently promised, and a disconsolate Ghalib had to call off his expedition. The Saudis had no success with the Bani Kalban and Al Yaᶜaqil shaikhs, and it was only through the agency of Sulaiman ibn Himyar that they were able to secure a declaration of allegiance to Saudi Arabia from a shaikh of the Labat section of the Duruᶜ – though what good this was to the Imam Ghalib was unclear. Sulaiman and the Duruᶜ shaikh were both rewarded for their efforts, 30,000 rupees being sent to the former in December 1954 through the medium of the Saudi police post set up in the Buraimi Oasis under the terms of the Anglo-Saudi arbitration agreement of July 1954. A similar sum was sent as consolation to Ghalib through the same channel a month later. The payments were not the first, nor were they to be the last, made to the triumvirate of Ghalib, Talib and Sulaiman by the Saudis. Assistance from this quarter, moreover, was not confined to money: between November 1954 and July 1955 at least 1,361 rifles and 183,000 rounds of ammunition were dispatched from Saudi Arabia to the Dhahirah and inner Oman, and in September and October 1955 further consignments of rifles and ammunition were said to have been sent to Oman. The Saudi police post at

Buraimi also facilitated the visit of a representative of the military government in Egypt to inner Oman in February and March 1955.

The Imamate in Eclipse

There is no space within the limits of this paper, nor is it one of its purposes, to recapitulate in detail the sequence of events within and without Oman since 1955 which have come to constitute what the United Nations Organization has of late years been pleased to call 'the Question of Oman'. Instead, attention will be confined to those aspects of Omani society and history with which this paper has been concerned, viz., religious particularism and tribal factionalism, the relative fortunes of the Ibadi imamate and Al Bu Sa^cid Sultanate, and the consequences for Oman of their respective rule.

To take first Ghalib ibn ^cAli's tenure of the imamate and its ramifications. Towards the close of 1955, after the breakdown of the Buraimi arbitration tribunal had led to the forcible removal of the Saudi police post from the oasis, the Sultan Sa^cid ibn Taimur made an armed progress through the interior of Oman to reassert Al Bu Sa^cid rule in the centre of the country and to challenge the authority and power of Ghalib and his brother. Talib was evicted from Rastaq with the help of Bani Ghafir tribesmen, whose *tamimah*, Muhammad ibn Nasir, was afterwards appointed *wali* of the town. Talib evaded capture and took himself off to Saudi Arabia to seek solace and plot revenge. When the Sultan's armed forces entered Nizwa in December 1955 Ghalib ibn ^cAli slipped away to the mountains, where the Sultan permitted him to remain, under a guarantee of good conduct from a shaikh of the Bani Hina and on condition that he kept within the bounds of his home village of Balad Sait. Sulaiman ibn Himyar came down from his eyrie in the Jabal Akhdar to pay his respects to the Sultan and to assure him of his fealty. Salih ibn ^cAli, however, tended to equivocate. Although he sent one of his nephews with a tribal force from the Sharqiyah to profess loyalty to the Sultan at Nizwa, two other relatives, at least,[6] travelled to Cairo to join with Talib ibn ^cAli in disseminating propaganda against the Sultan from an 'imamate of Oman office' set up to promote abroad the concept of a sovereign and independent imamate of Oman, separate from the sultanate. Talib's main pre-occupation during 1956 and the early months of 1957, however, was with equipping and training an Omani 'Liberation Army' at Dammam in Saudi Arabia, and with smuggling arms and men into Oman in preparation for an uprising at a suitable opportunity. Apparently oblivious or indifferent to what was going on, the Sultan did not venture into the

---

[6] The number varies according to the source, and so also does the identification of them as Salih's sons, brothers, and cousins.

interior again after December 1955, preferring to spend the greater part of his time in the languid confines of Salalah, on the coast of Dhufar. The government of the country was largely left to his elderly *wazir*, Saiyid Ahmad ibn Ibrahim, who conducted it by the normal Al Bu Saᶜid methods of persuasion and coercion: *sharhas*, or cash presents, and other gifts for the more influential shaikhs, meaningful references to the Sultan's standing army for the ill-disposed or recalcitrant. Neither method was very successful: Saudi Arabia could furnish more splendid bribes and the Muscat and Oman Field Force, recruited mainly from the heterogeneous population of the coast, ill-equipped and short of officers, was scarcely of a calibre to intimidate the highland tribes.

The uprising of 1957, which broke out within months of the Suez crisis, although it was tinged at times with religious fervour, did not originate in the spiritual hunger and passion of the Ibadiya of Oman but in the secular ambitions of Ghalib and Talib ibn ᶜAli and their circle, and, at a further remove, in the calculations of their backers in Riyad and Cairo. The first signs of trouble occurred in the Sharqiyah in April, when Ibrahim ibn ᶜIsa, a brother of the *tamimah* of the Hirth, quarrelled with his nephew, Ahmad ibn Muhammad al-Harithi, who had led the tribal contingent to Nizwa in December 1955 to swear fealty to the Sultan. Ahmad ibn Muhammad appealed for help to the Sultan, who sent a detachment of troops to the Sharqiyah. These proved no match for the dissidents, who were by this time in fine fanatical fettle as a consequence of the preaching of the *mutauwaᶜ* shaikh, Muhammad ibn ᶜAbd Allah al-Salimi, the quondam candidate for the imamate. Somewhat at a loss to know what to do, the Sultan invited Ibrahim ibn ᶜIsa to Muscat. Surprisingly, Ibrahim came, early in June. Less surprisingly, the Sultan incarcerated him on arrival. Another guest of the Sultan at Muscat that month was Sulaiman ibn Himyar, whose disposition and intentions the Sultan was anxious to gauge. The Bani Riyam chief noted the imprisonment of Ibrahim ibn ᶜIsa, and he also knew that Talib ibn ᶜAli had secretly returned to Oman in the middle of the month, landing on the Batinah coast with a consignment of arms. What tipped the scales for Sulaiman, however, was the closing down that month of the PDO base at al-Daqm in southern Oman. Henceforth the main supply base was to be at Azaiba, on the Batinah coast. When Sulaiman learned of the company's decision while visiting Azaiba, he realized at once that, with the company's supplies for their operations at Jabal Fahud no longer travelling by the al-Daqm route, he would have to seize and hold the Samail Pass if he was to exert any influence over the company's progress. He therefore slipped away from Muscat early in July and hurried back to his stronghold at Tanuf.

Talib ibn ᶜAli had meanwhile made his way across the Hajar to the Jabal Kaur region, where he assembled the tribesmen whom he had trained at Dammam. Dividing up his force, he proceeded with one half to Bahlah, where he was reinforced by a contingent of Bani Riyam sent by Sulaiman ibn Himyar, who was now in open league with him. Along the way Talib had been joined by his brother, Ghalib, who had emerged from seclusion at Balad Sait and declared that he was resuming the active functions of imam. Bahlah fell without a fight to the triumvirate's followers, and almost on the same day Nizwa surrendered to the other half of Talib's force, also without resistance. The two brothers now made Nizwa their headquarters. The white *mutauwaᶜ* banner was broken out over the great fort, and by the third week in July it was flying also over Firq, Izki and Yabrin. Beyond the heart of central Oman, however, it was seen only at Mintirib in the Wadi Bathaᶜ, and its appearance there was of little significance since the Sharqiyah as a whole remained quiet. So also did the other provinces – the Batinah, Dhahirah and Jaᶜalan – and the Duruᶜ of the steppes sent messages of loyalty to the Sultan. Saᶜid ibn Taimur was incapable of quelling the uprising, and it was only with British help that it was finally suppressed in the early part of August. Talib, Ghalib and Sulaiman retired to the fastnesses of the Jabal Akhdar, from which they and a band of resolute tribesmen kept up a spasmodic, running fight with the Sultan's forces. They were not overcome until January 1959, when their redoubt was assaulted and taken by British and Muscat troops. The three leaders escaped, and later managed to slip out of Oman to find refuge in a succession of Arab capitals.

One casualty of the uprising of 1957 was the agreement of Sib. Each side charged the other with having violated it at one time or another. The Sultan accused the Imam Ghalib of having broken the agreement by attempting to assert his independence from 1955 onwards. Ghalib's supporters accused the Sultan of having broken it in 1937 by the award of an oil concession without the previous imam's permission, and of breaking it again in 1955 when he asserted his authority in central Oman. The accusations were a little inconsistent: if the Sultan had really broken the agreement in 1937, would it still have been in operation in 1955? Obviously Ghalib's supporters considered it to be still valid in that year, otherwise they would not have charged the Sultan with a breach of it. The question was rendered academic by the Sultan's avowal in August 1957 that the rebellion had invalidated the agreement, and in this he was supported by the British Government, which stated later in the month that it considered the agreement, in any case, to have been merely one of a kind, familiar to the area, between a ruler and certain of his tribes, which allowed them a measure of autonomy. This interpretation is accepted, albeit grudgingly, by Dr Husain Albaharna, the latest eludicator of the nature of the agreement, who also implies, for he apparently cannot bring himself to say as much openly, that the agreement was breached by the Imam Ghalib and his supporters in 1955.[7]

Over the past ten years Ghalib ibn ᶜAli and his partisans have tried to keep up the struggle against the Sultan Saᶜid ibn Taimur by desultory acts of terrorism and guerrilla warfare inside Oman, and by enlisting political support for their cause from several Arab states and other sources. The Sultan, for his part, has, with British assistance, steadily consolidated his administration in Oman and has made Al Bu Saᶜid rule in central Oman a reality. His success in gradually eliminating guerrilla activity was attested to in the report submitted in October 1963 by Herbert de Ribbing, the special representative of the Secretary-General of the United Nations, who had visited Oman earlier in the year at the Sultan's invitation. With the discovery of oil in exploitable quantities in recent years, it may be surmised that the Sultan's administrative hold on the country has continued to improve since 1963. His administration bears many of the characteristics of traditional Al Bu Saᶜid rule, that is to say, its guiding principle is decentralization. Where tribal power still pre-dominates, e.g. in the Sharqiyah, the Duruᶜ steppes, and Jaᶜalan, the *tamimahs* of the leading tribes retain their authority and enjoy a quasi-independence. Elsewhere, as a consequence of the defeat or absence of local magnates, there has been a spread of the practice long employed in the Batinah and lowland districts of appointing *walis* to carry out the Sultan's orders directly. Saᶜid ibn Taimur has been greatly assisted in the imposition of his authority in the interior in the past decade by the dis-array among the tribes brought about by the events of the years 1954–9, and by the disruption of their normal alliances and alignments. According to the de Ribbing report, approximately four hundred dissident tribesmen (mainly Bani Riyam, Bani Hina, and Bani Bu Hasan) fled the country after their defeat between 1957 and 1959. About half of these had returned home by 1963, under a guarantee of amnesty from the Sultan, and pre-sumably more have followed in the years since then. The continued absence of Sulaiman ibn Himyar has meant that the Ghafiri tribes of the high Oman are without their customary leadership; and similarly the disappearance of the *tamimah* of the Hirth, Salih ibn ᶜIsa, has deprived the Hinawi tribes of their traditional head. Although Salih's nephew, Ahmad ibn Muhammad al-Harithi, has replaced him as *tamimah* of the tribe, he does not possess the standing to assume the leadership of the Hinawi faction as a whole, especially over the heads of such rivals as the *tamimah* of the Yal Saᶜad and the nephews of the Imam al-Khalili. The

[7] See *The Legal Status of the Arabian Gulf States*, pp. 243–4.

consequence of all this may well be that the long-established Hinawi-Ghafiri division among the tribes will henceforth count for less and less in the politics of Oman.

Can the same be said with any accuracy of the Ibadi imamate? That the institution has been harmed by the events of the last decade and a half is beyond question. From the moment that Ghalib ibn ᶜAli applied for admission to the Arab League he began to divest the imamate of its traditional character and to deprive it of its historical continuity. Whether or not he intended to do so is beside the point: the consequences are what matter. It has not been so much the way in which Ghalib and his associates have sullied the office of imam by their furtive transactions with the Saudis and others from 1954 onwards, by their acceptance of arms and bribes from the historic foes of the Ibadiya, that has brought the imamate into disrepute, as the compromises which have been made with ideas and concepts alien to its true nature and function, such as Arab nationalism and revolutionary socialism, and its subordination to the interests and purposes of states beyond the frontiers of Oman, whether they be Saudi Arabia with its territorial ambitions, Egypt with its illusions of imperial hegemony, or Iraq with its neo-ᶜAbbasid fancies – to mention but a few. To the Ibadiya of Oman their imam is *imam al-Muslimin*: he cannot acknowledge the spiritual supremacy of any other Muslim ruler or accommodate Ibadi doctrine to the tenets of the Sunni schools or the Shiᶜa. He is the spiritual and temporal ruler of his people and his prime duties are to guide the community in the way of the Koran, the *sunnah* of the Prophet, and the example of the early 'rightful' imams. He is required to defend the community against its enemies, although as a *Dafᶜi* and not a *Sharᶜi* imam he is not expected to sacrifice his life in battle with the enemies of the Faith rather than yield or flee. It is difficult to see how these limited concepts can be squared with the conduct of Ghalib ibn ᶜAli since 1954, with the activities of his close supporters and distant apologists, with the submissions of an 'imamate' delegation before the United Nations, with the affirmations of solidarity with a miscellany of governments and causes, with the professions of faith in Arab socialism, with the soliciting of aid in capitals as far apart as London and Peking, and with the portrayal of the imamate as an instrument of revolutionary nationalism.

There is also some doubt whether Ghalib ibn ᶜAli can still rightfully claim to be imam of the Omani Ibadiya. According to Wendell Phillips, Ghalib resigned the imamate at Nizwa on 16 December 1955, before he fled the town at the approach of the Sultan's troops.[8] If this is so, and leaving aside the question whether a legally elected imam can, by Ibadi

---

[8] *Oman: A History*, p. 194.

Law, resign his office at will, then presumably Ghalib would have had to be re-elected in 1957, when he emerged from banishment at Balad Sait and announced that he was resuming the active functions of imam. As there is no record of an election having been held at Nizwa or elsewhere in the summer of 1957, and as Ghalib was apparently accepted as imam, at least by those who fought for him, there would seem to be grounds for concluding that he may well have remained imam after December 1955, although exercising *taqiyah* or caution, as was his right. What is incontestably novel in the present situation, as compared with the rule of his predecessors, is his prolonged absence from Oman and from the discharge of the duties of his office. While in theory an imam is not supposed to absent himself from the Ibadi community, and therefore from Oman, it is possible that instances exist of past imams, particularly of the Ya'aribah dynasty, having gone abroad on military expeditions for short intervals of time. None, however, has ever been away from Oman for as long as Ghalib ibn 'Ali. De Ribbing reported in 1963 that some religious shaikhs had expressed the opinion that even if Ghalib were to return, he would not automatically resume office. Not only would his long sojourn abroad require his formal re-election by the Ibadi community, but it was also possible that another candidate might be put forward in his stead. At the very least, therefore, it is reasonable to conclude that Ghalib's entitlement to the style and dignity of imam is questionable.

The conclusion is reinforced by de Ribbin's findings that, while many tribesmen felt troubled by the absence (as opposed to the absenteeism) of an imam, only a minority wanted a return to an imamate form of government. Nowhere did de Ribbing find evidence to substantiate the thesis, which is central to the political campaign waged abroad by Ghalib and his associates and sympathizers in recent years, of an imamate state of Oman, separate from the sultanate. This thesis, which visualizes or presupposes the existence of a distinct territorial state, cloaks the reality of Omani life with illusion. Throughout the greater part of the country's existence the interior and the coastal region have dwelt in a symbiotic relationship. Their social and economic interdependence is a natural fact: together they form an organic whole, and the likelihood of their separation is scarcely a serious subject for discussion. What is more at issue is Oman's political destiny, whether the future government of the country will be the Al Bu Sa'id Sultanate, a revived and possibly modified imamate, or a revolutionary republic.

Trucial Oman: Some Random Considerations
A surprising feature of the struggles of sultanate and imamate in Oman in this century is that, unlike the internal conflicts of the nineteenth

century, they have failed to draw in the tribes of northern and Trucial Oman. There are obviously good historical, economic, and political reasons for the progressive disengagement of the tribes of the Trucial States from the politics of Oman from the late nineteenth century onwards, reasons which cannot be adequately discussed here. It might be noted, however, that these tribes, which are almost to a man Sunni in religious belief, and many of whom adhere to the Hanbali rite as a result of the spread of Wahhabi influence among them in the nineteenth century, felt and feel little interest in the vicissitudes of fortune suffered by the Ibadi imamate far off in the central Hajar. To the extent that they concerned themselves with Omani politics in the last century, the Trucial Coast tribes usually aligned themselves with the Ghafiri faction, though as often as not their partisanship was dictated solely by self-interest and was directed primarily towards reaping the spoils of war. The most conspicuous exception to the general Ghafiri affiliation was the Bani Yas of Abu Dhabi. What little part the Trucial shaikhs have played in the political life of Oman in this century has normally developed from their own rivalries, ambitions, and animosities.

The tribal composition of Trucial Oman, especially in the northern shaikhdoms, is highly variegated. The western slopes of the Hajar from Ru'us al-Jibal southwards, and the plains stretching southwards from Ras al-Khaimah, are inhabited by a mixture of Shihu, Habus, Mazari° Na°im (Khawatir and Al Bu Khuraiban), Al Bu Shamis, Shawamis, Ghafalah, Bani Qitab, Bani Ka°ab, and several other tribes. The ports from Ras al-Khaimah to Dubai are populated by heterogeneous conglomerations of tribesmen from these and other tribes, many of whom have lost their tribal identity or have suffered a considerable disorientation from it. Further complexity is lent to the population of the ports by the presence of Persians, Baluchis, Indians, Pakistanis, and Arabs from other parts of the Gulf. Abu Dhabi is, or was, inhabited mainly by Bani Yas and some Manasir, as well as by a floating and changing population from Oman and its borderlands. For the greater part of the nineteenth century the politics of Trucial Oman was dominated by a contest for ascendancy between the Wasimi confederacy, which controlled most of the northern ports, and the Bani Yas of Abu Dhabi, under the leadership of the Al Bu Falah shaikhs. The Qawasim, whose shaikhly family has ruled Ras al-Khaimah and Sharjah since the late eighteenth century, are a comparatively small tribe, most of whose members dwell in these two ports while the remainder are scattered through the Wadi Qaur to Kalba and Khaur Fakkan, on the Gulf of Oman. In this century a more conspicuous rivalry has been that between the Al Maktum, the ruling family of the Al Bu Falasah, who have controlled Dubai since the early decades of the nineteenth century, and the Al Nahaiyan, the ruling family of the Al Bu Falah of Abu Dhabi. Their rivalry deteriorated into open warfare in the 1940s, and although a truce brought most of the fighting to a close in 1947, the rivalry has endured, even though shorn of much of its acrimony. It remains a political issue of some consequence in Trucial Oman.

The present ruler of Dubai, Shaikh Rashid ibn Saᶜid Al Maktum, resembles the Al Bu Saᶜid rulers of Oman in that he is fundamentally a merchant prince, deriving most of his power and influence from the position of Dubai as an entrepot of trade and the leading port on the Trucial Coast. Lately, his revenues have been increased by the discovery and exploitation of oil off-shore. The ruler of Abu Dhabi, Shaikh Zayid ibn Sultan Al Nahaiyan, is first and foremost a territorial chieftain, just as Abu Dhabi has always been a land power, in contrast to the northern shaikhdoms of the Trucial Coast, which were, in the past, predominantly maritime powers. As Shaikh Zayid, too, derives great wealth from oil revenues, it is only to be expected that he should exercise greater authority in the hinterland than Shaikh Rashid. His family has done so, in fact, for a good century and a half now. The Al Maktum family, in contrast, have wielded little influence in tribal affairs in the hinterland, and even less in this century than in the last. On the occasion of ᶜIsa ibn Salih al-Harithi's expedition to the Dhahirah in 1925, Shaikh Rashid's father, Saᶜid ibn Maktum, offered to co-operate with him in resisting any Saudi incursion into the area, and so also did Shaikh Sultan ibn Zayid, the father of the present ruler of Abu Dhabi. Again, in the late 1940s, at the height of the Dubai-Abu Dhabi quarrel, Shaikh Rashid tried to enlist support for himself and his father from the Imam al-Khalili, the Duruᶜ, and the Dhahirah tribes, but without success. Beyond such spasmodic moves, the Al Maktum seem to have had little to do with Omani affairs.

The area where the politics of Trucial Oman most impinge upon that of Oman is the Dhahirah, the province stretching from the Buraimi Oasis southwards over the steppes and southeastwards along the foothills of the western Hajar as far as the Hamra Duruᶜ. The principal tribes of the region, settled and nomad, are the Bani Ghafir, the Baluchis, the Bani Qitab, the Naᶜim, the Al Bu Shamis, and, at its northernmost extension, the Bani Kaᶜab. All except the Baluchis and sections of the Bani Ghafir are Ghafiri by political affiliation, and all except these same sections of the Bani Ghafir and Sunni by religious persuasion mainly following the Hanbali rite as a consequence of Wahhabi proselytism in the nineteenth century. With the possible exception of the Ibadi elements among the Bani Ghafir, they have not acknowledged the imamate in this century or submitted to any of the imams. They have displayed much the same independence towards the Al Bu Saᶜid sultans.

Those Bani Ghafir who dwell in and around Dariz, in the foothills of the Jahar, are only a branch of the tribe, the main body of which lives in the Wadi Bani Ghafir, on the eastern slope of the Hajar. Information about the tribe, from which the Ghafiri faction originally derived its name, is scarce and contradictory. Because the political allegiance of some sections in the last century has swung backwards and forwards between the Ghafiris and the Hinawis, the tribe has gained the name of the *Miyayihah*, or waverers. As already indicated, some of its sections are Ibadi, some Sunni. They have maintained friendly relations throughout this century with both the Al Bu Saᶜid Sultans and the Al Bu Falah shaikhs, although their allegiance to the former has not been as firm as that of the Bani Kalban and Bani ᶜAli, their neighbours to the north, or that of their fellow tribesmen across the Hajar. The Baluchis, whose principal settlements of ᶜAraqi and Mazim lie to the west of Dariz, are Hinawi in politics although Sunni in religion. Because of this, and because at the time they stood in some fear of their neighbours, the Bani Qitab, they cultivated fairly close relations early in the century with the Al Bu Falah, and the connection remained friendly until about twenty years ago. To the north-westward of Mazim lies the collection of settlements known as Aflaj Bani Qitab, the home of the southern or settled branch of the Bani Qitab. The northern branch of the tribe is nomadic, and its *dirah* lies mainly in the Trucial shaikhdom of Sharjah. It ranges as far westwards as the Khatam, the district lying to the west of the Buraimi Oasis, and it has participated in tribal conflicts in the Dhahirah. The settled Bani Qitab of the Dhahirah are Sunni and Ghafiri.

The *dirah* of the Naᶜim and Al Bu Shamis begins in the Khatam and stretches over the northern part of the Dhahirah and along the western flanks of the Hajar to Dhank. Al Bu Shamis were once one of the three branches of the Naᶜim – the other two being Al Bu Khuraiban and Khawatir – but they have been accorded a separate identity for a good century now, the name 'Naᶜim' generally being reserved to the other two branches; although occasionally in the Dhahirah all three branches are grouped under the generic classification of 'Naᶜim'. Al Bu Shamis and Naᶜim have both settled and nomadic sections, although the latter are not true Bedouin in that they remain in the vicinity of their settlements. Al Bu Shamis live at Dhank, at al-Sunainah to the westwards, in Hamasa village in the Buraimi Oasis, and in the defiles at the western end of the Wadi al-Jizzi, to the east of Buraimi (where they are sometimes confused with elements of another tribe, the Shawamis). The Bedouin Al Bu Shamis wander between Dhank, al-Sunainah, and Qabil (about thirty miles to the northward). Al Bu Khuraiban live in Buraimi and Saᶜara villages in the Buraimi Oasis, at Hafit, several miles to the southward, and in Dhank.

Their Bedouin elements remain in the vicinity of Hafit. The ruling family of the Trucial shaikhdom of ᶜAjman is Al Bu Khuraiban, and it has in the past expressed resentment against the encroachment of the Al Bu Falah shaikhs upon the power and land-holdings of their kinsmen at Buraimi. Khawatir live at Hafit, and at Ras al-Khaimah, and elsewhere on the Trucial Coast. All the Naᶜim and Al Bu Shamis are Sunni, usually of the Hanbali rite, and Ghafiri. So, too, are the Bani Kaᶜab who dwell in the western half of the Wadi al-Jizzi and in the country to the immediate north, with their main settlement at Mahadhah.

Because the life of the Buraimi Oasis is linked so closely with that of Abu Dhabi, on the one side, and that of the Dhahirah, on the other, the Al Bu Falah shaikhs have exerted considerable influence in the Dhahirah for several generations now. They have certainly wielded more authority there than the Al Bu Saᶜid, and after the expulsion of the Wahhabi garrison from Buraimi a hundred years ago they fell heir to the authority previously exercised in the region by the Al Saᶜud. Al Bu Falah power in the Dhahirah reached its height during the chieftainship of Zayid ibn Khalifah (1855–1909), who by the turn of the century was the acknowledged arbiter of tribal disputes as far south as ᶜIbri. He also acted as the guardian of Al Bu Saᶜid interests in the Dhahirah, receiving in return an annual *fariẓah*, or payment, from the Sultan. The Al Bu Falah – Al Bu Saᶜid alliance dates back to the early nineteenth century, when it was exercised chiefly against the Qasimi confederacy. Later it was directed against the Wahhabis or Saudis. Like the Bani Yas in general, the ruling Al Bu Falah section is Sunni of the Maliki rite, and the tribe as a whole has been aligned with the Hinawi faction in Omani politics.

After the death of Zayid ibn Khalifah in 1909 the Naᶜim and Al Bu Shamis assumed a greater role in the political life of the Dhahirah, a role to which their numbers and importance entitled them. Up to this time their *tamimah*, the head of the Al Hamuda clan of the Al Bu Khuraiban residing in Buraimi village, who was also recognized as paramount shaikh by the Al Bu Shamis, had been overshadowed by the figure of the Al Bu Falah ruler. Now he began to contend for power in the Buraimi Oasis and beyond with Zayid ibn Khalifah's successors, whose position in the oasis was based upon their own holdings and upon their overlordship of the Dhawahir tribe, which constituted the larger portion of the settled population of the oasis. An early measure of the success of the *tamimah* of the Naᶜim in asserting his position was his rapid assumption of the role of Al Bu Saᶜid representative in the oasis, for which he received half the *fariẓah* formerly paid to Zayid ibn Khalifah. Thereafter, until the early 1950s, the *tamimah* and his successors continued to receive an annual allowance from the Sultan. The Naᶜim's power grew steadily throughout the 1920s and 1930s, its growth being linked to the fluctuations of Al Bu Falah power caused by quarrels and murders within the ruling family. No fewer than five changes of ruler took place among the Al Nahaiyan in the twenty years after Zayid ibn Khalifah's death, and during this time the Al Bu Falah position in the Buraimi Oasis and its vicinity was largely upheld by Ahmad ibn Hilal, the principal Dhahiri shaikh. His death in 1936 brought a considerable accession of strength to the Naᶜim, which was not reduced until a decade later, when Zayid ibn Sultan, the brother of the ruler of Abu Dhabi, Shakhbut ibn Sultan, was appointed Al Bu Falah *wali* in the oasis.

It was at this juncture, in the immediate post-war years, that the Sultan Saᶜid ibn Taimur decided to assert his authority in the Buraimi Oasis and in the northern Dhahirah, a decision which was not unconnected with the resumption of oil exploration in Trucial Oman. Several of the Naᶜim and Al Bu Shamis shaikhs of the region, excited and alarmed by reports of the imminent arrival of an oil-prospecting party from Trucial Oman, had clamorously declared that they would not permit it to enter their territories. Their excitement, which arose from the speculation that oil might indeed lie under their lands, was largely offset by their alarm that the operations of the prospecting party, which was being assisted by Zayid ibn Sultan, might lead to an extension or revival of Al Bu Falah power in the Dhahirah. Some thought of appealing for support to the Saudis, as they had in the early 1920s during an outbreak of tribal warfare in the Dhahirah, and again in 1925 when the Imam al-Khalili and ᶜIsa ibn Salih al-Harithi had threatened to bring the Dhahirah under their control. Others thought of invoking the aid of Saiyid Saᶜid ibn Taimur. The Sultan was not slow to seize the opportunity offered him, and in July 1948 he sent his *wazir*, Ahmad ibn Ibrahim, to Buraimi to persuade the shaikhs to recognize the *tamimah* of the Naᶜim, Saqr ibn Sultan Al Hamuda, as his, the Sultan's, representative, and to entrust all questions which might arise in the area, as well as their relations with the Sultan, to him. The shaikhs agreed to do so and they incorporated their consent in a written agreement.

The flurry over the question of authority and jurisdiction in the northern Dhahirah had barely died away when it was aroused afresh by the assertion of Saudi Arabia's frontier claim in 1949 and by the train of events set off by it. During the next half-dozen years the whole pattern of tribal life and alignments in the Dhahirah was upset by Saudi activities, and particularly by the infusions of money and arms into the region. Hardly a single tribe was unaffected by the campaign of subornation and subversion, and by the time the dust had settled, the *tamimah* of the Naᶜim, the chief of the settled Al Bu Shamis of Hamasa, the chief of the Bani

Kaᶜab of Mahadhah, and several lesser tribal figures were all refugees in Saudi Arabia. The affirmation of Al Bu Saᶜid authority in the northern and southern reaches of the Dhahirah respectively was symbolized by the establishment of the Sultan's *walis* in Buraimi village and at ᶜIbri. It was not Al Bu Saᶜid power in the region, however, which benefited most from the disorders of 1949–55 but that of the Al Bu Falah, and of Zayid ibn Sultan, in particular. His reputation with certain tribes of the Dhahirah had steadily increased from the time that he took up residence in the Buraimi Oasis in 1946. It was, for instance, largely through his influence with the Duruᶜ and the western Janabah at ᶜIzz, in Oman proper, that Thesiger was able to travel through inner Oman in 1949–50. Zayid's resoluteness during the Saudi lodgement in the Buraimi Oasis from 1952 to 1955 increased his stature still further, and in the succeeding decade it continued to grow.

Much of Zayid's authority derives from his standing with the bedouin tribes, like the ᶜAwamir, which frequent the vicinity of the oasis in the course of their wanderings. The ᶜAwamir are a far-ranging tribe which roams the borderlands of Oman from the Hadhramaut in the south to the Ramlat al-Hamra and the Dhafrah in the north. There is a settled branch around Nizwa and on the Batinah coast, which is Hinawi by political allegiance. The Bedouin ᶜAwamir can also probably be classed as Hinawi, particularly in view of their close connection with the Al Bu Falah since the early nineteenth century, although they seem to have played little part in Omani politics since that time. Zayid also has strong links, as indicated above, with the Duruᶜ and with the powerful Wahibah of the eastern sands, whose shaikhs visit him frequently. These connections have obviously been strengthened since he replaced his brother as ruler of Abu Dhabi in August 1966. With the increased revenue which oil production has brought him, and with the sound basis of territorial and tribal strength which he has long possessed, he will undoubtedly, if he does not already, command as much power in the Dhahirah and along the desert marches of Oman as his grandfather, Zayid ibn Khalifah, commanded in his time. What the eventual consequences of this may be for the Al Bu Saᶜid's standing in the region are unpredictable.

PART II

POLITICAL DEVELOPMENTS
AND
INTERNATIONAL RELATIONS

7

THE ARABIAN PENINSULA IN
ARAB AND POWER POLITICS

A. R. KELIDAR

A dominant feature in the modern history of Arab politics has been the struggle for the leadership of the Arab countries. This has invariably been undertaken in the name of Arab unity. The unity of the Arabs has been the most compelling idea of Arab nationalist thought. The Arabs have been expressing their allegiance to their unity ever since they recognized themselves to be different from their co-religionists, the Turks, when they seemed to have acquired a corporate national identity. The desire for unity was accentuated by the dismemberment of the Arab possessions of the Ottoman sultan into many and separate political entities after the First World War. Thus the Arabs have felt inclined to blame the European Powers for their division. There is little doubt that the Powers took the initiative in dividing the Arab territories into artificial and sometimes clumsy states and saw it in their interest to keep them divided. Although the idea of unity has been accepted by all Arabs, none dare resist nor denounce it, yet after more than fifty years of attributing their division to imperialist designs and Western diplomatic machinations, a fresh look at Arab unity is required by none more than the Arabs themselves. The struggle which the Arabs have waged for their unity has produced nothing, with the exception of the short-lived Syrian-Egyptian union, but invective, recrimination and the active intervention by some Arab states with the backing of one or more of the Great Powers to keep the Arab world divided and maintain the *status quo* which was established in the 1920s.

Furthermore, the movement for unity has always been constrained by the power struggle among the Arab states for the leadership. From the beginning the Arabs were divided into three camps – on one side the Hashimites who led the Arab movement for independence and found kingship in Iraq and Jordan, the Saudis who ousted the Hashimites from the Peninsula and established their own domain, and finally the Egyptians who at first expressed little interest in Arab political affairs but found themselves embroiled later on. The League of Arab States set up in 1945 as a first step towards the desired unity has served more as an obstacle to its primary purpose than a contribution. Apart from recognizing the political sovereignty and acknowledging the territorial integrity of its member-states, the League has served to institutionalize the conflict between the various Arab rivals instead of becoming a vehicle to further their unity. It has become the main safeguard for their independence and therefore their division. The League has always been hampered in its effort for positive action by the Egyptian-Saudi-Hashimite rivalry for the leadership of the Arab world. The development of the ideological schism of the late 1950s and the 1960s between the 'revolutionaries' and the 'reactionaries' among Arab regimes did not alter the nature of this rivalry, as ideological differences had to give way to political exigencies from time to time.

Given this inherent discord among the Arabs which manifests itself in their rivalry, all the attempts undertaken by the Arabs to unite their countries has meant partial unity, that is, the merger of two or more states and not all of them. This was seen by the others, mainly those who were left out, as a contrivance to extend the authority of a dynastic house or the interest of a ruling clique at the expense of others through the creation of a threatening power base. Thus Iraq's plan for a Fertile Crescent union, her desire to unite with Syria, and her claim to Kuwait; Jordan's design for a union of Greater Syria; Egypt's union with Syria and her involvement in the Yemen, were all seen by the largest Peninsular state, Saudi Arabia, as threats to her political independence and territorial integrity. The Saudis felt it their right and duty to disrupt any such plan, encouraged by the fact that most of the attempts undertaken lacked genuine public support and approval on the part of the peoples of the countries concerned. The pattern which has characterized the approach of the Peninsular states to Arab politics has been first and foremost to protect their own independence and territorial integrity and secondly to maintain the independence and sovereignty of the other Arab states. So jealously did they regard the attributes of their statehood that until the establishment of the Arab League in 1945 their policy towards the other Arab states was tantamount to isolationism.

The struggle between the Wahhabis under the leadership of Ibn Sa‘ud and Sharif Husain of Mecca for the control of the Peninsula was concluded when the Saudis succeeded in driving the Hashimites out of Hijaz in 1926. Henceforward and until about 1957 the main preoccupation of the Saudis had been to stamp out Sharifian influence and appeal in the Peninsula and to contain it in the Arab world. The repercussions of the dynastic antagonism were to determine the nature of the relationship not only between the two parties immediately concerned, but of all the Arab states towards one another. Thus when Sharif Husain declared himself King of the Arabs in October 1916 the Saudis who were busy consolidating their position in

Najd did not dispute his claim but when he asked them to acknowledge his authority over some territory and tribes which the Saudis believed theirs they resisted.[1] Their resistance turned into an open war when the Sharif assumed the caliphate in March 1924, three days after Atatürk had abolished it in Turkey. In his war against the Sharif, Ibn Sa^cud found a willing ally in King Fuad of Egypt who entertained the desire to assume the caliphate himself.[2] When Hijaz became part of his domain in the Peninsula Ibn Sa^cud saw no reason to support the pretentions of the Egyptian king thereby subjecting himself to a superior Muslim authority in the holy cities under his control. In 1926 another crisis over the Egyptian litter, the Mahmal, which in 1924 led to a rupture between Sharif Husain and King Fuad, was to precipitate a bloody clash between the puritanical Saudis and the Egyptian guards accompanying the litter. The Saudis found the ceremony too offensive for their simple taste and the musical accompaniment an outrageous profanation of Muslim teachings. The incident led the Saudis to suspend the Mahmal and caused the Egyptians to withhold diplomatic recognition from Ibn Sa^cud until King Fuad's death in 1936.[3]

Having ousted the Sharif from Hijaz and having rebuffed Fuad over his aspiration to the caliphate, Ibn Sa^cud turned his attention to improving his relations with his neighbours by the settlement of border disputes and the control of tribal movement across the frontiers. To the north the border with Iraq had been the scene of tribal raids and clashes. The establishment of police posts on the Iraq side of the border in 1925 caused considerable resentment as they were seen by the Saudis to be detrimental to Najdi interests and consequently led to renewed clashes of increasing violence. In 1930, however, Britain, before granting Iraq her independence, sought to reconcile the heads of the feuding dynasties and a meeting between King Faisal of Iraq and Ibn Sa^cud took place on board a British warship in the Gulf. Friendly relations between the two states were established and steps were taken for the settlement of border disputes as well as measures for controlling the movement of tribes across the boundaries. After the death of Faisal in 1933 and with the rise of pan-Arab sentiment in Iraq under the leadership of Yasin al-Hashimi, friendly visits between the two countries were exchanged in 1935. A year later a Treaty of Arab Brotherhood and Alliance was officially signed in Baghdad. A significant feature of the treaty was the emphasis on the religious bonds

---

[1] Hafiz Wahbah – *Jazirat al-^carab fi al-qarn al-^cishrin* (1935), pp. 231–9; Philby, H. St John, *Sa'udi Arabia* (London, 1955), pp. 273–80,

[2] Kedourie, Elie, 'Egypt and the Caliphate 1915–1946', *Journal of the Royal Asiatic Society*, iii and iv (1963), pp. 208–48.

[3] Twitchett, K. S., *Saudi Arabia* (Princeton, 1958), pp. 159–60.

between the two countries on which the Saudis laid great importance as well as Arab kinship, a feeling highly valued by the Arab nationalists of Iraq.[4]

The reconciliation between Hashimite Iraq and the Saudis did not end the dynastic confrontation. Amir Abdullah of Trans-Jordan was not to abandon his father's cause but continued to pursue the Hashimite vendetta with Ibn Sa'ud, especially as the Saudis remained adamant in their claim to the district and port of Aqaba as part of the Hijaz territory and therefore their own. Abdullah continued to stir up trouble for the Saudis by his incitement of the tribes of northern Hijaz to rebel against the authority of Ibn Sa'ud. These attempts coincided with similar action undertaken by the Imam of Yemen on Ibn Sa'ud's southern border. It seems that in 1932 the Amir of Trans-Jordan and the Imam of Yemen had an understanding to launch a two-pronged attack on the Saudis to drive them out of Hijaz. The attack from the north, in which the deposed Khedive of Egypt, 'Abbas Hilmi, was thought to be implicated, was quickly stemmed when Saudi troops put down the rebellion.[5] However Saudi relations with Abdullah were to deteriorate further in the aftermath of the first Arab-Israeli war in 1948, and to remain strained until the assassination of King Abdullah in Jerusalem in 1951. In the south the Saudi armies occupied large areas of the Yemen including the port of al-Hudaidah. Hostilities were terminated with the signing of al-Ta'if agreement between Ibn Sa'ud and Imam Yahya in 1934 whereby the major portion of the Saudi-occupied territory was restored to the Yemen. In 1936 the imam was invited to adhere to the Saudi-Iraqi pact of the same year, and after some hesitation Imam Yahya, who disliked every kind of international commitment on the part of his country, felt obliged to sign the pact.

It was about this time that the Arab states became concerned and alarmed about the situation in Palestine where continuous outbreaks of violence were taking place. The violence was the manifestation of Arab resistance to the British policy which sought the implementation of the Balfour Declaration in establishing a national home for the Jews in Palestine. The British had conducted many fruitless enquiries and drafted several reports and White Papers. While other Arab leaders felt mistrustful of British and French intentions in the area, Ibn Sa'ud seems to have placed too much confidence in Britain and France on the assumption that

---

[4] Khadduri, Majid, *Independent Iraq – A Study in Iraqi Politics from 1932 to 1958* (London, 1960), pp. 321–4; 'Abd al-Razzaq al-Hasani, *Ta'rikh al-wizarat al-'iraqiyah* (Saida, 1966), Vol. iv, pp. 193–200.

[5] Salah al-Din al-Mukhtar, *Ta'rikh al-mamlakah al-'arabiyah al-sa'udiyah fi madiha wa-hadiriha* (Beirut, n.d.), Vol. ii, pp. 455–6; Wenner, M. W., *Modern Yemen 1918–1966* (Baltimore, 1967), pp. 144–5.

they would not act against the real interests of the peoples of the area. He advised moderation on the part of the leaders of the Palestine Arabs as well as of the Arab states in their dealing with Britain; and he was reported to have warned the pro-Axis regime of Rashid ᶜAli al-Gailani in Iraq not to antagonize Britain or act against her interests.[6] None the less, the Saudis have always been suspicious of Hashimite ambitions in Syria and Palestine.

Iraqi interest in Syria dates back to the Arab kingdom of Faisal set up in Damascus in 1918 and driven out by the French in 1920 when the mandate for Syria was awarded to France. Faisal, it seems, could not readily forget his old capital, nor did his supporters – Iraqis as well as Syrians – who continued to campaign for Syrian independence. His hope to regain Syria received fresh stimulus when some Syrian nationalist leaders met Faisal, then the King of Iraq, in Paris in 1931 and pledged themselves to work for the unity of the two countries.[7] However it was not so much the efforts of the Syrian nationalists that revived the issue of unity and gave it some credence but rather the Second World War. Both contestants in the great conflagration made some friendly overtures to the Arabs and offers to help in the realization of their national aspiration for unity. The British, having liberated Syria from the Vichy administration and promised her independence, having suppressed the Gailani regime in Iraq and imposed a pro-British cabinet on Egypt, could wield greater influence in determining the destiny of the Arabs. Thus in 1941 Anthony Eden, the British Foreign Secretary, made a speech in which he said that the British Government would give full support to any scheme that commanded general approval among the Arabs to strengthen the cultural, economic and political ties between the Arab countries. In December 1942 Nuri al-Saᶜid, Prime Minister of Iraq, put forward a plan for an Arab union in two stages. First, he recommended the formation of a single state – unitary or federal – comprising Syria, Lebanon, Trans-Jordan and Palestine with special autonomous status for the Jews of Palestine and the Christians of Lebanon. Secondly, Nuri proposed an Arab confederation to begin with of the new state and Iraq, but open to any other Arab country that wished to join. The plan was known as the Fertile Crescent Union.[8]

Nuri's plan was opposed by more than one interest in Arab politics. Amir Abdullah who had set out from Hijaz in 1920 to reconquer Syria and restore Hashimite authority but had to make a permanent stop in Amman on British advice, rejected the plan. Instead he proposed the

[6] Twitchett, op. cit., pp. 166–8.
[7] Muhammad Jamil Baihum, Qawafil al-ᶜurubah wa-mawakibuha (Beirut, 1950), Vol. ii, pp. 237–8.
[8] Khadduri, op. cit., pp. 335–6.

unity of Greater Syria under his throne. To Ibn Sa^cud the view of his old Hashimite enemies ruling Iraq and Greater Syria, dominating the land bridge between the Mediterranean and the Persian Gulf sealing off the Peninsula from the rest of the world, was a daunting prospect. Egypt, which was beginning to express some interest in Arab politics, because of British encouragement to her leaders to assume the leadership of the Arab countries, saw the extension of Hashimite authority to Syria as a threat to her own claim. Thus she too rejected the plan and ranged herself along Saudi Arabia in opposition to the Iraqi plan. Egypt, therefore, found in Saudi Arabia a willing ally to challenge Hashimite Iraq's claim to the leadership of the Arab world, forming the nucleus of a group which was to contribute so much to the polarization of Arab politics in the years to come. In the course of 1943 the initiative passed from Nuri to Nahhas, from Iraq to Egypt where a general Arab conference was held in 1944 the result of which was the establishment of the Arab League in 1945. From its inception, therefore, the League was rendered impotent for its primary purpose by the rivalry and the alliances of its member states; and Arab unity as the national ideal of the Arabs was to be hamstrung by the very machinery which was designed to give it life.[9]

Henceforward the Arab states had to fall back on an enabling clause in the League's charter to contract bilateral agreements of close co-operation or union but the division among them was so pervading as to make this an impossible task. A year after the establishment of the League Sa^cd Allah al-Jabiri, the Syrian Premier, expressed some doubts on the advisability of union with Iraq when he was approached by Nuri because Syria did not want to displease Saudi Arabia or Egypt.[10] Later when some Syrian politicians started making contact with Iraq, Ibn Sa^cud intervened to check this trend. Both countries became embroiled in a tug of war over Syria by supporting different Syrian political factions. They had to pour a considerable amount of bribe money in the direction of Shaikh Yusuf Yasin, a Syrian supporter of the Hashimites, who had defected to the Saudis in the 1920s, and the whole weight of Saudi resources was directed at driving a wedge between Iraq and Syria.[11] After the Arab defeat in the first Arab-Israeli war in which Saudi Arabia played an insignificant role – she sent only a token force – the Saudis and the Egyptians faced a further Hashimite threat to extend their authority. Abdullah of Trans-Jordan

[9] For a study of the Arab League, see Robert W. Macdonald, *The League of Arab States* (Princeton, 1965); also Tom Little, 'The Arab League: A Reassessment', *Middle East Journal*, Vol. x, pp. 138–50.

[10] *Majra al-hawadith al-muta'tiyah min al-inqilab fi Dimashq bima yata^callaq bi-al-hukumah al-^ciraqiyah* (Baghdad, 1949), cited by Patrick Seale in *The Struggle for Syria* (London, 1965), pp. 47–52.

[11] *Ibid.*, pp. 47 and 140.

intended to annex the part of Palestine under the occupation of his army, and a coup in Syria brought to power Colonel Husni al-Za^cim who sought to stop a defence pact with Iraq. The opposition failed to stop Abdullah but succeeded in foiling Iraq's union with Syria. Za^cim, it seems, turned to Iraq only because President Quwatli whose regime he had overthrown had been an ally of the Saudis and the Egyptians, and therefore Iraq was the obvious choice against them. He also wanted to strengthen his hands against the Israelis at the armistice talks which were imminent by concluding a defence agreement with Iraq. The Saudis and the Egyptians were alarmed and Ibn Sa^cud issued a warning to King Abdullah, who greeted the overthrow of Quwatli somewhat too gleefully, that he would consider any attack on Syria as an aggression against himself. However, their anxiety was allayed when Za^cim dispatched envoys to Cairo and Riyad to offer King Ibn Sa^cud and King Faruq his respects and to assure them that his regime would jealously defend Syria's independence. The promise of financial assistance from Saudi Arabia and military aid from Egypt led Za^cim to drop his proposals for co-operation with Iraq. Having paid a brief visit to King Faruq, Za^cim returned to Damascus to declare: 'The Lords of Baghdad and Amman believed that I was about to offer them the crown of Syria on a silver platter but they were disappointed. The Syrian Republic wants neither Greater Syria nor the Fertile Crescent.' He went on to claim Trans-Jordan as the tenth Muhafaza (province) of Syria. Following this, Iraq launched a virulent propaganda campaign against Za^cim which he brushed aside by announcing that he counted for support on a Cairo-Damascus-Riyad triangle. Ibn Sa^cud followed by stating that neither he nor King Faruq would stand idly by in the face of an attack on Syria.[12]

However, to attribute Iraq's failure to unite with Syria under Za^cim as well as under subsequent regimes to Saudi and Egyptian diplomatic machinations would not be the whole truth. The Great Powers, particularly France, which regarded Syria as her sphere of influence expressed strong objection to the union of the two countries; Britain did not feel very enthusiastic in deference to her good relation with France as well as Iraq's Arab rivals. More important than all these considerations seems to be the evolution of a Syrian interest in the independence of their country and the sovereignty of their own state. Many of Syria's leaders, including some of those who sought union with Iraq, did not wish to replace the country's Republican institutions with a Hashimite monarchy, others expressed grave reservations about Iraq's commitments under the Anglo-Iraqi Treaty of 1930; and some realized that to unite with Iraq would stem the flood of gold particularly from Saudi Arabia. The Saudis made

---

[12] *Ibid.*, pp. 56–9; also Baihum, *op. cit.*, pp. 238–40.

three loans to Syria; $6 million in 1950, $10 million in 1955, and again $10 million in 1956.

The early 1950s introduced major shifts in world power politics that led to a new confrontation between West and East. The whole world was gripped by the fever of the cold war, but these changes were not of immediate or direct importance to the Arab world. Nevertheless Western policy in the Middle East was determined largely by such issues as the communist take over in Czechoslovakia and China, the Berlin blockade and the Korean war, representing Russian policy as an 'international conspiracy'. Thus Western plans for the defence of the Middle East were motivated by the need to secure oil supplies for European industry and the safeguarding of transport routes. The Arab world too saw some changes that were eventually to radicalize Arab politics. King Abdullah of Jordan was assassinated in 1951, Faruq of Egypt was overthrown by a military coup in 1952 and King Ibn Saᶜud died in 1953. However, the Arabs were more concerned with the containment of Israel, the creation of which they blamed on the West, rather than international communism; with the effective assertion of their political and economic independence from the Western powers rather than join their defence system. Finally, the Arab political scene was completely overshadowed by a fresh and a more vicious rivalry between Iraq under the old man of Arab politics, Nuri, and Nasser's radical Egypt. Iraq wanted the Arab states to join the Western-sponsored defence system. Egypt stood for neutralism in international politics and self-help in Arab politics, policies advocated for some years by the Syrian Baᶜth party which became Nasser's ally. King Saᶜud who lacked the dynamism and the cunning of his father joined the radical front for reasons of his own, mainly his dispute with Britain over the Buraimi oasis.[13]

By 1955 the new leadership in Egypt had made sufficient inroads into Syrian politics to make possible the conclusion of a military alliance between Egypt, Syria and Saudi Arabia. Thus the Cairo-Damascus-Riyad triangle was reformed under new leadership to challenge Iraq. A year later a similar pact was signed in Jiddah between Egypt, Saudi Arabia and Yemen. The Yemen, it seems, joined basically because of her dispute with Britain over Aden and the protectorates which she claimed to be part of historic Yemen. It had been the policy of the rulers of Yemen to seek the support and friendship of Britain's most outspoken and powerful opponents. As it was the Italians in the 1920s and 1930s, it had come to be the Russians on the international scene and Egypt locally; thus a friendship pact with the Soviet Union in 1955 and the Jiddah pact with

[13] See Kelly, J. B., *Eastern Arabian Frontiers* (London, 1964).

Egypt and Saudi Arabia in 1956 were concluded.[14] However none of these pacts was useful or effective. Of the Egyptian-Syrian-Saudi pact, Patrick Seale writes that it 'was never either militarily effective or economically stimulating. These are not criteria by which it should be judged. It was no more than a diplomatic coup, swiftly conceived and executed, to counter a challenge from Nuri al-Saᶜid. King Faruq acted in much the same way to save Colonel Husni al-Zaᶜim from the Hashimites in April 1949. For both Cairo and Riyad, the only *raison d'être* of the alliance was to prevent Syria from falling into Iraq's sphere of influence'.[15] The Baᶜthists, on the other hand, were motivated by the ideal for Arab unity. The pact was seen as constituting the first step towards a federation of the three countries, but on the admission of the leader of the Baᶜth, Michel ᶜAflaq, the pact remained a dead letter.[16]

When Nasser nationalized the Suez Canal in 1956 the Government of Saudi Arabia supported his right to do so; and later when Egypt became the victim of an aggression the Saudis broke off diplomatic relations with Britain and France and suspended oil shipments to them. The aftermath of the Israeli-British-French attack on Egypt saw the emergence of Nasser as an Arab national hero. With Syria secured, the battleground in the Nasser-Nuri confrontation shifted to Jordan. Nationalist agitation did not only stop Jordan from joining the Baghdad Pact but led to the dismissal of General Glubb, the famous commander of the Arab Legion, by young King Husain. Moreover, under Nabulsi, Jordan for the first time in its history possessed a cabinet that was veering towards the Cairo-Damascus-Riyad triangle rather than Hashimite Baghdad. In Jordan the Anglo-French intervention in Egypt was seen as a deliberate move to assist Israel, and therefore intensified the anti-Western mood of the country. Thus, two weeks after the announcement of the Eisenhower Doctrine which Nabulsi rejected, Jordan signed an agreement with Saudi Arabia, Egypt and Syria under which the three countries were to pay Jordan £12½ million to replace the British subsidy paid to her armed forces. Nabulsi also pronounced in favour of economic union with Syria which was considering some form of integration with Egypt. Earlier, Jordan had asked Iraq and Syria to send troop reinforcements to her territory as a precautionary measure against Israeli threats. The changed political situation led King Husain to demand the withdrawal of these troops. Iraq complied immediately but the Syrians, who were under Egyptian command by virtue of the joint defence pact, were reluctant to

---

[14] Macro, Eric, *Yemen and the Western World since 1571* (London, 1968).

[15] Seale, *op. cit.*, p. 224.

[16] *Ibid.*, p. 225.

leave the country and therefore roused the suspicions of both King Husain and the Saudis.

Indeed, King Saᶜud had been moving away from Egypt for some time as he grew increasingly uneasy about Nasser's intentions. He especially disliked Egypt's flirtation with communist Russia. In their foreign policy the primary concern of the Saudis has always been Islam. This has made them instinctively anti-communist. The development of American oil interest made them doubly aware of the dangers of communism to their wealth. They have also come to rely on American support and advice in dealing with the outside world. In January 1957 Saᶜud paid a visit to the United States. He brought back a promise of military aid in return for an extension of the Dhahran air base as well as an appreciation of the Eisenhower Doctrine which was tantamount to approval. The Egyptian-Saudi harmony was broken when Saᶜud publicly sided with Husain against the Syrians in April. A month later he showed complete independence by visiting Baghdad where a government spokesman said 'He [Saᶜud] does not want to fight Nasser openly, and we do not want to embarrass him but we must keep Egypt and Syria from interfering in Jordan.'[17] Although the official communique called on the Arab states not to interfere in each other's domestic affairs; it has been suggested that the Americans encouraged Saᶜud to challenge Nasser to the leadership of the Arab world.[18]

Following the foundation of the Egyptian-Syrian union in 1958 the radical notions of nationalism and revolutionary socialism of the pan-Arab movement acquired a particular significance, since the establishment of the U.A.R. was seen as its finest achievement. A tumultuous wave of enthusiasm greeted the union in the two countries concerned and in the rest of the Arab world. It was regarded as the turning point in the history of the movement; the initiative had passed to the revolutionary nationalists who expected the peoples of the other Arab states to rise against their oppressors and join the union. These expectations were misplaced. Iraq and Jordan were quick to protect themselves with a Hashimite federation of their own, but the Iraqi revolution of July 1958 soon brought this to an end. In the Peninsula King Saᶜud dropped out of his pacts with Syria and Egypt and sought to disrupt the Syrian-Egyptian union, when it was alleged in Damascus that he offered ᶜAbd al-Hamid al-Sarraj, the chief of the Syrian Army Intelligence, £2 million and the Presidency of Syria if he would assassinate Nasser and frustrate the union between Egypt and Syria. This allegation made Saᶜud the object of a virulent propaganda campaign in the press and radio of both Egypt and Syria. Saᶜud had to give way to his younger brother Crown Prince Faisal, who tried to

[17] *Middle Eastern Affairs*, Vol. viii (1957), pp. 262–3.
[18] Holden, David, *Farewell to Arabia* (London, 1966), pp. 118–20.

placate Nasser rather than fight him, a move for which he was thought to be pro-Egyptian.

Imam Ahmad of Yemen was shrewder and had more foresight than Saᶜud. He avoided the acrimony of Egyptian propaganda by associating the Yemen with the UAR to form the UAS. At the same time, however, he did his utmost to keep the Egyptians out of his country. Emboldened by Syria's secession in 1961 and encouraged by mounting Saudi and Iraqi opposition to Nasser, Ahmad ventured a public criticism of the Egyptian leader. He composed a poem in which he condemned the socialist policies of Egypt declaring them to be incompatible with the tenets of Islam. Nasser who, following the break-up of the UAR, decided to contract out of Arab politics to build up socialist Egypt, seized the opportunity to terminate the UAS. Ahmad was to regret his indiscretion as he incurred the wrath of the Egyptian propaganda machine which condemned him as the *qat*-chewing Imam. Furthermore, the Egyptians began to cultivate the friendship of Yemeni revolutionary groups, a process which hastened the revolution of September 1962.[19] It was this coup as well as those in Baghdad in February 1963 and Damascus in March 1963 that brought Egypt out of her isolation and led to her involvement in the Yemen and the wider sphere of Arab politics.

In recent years the concept of Arab unity has been accompanied by the idea of revolutionary socialism. In 1958 a shift of emphasis in the radical political currents had taken place in the Arab world. This was given a strong impetus by the rise of the UAR and the Republic of Iraq. The appearance of the two republics on the Arab political scene led to the identification of the opponents of the Arab unity as the 'reactionaries', i.e. the hereditary monarchs, the oligarchic politicians, and wealthy land-owners and businessmen who had found it easier to protect their political and economic interest by keeping the Arab world divided. Their commitment to the protection of Western interests in the region was seen as a facet of their reactionary outlook.[29] At first sight, the division in the Arab world may be seen as a contest between the monarchies, with their accepted and traditional basis of legitimacy, and the newly-established republic, seeking a fresh formula to legitimize their rule by responding to the political aspirations of the masses in their own territory and further afield. But on closer examination it is clear that the division is really the same old struggle between the contending parties for the leadership of the Arab world. Furthermore, this division is not as clear cut as many people seem to think, nor has it any real ideological basis as indicated by the dispute between the Baᶜth and Nasser, the feud between the two

[19] Wenner, *op. cit.*, pp. 184–9.
[20] Kerr, Malcolm, *The Arab Cold War* (London, 1966).

ruling factions of the Baᶜth in Iraq and Syria and the conflict between the republic of Yemen and the People's Republic of South Yemen.

Nothing could illustrate this better than the rise of General Qasim in Iraq to pose a challenge to the revolutionary leadership of the UAR. Qasim, unlike Nuri, was no reactionary but an Arab revolutionary whose political behaviour did not conform to the conventional expectations of the UAR. He failed to join the march towards Arab unity and refused to acknowledge Nasser as the leader of the revolutionary movement. To oppose him, Nasser had to adjust his position *vis-a-vis* the other Arab countries such as 'reactionary' Jordan and Saudi Arabia. In April 1959 the UAR sought to condemn Iraq at a meeting of the Arab League Council but neither Saudi Arabia nor Jordan would agree unless they were given assurances that the independence and integrity of their regimes would be respected. This seems to have been agreed, for soon afterwards diplomatic relations were restored and King Saᶜud paid a state visit to Cairo. The two countries were to work even closer in 1961 when Qasim renewed Iraq's claim to the newly-independent State of Kuwait. Iraq first claimed Kuwait in the 1930s. The Saudis have had a lifelong interest in an outlet to the Gulf and Kuwait as well as the rest of the Trucial Coast had been the obvious target. The Egyptians could not allow Qasim to extend his authority to the oil rich shaikhdom. Thus they co-operated with Saudi Arabia and Jordan in creating a force under the auspices of the Arab League to replace the British troops who were sent to defend the independence of Kuwait under the Anglo-Kuwaiti treaty. Revolutionary Egypt, therefore, not only co-operated with 'reactionary' Saudi Arabia to defend the independence of 'reactionary' Kuwait, but in the final analysis she did so to protect what must be described as British imperial interest in the Gulf. Kuwait's independence was acknowledged by the Arab League whose member-states, with the exception of Iraq, offered the new state prompt recognition. The price was a share in the country's oil revenues. The Kuwait Fund for Arab Economic Development, which began in 1962 with a capital of £150 million, proved an entirely new source of investment capital for development projects anywhere in the Arab world. Unofficially, however, it was understood everywhere from Casablanca to Baghdad as the first instalment of Kuwait's protection money. The more immediate the menace, the higher the cost of this protection. £25 million to Egypt and £30 million were required to buy off Iraq's claim to sovereignty over Kuwait and to recognize the shaikhdom's independence in 1963 following the overthrow of Qasim.[21]

In 1962 Prince Faisal assumed real power in Saudi Arabia again. The reason for the transfer was once more King Saᶜud's failure to deal with

[21] Holden, *op. cit.*, p. 169.

the Egyptian threat, this time from the Yemen. In September of that year Brigadier ᶜAbd Allah al-Sallal carried out a successful coup which overthrew Imam al-Badr and declared a republic. From its very beginnings the republican regime of Sallal sought Egyptian support and military aid to sustain it against the guerilla forces, formed with the assistance of Saudi Arabia, by the deposed Imam. Egyptian paratroopers arrived in Sanᶜa only four days after the coup. Seven days later Egyptian ships were landing troops and material in Hudaidah. By November, a mutual defence treaty was signed between the republic and Egypt to replace the Jiddah pact of 1956. The Saudis could not remain idle while Egypt introduced a considerable force into the Peninsula. Sallal made matters worse when he declared his intentions of eventually establishing a Republic of the Arabian Peninsula. The Egyptian argument that they were in the Yemen to protect the republican regime against Saudi Arabian aggression did not cut much ice with the Saudis. They were convinced that the purpose of the Egyptian expeditionary force was first and foremost to gain a foothold in the Peninsula from which to work for the overthrow of the Saudi monarchy and control of the oil resources. Furthermore, they saw the establishment of an Egyptian power base in the Yemen as a means for the propagation of Egyptian revolutionary ideas not only northward into their own country but southward into the Arabian Federation and Aden where the Egyptians were enjoying some support. The United States, where the security of Saudi Arabia is regarded as an American responsibility, was becoming concerned about Soviet penetration, and offered to mediate by drawing up a disengagement plan for both Egypt and Saudi Arabia. To the Saudis the American proposals were meaningless as Sallal would have been left in power to keep up the propaganda campaign against them. Instead they advocated the restoration of the imamate as the legitimate government. The civil war had to go on.

The Egyptians soon found the expedition too costly and were desperately in search of a face-saving formula to extricate themselves from the Yemen. In the meantime a considerable number of Yemenis were becoming increasingly resentful of the Egyptian domination of their country and were prepared to entertain a solution. They came to the conclusion that some approach to the imam and his forces must be made to obtain peace. They sought to create an atmosphere condusive to some kind of a compromise with the royalists, thereby ending the war. They formed the nucleus of what was to become the 'third force.[22] At the second Arab League summit conference held in September 1964 Faisal and Nasser agreed on a disengagement plan similar to that proposed by the United

[22] Wenner, *op. cit.*, pp. 215–21.

Nations a year earlier but with a joint Saudi-Egyptian force to play the role of peace-keeping. Abortive talks between the republicans and royalists were held, but the agreement came to nothing. Two months after the signing of the agreement Faisal deposed his brother and proclaimed himself king. Following the intensification of the civil war by the royalists with Saudi and Jordanian help, Nasser flew to Jiddah in 1965 to sign the Jiddah agreement with King Faisal. The agreement provided for a disengagement plan as well as a plebiscite for the Yemenis to determine their own system of government. Protracted negotiations between the republicans and royalists once again proved inconclusive and the Jiddah agreement remained a dead letter until the Khartoum summit conference held in September 1967, following the third Arab-Israeli war.

The apparent failure of the Jiddah agreement, followed by the abandonment of the Arab summit conferences, renewed the struggle for Arab leadership, with the emergence of Faisal as a contender. Faisal called for the establishment of an Islamic alliance in which all the Muslim states would participate. His government undertook the holding of several Muslim seminars, where Muslims from all parts of the globe discussed common issues and resolved to work for the revival of a vigorous Muslim community. In Egypt this was seen as a threat to the Arab nationalist movement and an attempt to reconstitute a regional defence pact like the old Baghdad pact. Syria condemned Faisal's initiative and called for an emergency conference of the five revolutionary states – Egypt, Syria, Algeria, Iraq and the Republic of Yemen – to counter the projected alliance. Throughout 1966, and until the third Arab-Israeli war broke out in June 1967, the main dividing line between the 'revolutionaries' and the 'reactionaries' had been that between the supporters of King Faisal's Muslim alliance and President Nasser's pan-Arabism. The result of the war came to blur the division in the Arab world further.[23] Egypt's defeat led to the reactivation of the Jiddah agreement of 1965 with Saudi Arabia, thereby evacuating her forces from the Yemen. The arrangement for the evacuation of Egyptian troops was finalized at the Khartoum summit conference.[24] By this move Egypt was to forfeit her guardianship of the Arab revolution in the Yemen, a task which she had undertaken ever since the overthrow of Imam al-Badr in 1962. The immediate repercussion of the Egyptian-Saudi *rapprochement* was the overthrow of President Sallal in November 1967, and the assumption of political power by the 'third force' in the Yemen. The Khartoum agreement has also given

---

[23] Kelidar, Abbas, 'Shifts and Changes in the Arab World' in *The World Today* (December, 1968).

[24] Watt, Donald, 'The Arab Summit Conference and After' in *The World Today* (October, 1967).

King Faisal a free hand in the Gulf, where British withdrawal will offer Saudi Arabia as the strongest power in the Peninsula an important role to play.

The containment of the Egyptian thrust into the Peninsula has affected the position of the great powers in the region. The United States, the staunch ally of the Saudi State has maintained its friendly relation with all the Peninsular states except the new Republic of South Yemen, but has caused public resentment because of her support for Israel. Britain relieved herself of the troublesome burden of southern Arabia in 1967 but has created confusion by her decision to withdraw from the Gulf by 1971, a confusion that is likely to lead to the polarization of Gulf politics into Arab against Iranian, with Saudi Arabia and Iran as the chief contenders for the leadership. Egyptian withdrawal has also led to the arrest of Soviet influence. Before the Egyptian departure from the Yemen and the closure of the Suez Canal, the Red Sea with the Egyptian ports in the north and Hudaidah and Aden in the south would have been open to Soviet naval and political activity. Though the Russians enjoy considerable political influence in several Arab states outside the Peninsula, within it only Southern Yemen maintains good and friendly relations with the communists. However, even in this area, the closure of the Canal has rendered the strategic port of Aden useless.[25]

[25] Lewis, Bernard, 'The Great Powers, the Arabs and the Israelis', in *Foreign Affairs*, vol. 47 (1968–9), pp. 642–53.

8

BRITAIN, IRAN AND THE PERSIAN GULF: SOME ASPECTS OF THE SITUATION IN THE 1920s AND 1930s

R. M. BURRELL

The attitude of the Persian Government to the Gulf area has, according to popular report, undergone a significant change in the last few years. The permanent preoccupation of Persian foreign policy since the Second World War – freedom from Russian encroachment – is supposed to have lessened, while desires for southward expansion have increased. Many factors are stated to have been involved; the recognition of potential sources of under-sea oil supply, the fear of Egyptian expansion which might block the Gulf to Persian shipping, and a desire to replace British power when this is withdrawn. The enabling factor has been the emergence of a *détente* with the Soviet Union, a *détente* which can be dated from the 1962 Agreement by which the Persian Government promised not to allow the erection of American missile bases on her territory, and which found culmination in the 1967 agreement to purchase Soviet armaments and a steel mill which would be paid for largely by exports of natural gas. Whether this *détente* is complete remains questionable and it should be remembered that the Persian Government may well be basing its current policy on the realization that, in the event of serious trouble, help would be forthcoming from the West to counter Soviet pressure. Whatever the forces at work, however, it appears that the Persian Government is taking the Persian Gulf as the focal area in its military planning. Large arms contracts in 1966 to buy American fighter aircraft and British destroyers were followed by the agreement with the Soviet Union in February 1967 mentioned above. An order for ten British hovercraft in September 1967 for patrol service in the Persian Gulf raised the level of arms expenditure in that year to $660 million. The significance of these purchases lies not in their size so much as in their content – chiefly for naval and air-cover purposes. The decision of February 1967 to concentrate the bulk of Persian military strength in the south of the country and the speech made by the Shah on the opening of part of the Isfahan steel mill (13 March 1968) warning other countries to honour Persian interests in the Gulf, appear to strengthen the view that Persian foreign policy is taking on a new aspect.

If a wider view is taken it will be seen that these recent moves do not constitute a radical departure from previous policy. In fact there are striking parallels with the past and a significant measure of continuity. Present activity re-emphasizes many recurrent themes in modern Persian history – the quest for naval power in the Gulf is an old one. It was with the aid of the fleet belonging to the East India Company that Persian control over Hormuz was established in 1622. Nadir Shah in the eighteenth century desired to establish a Persian fleet and Karim Khan foreshadowed recent events on the Arab side of the Gulf when, in 1764, he wanted to subsidize a British naval presence. (He offered a price of 40,000 rupees annually for the use of two cruisers.)[1] The following century was one of general Persian retreat in the Gulf as energies were devoted more to combating Russian advances in the north. Interest in a Persian fleet was revived by Nasir al-Din Shah but his plans were discouraged by the British Government on the grounds that Persian claims – particularly to Bahrain – might have been pursued more vigorously had a fleet been available.[2] In 1883, however, an order was given to a German firm for two steamers which arrived in the Gulf in 1885. Neither of these two ships seems to have given much trouble to the British authorities. The same cannot be said for the six ships ordered by Riza Shah from Italy which arrived at Bushire on 29 October 1932. The role of these ships in various events will be considered later in this paper.

The desire for a navy is but one element in a complex series which surround Persian attitudes to the Gulf. Interest in a navy was expressed by the stronger and more determined of the shahs. The establishment and consolidation of power by Riza Shah gave Iran such a ruler in the 1920s and 1930s. The renewed desire for a navy was both cause and effect of his policy of creating a greater degree of central control. The desire to extend that control – particularly for the purposes of preventing smuggling and gun-running – made a navy necessary. In turn the presence of a navy meant that elements of national pride could be assuaged by a series of pin-pricks at British authority in the Gulf and the Shatt al-ᶜArab. In analysing Persian governmental attitudes to the Gulf there are, therefore, many elements which need to be considered: the strength of the central government and the extent of its control, the policies pursued by Great Britain and Russia – for without a relatively quiescent Russia Persian

---

[1] Lorimer, J. G., *Gazetteer of the Persian Gulf,* '*Oman and Central Arabia* (Calcutta, 1915), (hereafter referred to as *Lorimer*), p. 1782.

[2] *Persian Gulf*, handbooks prepared under the direction of the Historical Section of the Foreign Office, no. 76 (London, 1920), section II (2) (hereafter referred to as *F.O. Handbook*).

energies cannot be turned to the south, the views and rivalries of Arab governments and rulers, the historical memory and the degree of expression of Persian national pride, and, in later years, the possibility of new, valuable oil discoveries and the difficulties involved in the shipping of oil from established sources.

The aims of Riza Shah were essentially the establishment of internal control and of external independence – aims which were by no means new in Persian history. In pursuing these policies the situation was made much more propitious by the attitude of the new Soviet Government. The Russo-Persian treaty of 26 February 1921 gave vital room for manoeuvre. With the threat of partition and extinction temporarily removed attention could be turned to the creation of internal authority. The retention of independence required, as Riza Shah saw, the establishment of effective national sovereignty. A series of campaigns was begun to subdue the provinces. In 1921 the rebellions of Colonel Muhammad Taqi in Khurasan and of Kuchik Khan in Gilan were crushed. In 1922 attention was turned to the Kurds and in 1922 their leader Ismaᶜil Shakkak Semiqu was forced to flee to Mosul, and in 1924 the pacification of Luristan was undertaken.[3] It was at this stage that international complications began. The effective ruler of what was then ᶜArabistan, now Khuzistan, was Shaikh Khazᶜal of Muhammarah. In 1898 the Shaikh had asked to be taken under British protection; this request could not be granted by the British government but he was assured by the British Minister in Tehran, Sir Henry Mortimer Durand, of British support.[4] The plans to reform the customs administration of Persia and to hand this over to Belgian control in 1902 did not please the Shaikh who had formerly administered the customs in ᶜArabistan. The Shaikh again requested British help and, in order to thwart Russian schemes to occupy Muhammarah, he was informed by Sir Arthur Hardinge (British Minister at Tehran) in December 1902 that 'we shall protect Muhamrah against naval attack by a foreign power, whatever pretext of intervention may be alleged; and also, so long as you remain faithful to the Shah and act in accordance with our advice we will continue to give you our good offices and support'.[5] The value of the Shaikh's friendliness to Britain had been greatly increased by the explorations and activities of the Anglo-Persian Oil Company which in 1909 obtained his permission to construct a pipeline from the wells to the refinery which was to be built at Abadan. As the *de facto* ruler of the area his acquiescence was essential for the security

---

[3] *Survey of International Affairs 1925* (Royal Institute of International Affairs, Oxford, 1927), vol. i, part III, section XIII, p. 538 (hereafter referred to as *RIIA Survey 1925*).

[4] Information on Shaikh Khazᶜal and his relations with the British, drawn from *Lorimer*, pp. 1748 ff.

[5] Letter quoted in *Lorimer*, pp. 1758–9. Also *F.O. Handbook*, p. 57 fn 1.

of the venture. In 1910 the Shaikh was made K.C.I.E. and was again assured of help against foreign attack and of British support in any endeavours to come to a *modus vivendi* with the Tehran authorities.[6] With the anarchy prevailing in Persia however, there seemed little danger of any attempt at control by the central government.[7] During the war the Shaikh assisted British efforts to capture Basra. The anomalies of his position became obvious when the centralizing policy of Riza Khan began to show fruits. In November 1923 a tentative agreement on the payment of taxation was worked out but in the summer of 1924 the Shaikh somewhat hastily denounced Riza who set out for ᶜArabistan in November of that year. An amnesty was signed at Nasiri on 6 December and after garrisons had been established at Shustar and Dizful the Shaikh was removed to Tehran. No serious British protest was sustained and a minor rebellion by the Shaikh's supporters was crushed in July 1925.[8] The question for the British government was could they afford to support the Shaikh in the face of determined opposition by the central Persian government. When the control exercised by Tehran was weak recognition by Britain of a relatively powerful local ruler was the most effective way to safeguard interests, but when internal Persian conditions altered, the over-riding need was to foster the establishment of an effective and independent Persia. The situation of the Shaikh of Muhammarah was analogous to many later problems on the Arabian side of the Gulf. In January 1939 Lord Halifax, Secretary of State for Foreign Affairs, wrote to Lord Zetland, Secretary of State for India, 'one of the main causes of the frontier difficulties which have arisen in this part of Arabia in recent years has been the fact that His Majesty's Government and the Government of India have in the past given undertakings to local rulers recognizing them as the possessors of certain territories, when those rulers had in fact little hold over the territories in question, or have since lost such influence there as they formerly possessed'.[9] The immediate occasion of this letter was the attempt to persuade the Shaikh of Abu Dhabi to give Saudi Arabia access to the Gulf at Khaur al-ᶜUdaid, but the truth of the statement had been made manifest by many earlier events.

The development of a strengthened and more effective Persian government was, generally speaking, welcomed by the British Foreign Office. Many of the problems in the Gulf during the 1930s arose from the unwillingness of the Government of India to adopt such an attitude. On several occasions the Government of India entered warnings against

---

[6] *RIIA Survey 1925*, pp. 540 ff.
[7] Millspaugh A. C., *The American Task in Persia* (New York, 1925), pp. 226–34.
[8] *RIIA Survey 1925*, p. 542.
[9] F.O. 371/21816 1938, Arabia E5861/150/91.

negotiations with Persia on the grounds that the regime of Riza Shah might be very temporary in its nature. On one side was the Persian desire to assert independence while on the other lay the unwillingness of the Government of India to countenance such an assertion. The British Foreign Office was often caught between the two. Within the Persian Government too it should be noted all was not at harmony, the Shah sought an active pursuit of national objectives whereas the Ministry of Foreign Affairs was more reticent in its endeavours. The two extremists – the Shah and the Government of India – resembled each other in that each gave very heavy emphasis to prestige and *amour propre*.

In a memorandum[10] of August 1934 G. Rendel, Head of the Eastern Department at the Foreign Office, pointed out that Persia must be treated on terms of equality, the idea of the Persian Gulf as a 'British Lake' had to be abandoned, Persian goodwill was needed to protect the interests of the Anglo-Persian Oil Company and it was necessary to ensure that Persian friendship did not go to Russia by default. The Government of India, Rendel argued, had not moved out of the nineteenth century; it believed that Persian control over the Gulf area was weak and must ever remain so. While the Foreign Office sought a general settlement with Persia on terms of greater equality, the India Office appeared to be happy with purely local arrangements confident in the knowledge that the Persian regime was ephemeral and that when it collapsed all British objectives could be more easily achieved. In a later memorandum of the same year[11] Rendel returned to the charge and commented upon the many reminders of a former subordinate status still existing as irritants to Persian pride – the position of the Political Resident at Bushire, described in a Foreign Office minute as 'virtually Governor General of the Gulf',[12] the consular posts in southern and eastern Persia still staffed from the Indian Political Service – all these served as reminders of the earlier times when no proper local administration existed. No formal demand for the withdrawal of the Residency was ever made but the Persian Minister of Court Taimurtash said that its existence was regrettable as a reminder of the past. The British Government and the Government of India agreed in principle to removal of the Residency from Bushire but the Government of India insisted upon the Resident having the title of 'Inspecting Consul General' with the right of unlimited access to all British consular posts in Persian ports.[13] The Persian Government could not accept this condition which would have involved very frequent visits of British

[10] F.O. 371/17893 1934, Persia E5177/139/34.
[11] F.O. 371/17893 1934, Persia E5648/139/34.
[12] F.O. 371/17895 1934, Persia E6456/139/34.
[13] F.O. 371/17892 1934, Persia E7322/139/34.

warships and the Residency remained at Bushire until 1946 when it was removed to Bahrain and when the Foreign Office took over responsibility for it.

A real clash of policies between the Foreign Office and the Government of India occurred over the British naval bases in the Gulf at Hangam and Basidu. Here the Foreign Office had great sympathy with the Persian case but found itself in opposition to the India Office and the Admiralty. The case of Hangam and Basidu is of great interest in revealing many aspects of the complex situation in the Gulf – the obscurities of earlier history, the maintenance of old attitudes by various departments of the British Government, the new assertiveness in Persian policy and the fact that the ambition of local Persian – and British – representatives some-times outstripped official policy. With regard to Hangam and Basidu the Persian Government found itself dealing directly with the British authori-ties and not, as in the case of other islands, with the British as representa-tives of Arab rulers. The bases in question were small – and by the early 1930s neither was continuously occupied.[14] The origin of the Basidu problem lay in the desire of the Government of Bombay to establish a base 'more central and commanding than either Bushehr or Basra'[15] for the suppression of piracy. Possible sites included the islands of Hangam and Qishm. It was believed by the Government of Bombay that, despite claims by the Shah, the islands belonged to the Sultan of Oman who had seized them in 1794 or 1795. Apparently the inhabitants of Qishm had invited such annexation as rule by the local Arab chief, Mulla Husain, who was regarded as the representative of the Shah, was oppressive. The Sultan of Oman gave written permission in 1820 for the establishment of a station on Qishm and denied, in 1821, that he held Qishm as a dependency from the Shah – he admitted, however, that his holding of Bandar cAbbas was such a dependency. The British station was set up at Qishm town in July 1820 but shortly afterwards the area was visited by a severe outbreak of cholera and the search began for an alternative base. The captured town of Ras al-Khaimah had been considered but was not regarded as convenient because adquate supplies of good drinking water were not available, the island of Tunb was discounted for the same reason. The island of Qais was also investigated but a request for per-mission from the Persian government to transfer the station there seems to have been dropped. Lorimer, however, notes Curzon's statement that for a time there was a British military settlement on Qais.[16] The base was

[14] F.O. 371/17893 1934, Persia E3557/139/34.

[15] *Lorimer*, p. 1936. Information on the origins of the base drawn from *Lorimer*, pp 1936–48 and F.O. 371/16073 1932, Persia E2787/423/34 Correspondence Foreign Office, India Office, Tehran, plus opinion of Foreign Office Legal Advisers.

[16] *Lorimer*, p. 1942.

finally moved to Basidu at the extreme western end of the island of Qishm in the spring of 1822. An evacuation of Basidu began at the end of 1822, or in the first days of 1823 apparently because of opposition by the Shah. The Government of Bombay felt, according to Lorimer, that the continuance (of a British garrison) at a place upon either coast would sooner or later involve the British government in the politics of the adjoining countries.[17] The Foreign Office was to appreciate the force of this prescient argument many times in the next century and a half.

Basidu was reoccupied, however, in the autumn of the same year – apparently without a Persian protest – but no firm boundary for the British base was established, this was to be a cause of dispute later. In 1855 an order was signed, on behalf of the Persian Government, by Prince Tahmasp Mirza, Mu'aiyad al-Daulah entrusting the government of Qishm – and various other areas including Bandar ᶜAbbas – to the Sultan of Oman for a period of twenty years.[18] The sovereignty of the island from that date on appears to have been Persian and not to have been challenged by other claimants. When reviewing the legal situation in 1932 the British Foreign Office view was that the British right to a base was founded upon the original licence granted in 1820 by the Sultan of Oman, and that this licence was revocable at will by the Sultan until 1855–6 – the right of revocation then passing to the Shah. The British base was in fact there on Persian sufferance only, an India Office memorandum 1928 stated 'the station cannot be regarded as British territory, and an absolute claim to the concession, in the face of a desire on the part of Persia to resume it, cannot be maintained by His Majesty's Government'.[19] The Foreign Office offered to cede their rights on the island in an article in the draft Anglo-Persian treaty of February 1929.[20] On this occasion the offer had been linked with a request for a twenty-year lease for the British naval station on the neighbouring island of Hangam. This station had been established in 1911 and the right to it rested on an even flimsier basis than that of Basidu.[21]

The situation in Hangam and Basidu was much aggravated by the lack of a clear definition of British rights and by the zeal of local officials on both sides. In combination these two factors caused a series of incidents. The erection of a flagstaff by the Persian authorities at Hangam in 1928

---

[17] *Lorimer*, p. 1943.

[18] Referred to in a minute of 24 June 1932 by W. E. Beckett (F.O. 371/16073 1932 Persia E2787/423/34) and given in full in Aitchison C.U., *A Collection of Treaties Engagements and Sanads Relating to India and Neighbouring Countries* (Calcutta, 1909), (hereafter referred to as *Aitchison*), vol. xii, appendix p. CXXXIX.

[19] Quoted in F.O. 371/17893 1934, Persia E3517/139/34. Minute by G. Rendel.

[20] F.O. 371/14543 1930, Persia E2445/522/34 (Annual Report 1929).

[21] F.O. 371/17893 1934, Persia E5177/139/34. Minute by G. Rendel.

gave rise to a British complaint and in the same year a permanent British guard was established at Basidu to forestall a rumoured Persian seizure of the station.[22] As has been noticed the British Foreign Office were prepared in 1929 to renounce the shaky British rights there in return for a regularization of the position at Hangam. Local trouble was caused in 1930 by accusations of pilfering by residents from the coal dump at Hangam and in the same year flags planted by H.M.S. *Ormonde* on Qishm and Hangam for surveying purposes were viewed suspiciously by the local Persian authorities as a sign of a British desire for annexation.[23] In June 1931 the British caretaker at Basidu (Shaikh Muᶜin) refused to let the Persian *mudir* of Customs visit a boat from Umm al-Qaiwain which was anchored near the British area.[24] Trouble arose at Hangam in 1932 because of what the British Senior Naval Officer in the Gulf described as the 'perversity' of the local quarantine officer.[25] In the same year the SNO reported that the local authorities on Qishm were trying to tax the owners of certain date groves which lay in the British area; the Foreign Office believed that it was difficult to decide in which area the date groves actually lay and gave the SNO no encouragement to pursue the matter.[26] The Foreign Office once more said they were willing to yield Basidu as part of a general settlement with Persia.[27] On 20 September, however, the Persian government requested the evacuation of Hangam – for which Britain was still seeking a lease – on the grounds that it would be needed by the ships of the new Persian navy. The Admiralty registered strong objections and the official British reply, in October, was that negotiations on the draft Anglo-Persian treaty would be broken off if the demand was not withdrawn.[28] This decision may well have been one of the factors which went to influence Riza Shah's decision to cancel the APOC concession in November. On 31 July 1933 one of the ships of the newly arrived Persian Navy called at Basidu and hauled down the Union Jack. The Government of India despatched the first destroyer flotilla to the Gulf 'to restore confidence on the Arab Coast' and the Political Resident at Bushire wanted the officers of the Persian ship in question to raise the flag and then for the ship to salute it. The British Minister at Tehran received an immediate official disavowal of the action by the Persian government who referred to excessive local zeal.[29] This quality seems to have been in

[22] F.O. 371/13799 1929, Persia E3676/3676/34 (Annual Report 1928).
[23] F.O. 371/15356 1931, Persia E3067/3067/34 (Annual Report 1930).
[24] F.O. 371/16077 1932, Persia E3354/3354/34 (Annual Report 1931).
[25] F.O. 371/16967 1933, Persia E2439/2439/34 (Annual Report 1932).
[26] F.O. 371/16073 1932, Persia E423/423/34.
[27] F.O. 371/16073 1932, Persia E1320/423/34.
[28] F.O. 371/16967 1933, Persia E2439/2439/34 (Annual Report 1932).
[29] F.O. 371/17909 1934, Persia E1620/1620/34 (Annual Report 1933).

abundant supply for when on 9 October the Persian *mudir* of Customs endeavoured to go on board a Persian dhow anchored near the British area he was promptly taken on board H.M.S. *Lupin* and removed to Bandar ᶜAbbas. This time it was the Persians' turn to complain and the Foreign Office regretted the impolitic arrest and noted the high level of Persian feeling on this matter[30] and managed to get the British guard withdrawn from the island.[31]

By the end of 1933 the Persian government was actively seeking permanent British withdrawal from these two areas, and with ships at its disposal, was endeavouring to assert sovereignty. The Government of India had grave reservations about the disastrous effects on British prestige if withdrawal took place. The Admiralty began to assert the need for both stations – previously it had agreed to give up Basidu if Hangam could be secured. The fact that the APOC had begun to prospect for oil on the island of Qishm may have had an influence on Admiralty thinking. The Foreign Office quite simply sought evacuation. The lesson it drew from previous events was that Hangam and Basidu were hostages in Persian hands; the British position was, in law, very weak; and as the British occupation of the stations was not continuous, it would be possible for the Persian government to send in forces to seize the areas while British ships were absent and thus any British attempt to reassert rights might have to be forceful. The Foreign Office, using the language of the India Office, argued that British prestige in the Gulf would suffer much more if British forces were compelled to leave rather than evacuating voluntarily.[32] In April a Foreign Office minute refers to 'the muddle-handed die hards of the Admiralty',[33] but by the middle of October the Admiralty view had changed and at a meeting of the Ministerial Middle East Sub-Committee of the Committee of Imperial Defence on 12 October 1934 the agreement was reached on the evacuation of Hangam and Basidu, the establishment of bases at Bahrain and Khaur al-Quwaiᶜ was accepted as an alternative.[34] Among the factors influencing Admiralty thinking was the announcement, in May 1934, of large oil strikes on the island of Bahrain.[35] The Foreign Office regarded the decision to withdraw as one which 'would extricate us from our present untenable position, remove the two most valuable hostages which the

[30] F.O. 371/16969 1933, Persia E7470/3062/34.

[31] F.O. 371/17909 1934, Persia E1620/1620/34 (Annual Report 1933).

[32] F.O. 371/17893 1934, Persia E3037/139/34. Minutes of Middle East (Official) Sub-Committee of the Committee of Imperial Defence.

[33] F.O. 371/17893 1934, Persia E2951/139/34.

[34] F.O. 371/17895 1934, Persia E6456/139/34. Minutes of Middle East (Ministerial) Sub-Committee of the Committee of Imperial Defence.

[35] F.O. 371/18995 1935, Persia E1606/1606/34 (Annual Report 1934).

Persians at present hold from us and free us from continued liability to blackmail'.[36]

The Foreign Office view that the Persian Government attached great importance to the issue of Hangam and Basidu was apparently correct. The evacuation of the two islands was completed by 5 April and 11 April 1935 respectively; in early May the Persian navy established small detachments there. By the end of the year the British Minister in Tehran could report that 'the Gulf had lost its position as the British-Persian "storm centre"'.[37] The transfer of the radio stations belonging to Cable and Wireless Ltd. at Hangam, Chahbahar and Jask was also agreed upon in 1935 but the evacuation of the station at Jask was delayed, at Persian request, until various connecting lines, to Bandar ᶜAbbas had been laid. By the end of the year therefore several of the more pressing claims of the Persian Government in the Gulf had been met. It should be noted that these claims were all directed at Britain, they were all designed to remove evidence of past inferiority and weakness. In fact the attitude of the Government of Persia to the Gulf was, at this time, but one aspect of the general policy of self-assertion. The Foreign Office was better disposed to recognize this than were other departments of the British Government, thus the Foreign Office recognized the link between the demand in September 1932 for the evacuation of Hangam and the cancellation of the APOC concession in November of the same year.[38] Other Persian demands – for the cancellation of a debt of £1,510,000 incurred during the First World War and for the re-opening of the Zahidan railway – were also received favourably by the Foreign Office. The Persian case regarding the loan was that the sums advanced to Persia during and immediately after the war were spent in British and not Persian interests – they should therefore be seen as a subsidy and part of British war expenditure. The Foreign Office admitted that 'there is a good deal to be said for this view'[39] particularly as interest on the pre-war Persian debt of £490,000 was paid regularly and the capital finally repaid in June 1933. (It was finally agreed by the British Government that the war debt could be waived if the Persian Government was to sign a general Anglo-Persian Agreement.)[40] The Foreign Office also proved less sensitive than the Admiralty in the question of Persian rights to search ships for evidence of gun running. In the past this had been a theoretical matter but the presence of the new Persian navy made it a live issue as will be seen in a later part of this

[36] Minute by G. Rendel on E6456/139/34 F.O. 371/17895 1934, Persia.

[37] F.O. 371/20052 1936, Persia E1147/1147/34 (Annual Report 1935).

[38] F.O. 371/16088 1932, Persia E6258/3880/34.

[39] F.O. 371/17892 1934, Persia E7322/1329/34 and F.O. 371/17893 1934, Persia E5648 139/34.

[40] F.O. 371/17892 1934, Persia E7322/1329/34.

paper. Generally speaking in the late 1920s and 1930s the British Foreign Office was prepared to recognize certain Persian rights in the Gulf – rights that were being increasingly sought by a strengthened and independent Persian ruler. The British departments with an older responsibility for the Gulf were less prepared to accept this self assertion by Riza Shah – difficulties were almost inevitable when Persian pride was confronted with the Government of India's preoccupation with 'British prestige'.

The general situation at this time is of great importance for the Gulf as a whole. By May 1934 the Foreign Office had abandoned hopes of a general Treaty settlement with Persia. A long memorandum of May 1934[41] speaks of the value of Persia as a bulwark for India against Russia and as a vital source of oil supplies, and of the Gulf as a focus of mercantile and communications interests: the need according to the author of the memorandum was not to temporize as the Government of India wished, but to accept the fact that Persia was no longer in its nineteenth-century state of weakness but was demanding treatment on grounds of nominal equality. The evacuation from Hangam and Basidu would help greatly to regularize relations, for it was believed that although Persian policy was 'nationalist and difficult',[42] there was no desire in Tehran for a real quarrel with Britain as such a quarrel could put Persia at Russian mercy. It is significant to note, however, that the Foreign Office attitude to the Arab side of the Gulf was not cast in a similar mould although withdrawal from Persian territory was felt desirable but in return 'an unassailable position on the Arabian side of the Gulf' was essential.[43] On this point the views of Foreign Office, Government of India and the Admiralty coincided. The transfer to Bahrain was advocated by the Foreign Office as the final and definitive answer to Persian 'pretensions' there. Although the Foreign Office desired to strengthen Persia as a barrier to Russia they also sought a strong British presence in the Gulf to protect interests there – now that the weak position over Hangam and Basidu had been abandoned it was possible to take the initiative and resist further Persian claims. The move to establish a firmer British hold on the Arabian coast had been argued in 1931 and 1932 when the Persian Government had demanded the cancellation of the 1928 agreement which gave Imperial Airways the right to fly over and land at certain specified points in Southern Persia as part of the service to India. The alternative route, via the Arabian coast, was used by the RAF but was recognized as more expensive, suitable landing grounds were fewer, and it was believed that flying boats – which Imperial Airways did not possess – might be the only form of aircraft able to fly

[41] F.O. 371/17893 1934, Persia E3557/139/34. Memorandum by G. Rendel.
[42] *Ibid.*, E5177/139/34. Second memorandum by G. Rendel.
[43] F.O. 371/17893 1934, Persia E3596/139/34.

the route.[44] In fact the Arabian route was established with relatively little difficulty at the end of 1932 and this was quoted, in 1935, as a further reason for establishing more extensive British control of the Arabian coast.

An interesting piece of evidence for this firmer Foreign Office line is revealed by answers given in reply to questions by the Board of Trade and the Customs and Excise Authorities about the status of the island of Abu Musa. Small amounts of iron ore were imported by Britain from this island and in the early months of 1935 the issue was raised whether this island was classed as a 'territory under His Majesty's protection' for the purposes of deciding the level of import duty. If the ore came from such a territory it was admitted duty free – otherwise the charge was 10 per cent *ad valorem*. In February 1935 the Foreign Office was inclined to believe that although the island was regarded as belonging to the Shaikh of Sharjah and ultimate international responsibility for the shaikhdoms of the Trucial Coast lay with His Majesty's Government, the island could not be regarded as falling within the British Empire as such a ruling would give rise to renewed Persian claims. By April 1936, however, when the same issue was raised again the Foreign Office regretted its earlier decision and sought to reverse it. The evacuation from Hangam and Basidu had freed British hands in the Gulf and now, therefore, there was a much greater willingness on the part of the Foreign Office to support the idea that the island was a territory 'under His Majesty's protection'.[45]

The case of Tunb and Abu Musa also serves as an example of the many factors which must be studied in any survey of events in the Gulf region. The history of the islands and their ownership was by no means indisputably clear, their value was a matter of speculation and in the early 1930s personal initiatives by the local officials often played a more important role in shaping events than did the deliberations of remote governments. One series of Foreign Office memoranda gives some indication of the apparent ownership of the islands in the eighteenth and nineteenth centuries.[46] (In these documents the two islands referred to are Tunb and Abu Musa; in fact there is a third island, Nabiyu Tunb, about seven miles west of Tunb, but for ownership purposes this appears never to have been treated separately from Tunb.) The ownership of the islands is very closely linked with the internal family history of the Qawasimi (Jowasimi). This family seems to have become established as a ruling family on the Arabian coast of the Gulf in the early eighteenth century.

[44] F.O. 371/16077 1932, Persia E3354/3354/34 (Annual Report 1931).

[45] F.O. 371/19977 1936, Arabia E2463/2463/91.

[46] See F.O. 371/18901 1935, Arabia E270/4/91, E970/4/91, E1986/4/91, E2336/4/91, and F.O. 371/17827 1934, Arabia E5652/3283/91.

When the islands were added to their dominion is uncertain. The ruler is variously described as the Shaikh of Sharjah and the Shaikh of Ras al-Khaimah. In the eighteenth century Ras al-Khaimah was apparently the more important centre of power. By the mid-eighteenth century one branch of the family had established itself at Lingeh and ruled over the islands of Tunb, Abu Musa and Sirri together with part of the Persian mainland as deputy for the principal shaikh of the family who had his centre of power on the Arabian coast. This extension of power across the Gulf was apparently undertaken on the invitation of the Persian Governor of Bandar ᶜAbbas and Hormuz who sought help against neighbouring chieftains. During the reign of Karim Khan the power of the Persian monarchy was reasserted in the Gulf and the Qawasimi were certainly driven from Persia and probably from the islands mentioned in about 1767 and 1768. By the end of 1780 the Qawasimi had returned (Karim Khan died in 1779 and Persian control of the Gulf coast was lost) to their former holdings which they maintained for a century as an Arab principality. By 1880 the control of the central Persian government was once more beginning to be established on the Gulf coast and the Qawasimi shaikh, who acted as Governor of Lingeh, paid tribute to the central authorities and became a Persian subject. It would appear that the shaikh on the Persian coast also ruled Abu Musa, Tunb and Sirri throughout this period and that when he became Persian vassal he ruled as such on both the mainland and over the islands. In 1887 the Persian Government expelled the shaikh from the Persian coast and also from the island of Sirri. A British War Office map of 1888 also showed the islands of Tunb and Abu Musa as Persian possessions but despite various attempts, effective Persian control over these islands was never established and they remained Qawasimi possessions.

The Qawasimi family on the Arabian coast had meanwhile split into at least two branches, one ruling in Sharjah and the other in Ras al-Khaimah. Abu Musa came under the rule of the former shaikh and Tunb under the latter. From 1900 to about 1920 the two shaikhdoms were effectively united under the rule of Shaikh Saqar ibn Khalid of Sharjah who gave permission in 1912 for the Government of India to erect a lighthouse on Tunb. In 1920 the two shaikhdoms became separated again and the ownership of the islands was divided as before. In 1921 the separation of the two shaikhdoms was recognized officially by the Government of India.

Problems arose in the late 1920s as the Persian Government began to suspect that Tunb, which was much nearer to the Persian coast than Abu Musa, was being used as a base for the smuggling of goods into Persia. (The general importance of smuggling in the Gulf at this period will be discussed below.) In May 1928 a verbal agreement was reached with the

Persian Government to recognize the *status quo* – Sirri as a Persian island, the other two as Arab islands.[47] This agreement was incorporated into the draft-treaty of 1929. In 1930, however, the refusal of the British Government to consider a Persian claim to Tunb was used as the occasion for the Persian Government to break off negotiations on the draft treaty. The British Minister in Tehran reported that the Persian military were thoroughly nationalistic and any settlement would have to provide some element of territorial acquisition.[48] In October 1930 Taimurtash offered to abandon the Persian claim to Abu Musa if the claim to Tunb was acknowledged.[49] An attempt was made to obtain a lease of Tunb for the Persians from the Shaikh of Ras al-Khaimah. The Political Resident pointed out the difficulties in a letter to the Government of India of 6 January 1931[50] – the Shaikh of Ras al-Khaimah was, in the Residents opinion, 'the most difficult of the Trucial shaikhs to deal with'; if he were to receive any rent for the island this sum of money would be small and would moreover have to be shared among the family and tribe in keeping with the tradition of land ownership in common. Finally the Arabs entertained a deep suspicion of the Persians and any expression of desire for the island by the Persians would serve to deepen this suspicion and strengthen the shaikhs' determination to retain possession. The usual order, that any such deal would undermine Arab confidence in Britain completed the list of objections. The Foreign Office, however, was pressing for a general settlement with Persia and believed that a lease to Persia would satisfy Persian opinion while at the same time serving as a recognition by Persia of the shaikh's sovereignty over the island.[51] A minor flurry was caused in the Foreign Office when a telegram came in reporting the presence of a 'garrison' belonging to the shaikh on the island. This was later revealed as a decoding error and the correct word was 'garden' – even this harmless report was later proved to be untrue!

The shaikh was approached by the Political Resident as to the conditions on which he would be prepared to lease the island to Persia. A Foreign Office hope 'that the conditions will be reasonable'[52] was disappointed on 11 May 1931; the stipulations were in fact so stringent and comprehensive as to nullify the value of the lease to the Persians for they satisfied neither *amour propre* – the Qawasimi flag would have continued to fly and the Persian Government would have had little control over the inhabitants – nor the desire to prevent Tunb being used as a smuggling

[47] F.O. 371/13799 1929, Persia E3676/3676/34 (Annual Report 1928).
[48] F.O. 371/15356 1931, Persia E3067/3067/34 (Annual Report 1930).
[49] F.O. 371/15276 1931, Arabia E390/280/91 (enclosure 1).
[50] *Ibid.*, E280/280/91.
[51] *Ibid.*, E390/280/91.
[52] *Ibid.*, E2215/280/91.

centre – article III would have prevented Tunb being used as a base for Persian ships in search of Arab smugglers.[53] By the time this reply was received Anglo-Persian Treaty negotiations had been suspended, but the Foreign Office regretted the stringency of the conditions (which were never put to the Persian Government) and when the issue was raised again in the autumn of 1933 the view was expressed in a Foreign Office minute that the Political Resident might not have pressed the shaikh sufficiently to make the conditions acceptable.[54]

In 1933 Tunb was again an issue of controversy. The Persian Government had begun to make plans for taking over the administration of the lights and buoys on the Persian side of the Gulf, most of these lights were administered by the Persian Gulf lighting service which was responsible to the Government of India. This policy received Foreign Office acquiescence but guarded hostility from the Government of India and the Admiralty – the former refused to believe that the Persian Government was sufficiently competent to maintain adequate lights.[55] (The senior Persian Naval Officer admitted privately in 1935 that the motive behind the Persian actions was one of prestige.[56])

In pursuit of the take-over policy the Persian Government hired the services of a French expert to survey the lights on Persian territory in the summer of 1933. A visit by this official to the island of Tunb on 23 July resulted in a British protest and a Persian apology.[57] Events in September, however, had a much more devious aspect.

The Political Resident in the Gulf reported in September 1933 that the Senior Naval Officer, at a meeting with the Shaikh of Ras al-Khaimah, had been informed that the shaikh had received a letter from Tehran requesting a lease of Tunb for the Persian Government.[58] The Political Resident and the Government of India wanted the shaikh to be reminded of his commitments under the treaty of 1892 – article I of which said 'I will on no account enter into any agreement or correspondence with any power other than the British Government', article III stating 'I will on no account cede, sell, mortgage or otherwise give for occupation any part of my territory save to the British Government'.[59] The Foreign Office agreed that a protest should be made about communications that were direct between the Persian Government and the shaikh but felt that reference to article III might be undesirable as the British Government

[53] *Ibid.*, E2812/280/91.
[54] F.O. 371/16852 1933, Arabia E5775/3263/91.
[55] F.O. 371/21889 1938, Persia E153/27/34.
[56] F.O. 371/20052 1936, Persia E1147/1147/34 (Annual Report 1935).
[57] F.O. 371/16969 1933, Persia E4778/3062/34.
[58] F.O. 371/16852 1933, Arabia E5697/3263/91.
[59] *Aitchison*, vol. xii, p. 185.

had already sought a lease for the Persians. In a minute the Foreign Office again recorded a hope that a long lease might be arranged through the proper channels but suspected that the present case was merely a bluff by the shaikh.[60] The Senior Naval Officer was instructed to look into the matter further; he found that the shaikh was unwilling to meet him and he too began to suspect a bluff.[61] This was confirmed in mid-November when the Political Resident reported that no such letter existed and that the story had been a device aimed at alarming the British and prompting them to lease the island themselves – thus providing revenue for the shaikh.[62] (No rent was paid by the Government of India for the lighthouse on the island.) The Foreign Office saw this as an example of the way in which officials in the Gulf were deceived by local Arab rulers who were adept at inventing crimes in the hope of stiffening the British attitude to the Persians.[63] It should be remembered that at the end of 1933 the Foreign Office was still seeking a general agreement with Persia and was loath to take any action while Hangam and Basidu were still unsettled issues.

In September 1934 decisive action was taken, however, following visits by two ships from the Persian Navy to Tunb in late August and early September.[64] Orders were issued to the Senior Naval Officer reminding him of the instructions of 15 November 1928 that any attempt by the Persians to occupy Tunb might have to be resisted by force in the last resort. The British Minister in Tehran reminded the Persian Government of the verbal agreement of 1928 to maintain the *status quo* and informed him of the renewed instructions issued to the British Senior Naval Officer.[65] These solemn inter-governmental warnings were soon overtaken by local events in the Gulf.

The Commander in Chief Persian Gulf reported to the Admiralty on 31 December 1934 that a visit by H.M.S. *Bideford* to Tunb had revealed the fact that the Shaikh of Ras al-Khaimah had withdrawn his flag and it was rumoured that he was in communication with the Persian authorities over a lease of the island to them.[66] The Foreign Office were somewhat alarmed by this and feared that Britain would look rather foolish if after making official protests on behalf of the Shaikh she now allowed this voluntary – and locally organized – transfer.[67] At the worst the Foreign

[60] F.O. 371/16969 1933, Arabia E5697/3263/91.
[61] *Ibid.*, E7139/3263/91.
[62] *Ibid.*, E7421/3263/91.
[63] *Ibid.*, E7139/3263/91.
[64] F.O. 371/18995 1935, Persia E1606/1606/34 (Annual Report 1934).
[65] F.O. 371/17895 1934, Persia E6083/139/34.
[66] F.O. 371/18901 1935, Arabia E4/4/91.
[67] *Ibid.*, E4/4/91 (minutes).

Office were prepared for His Majesty's Government to depose the shaikh on the grounds of treason in handing over national property.[68] This somewhat extreme policy was not seriously considered but the idea of hoisting a British flag on the island was given much thought. It was believed to be better to have the island under direct British control rather than in the hands of an 'unreliable' shaikh – or in the hands of the Persians without any promise of a general Anglo-Persian Treaty.[69] On 5 January the Political Resident reported that the shaikh's motives, as in September 1933, were probably pecuniary – his aim was to receive a rent for the lighthouse similar to that received by his relative the Shaikh of Sharjah for the British aerodrome on his territory.[70] The Shaikh of Sharjah was more than willing to take over Tunb reported the Political Resident.[71] A lengthy inter-departmental correspondence followed[72] on the earlier history of the ownership of Tunb in which it was argued that when the branch of the Qawasimi family became established for the second time on the Persian coast, and ultimately became vassals of the Persian Government, they held Tunb, Abu Musa (and presumably Sirri) under a different title than that by which they ruled on the mainland. In Persia proper the particular Qawasimi shaikh ruled as a tribute-paying vassal from about 1880 to 1887 but with respect to the islands he paid no tribute but ruled as a deputy of the leading Qawasimi shaikh on the Arabian Coast. By this argument there had been no Persian sovereignty exercised over Tunb and Abu Musa since before 1750. This argument was adopted by the Political Resident and the Government of India; the Foreign Office, however, believed that the shaikh on the Persian Coast may well have acted as a Persian vassal, between 1880 and 1887, over the islands as well as over the mainland.

Apart from these complex and inconclusive arguments, policy had to be shaped. The Political Resident reported on 22 January 1935 that the Shaikh of Ras al-Khaimah had not actually offered the island to the Persians but was acting in the belief that Britain would step in and lease the island.[73] The Foreign Office was relieved to hear of the absence of a Persian intrigue and expressed themselves as none too pleased with the actions of the Shaikh whose previous attempts to maintain his sovereignty over the island had frustrated the attempts at an Anglo-Persian settlement. This feeling of frustration found heartfelt expression in a minute[74] of

[68] *Ibid.*, E57/4/91.
[69] *Ibid.*, E57/4/91.
[70] *Ibid.*, E454/4/91.
[71] *Ibid.*, E454/4/91.
[72] See documents under reference 46 above.
[73] F.O. 371/18901 1935, Arabia E531/4/91.
[74] *Ibid.*

31 January. After recording dismay at the shaikh's past activity G. Rendel wrote:

'It looks to me rather as though this miserable little island were becoming little more than an empty symbol. If on the other hand the island *has* the slightest value it seems that we have an extraordinarily favourable opportunity to acquire it for ourselves. Most of our troubles on the Persian Gulf are due to the fact that we have always hesitated to take such opportunities in the past, and, instead of annexing places like Hangam, Bahrein and even Muscat, when it would have been easy, and indeed almost laudable to do so, we have embarked on the most complicated and peculiar treaty arrangements which were intended to give us the advantages of annexation without its responsibilities, but which are in danger of producing the opposite result and landing us with responsibilities but not its compensations. . . . My feeling therefore is that if Tunb is worth anything we should do much better to take it and that if it is worth nothing it is foolish to let it affect our policy on major issues; and that in any case the Shaikh of Ras al-Khaima has shown no real interest in it and has no further claim on us to protect his rights over the island unless we are quite sure that it is in our own ultimate interest to do so.'

Rumours of activity by Persian officials in the Gulf to take over the island added a note of urgency to the discussions[75] in early February and H M S. *Fowey* was ordered to remain at Tunb until further notice. The Foreign Office did not believe Tehran to be implicated[76] but felt that the island could not be allowed to continue for long without someone exercising sovereignty over it. The India Office preferred the island to go to Sharjah as a piece of Qawasimi tribal property but were firmly opposed to any suggestion that the island might end up in Persian hands.[77] The Minister in Tehran believed that the Tunb issue would be revived in any future Anglo-Persian negotiations and for this reason British control over it should not be weakened – he believed, however, that Tehran was by no means involved in the current events as the warning over Tunb of September 1934 had had a significant deterrent effect.[78] Many views were expressed at the meeting of the Committee of Imperial Defence on 8 March 1935.[79] The Admiralty had no use for the island but was opposed to any hint of Persian control other than the need for the lighthouse (a later Admiralty report of 31 July said Tunb might be used as a

[75] *Ibid.*, E712/4/91.
[76] *Ibid.*
[77] *Ibid.*, E814/4/91.
[78] *Ibid.*, E923/4/91.
[79] *Ibid.*, E11171/4/91.

recreational centre for the Navy and the possibility of a golf course and football fields was mentioned.)[80] The Air Ministry had no use for the island either. The India Office was alarmed by the idea of a British claim – which it was believed would do untold damage to Arab confidence – and wanted the Shaikh of Sharjah to accept responsibility for the island. The Foreign Office view was, at this stage, one of preserving the island as a bargaining counter against the Persians – when it was seen that the island was of no real value the idea of a British bid was rapidly dropped. (It does not appear that the question of oil resources existing near the island was raised by any of the departments.)

Finally it was agreed that the Shaikh of Ras al-Khaimah should be given ten days to re-raise his flag and that he should be told that failure to do so would result in the transfer of the island to Sharjah.[81] The shaikh complied with the wishes of the British Government and rehoisted the flag on Tunb on 10 April.[82] In May the issue of the local Persian intrigue was uncovered finally when the Senior Naval Officer sent to the British Minister in Tehran a copy of a letter addressed to the headman of Tunb from the Governor of Bandar ʿAbbas.[83] This letter had included three copies of 'the esteemed decree of His Imperial Majesty relating to elections for the tenth period of the Majlis for immediate circulation'. There was no evidence to show that the Persian Government was behind the manoeuvre and the Foreign Office view was that as this was a purely local initiative and as the papers in question had been acquired by the British authorities in an unusual manner an official protest was unnecessary and impossible.[84] Apart from a Persian claim to build a separate lighthouse on Tunb in 1938[85] the island never again figured prominently in Persian policy until the early 1960s by which time external conditions had changed greatly.

When Persian interest in these islands revived the factors affecting the situation were very different. No longer was the primary motivating force behind the Persian Government's Gulf policy a desire for self assertion *vis-à-vis* Britain but rather the recognition that well established Persian interests could suffer very greatly if the Gulf were ever to be closed to Persian shipping. The primary factors now were not so much pride and *amour propre* as the recognition of vital defence interests. As was noted earlier, from the early 1960s Persia began to turn her eyes increasingly to the need for military forces capable of acting in the Gulf area. The announcement of the withdrawal of British forces from the area gave an

[80] *Ibid.*, E4701/4/91.
[81] *Ibid.*, E1857/4/91.
[82] *Ibid.*, E2382/4/91.
[83] *Ibid.*, E3204/4/91.
[84] *Ibid.*
[85] F.O. 371/21889 1938, Persia E7841/27/34.

added intensity to this quest for security. Iran was becoming a well-equipped – indeed the dominant – local power but the problem remained of certain key areas which she did not control. In February 1968 urgent discussions took place between Iran and Britain soon after the decision to withdraw British forces had been announced. The topic of these discussions was the islands of Tunb, Nabiyu Tunb and Abu Musa. The first two still belonged to the Shaikh of Ras al-Khaimah and the third to the Shaikh of Sharjah. The significance of the islands now lay in the fact that should they be fortified they would be capable of blocking the narrow Strait of Hormuz to shipping. The Persian aim was to prevent this from happening and their case was for a redivision of the islands' ownership on the lines of the agreements reached elsewhere on the Gulf for oil exploration purposes. The Iranian contention was that division of the area by a line equidistant from the coast lines of the Arab and Persian shores would place two of the islands (Tunb and Nabiyu Tunb) under Persian control. Thus their defence needs would be met. There is no evidence available of what settlement, if any, has yet been reached on this issue.

The changed importance attached to Tunb and Abu Musa by the Persian Government is but one example of far-reaching alterations in the many factors which affect the Gulf. The greatest of these changes has probably been the discovery of under-sea oil and the introduction of new methods for its exploration and subsequent exploitation. Coupled with this has been the gradual emergence of new principles of international law governing the ownership of such resources – and for specific geographical reasons the Gulf has been an area of peculiar complexity. The existence of offshore oil supplies had been recognized as geologically possible for a long time before the necessary techniques for exploitation became available. Several of the oil concessions granted in the 1920s and 1930s had included allocated areas within the territorial waters of the country. The seeds of difficulty existed over the Persian Law, establishing a territorial waters limit of six miles offshore, passed by the Majlis on 19 July 1934.[86] The British Government stated at the time that they could not recognize such a limit, neither could they recognize the Persian claim for a single belt of territorial waters to embrace a given group of islands – each island must, it was stated, stand on its own. At the time the acknowledged reason behind the declaration was to aid the Persian attempt to reduce smuggling and this motive was not questioned by the British Government. There was at the time no mention of oil claims, and even when the Persian territorial waters limit was extended to twelve miles, by the law of 17 April 1959, no specific reference to oil was made.

[86] F.O. 371/18995 1935, Persia E1606/1606/34 (Annual Report 1934) and F.O. 371/16969 1933, Persia E5214/3062/34.

In 1949 the King of Saudi Arabia and the nine shaikhs of the Arab Coast issued separate statements claiming that the sea-bed and sub-soil lying beneath the high seas of the Persian Gulf belonged to them subject to the drawing of future boundaries. In this matter the rulers were, as Sir R. Hay has pointed out,[87] following the 1945 declaration of President Truman which claimed for the United States of America the natural resources of the sea-bed and sub-soil of the continental shelf beneath the high seas but contiguous to the coasts of the USA. The problem in the Gulf was that the continental shelf was continuous from one coast to the other. The waters of the Gulf are shallow, rarely over fifty fathoms, and the internationally accepted depth for the edge of the continental shelf is 100 fathoms. Thus the whole of the floor of the Gulf was open to conflicting claims which were pressed vigorously in the late 1950s and early 1960s, as oil drilling at such depths became a viable proposition. Settlements in other areas of the world with similar problems (e.g. the North Sea) have generally taken the form of drawing a median line between the two coasts. The problem in the Gulf was complicated, however, by the existence of many islands for which the owner countries demanded treatment as if they were an integral part of the mainland. Thus the Persian Government in its negotiations with the Kuwait and Saudi Arabian governments demanded that the median line should be drawn equidistant between the island of Kharg and the Arabian shore and not equidistant between the two coastlines. As the island of Kharg is over twenty miles off the Persian coast the arrangement was much to the Persian advantage (it should be noted that the richest area of under-water oil lies nearer to the Arabian coast). In return for this concession the Persian Government had to grant similar status, in the agreement of January 1968, to the Kuwaiti island of Failakah about ten miles off the Kuwait shore. Generally speaking islands have not been included as an integral part of the coast for the purposes of determining the base line for median division but their potential value in such claims gave a new value to often very barren pieces of rock over which previously no ownership at all had been effectively exercised or claimed.

The conflict over sea-bed division has been most intense in the Northern Gulf where the oil potentiality is greater. Negotiations began in July 1963 after the Iraq government had been dismayed by an Iranian offer of 40,000 square kilometres of sea-bed for tender as an oil concession area. Talks were pursued in Geneva, Copenhagen and Tehran up to 1966

[87] Sir R. Hay, 'The Persian Gulf States and their Boundary Problems' in *Geographical Journal* 1954, pp. 433–45. On the legal problems involved in determining submarine boundaries in the Gulf see Husain M. al-Baharna, *The Legal Status of the Arabian Gulf States* (Manchester 1968), chap. 17.

when a provisional Saudi Arabian–Persian agreement was initialled. A modified version of this – more favourable to the Persians – was finally signed in October 1968. A Kuwaiti–Persian agreement was reached in January 1968 but was immediately rejected by Iraq who has so far not come to an agreement with either Iran or Kuwait. There remains therefore the possibility of future disputes at the head of the Gulf.

The Saudi Arabian–Persian agreement of 1968 settled an issue that had been discussed in the late 1930s. In 1936 the British Political Resident in the Gulf raised, apparently with no specific prompting from either Simla or London, the question of the ownership of the ⁏Arabi and Farsi islands.[88] Linguistic evidence would appear to resolve the issue immediately but as with all Gulf problems the complexities were great. These islands had been discussed in 1929[89] together with the islands of Harqus and al-Qiran. At that time the Air Ministry had expressed an interest in them but the development of longer range aircraft meant that by 1936 the Air Ministry saw no real use for these islands.[90] The existence of oil on the islands had been recognized as early as 1914 but apparently this information was known only to the British Government.[91] The Foreign Office view in 1936 was one of seeking to find a settlement on the ownership of the islands such that the ultimate supply of oil would be available to Britain. If Persia were to take two of the islands, as had been suggested in 1929, the Anglo-Iranian Oil Company would have the right, under the 1933 agreement, to include them in its 100,000-square-mile concession, the limits of which had to be fixed by the Company before 31 December 1938.[92] In November 1936 the Political Resident reported that the Shaikh of Kuwait had claims to ⁏Arabi and Farsi, on grounds of proximity he could claim Harqus while al-Qiran appeared to be a *res nullius* and therefore available for the first comer.[93] The Political Resident suggested that the Shaikh of Kuwait should be prompted to hoist his flag over these islands. A long correspondence followed on the likely ownership of some forty miscellaneous Gulf islands[94] but ⁏Arabi and Farsi were the only ones to cause much comment. This was because they lay farther out in the Gulf than did the others and had potential use as landing grounds and, more importantly, as likely sources of oil. Local opinion – both native and British – appeared to regard the islands as Kuwaiti property.[95]

[88] F.O. 371/19979 1936, Arabia E2902/2902/91.
[89] F.O. 371/13721 1929, Arabia E401/52/91.
[90] F.O. 371/19979 1936, Arabia E4022/2902/91.
[91] *Ibid.*, E4022/2902/91.
[92] *Ibid.*, E4022/2902/91.
[93] F.O. 371/20775 1937, Arabia E184/184/91.
[94] Summary given F.O. 371/20775 1937, Arabia E7330/184/91.
[95] F.O. 371/20775 1937, Arabia E941/184/91.

The Admiralty had no desire for direct annexation by Britain but was not happy about the prospect of Persian ownership. The Air Ministry were likewise opposed to Persian control as flying boats made use of Harqus as a navigational check when flying from Bahrain to Basra.[96] The Foreign Office reaction was to let sleeping dogs lie as it was believed that any overt attempt by the Shaikh of Kuwait to assert sovereignty would evoke both Persian and Saudi Arabian protests – and possibly retaliation elsewhere in the Gulf. It was admitted that neither Persia nor Saudi Arabia had exercised effective control over any of the islands but neither had Kuwait. The Foreign Office noted that when the Shaikh of Bahrain had erected a small cairn on one of the small islands of the Hawar group, the Saudi Arabian government had made a swift and unexpected protest.[97] On these grounds a Foreign Office minute hoped 'the Political Resident would leave these islands alone'.[98]

The issue of oil was present, however, and this meant Admiralty interest. The need, according to the Admiralty, was to see that the islands did not fall into such hands as would threaten the oil supply in time of difficulty.[99] It did not matter if the exploiting company was British or American owned – what counted was the attitude of the local ruler. For this reason the Admiralty preferred Kuwaiti ownership or failing that Saudi Arabian. Persian ownership was to be ruled out. The Foreign Office, in view of problems elsewhere in the world, did not feel that the islands were worth a real dispute as this was not the time 'to provoke unnecessarily even a second-rate power like Persia'.[100] The Petroleum Department too, in view of the recent nationalization of the oil companies in Mexico, was anxious not to provoke the Persian Government to similar action.[101] (It should be noted that in 1937 Mexico, which produced more oil than Iraq, was Britain's second largest supplier.)

When it was pointed out to the Political Resident that the islands lay a long way from the Kuwaiti shore, he replied, interestingly, that the Kuwaitis regarded their rightful frontiers as those established by the Anglo-Turkish Convention of 1913 and although territory had been lost since then to Saudi Arabia these islands lay opposite what they believed was rightfully Kuwaiti territory.[102] The Political Agent in Kuwait also informed the India Office that the islands were visited in the late summer and early autumn by sailors from the Oman coast who came to catch

[96] *Ibid.*, E2277/184/91.
[97] *Ibid.*, E2399/184/91.
[98] F.O. 371/21831 1938, Arabia E7220/1154/91.
[99] *Ibid.*, E1154/1154/91.
[100] *Ibid.*, E1154/1154/91.
[101] *Ibid.*, E2404/1154/91.
[102] *Ibid.*, E2109/1154/91.

sharks and turtles which they then sold in Basra before returning home with a cargo of dates. The islands were also used by Kuwaiti fishermen. For these reasons any attempt to let the islands fall under Persian rule would result, inevitably, in a significant loss of British prestige.[103]

It was finally agreed in June 1938 that the issue should be allowed to rest on the grounds that any decisive move by the Shaikh of Kuwait might provoke undesirable reactions by Saudi Arabia and/or Persia. A Foreign Office minute reflected the difference between local and central opinion.[104] In the Foreign Office view, the whole issue was begun by the local British authorities, and it was to be doubted whether local native opinion had ever even considered the issue of ownership until such enquiries began. The man on the spot saw the issue as one of prestige but in London it appeared as an unnecessarily distracting nuisance. It is more than likely that some of the local initiatives by Persian officials raised similar sentiments in Tehran.

The issue of Persian claims to Bahrain is one on which much has been written[105] and the problem will be touched upon only lightly here. The claim has often been used as a device by the Persian Government for releasing internal political pressures but it has rarely been pursued in a sustained manner with any degree of seriousness. The Persian control of the island ceased in 1783 when the ᶜUtubi Arabs under the Al Khalifah shaikhs seized the island. The claim of the Persian Government to Bahrain was intermittently pressed, however, even when the power to assert the claim was sadly lacking. Thus in January 1906 the British Chargé d'Affaires in Tehran, Mr Grant Duff, received a protest from the Persian authorities about illegal interference with Persian territory and 'the compromising of Persian rights over ancient subjects'.[106] The immediate cause of the protest seems to have been a series of attacks made by Arabs on Persian traders in Bahrain during the winter of 1904–5. The real cause, however, in Grant Duff's view, was the Shah's desire to emulate Japan and show that Persia too could defy a European power.[107] Such aspirations, the British representative said, were not to be treated seriously.

During the reign of Riza Shah protests were again made particularly

[103] *Ibid.*, E2109/1154/91.
[104] *Ibid.*, E3333/1154/91.
[105] See Majid Khadduri, 'Iran's Claim to the Sovereignty of Bahrayn', in *American Journal of International Law* (1951), pp. 631–47; J. H. D. Bellgrave, 'A Brief Survey of the History of the Bahrein Islands' in *Journal of the Royal Central Asian Society* (1952), pp. 57–68; Fereydoun Adamiyat, *Bahrein Islands: A Legal and Diplomatic Study of the British-Iranian Controversy* (New York, 1955). J. B. Kelly: 'The Persian Claim to Bahrein' in *International Affairs* (1957), pp. 51–70; Gholam-Reza Tadjbakhche, *La Question des Iles Bahrein* (Paris, 1960); and Husain M. al-Baharna, *The Legal Status of the Arabian Gulf States*, ch. 12.
[106] F.O. 371/105 1906, Persia, Grant Duff to Sir E. Grey, 25 Jan. 1906.
[107] *Ibid.*

when British action could be construed as an endeavour to tighten control and threats to take the issue to the League of Nations were made several times by the Persian Government but received with equanimity by the British Foreign Office. Action was largely confined to a series of pinprick activities – the non-recognition by the Persian Post Office of the Indian postage stamps over-printed 'Bahrain' for use in the Gulf[108] and endless disputes about the right of Persian subjects to enter Bahrain without a passport but with a simple identity card (*ᶜilm o khabar*.)[109] When treaty negotiations were being pursued in 1929 the Persian Minister of Court offered to sell Persia's claim to Bahrain but the British Government was loath to take up this idea in case the necessary Bill failed to pass the Majlis – for the very admission of a Persian claim would weaken Britain's position in any subsequent arbitration.[110] The Foreign Office did not believe that the Persian Government was desirous of making a serious claim for Bahrain in the 1930s but acknowledged the difficulty experienced by the Persian Ministry of Foreign Affairs in dropping a claim 'that had been so sedulously fostered'.[111] The announcement, made in May 1934, of oil discoveries on Bahrain brought a protest from the Persian Government, to the American Government, that the concession granted to the Standard Oil Company in Bahrain could not be recognized as it had not been obtained in Tehran.[112] The establishment of a British base in Bahrain also produced a Persian protest in 1934.

Hostility to Britain during the oil crisis of 1950 brought a spate of renewed protests about Bahrain. Press comment was vociferous and violent[113] but official activity was again limited as the Persian Government sought not to alienate American sympathies. Once more activity was largely confined to small-scale gestures, some of which were, by now, almost traditional – non-acceptance of letters with Bahraini stamps and a refusal to attend a World Health Organization Conference in Istanbul because of the presence of a Bahraini delegate. In December 1952 an officially published list of Persian electoral districts included the Bahrain islands and in November 1957 Bahrain was specified one of the areas covered by the new Persian administrative area 'ports and islands of the Persian Gulf'. This latter declaration brought Saudi Arabian – and, significantly, Egyptian – protests. The reported announcement by the Shah in November 1968 that Iran would not pursue her claims to Bahrain

108 F.O. 371/17895 1934, Persia E584/156/34.
109 F.O. 371/16967 1933, Persia E2439/2439/34 (Annual Report 1932)
110 F.O. 371/14543 1930, Persia E2445/522/34 (Annual Report 1929).
111 F.O. 371/17893 1934, Persia E4352/139/34.
112 *Ibid.* E3558/139/34.
113 See the Anglo-Iranian Oil Company weekly press digests (at Royal Institute of International Affairs, Chatham House), particularly for the months August–December 1950.

by force may be seen as a Persian gesture to gain Saudi Arabian support in the attempt to exclude outside influences from the Gulf after the British withdrawal. Whether or not such a claim, which has had value as an internal political 'safety valve', can be discarded is still an open question.

Reference was made earlier to the recurring theme of a navy in Persian history. The ships ordered by Riza Shah from Italy arrived in the Gulf in the late autumn of 1932 and provided a further means of self assertion *vis-à-vis* Great Britain. The new navy had other tasks to perform too, tasks which derived from internal policies being pursued by the Persian Government. As part of the desire for independence from foreign indebtedness Riza Shah had decided that the capital for the Trans-Iranian railway would come from internal sources – chiefly taxes on tea and sugar – and not from international loans. The desire for national autarchy had also helped to promote high tariffs on goods entering Persia. The profits were therefore great if tea and sugar could be purchased cheaply on the Arab coast of the Gulf and run to Persian ports. A further feature, according to a fascinating report[114] on the organization of smuggling in the Gulf area written by Colonel Dickson, the Political Agent in Kuwait, was the fact that the world depression had severely reduced the value of the pearl trade. The report speaks at great length of smuggling into Saudi Arabia, Persia and Iraq and says that the incentive – and the profit – stemmed from the high import tariffs levied by these countries, some Persian tariffs were at levels in excess of 200 per cent *ad valorem*. These three countries saw the sole object of tariffs as the increase of revenue whereas the rulers of the Trucial Coast saw that low tariffs would attract much trade. (Once again it is necessary to note that at this time income from oil exploitation was very small indeed on the Arabian side of the Gulf.) The smuggling of goods to Persia was apparently in the hands of Tangistani tribesmen who sailed from Persia with cargoes of grain, fruit, fodder and cloth, returning with contraband in the form of tea and sugar. The two receiving ends of the trade were conducted by Persian merchants whose family connections spanned the Gulf. The favourite stretch of Persian coast was that between Bushire and Lingeh and it was here that the new Persian navy successfully concentrated its efforts to arrest the smugglers. This aspect of the Persian navy's work may be regarded as an extension of internal policies – so too may another task they performed – the suppression of gun-running, but here the Persian Government came up against British opposition again.

The task of preventing gun-running in the Gulf had been a traditional one for the Admiralty but Britain had recognized Persian rights in this

[114] F.O. 371/16852 1933, Arabia E3688/2079/91.

matter. While the Persians lacked a navy, this recognition was an easy matter but when Riza Shah got his ships and started carrying out searches the Admiralty felt somewhat resentful. The essential Persian demand was for reciprocity of rights with the British Navy, with ships of both fleets having the right to search both Arab and Persian ships on the High Seas of the Gulf. The Admiralty were prepared to allow the Persian Navy to investigate ships of their own nationality but not Arab vessels.[115] The Government of India also resented this new element of Persian assertiveness and believed that any attempt to give Persia the right to investigate Arab ships would, once more, be a grave blow to British prestige.[116]

The incipient national pride of Persia had been affronted by the Arms Traffic Convention signed at Saint-Germain-en-Laye on 20 September 1919.[117] Section II Article VI (Part 3) of this Convention established the Persian Gulf as one of the special maritime areas where the High Contracting Parties had the right to search all ships suspected of running specified types of arms and ammunition. The Convention received no general ratification and appears to have been abandoned when it became clear that the American Government would not accept it. A League of Nations Temporary Commission on Armaments called an Arms Traffic Conference in 1925 when a proposal along the lines of the 1919 Convention was again suggested.[118] This document would have allowed the right of inspection by the High Contracting Parties of all ships on the High Seas in the Persian Gulf. This suggestion also proved abortive as too few countries ratified their acceptance of the scheme, and Britain continued to rely upon the series of agreements made within the Gulf during the nineteenth century. The Persian counterclaim repeated in 1934 was for a bilateral (i.e. Anglo–Persian) Arms Traffic Convention which would have given ships of the two fleets equal rights of search[119] but the Admiralty and the Government of India proved hostile to any sharing of British rights and the Foreign Office saw the Persian claim as providing an opportunity for Persian interference with Arab ships.[120] Generally

---

[115] F.O. 371/17909 1934, Persia E1620/1620/34 (Annual Report 1933).

[116] F.O. 371/16077 1932, Persia E2529/2529/34. It appeared that by the Muscat Arms Proclamation of 1898 (*Aitchison*, vol. xii, p. 241) the Persian Government already had the authority to search Arab vessels for arms in Persian, Muscati or Indian waters. It also appeared that the ministers of Riza Shah were unaware of this right and the British Foreign Office was prepared to arrange for its immediate cancellation, by the ruler of Muscat, if the Persians ever began to exercise such a right of search. See F.O. 371/17909 1934, Persia E1620/1620/34 (Annual Report 1933) for summary.

[117] British and Foreign State Papers 1922 London. H.M.S.O. volume 112 (1919), pp. 909–24.

[118] F.O. 371/16077 1932, Persia E2592/2592/34.

[119] F.O. 371/18995 1935, Persia E1606/1606/34 (Annual Report 1934).

[120] F.O. 371/17893 1934, Persia E4485/139/34.

speaking, the arms trade in the 1930s appears to have been quite small and incidents were few in number.

In the Annual Report from Persia for 1935 the foreign policy of Iran was described as a mixture of pride, self-consciousness, a stinging sense of past indignities, a desire to pay off old scores, face-saving and administrative inefficiency.[121] This paper has been an attempt to outline some of the issues which influenced the local situation in the Gulf – the complexities of earlier events, the desire by the Government of India to maintain the British role of supervisory power, the degree of initiative which remained in local hands, and the relatively late appearance of oil as a decisive factor. In the 1920s and 1930s the Persian Government did not have a Gulf policy as such. Riza Shah's aim was to establish Persian independence on a sound basis. This involved the imposition of effective central control – a policy which was applied by stages and brought Persia and Britain face to face in the Gulf. The desire to establish a new Persia meant the eradication of reminders of former inferiority. The early policies of Soviet Russia removed many of the Persian grievances relating to the North and allowed Riza Shah to concentrate energies upon the internal consolidation of power and the exercise of effective sovereignty in the south. The Gulf was, in effect, an area for the exercise of self-assertion and many of the actions taken in the Gulf are extensions of internal aims rather than foreign policy as such.

The attempt by a powerful Shah to assert control in the Gulf was an old theme in Persian history but in endeavouring to do so in the 1920s and 1930s Riza Shah was confronted by a well-established and confident British presence. Thus in the Gulf the two threads of Persian policy intertwined, the desire to establish both an effective and an independent state. In this task progress was relatively slow but quite constant, from the abolition of the capitulations in 1928 and the handing over to Persian control of the Persian Quarantine Service in the same year to the negotiation of the new oil agreement in 1933 and the evacuation from Hangam and Basidu in 1934. By this time many Persian demands in the Gulf had been met and attention turned to problems elsewhere, particularly in south-eastern Persia. Thus, despite the interruptions of the Second World War, the period from the late 1920s had seen a gradual fulfilment of Persian aims and a great strengthening of her power. During the 1950s new factors – such as under-sea oil and Arab self-assertiveness – began to enter the scene, while at the same time older factors – such as the desire, and ability, to preserve British prestige – were apparently on the wane. As the strongest local power Iran had to reconsider the guidelines of

[121] F.O. 371/20052 1936, Persia E1147/1147/34.

policy and although this process is by no means at an end it seems safe to say that Persian attitudes to the Gulf have altered considerably in the last forty years and Persia, like Britain earlier, has begun to approach the position of a satisfied power whose interest lies in the preservation of an acceptable *status quo*.

[*Excerpts from Crown copyright records in the Public Record Office appear by permission of the Controller of H.M. Stationery Office.*

Most place name transliterations are based on those of the Persian Gulf Pilot *published by the Hydrographic Department of the Admiralty, tenth edn., 1955.*

I should like to thank the staff of the Press Library, Royal Institute of International Affairs, for their help and efficiency in making available press cuttings.]

9

SOCIAL AND POLITICAL CHANGE IN
THE THIRD WORLD:
SOME PECULIARITIES OF OIL-PRODUCING
PRINCIPALITIES OF THE PERSIAN GULF

FRANK STOAKES

My immediate purpose is to consider how phenomena characteristic of the Persian Gulf situation may modify typical patterns of social and political change in the Third World. This chapter is, however, an abridgement of a more detailed and comprehensive exercise in structural-functional analysis which poses the questions: first, what amount of political disintegration is inevitable in the oil-producing principalities of the Gulf and what are the optimum and pessimum positions; second, what type of political organization is likely, at different stages of social change, to prove most appropriate there; and third, whether such organization can be expected to emerge spontaneously or with a practicable measure of political engineering. These questions, though not integral to our present purpose, are also touched on here. For reasons of brevity conceptualization and empirical detail have been virtually excluded or relegated to the notes; it should, moreover, be mentioned that the principalities under review are Kuwait, Qatar and the more developed of the Trucial States, the rather different circumstances of Bahrain calling for separate treatment. Also in the interest of brevity, domestic relations of existing principalities are considered in abstraction from foreign or even regional relations. Abstraction of this kind must clearly constitute one approach to comprehensive analysis; but it must equally clearly be supplemented, particularly in view of current discussions and decisions on federation. Federation, however, retains many of the existing problems and adds more, while incorporation by force or diplomacy in an external state would require a change of focus.

Typical Political Problems of Social Change
First of all, let us glance at some typical problems of social change in the Third World and at the strains they impose on political relationships. The stimuli which set the forces of change in motion may be such

economic developments as industrialization, the attraction of urban employment, and the spread of roads and other physical communications; or cultural ones, like the introduction of Western ideas, modern education, the press and broadcasting; or political ones like the creation of a modern civil service. Each stimulus is likely to have consequences which stimulate further change. So modern education may prepare the ground for modern political ideas, which inspire governments to agrarian reform, which changes the social structure. The proliferation of cause and effect – or, in other terms, the sequence of input, output and feedback – may be extremely complicated, and it may simplify and systematize the complexity if we consider the combined effect of the various stimuli upon the basic components of social action;[1] that is, upon first the values or norms which set guide-lines for our conduct, secondly the psychological mechanisms which move us to follow or abandon these guide-lines, and thirdly the social structures – families, businesses and political groupings – which represent, however imperfectly, the combined operation of norms and psychological motivation.

In these terms, the fundamental problems of a changing society may be briefly stated. In the first place, the value patterns are in conflict, old against new and various brands of new against one another. The conflict may occur between social structures which embody different values, as when progressive businessmen compete with conservative landlords to determine national policy, or it may occur within the individual psyche, when transitional man does now know whether he should follow tradition or his reason, or whether he is primarily a Muslim or an Arab. In the second place, and it may come about from precisely this uncertainty, the motivation for accepted action may fail, so that no code of conduct is seriously followed, or behaviour is determined by unfettered emotion, ambition or fantasy.

The basic political problem of a changing society is in practice the same whether we adopt a functional or structural definition of the polity. In either case, if political relationships are to persist over the area concerned, government – or the political system – must play a major part in meeting these stresses, both as affecting society as a whole and as impinging more directly upon political relationships themselves. The catastrophe of many new states is that government has been incapable of doing so. In place of a steady change from old to new, the ring socially or politically held while old structures dissolved and new ones crystallized,

[1] As expounded particularly by Parsons, Talcott et al. *Toward a General Theory of Action* (Cambridge, Mass., 1951) and Parsons, *The Social System* (New York, 1951), and modified, for example, in Parsons and Smelser, N.J., *Economy and Society* (London, 1956), and Parsons, 'The Political Aspect of Social Structure and Process' in Easton, D. (ed.) *Varieties of Political Theory* (Englewood Cliffs, N. J., 1966).

societies as a whole, and their political subsystems, have been caught in what Riggs, in a political context, has called a developmental trap.[2] There is a deadlock between old and new or between other antitheses, or there is temporary resolution in a swing between the extremes; in either case the capacity is lacking to carry relationships to a higher plane, where both elements may be fruitfully integrated.

These are our problems in brief; we may now examine them in rather more specific terms both for society at large and for the political system. As the forces of change invade society, blueprints are imposed and to a greater or lesser degree institutionalized. In the first place these blueprints are for new instrumental organizations, such as governmental and political agencies (like ministries and parties), commercial and industrial firms, trade unions and other occupational associations, and recreational and social clubs. In the second place they are for new solidary organizations of which the most revolutionary is no doubt the small family. Some of these structural innovations are involuntary, others inspired by new values; once introduced with any vigour, they are crucial for institutionalizing an abstract new culture and extending it beyond the confines of a modernizing elite. At the same time old structures are weakened or destroyed, under economic pressure or on ideological principle; these declining structures may include the village unit and extended family, the tribe and traditional craft organization. In consequence, the norms of the old society may disappear and its ultimate values be replaced in favour of such new values as progress and perfectibility, efficiency, individual freedom; and on an intellectual level old norms and values are also under attack from the pure ideas of a newly imported culture.

These processes of change provoke serious social and personal stresses. On the level of social organization, old groupings, classes and occupations suffer devaluation and deprivation, while new groupings have still to attain the prestige and even the material affluence and satisfying employment to which their new culture is presumed to entitle them; intellectual underemployment is a well-known phenomenon. Social security passes with the old structures in which it inhered, and it may take time for patron-client groups, political parties, social clubs and perhaps religious brotherhoods to fill the gap, let alone adequate governmental provision. Formerly integrated structures, embracing father and children or employer and employee, now dissolve in conflict, and new mechanisms of adjustment have still to emerge. Social classes diverge more widely as a money economy and new opportunities for spending broaden and advertise the financial gulf, and the twofold link of responsibility and respect gives

---

[2] Riggs, F.W., 'The Theory of Political Development', in Charlesworth, J.C., (ed.) *Contemporary Political Analysis* (New York, 1967).

place to plutocratic disregard and proletarian hatred. Economic stringency is aggravated by organizational and educational inadequacy. Modern administration, laid down in terms of organizational charts, takes time to develop adequate modern norms in its functionaries; and the functionaries come to their employment from an education which implants all the ultimate goals of modern industrial society but few of those instrumental values through which the Ultimate is at the same time approached and brought closer to sordid earth.

The psychological and motivational implications of these changes is profound. Many modernizers are individual microcosms of their unintegrated society, which is to say a personification of uncertain or conflicting values, anxiety, vacillation and perhaps paralysis. Old elements and the varied new tend, it is true, to occupy separate compartments; but there is still enough intellectual and spiritual confusion, enough economic and social insecurity and frustration, enough conviction that malignant forces must be in motion, to provide ample basis for those unsettling social and political phenomena which are commonly termed oppositionalism and collective behaviour. Moreover, with social and political fact and theory to provide real and imaginary devils, like imperialism, feudalism and capitalism, such behaviour may be almost universal at sensitive times among sensitive groups; its most important manifestation is perhaps the ideological possession – as opposed to mere ideological conviction – of students and of those educated adults who have been subjected to particular uncertainty or humiliation. The ideology, like the age, tends to be political; some of the most obvious frustrations – and particularly foreign occupation – are political; and when the social order is impotent it is to politics that it looks for salvation, in the touching raith that government may be stronger and more inspired than society itself.

We must now turn in rather greater detail to the political system and observe the effect on it of these various changes and stresses. For this purpose it may help us to adopt a simple model of the political processes. For the principalities of the Gulf, as also for much of the rest of the Middle East, we may find it sufficient to think, in structural terms, of a government which makes ultimate decisions in an area and implements them; it implements them by making demands on the various groups which constitute society and the state machine – demands, for example, for resources or obedience – and by reinforcing these demands with adequate sanctions. The reinforcement lies in the capacity to issue inducements, threats or appeals on cultural, psychological or material grounds. The public groups on their side, as also the organizations of state, make demands on government and reinforce them with similar sanctions. The character of the regime – that is, of the longer-term relations between government and society – is determined partly by the sort of balance which is struck between the two sides: whether government extracts much and grants little, or is a puppet of social forces, or lies somewhere on the long scale between. The regime, viewed in these terms, persists if the pattern of demand and reinforcement between the two sides remains as it is, and changes if that pattern is changed. Whatever the pattern, the reinforcement at government's disposal will depend mainly on government's ability to meet the demands or expectations of others; police will take orders if they are paid, tribes will give their support if they receive their subsidies, and customary obedience will be extended if government itself conforms with custom. It follows that government's output of action feeds back not only, in the first place, to the demands of society on government (so that government action of one sort will reduce demand and of another sort will intensify it), but also, in the second place, to the reinforcement with which government can press home its own demands, and so in the third, to the resources available to government for meeting the demands of society. All this supposes that the resources are not only granted when required but actually exist – that when government calls on police or civil service or businessmen, the skill or organization or capital are present as well as the will to offer them. It is typical of a changing society that they are often not (see diagram).

We may now introduce the changes and stresses of society into our political model, and shall do so through the channels of demand and reinforcement as controlled both by public and by government. In the first place, social and cultural change vastly alters the nature and volume of demands on government, their source, and the capacity of their authors to press them. New social groups set themselves new goals, at first material, then, with the spread of modern education and communications, in terms of ideas – the establishment of a modern, efficient, powerful nation state with international influence and dignity, an ideologically acceptable foreign policy, social reform, participation of new elements in government, and possibly some specified form of regime. In the absence of other agencies and in the presence of foreign examples, these demands are naturally directed to government; and, given the lack of practical experience and logistic sense, which education has still to impart, they may well be quite unrelated to the capacity and resources of government, state machine and society itself to implement them. When the initial, material demands cannot be met, they are pressed more bitterly, and it is then that ideological demands are more seriously presented, at first, perhaps with moderation, then in an uncompromising spirit of millenarian certitude. Initially neither material nor ideological demands control more reinforcement than deputations, riots and demonstrations, which any

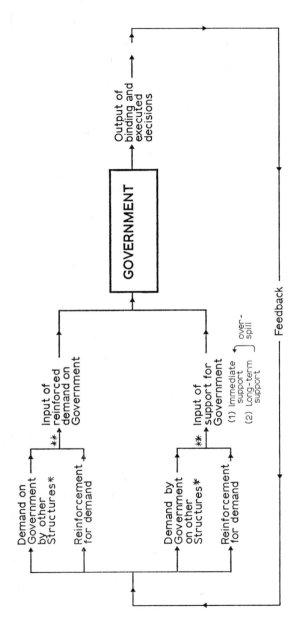

DIAGRAM: Simplified Model of Political Processes

* 'Other structures' = state machine and the various public groupings; they may also be taken (according to the definition of 'government') to include subunits or peripheral units of a governmental complex.

** These connections may, if required, be expressed in an input-output form.

NOTE: This simplified diagram does not specify the various public groupings and their relationship with one another and with government and the state machine.

strong-willed government can suppress. With wider education, however, they may inspire enough fear or guilt to weaken the will of more sensitive governments; and eventually alliances may be contracted between intellectuals, who command no serious sanctions, and army officers or organized labour, who do.

The demands of government and their reinforcement are also likely, during this process, to change. Government may well have come to accept some of the public demands upon it, such as responsibility for the welfare of all its subjects; but it will certainly, on its side, expect to penetrate the public more deeply and to command more positive and more frequent services from it. Indeed, to meet new demands government *must* mobilize new material and human resources, and must do so from society if no other provision, such as foreign aid, exists. These new demands of government, diffuse and specific, are not sanctified by custom; and even if they were, the social groups in whom custom inhered are already passing. Appeals to common interest and future benefit may serve, but they must be buttressed by the outputs of an inadequate state machine, and so must the appeals of charisma and a common ideology; these are wondrous tighteners of belts, but they must nevertheless afford the occasional glimpse of heaven realized on earth, even if gratifying foreign policies offer a temporary surrogate. Nor can government still control the public through a few social leaders; *their* day is passing, and, perhaps for the first time, government stands face to face with the individual. A dynasty may sometimes elicit support for its numen, a ruler for his personal authority; but political dogma may reject this prop and knock together democratic regimes where there is no social or cultural basis for democracy, or ideological regimes where ideology is less compelling than social or individual claims. Force always remains, and a modernizing government has usually a more concentrated command of it than its predecessors. But demands on the security forces must also be matched by reinforcement; and, even if conditions of service are better than they often are, individual alienation always exists, and an educated army is likely to share the aspirations and frustrations of the educated public and to equip public demands – now challenges to the regime – with decisive reinforcement.

The interaction of reciprocal demand and reinforcement has now generated a revolutionary situation, whether under a modernizing regime of traditional type, under a successor democracy or dictatorship, or even under army rule. On rare occasions the revolutionary regime is more glorious and permanent; more often it has marked a descent into deepening squalor. But let us turn from this disturbed, though not untypical pattern, first to the Gulf regimes in their pre-petroleum innocence, and next to the peculiar features of their situation which might modify the outcome.

Political Systems of the Gulf Principalities

Immediately before oil was produced in the Gulf principalities they were governed by similar forms of regime. Governments (as defined above) consisted of an individual ruler – shaikh – drawn from and legitimized by his membership of a ruling family, and of a lesser or greater number of other members of the ruling family, depending on the structure of authority and power – the allocation of reinforcement – within the family itself. Optional elements in the political and social system, which varied from one principality to another, were other aristocratic families, nomadic or semi-nomadic tribes, retainers and clients of the ruling family and of other aristocratic families, non-aristocratic elements, and foreigners.

The complexes which were later to constitute states, and the form of control they embodied, differed in each case. The nucleus might be a town, as in Kuwait and Dubai, or a combination of town and coastal villages, as in Qatar, or a coastal fortress and an inland oasis, as in Abu Dhabi. In Abu Dhabi and Dubai this nucleus was dominated or virtually owned by a single family. In Kuwait and Qatar it had once been controlled by a merchant oligarchy, but one leading family eventually became *prima inter impares* and in the end vastly predominant as a result of Ottoman or British recognition,[3] of an increase in state affairs which had few implications for other families, of the decline of the pearl trade,[4] of the payments and deferential attitude of oil companies even before oil was discovered, or of simple inter-family politics. In consequence, the dominant family came to regard the embryonic state as their private domain, particularly in matters like mineral resources which fell outside the scope of customary rights. Other aristocratic families continued to be treated with courtesy by the ruler and his family and enjoyed adequate reinforcement – though increasingly moral rather than material – for their sectional demands; but supreme matters of state had long been the responsibility of the ruler, who might, however, expect to consult other families on them, whether he took their advice or not.[5] This decline in aristocratic status was not accepted without protest. In Kuwait the aristocratic families tried to participate in the selection of a new ruler in 1921, and in the same year insisted on the formation of an (in fact ineffective) advisory council, while the constitutional movement of 1937–9 was pro-

[3] In the case of Qatar, until 1867–72 Muhammad ibn Thani had the status, however unwelcome, of vassal of Al Khalifah of Bahrain.

[4] Profoundly damaging to the coastal villages of Qatar.

[5] ʿAbd Allah Salim of Kuwait continued the practice until his death, well within the petroleum era.

voked largely by the autocratic attitude of Ahmad Jabir to the other families, following the example of Mubarak Sabah; on this occasion, before the access of oil revenues, the aristocrats commanded material force. In the post-petroleum era of Qatar, the so-called strike of 1963 had little, if anything, to do with industrial relations and represented a rebellion of aristocratic village families, many of whose members were employed in the oil companies, against the Al Thani monopoly.[6]

The nucleus, organized in this way, had in some cases a relationship with a nomadic or semi-nomadic tribal population. This was the case in Kuwait[7] and to a minor extent in Qatar and Dubai, but the supreme example was Abu Dhabi, where, at the turn of this century, Zayid ibn Khalifah controlled a considerable tribal empire. His family, the Al Bu Falah, itself belonged to the major tribal confederation[8] and was closely related by marriage to the second large tribal group,[9] while individuals of the family have maintained a careful policy of matrimonial alliance with other tribes.[10] Tribal relations have indeed been central to Al Bu Falah policy, for it has been essential to maintain goodwill or a precarious allegiance which might otherwise gravitate, in particular, to the Saudi rulers; and although the relationship has been partly of lineage or marriage, it has rested even more on an instrumental or tacitly contractual basis, which is to say on favours – and particularly subsidies – accorded by the rulers. In the hands of men like the present ruler, when he was warden of the marches of Buraimi, the balance of reinforcement has been skilfully

[6] The rising began on 19 April 1963, during demonstrations to celebrate the abortive union agreement between Egypt, Syria and Iraq. A young nephew of the ruler, ᶜAbd al-Rahman ibn Muhammad ibn ᶜAli, finding his car blocked by a carload of demonstrators, got into argument with them and eventually opened fire, causing one non-fatal casualty. Two days later a general strike began in protest against this incident, a 'National Unity Front' was formed, and a list of demands on the regime was circulated; these mainly concerned the special privileges of the ruling family, the employment of foreigners and the need for certain welfare facilities, and important additional items were that a representative municipal council should be elected, the state budget be published and trade unions be officially recognized. The movement came to centre upon a potentate of Khaur, in the north of the peninsula, whom the more reactionary members of the ruling family would have liked to bombard with artillery. In the event there was little violence on either side, the ruler and deputy ruler remained reasonably flexible, and at the beginning of May the strike ended, against some not very precise promises of reform. One outcome was legislation for a partially elected municipal council, whose actual formation, however, hung fire.

[7] In Kuwait the bedu have tended to suffer from economic development, having no land to sell, finding it difficult to obtain nationality papers, and losing their direct contact with the ruler; in consequence their impact on government has in some cases tended to change to that of a proletariat which might be mobilized by radical politicians. For example, in the elections of January 1963 Khalid Masᶜud al-Fuhaid was able to organize support from the Mutair tribe.

[8] Bani Yas.

[9] Manasir.

[10] Not least the present ruler, Zayid ibn Sultan.

maintained. In all principalities with a tribal population rulers have tended to treat it circumspectly, the relationship varying from that of allies to something approaching that of suzerain and vassal, but always with a wary balance of reinforced demand. At times more concrete services have been required of the tribes than expressions of allegiance or acquiescence; in 1946–47 they fought the war between Abu Dhabi and Dubai, they have been brought into disputes of the ruling family, as when Saqr ibn Zayid of Abu Dhabi was murdered by a group of Manasir in 1926, on his nephew's initiative, and in the 1963 rising in Qatar the Al Thani could count on the support of certain but not all of the tribes.

The principal relationships remaining were first that between the ruling family or other aristocrats and their retainers or clients, which accounted for much of the commoner population of fishermen and craftsmen, and secondly one of protection and petition as between rulers and the foreign population. In some principalities, even before the discovery of oil, foreigners formed a considerable proportion of the merchants, chandlers and craftsmen; they consisted largely of Persians (Kuwait, Dubai), Hawali (Sunni Persians of allegedly Arab origin, as in Qatar, Dubai and Abu Dhabi), Baluchis (as in Abu Dhabi and Dubai), Indians, and migrants from other Gulf communities, many families of all origins being of long residence. In general, there was no place for foreigners in the existing pattern of relationships, tribal, aristocratic and patronal, and a common attitude of rulers has been that even those of long standing had no claims of any kind on themselves, but rather owed them a debt for the privilege of residence; any reinforcement for their requests would lie in personal relations with the ruler or his family, or in their capacity to pay.[11] There has been one notable exception. Rashid ibn Sa\ʿid of Dubai, though commanding autocratic power, was brought up in a partly foreign merchant community, was sympathetic to the merchants' aspirations and was conscious, before the days of oil, that the prosperity of the community depended on them; in consequence he has treated them, whatever their origin, as an element to be propitiated, and has maintained an instrumental and quasi-contractual relationship with them, of protection, fair treatment and consultation in return for taxes[12] and continued residence. Even so, merchants from the old Arab families have enjoyed closer social contact with him than those of foreign origin.

[11] While acquiring no aristocratic rights, foreigners have at times gained considerable influence – always terminable at the ruler's will or whim – as agents, go-betweens and factotums, particularly when rulers were suddenly brought into contact with an unknown modern world; so the Hauli \ʿAbd Allah Darwish Fakhroo (his spelling) with Al Thani of Qatar, and Mahdi Tajir the Bahraini with Rashid ibn Sa\ʿid of Dubai.

[12] The taxes have, however, in déference to merchant opinion, been kept low.

There remains the ruling family, a small political system in itself. Its status has varied from that of collective government, taking oligarchic decisions on all matters of state,[13] to that of scantily reinforced petitioner of an authoritarian ruler;[14] intermediate positions include the ability and interest to determine or be consulted on some matters of state, and the ability to determine all sectional or personal matters. That reciprocal reinforcement on the side both of ruler and kinsmen which determined relative authority was based on size of family, degree of kinship, size and relationship of the generations, force of character, personal ties, vague or specific threats of deposition, and (especially in Abu Dhabi) almost institutionalized liquidations. Once state machinery is established, these relationships may be more or less formalized as between office-holders. Except where the Family has been held in a strictly subordinate position, a feature of its relationships has often been a family council,[15] and this, as in Kuwait, might be expected to continue after modern instruments of government have been established. Family cohesion varies, and owes much to individuals, as to ᶜAbd Allah Salim in Kuwait and Salama bint Butti in Abu Dhabi. But rivalries between branches and individuals are rarely wanting beneath the surface, particularly – in the absence of primogeniture – for the rulership,[16] and in most of the principalities assassination or rebellion have been employed to seek or secure it.[17]

Regimes before oil were thus of a dual character. They comprised in the first place relations between the ruler and his family, and in the second, relations between this small system – oligocracy, monocracy or a mixture of both – with other aristocratic families and with tribes, supplemented

[13] So Al Thani during the 1963 'strike'; but in general it is in support of dourly pursued personal and sectional interests that the enormous Al Thani has badgered successive rulers almost to distraction. In Kuwait, ᶜAbd Allah Salim sometimes gave the impression of being the simple chairman of a family council – the government, as it were, of a tiny reconciliation system (see p. 211), mediating its differences and expressing its consensus; but at any rate in major matters he seems to have guided its affairs shrewdly if unobtrusively.

[14] So with Shakhbut ibn Sultan of Abu Dhabi and Rashid ibn Saᶜid of Dubai. Rashid crushed family opposition in 1937–8 and again in 1955.

[15] Always informal and most regularly held in Kuwait; in other principalities held usually in a crisis or when matters of family importance are to be decided.

[16] Competition for the rulership between brothers and their descendants is not uncommon and sometimes results not so much in conflict as in a semi-institutionalized or even formalized balance of power (as embodied in official office), amounting in Qatar to a sort of dyarchy. So in Kuwait there is the dichotomy of Bani Jabir and Bani Salim, in Qatar of the Bani ᶜAli and the Bani Hamd, formerly in Dubai of the Bani Hashar as against the Bani Rashid and Bani Butti, and now mildly in Abu Dhabi of the Bani Sultan and Bani Muhammad Khalifah.

[17] Qatar is an exception. The family frequently threatened ᶜAbd Allah ibn Jasim (Qasim) and ᶜAli ibn ᶜAbd Allah with violence, if they were not more amenable to family demands, but no ruler has in fact been assassinated; the murder of Ahmad ibn Muhammad ibn Thani, the effective ruler during the later years of Jasim ibn Muhammad ibn Thani (1876–1913), by a tribesman of the Bani Hajir seems to have been personal in motive and without political significance.

by minor relationships or clientship and protection. In most cases the political nexus was equalled, dominated or obscured by the social, and it very rarely corresponded with the modern Western relationship of ruler and subject or state and citizen. Relationship between government and rank and file was not usually direct, but mediated through family heads or other social leadership. A ruler's control was often reinforced by awe and sometimes by affection, but only in Qatar was there anything approaching an ideological bond between rulers and public; there Wahhabism imposed obligations on both sides alike and has more recently confirmed the reluctance of the ruling family for change. In most of the principalities the *ahl al-din* have tended to be well under the ruler's influence, adding a certain (but not fervent or indispensable) Islamic basis of legitimacy.

In general, interaction between rulers and the various categories of public was not intense. In times of crisis there might be mobilization of townsmen[18] or tribes and there might also be a degree of taxation, matched by the payment of subsidies; but for the most part the ruler expected and was expected to do little more than to protect the community, and to maintain Islamic Law and local custom and adjudicate disputes in their light, while he on his side demanded little more than that the public should remain law-abiding and loyal. It was, moreover, by social pressure rather than by shaikhly coercion that these norms were observed; means of coercion were certainly present, originally in the form of the bedu retainers of the ruler and his family, but on the whole the instruments of political control were rather those of manipulation and a good intelligence service.[19]

Peculiarities of the Gulf Situation

We must now isolate those features of the regimes, of the initial stimuli to change and of the resultant processes which are characteristic of these Gulf principalities and might conceivably impart an individual character to their political development.[20]

Of all these phenomena the most spectacular – in fact, the very essence of the situation – is the environmental fact of oil and the revenues which it generates. This is all the more environmental in that indigenous economic structures need be very little involved and can often, for lack of a 'natural' economy, capable of development, be little affected by it. The

[18] As in the famous building and manning of the Kuwait wall against the Ikhwan in 1920.
[19] In a tribal context the intelligence service of Zayid ibn Sultan of Abu Dhabi was famous,, in an urban context that of Rashid ibn Sa^cid of Dubai.
[20] To save space, no attempt is made here to group these phenomena under the structural, cultural, psychological and environmental headings used above; instead, they are presented in a form which will permit their readier introduction into the political model.

most important political consequences, or consequences impinging on the political system may, for the sake of brevity, be enumerated as follows:

(1) Demands on government increase enormously, especially in view of the quasi-contractual relationships already existing.

(2) The capacity to meet material demands may be virtually limitless, given adaptable rulers, sage advice, proper recruitment and training for the state machine, and some policy of subsidizing the public which does not clog that machine with sinecures.[21] It is, in fact, possible to create a public with a stake in the existing political community and even in the regime.

(3) The capacity for persuasion, manipulation and coercion is equally great, with every opportunity – as far as that goes – of conciliating the administrative and security organizations on material grounds.

(4) There is an unusual bonus of political time. In many other areas a fantastically increased national income is possible, if at all, only in consequence of preceding social changes which are disruptive of the regime. In this case, however, it is possible, given counsel and speed, to satisfy initial demands and to prepare the public for political participation and even democracy before cultural evolution has turned aspirations into issues or even created some of the aspirations themselves.

(5) Given the 'natural' economy and existing cultural factors, the tone of society and its politics may be set, in an intermediate stage, by groups not widely typical of the Third World; that is to say by organized petroleum labour[22] and vehicle drivers,[23] some of them still with aristo-

---

[21] This omits the possibility, recently so disturbing to Qatar, that oil reserves might rapidly be exhausted.

[22] The floating regional labour force, with experience of association and strikes elsewhere, as well, perhaps, as radio news and incitation, can be expected to produce attempts at labour organization wherever oil is found. Such organization, whether or not officially recognized, is a potent political instrument, and even initially industrial action can quickly incorporate political objectives. Bahrain in 1954–6 (if we may stray beyond our self-appointed limits) offers an excellent example of labour, including petroleum labour, organized for both industrial and political ends, as also does the Eastern Province of Saudi Arabia in the earlier 1950s. Within our own boundaries, Qatar in 1963 is the supreme example. The Abu Dhabi strike which immediately followed it could, had it continued, have developed political overtones, but was checked in time. Industrial action may, in addition, be turned by radical politicians into a political issue, as it was by the Khatib group in the Kuwaiti parliament in 1963.

[23] Vehicle (mainly 'taxi') drivers, the new knights of the desert, honoured, conscious of their dignity – it is a vocation worthy of a noble (in the social sense) tribe – and possibly composing qasidahs to their Land Rovers, have become an important element, both socially and politically, in certain of our states. In Qatar, though far less numerous than organized labour, they formed a pressure group second only to labour, led by the radical nationalist brother-in-law of Shaikh ᶜAli ibn ᶜAbd Allah, Hamid ibn ᶜAbd Allah Al ᶜAtiyah. At one time they had some influence with the rulers, and they used their organization for political purposes in the 1963 'strike', though with indifferent solidarity. In Abu Dhabi they have

cratic pretensions, to a lesser extent by business men and contractors (among whom the distinction between aristocrat and plebeian is fading), and hardly at all by students and intellectuals, who will require at least a decade to form a matrix of political thought and action.[24] In one respect, however, the situation may prove atypical for the contrary reason; it is possible that the armed forces may come to play a more important part than is usual even in the other areas of the Arab world. Hitherto, except in Kuwait and to a lesser extent in Qatar, the British presence has reduced local security forces to secondary importance. With British withdrawal imminent, a change has already begun, particularly as the Gulf States need armed forces genuinely for defence and not merely for prestige. Now in most other areas the army, although a prime political striking force, has hardly served society as a principal incubator of political thought; its ideas, if not accepted ready-made from civilian intellectuals, have tended to lie somewhat apart from the main political stream and to be mixed with professional principles or professional expediency. In the Gulf, on the other hand, the necessities of defence may produce an officer corps with modern training and education before a considerable body of civilian intellectuals emerges, and it could be the officers who initially set the modern political tone and provide the matrix as well as the instrument of political change.

(6) Depending on oil company and other policies, the traditional social structure and culture may break down much more quickly in these small communities than is usual elsewhere,[25] and a modern type of man may be moulded with unusual speed. This, combined with factors (2) and (5), could lay down a pragmatic, prosperously occupied social stratum, tending to constructive citizenship and able to counterbalance ideological oppositionalism if it arose.

(7) Where environment, culture or policy tend to keep commercial and technical groups small and where modern education is widely diffused (as it is very likely to be), the major problem arises of occupying as

[24] Even in Kuwait the students do not yet constitute a substantial political force, let alone a matrix of political thought and action, though they have at intervals mounted mass demonstrations, sometimes in conjunction with radical politicians; so the celebrated Shuwaikh Secondary School rally of 1959, commemorating the anniversary of the formation of the United Arab Republic, in which Dr Ahmad al-Khatib and Jasim (Qasim) al-Qattami were involved. So also the demonstrations during the visit of the Algerian heroine Jamila Bouhaired in 1962.

[25] In Qatar, on the other hand, village rehabilitation has had a somewhat different effect.

formed a potentially still more important group. Constituting five years ago a fifth of the indigenous working population, indispensable, resourceful, carriers of ideas, united (despite factions) in an *esprit de corps*, they here too came to constitute an important pressure group and might be expected to align themselves with organized labour.

well as supporting the educated population. Failing subsidized residence abroad, there may be a temptation to seek a solution in paid idleness, whether at home[26] or in a government office,[27] the latter to the detriment of administration, both with the possible danger of over-politicization and accelerated demands on government.

(8) Oil revenues and the development projects they finance, combined with the initial barrenness of indigenous culture, may lead – as most notoriously in Kuwait – to a vast influx of foreigners. Some of these represent that regional body of floating labour which is a feature of the Gulf littoral, or are drawn from the Persian proletariat; these may introduce ideas of labour organization and action, and in some cases affiliations with politically oriented labour movements in the Arab world[28] or with movements allied to communism.[29] Others are from more advanced Arab countries, and these present major problems. If they are granted naturalization in great numbers, they threaten to change indigenous culture in a way that is initially unacceptable to rulers and public alike. If they are denied it, they may become an element of political opposition and a channel of domestic or foreign subversion. In any case they may disseminate modern political ideas of too specific a type to be automatically beneficial to the Gulf States, and certainly inimical to existing regimes, however these regimes might modify their form. On the other hand, a foreign population, not least when it originates from more advanced areas, is usually regarded as suspiciously alien and offers a ready target and scapegoat[30] to which grievances against the regime may be diverted and by recourse to which opposition to the regime may be split;[31] and it may even stimulate

[26] Note particularly the fictitious land transactions in Kuwait, to the benefit of part of the public.

[27] The notorious Kuwaiti ferrashes, giving lifts, in their new American cars, to their departmental advisers; and, on a higher level, the danger of educated young men, denied the commercial career they would prefer, clogging the works of government offices.

[28] i.e. AFPW (Arab Federation of Petroleum Workers), affiliated to ICATU (International Confederation of Arab Trade Unions) and with the strongest connections with the Egyptian Government.

[29] It has been suggested that some of the large body of Persian labour in Kuwait, especially skilled labour, have had Tudeh connections.

[30] Most clearly in Kuwait, by reason of numbers, and apparent also among the Abu Dhabi merchants, in the demands of the Qatar 'strikers' and in the Arab-Persian division in Dubai. In Dubai, consciousness of ethnic origin flared up in April 1963, after the Egyptian-Syrian-Iraqi unity talks, when a body of Arab nationalist students, adding criticism of the Shah to their eulogies of President Nasser, were set upon by a handful of Persians and routed, with one fatal casualty. The Arab crowd thereupon wanted to lynch the two Persians accused, but the ruler managed to calm the passions.

[31] Dr Ahmad al-Khatib was vastly embarrassed in 1963 after making a parliamentary speech urging that the privileges of Kuwaiti workers should be extended to other Arab workers in Kuwait and that there should be no truck with *iqlimiyah*. Kuwaiti opinion proved so

the crystallization of some form of modern national sentiment round the regime.

(9) The influx of oil revenues is likely, on grounds of interest or principle, to excite the interest of neighbouring and regional states. This, like the presence of foreigners, is likely to affect the domestic situation in two ways: first, by attempts at subversion, possibly through the foreign population itself; and second, as tending to promote national sentiment,[32] to focus it on reasonably acceptable rulers, and to modify current ideologies both in content and in fervour. On the other hand, security forces and foreign alliances become the more necessary, with the political dangers they may involve.

The second major factor lies in the existing regime itself, namely the existence of a ruling family with relatively deep-rooted authority and considerable capacity for withstanding shock. This ensures (and decreasingly through assassination) that there is a single formal ruler, however beset by family pressures; and the outcome is not infrequently rulers of character and capacity, adaptable themselves and capable of controlling their family. But when, for example, untimely death brings an inexperienced and uncle-ridden young man to supreme office,[33] the family can exercise an appalling influence for ill. Clinging in some cases to traditional privileges and vastly extending them, monopolizing oil revenues[34] and the offices of a growing state machine,[35] arrogant, brutal, corrupt and even degenerate,[36] they may nullify the efforts of a public-spirited ruler and destroy those reinforcements of customary acceptance, mutual interest and personal popularity or respect which a number of rulers have commanded. For, given that initial public demands may be met or anticipated before ideological demands gain serious reinforcement, and that a satis-

[32] Local sentiment, of diffuse city-state type, already exists, to become quite specific in moments of foreign threat (as in Kuwait when menaced by the Ikhwan or, in 1961, by ᶜAbd al-Karim Qasim of Iraq), but habitually implied, in a mild form, in relations to foreign states (especially regional states) and their nationals; Iraq, in particular, seems to be distrusted throughout the Gulf.

[33] In Qatar the untimely death of the forceful Hamd ibn ᶜAbd Allah ibn Jasim in 1947 led first to the unwilling succession of ᶜAli ibn ᶜAbd Allah ibn Jasim, and after his abdication in 1960, to the succession of the young Ahmad ibn ᶜAli ibn ᶜAbd Allah, who would seem at one time to have had over thirty uncles and great uncles.

[34] Initially every new-born member of Al Thani of Qatar received a pension.

[35] Which in Kuwait have been ruled like baronial fiefs.

[36] Not in every state nor in every branch of a ruling family; but where it has occurred, aggression against the public has ranged from forced loans and acquisition, through assault, to attempted murder, and the *fidawis* (tribal retainers) of ruling families have behaved with no less arrogance.

uncompromising on the matter that he was later forced to hedge about his attitude. The radical Arabist dilemma has been that it is impossible both to pursue strong Arabist policies and to maintain public support.

factory response to these initial demands may delay the onset and dilute the vehemence of ideology, the implication of the traditional regimes is this: Whatever changes may occur in the basis of political authority (that is, in the reinforcement of governmental demands), a sound umbrella or parasol may well exist beneath which new bases may be consolidated. This umbrella is the continued rule of a such respected ruler – which may be enough to span the most crucial period of change – or of a succession of respected rulers from an accepted ruling family. Their authority will inevitably diminish as modern ideology gains ground, but they may nevertheless retain it long enough to lay the foundations of a stable successor regime.

A third factor lies in the history of external relations. There has been no colonial occupation, and the British presence is likely to disappear before it provokes elsewhere the same animosity as it has among some elements in Bahrain and Kuwait; a major impulse to ideological zealotry will consequently be absent. Frontiers, moreover, if adjusted under imperial auspices, have not been imposed capriciously by imperial force. The Gulf States, that is to say, are in no danger of closing their eyes to the differences between them on the ground that they do not exist.[37] This may delay comprehensive unification, but at any rate there will be no premature idea of unity to impose unrealistic demands and to invite frustration.

Possible Peculiarities in the Political Development of the Gulf Principalities
In the light of these regional factors we may now modify our model of a political system labouring under the stress of social change. We shall curtail our investigation by emphasizing the factors of stability and eliciting the most favourable outcome. If malfunctional factors should triumph, such as inflated public demands, universal education of low quality, and the excesses of a ruling family, there could be at least as much instability as in the fairly typical Third World case we have considered. The actual consequences are likely to lie somewhere between, and in any given case this medial position, as well as the pessimal, could be plotted in some detail.

In terms of public demands on government, the accession of oil revenues to a partly contractual relationship is likely to increase demands enormously, and has in fact already done so.[38] On the other hand, a ruler who possesses or acquires a feeling of responsibility to the public and can resist the monopolist claims of his family, may meet or anticipate

---

[37] The rivalry and mutual suspicion of rulers is to some extent echoed by public opinion.
[38] Almost immediately in Abu Dhabi.

material demands as they arise, developing a state machine to keep pace with their growing complication;[39] of this, also, there are examples. If material demands are met and channels of communication kept open,[40] if the quality of education is high, if the growing body of educated public can be kept busy to its gain and satisfaction, if too conspicuous differences of wealth are discouraged outside the ruling family[41] (though inside it a degree of ostentation can hardly be avoided),[42] then political ideology, when it takes hold, is more likely to present its demands in a realistic and moderate manner and to avoid those psychological excesses which arise from uncertainty, frustration and the need for scapegoats. If, moreover, the ruler is ideologically orthodox in his foreign policy, this, and a natural distrust of foreigners within and without the frontiers, may for a time help consolidate even educated opinion behind him, in practice if not in principle; and if he is seen to make sincere preparations for public participation in government, in the form of widespread education, commoner

[39] Administration, with foreign underpinning, has usually proved adequate to meet demand. Qatar has been particularly fortunate; with a much smaller organization, few family members involved, and their spheres of influence demarcated and accepted, there has been none of the personal and factional competition, the empire-building, the unco-operative isolationism and barefaced trespass that marked the administrative relations of potentates like ᶜAbd Allah Mubarak and Fahd Salim, in Kuwait.

[40] Before development began every member of the public had access to the ruler and some rulers have done their best to maintain personal access to themselves: so Ahmad ibn ᶜAli of Qatar, Zayid ibn Sultan of Abu Dhabi and Rashid ibn Saᶜid of Dubai, though in Kuwait ᶜAbd Allah Salim abandoned the attempt. But business is increasingly with government departments, and it is frequently true that the more conscientious the family member who controls the department, the more bureaucratically he organizes himself, the more difficult he is to see and the more secretaries and clerks interpose themselves between the administrator and the public. So Khalifah ibn Hamd in Qatar and to some extent Hamdan ibn Muhammad Khalifah in Abu Dhabi.

[41] A general characteristic of the relationship between rulers and businessmen is that any reinforcement which the latter command resides in the ruler's feeling of social solidarity with aristocratic families (as in Kuwait) or in his consciousness of the importance of commerce for his state (as was the case in Dubai). In themselves, businessmen command no sanctions and they are often precluded by mutual suspicion and competition from combining even the tenuous moral appeal they might muster. That is to say, in the petroleum era, when rulers are no longer dependent on merchants' loans, they can treat merchants as strictly as they wish, and have sometimes done so. In Abu Dhabi Shakhbut ibn Sultan showed considerable suspicion of merchants after the ᶜUtaibah family were caught in correspondence with the ruler of Dubai; partly, perhaps, because of this experience, he seemed subsequently to oppose, almost as a matter of policy, the enrichment of any of his subjects, unless they were strictly under his own control, and it was a feature of his dealings with them to impose heavy profit-sharing arrangements. In Dubai, before oil revenues commenced, Rashid ibn Saᶜid, however, sympathetic to his merchants, also seemed anxious that they should not become too powerful. Once oil is produced in a state, there is a danger that the ruler may command such overwhelming resources as to lose these promptings of caution and allow, as in Kuwait, a vast accumulation of wealth in a limited number of hands.

[42] Though ᶜAbd Allah Salim of Kuwait did eventually make some attempt to curb the worst excesses.

appointments to ministerial office,[43] increasingly elective municipal government,[44] and a promise of constitutional representation, of however guided a type, demands may still remain within bounds.

Throughout this initial period, if public demands are not later to explode in his face, the ruler may have himself, at times, to articulate and reinforce them, for a matrix of effective political action may be slow to emerge, even in military form.[45] From the initial export of oil, the ruler may for ten years or more be relatively free from serious public pressure and almost completely free from serious ideological demands. If this period of grace is profitably spent, subsequent stability may possibly be assured. If not, the failure of the public to organize may be a disservice where family pressures are in play, and early associations of petroleum labour, taxi drivers and merchants (if, indeed, merchants can subordinate individual gain to their collective good),[46] may play a useful part if only in dispelling complacency and, in some cases, in helping counterbalance the army. Student organization of sufficient scope is likely to emerge far too late.

On the side of the ruler, *his* problem is gradually to adopt a fairly modern view of the state and to dragoon his family into accepting it, so that his diffuse or long-term demands on the public will conform with

[43] In Kuwait, departments were established and placed under commoners in the constitutional reforms of 1937, but were subsequently replaced by members of the Sabah family, with the addition of the commoner ᶜAbd Allah Mulla Salih in a quasi-ministerial position. As part of the constitutional reforms of 1961 onwards, commoners were appointed to some of the newly-designated ministries. In Kuwait of all places, one feels, there should have been an attempt to associate commoners with government long before it was in fact done; in fact, precisely in 1937.

[44] Also introduced in Kuwait as part of the post-independence reforms, and projected in Qatar after 1963.

[45] It is the matrix which has so far been lacking rather than instances of political activity. In Kuwait it existed, in the merchant aristocrats opposed to Sabah pretensions; but these could hardly foster a modern political movement and in any case lost their opportunity with the crushing of the constitutional cause and the transformation of their class with the influx of oil revenues. Their successors, the radical nationalists, though vocal in parliament and without, are still too limited in number to constitute a movement; they have, however, sponsored isolated incidents of protest. In Qatar, political incitement has radiated mainly from Hamd Al ᶜAtiyah, the brother-in-law of Shaikh ᶜAli ibn ᶜAbd Allah (see footnote 23), who professes Arabist sentiments and possibly harbours republican ones. He was suspected in connection with the oil-pipeline sabotage of November 1956, and, but for his arrest, would clearly have played a major part in the 'strike' of 1963. In Dubai the Ghurair family has been a centre of Arabist sentiment and mild Arabist activity. For the political stances of members of ruling families see Note 50.

[46] See footnote 41. In Qatar, Abu Dhabi and Dubai they have had difficulty in subordinating private interest to their collective good and in organizing effectively. In Qatar they have been unable to block labour legislation or recover debts from Al Thani; in Abu Dhabi the extent of their co-operation has been to make reasonably successful representations against the share of foreigners in trading and contracting; in Dubai their interests have been safeguarded rather by the ruler than through their collective efforts.

political ideology when it takes root.[47] The family must not be allowed to preempt the state and its revenues at the moment of its birth, though some diversion of revenue and office to their hands may for a time be unavoidable and may, if other public demands are met, be viewed without bitterness; experience has shown that family wings are hard but not impossible to clip.[48] With regard to his short-term demands on the public, the ruler is in the happy position of having to make none at all, beyond the acceptance of traffic and labour legislation and the other restrictions inherent in industrialization and urbanization; indeed, with oil revenues to take the place of taxes, there is a danger that the public may come to look on the state as a cornucopia, independent of their own efforts and involving no responsibility on their part for its maintenance – a poor but not untypical foundation for Third World democracy. Ideally, as soon as oil revenues are used mainly for the public benefit, light taxation should be imposed against this future danger; and in the case of certain social groups measures must certainly be taken to prevent land speculation and the accumulation of vast commercial or industrial fortunes.

The reinforcement of government demands – that is to say, public support for the regime – depends inevitably on the ruler's character and the ruler's policies. Respect initially exists for his office and often for his person; if this is maintained, it may, as we have seen, hold the evolving state together while new bases of authority take shape. These might include a consolidation of local sentiment round the ruler,[49] perhaps strengthened by the vicissitudes of foreign relations; but they will consist largely of a sense of common interest, confidence in the ruler's goodwill, and in time the conviction that he is working in his own way towards ideologically acceptable goals. A bond of ideological fervour between ruler and public is perhaps conceivable in only three situations. The first is – *per improbabile* – a prolonged and public dispute between ruler and family in the interests of progress. The second is continuous hostility from foreign states or a serious threat from a resident foreign population. The third is a successful attempt of some member of the ruling family to seize supreme power as head of an Arabist or other ideological movement.[50] It is questionable, even so, how long an ideological bond could

[47] In Kuwait an Al Sabah decision to adopt a calculating and pragmatic (but by no means ideological) liberalism was made implicitly with the expulsion of ᶜAbd Allah Mubarak in April 1961. In the subsequent family division over the constitution (1961–2) the progressives won – possibly because the family did not see the implications of the constitution. During the Qatar 'strike' of 1963 the more progressive side, including the ruler and deputy ruler, tipped the scale, but with no very significant long-term consequences.

[48] As the experience of Kuwait shows.

[49] Attempted in school text books from Kuwait to Dubai (which is Biladuna Dubai).

[50] So far the appeal of individual family members to Arabist or popular forces has not been very serious. In Kuwait Jabir Ahmad seems to have made some small attempt to win edu-

last. Inherently the traditional regime is at odds with modern ideology, and even a ruler or member of a ruling family who turned himself into a republican president would be suspect.

There remain manipulation and coercion. Manipulation, mainly in the form of propaganda, will no doubt be employed; a powerful national – or, if federation proceeds, regional – radio and television station would represent a wise investment of oil revenues for any ruler. As for coercion, in most conceivable situations its use against the public would be a confession of failure. Even so, it might, up to the present time, have been successfully applied through bedu forces, though at the expense of alienating the educated part of the public still further. But even bedu forces, if they have modern equipment, require officers with modern training, who may not remain eternally loyal in despite of their modern principles.[51]

But the security forces present a still greater problem. The near future, as we have noted, is likely to bring armies of a far more modern type, whose officers may affect the evolution of politics more comprehensively than has been usual elsewhere. However enlightened the ruler may be, his position and the possibility of orderly transition are likely to depend largely on his relations with the army. This could perhaps be considered a reason for the deepest pessimism. Might not a group of officers imbued with socialist Arabism take over the government on principle, however wisely it was already operating, only to divide immediately on personal grounds or on details of ideology? Might not the same occur out of professional impatience with a ruler who adjusted the pace of reform to the comprehension of society as a whole? Is there not always enough personal resentment among ambitious or politically active officers to drive them to violent action, in the absence of any deep-rooted loyalty to the regime? Or might not the almost inevitable conflict between civilian and military influence equally impel the army to take control?

---

[51] During the Qatar 'strike' in 1963 there was some doubt how the security forces, which contained Yemeni other ranks, republican in sympathy, and some Palestinian officers of liberal views, would behave. In fact they supported the regime loyally, though they were admittedly not called on to take very forceful action.

---

cated public support, though on modernist rather than political grounds. In Qatar, Nasir ibn Khalid of the Bani Ahmad branch of Al Thani has close relations with commoner merchants and organized them in resistance to the labour law, while the Bani Hamd (and especially 'Suhaim' and Nasir ibn Hamd) have courted the public with professions of reformism and of sympathy with labour and with Arabism. In Abu Dhabi Sultan ibn Shakhbut seemed inclined to woo labour until the strike of 1963. In Dubai Maktum ibn Rashid seemed for some time to be a nucleus for Arabist, anti-imperialist, anti-Persian sentiment. So far there has been too little modern political sentiment in any of the states to make an appeal to it, against the family, worth while; the situation may, however, change.

True; but it is likely that policies which are acceptable to the politically-conscious public in general will also be acceptable to politically conscious officers, with the proviso that officers may demand a higher standard of superficial efficiency than the civilian public; whether or not military ideologists nevertheless decide to seize power will depend largely on the ruler's expressed sympathy with their principles and particularly on his foreign policy, not least towards those Arab governments which are setting the ideological trend of the moment. As for those internal army disputes which have played a part in most military *coups d'état* in the Middle East, these are a hazard with which several existing rulers might be thought quite capable of dealing; a younger generation of rulers might, like King Husain of Jordan, learn the trade, others possibly not. There is another factor worth considering, though this might well take effect after rather than before a military coup: no group of people except governments themselves are more jealous of their regional autonomy, status and privileges than an officer corps. And finally, the will and capacity even for a military coup take some years to mature.

To summarize: optimistic – perhaps wildly so – despite the manifest dangers, we have supposed that the situation has progressed to the point where respected and public-spirited rulers have been flexible enough to modify their own and their family's long-term demands on the public and to meet the most pressing of the public's material demands, while complying with sensitive ideological requirements in foreign policy, listening sympathetically to all aspirations, conciliating the security forces, giving hope for gradual public participation in government, controlling business interests sufficiently to prevent too obvious an income gap, and preventing the older members of the ruling family from behaving like rogue barons[52] and the younger members like juvenile delinquents.[53] In the course of this advance, a state machine of reasonable efficiency has been established, preferably not overloaded with sinecures and preferably with indigenous replacements for foreign employees under training. For a period these beginnings should be more than enough to ensure stability. They have never in practice been completely realized and in some principalities there have been striking provocations to the public, yet none of them is close to revolution. Kuwait, at this stage, survived its perplexities. Dubai, in simpler circumstances, has so far flourished. Qatar, despite the conduct of Al Thani, has been saved by the personal popularity of its dyarchs Ahmad and Khalifah, by diffused affluence, due to no small extent to the personnel and operating policy of the oil companies, and to efficient administrative and security services. Abu Dhabi, after family

---

[52] The most exotic of whom have been ᶜAbd Allah Mubarak and Fahd Salim of Kuwait.
[53] As only too many of them do; in this respect family control frequently breaks down.

and public opinion had come to resent the caution of Shakhbut ibn Sultan, has now a popular and devoted ruler whose principal problem may be the vortex of change. But stability of this kind cannot endure indefinitely. Sooner or later all rulers will be confronted with a specific and reinforced demand for public participation in government. So far only Kuwait has advanced to this further stage; and this, in response to a certain public demand but by no means under its pressure, was effected by the ruler himself, in establishing constitutional and parliamentary rule in 1961–2.[54] If only because of this example, the aspiration is certain to spread; participation, in a limited form, was a demand even of the Qatar 'strikers' in 1963.[55] Let us assume that the ruler is prepared to concede or anticipate the demand; what are the relative prospects of stability and chaos?

Here, if we were to proceed systematically, we should analyse the utility, the requisites and the likely fate of various types of regime which are likely to emerge in the area or could be induced to do so, and should then determine what application of political engineering could increase the persistence and utility of the toughest and most serviceable. We might adopt, as particularly suited to conditions of change, the original typology of David Apter,[56] which establishes a continuum of regimes, with 'reconciliation' and 'mobilization' regimes (systems) at the extremities, and what we might, more simply, call a mixed regime in the centre; the Gulf regimes, in their pre-petroleum form or at the point of development at which we have left them, are of the mixed type.

These three types of regime may readily be classified in terms of our reciprocal demands, of their sectional or collective nature, and of the volume and quality of their reinforcement,[57] but we shall here outline them more economically. The reconciliation regime (with democracy an

[54] After false starts in 1921 and 1938.

[55] See footnote 6.

[56] 'System, Process and Politics of Economic Development' in Hoselitz, B.F., and Moore, W.E. (eds.) *Industrialization and Society* (The Hague, 1963), as opposed to his modified typology in *The Politics of Modernization* (Chicago, 1965). In the later typology the intermediate system, originally called 'modernizing autocracy', is divided into 'modernizing autocracy' and 'neomercantilism', whose difference, in practice, seems to be that they come respectively before and after a mobilization or highly ideological regime. Our purpose requires the initial, more general, category, which we have generalized still further by eliminating modernization as a mandatory value; we have also dispensed with the term 'autocracy' which (in our Gulf context) would tend to obscure the considerable reinforcement of some public demands on the ruler, and used the non-committal term 'mixed regime'.

[57] Our model has been adopted partly because it permits such classification. Apter's hierarchical-pyramidical-segmental distinction is converted into our balance of reciprocal, reinforced demands, with particular reference to the source of demands on government and whether their substance is sectional or collective. Apter's distinction between consummatory and instrumental values is represented in the character of the reciprocal demands and the bases of their reinforcement.

extreme subtype) is a pluralist system in which government holds the ring for conflicting public demands, both sectional and collective (national), mediates between them, and implements those of them on which agreement has been reached; government is the instrument of society. The mobilization regime (with totalitarian dictatorship an extreme subtype) is ideally a one-way system in which public demands are obviated because government imposes elitist policies for the public good; society is the instrument of government. The mixed system tends to work autocratically where collective issues are concerned and as a reconciliation system on sectional issues. The typical cultural and psychological tone of the three regimes is respectively one of pragmatic and institutionalized bargaining within a revered framework of law; one of ideological zealotry and charisma; and a combination of institutionalized ideology, or custom, and pragmatism. These cultural and psychological differences are expressed in the nature of demand and the bases of reinforcement. The main requisites of the three regimes are as follows. For the reconciliation: plural groups with adequate reinforcement, the temperament and institutions for reconciliation, reasonable cultural homogeneity, adequate information, a concern for collective as well as sectional interests, and leadership which shall pursue the common interest in changing circumstances. For the mobilization: a party of unity and fervent ideological certitude, commanding wide public acquiescence or support, possibly a charismatic leader, and a backstop of specific and diffuse fear. For the mixed: institutionalized goals and leadership and a sense of common material interest, braced if possible by the personal authority of a ruler or dynasty. In terms of context and utility, the reconciliation regime is one of social crystallization or recrystallization, and in these conditions it can perhaps operate more efficiently than any other type. The mobilization regime is the regime of flux, which, by forced integration and power of will, it may recrystallize at a new level. The mixed regime is based on the coexistence of divergent institutions (such as traditional and modern) and is ideally one of smooth transition, in particular exploiting the old culture, while it lasts, to ensure reinforcement for government demands and to sanctify innovation, but holding the confidence of emerging groups and preparing them to inherit the kingdom; its main instrument is evolving but unbroken authority.

All these regimes and their many subtypes may exist in more or less operative forms, according to whether or not their requisites are met. In the case of a particular Gulf State it would not be too difficult, at a given time and for a limited period, to predict what type might spontaneously or with practicable encouragement emerge, and to prescribe the structures through which the requisites of persistence and utility could best be satisfied. The capacity to meet requisites and retain power of manoeuvre will depend largely on policies adopted by government in the first stages of change; these will include the following, which may readily be related to the scheme which precedes:

(1) nature and phasing of plans for economic development and social services; on the phasing will largely depend, inter alia, the extent of foreign immigration;

(2) policy towards private wealth, capital and enterprise;

(3) policy towards occupying and financing the public, whether one of dole, fictitious land dealings and sinecures, or of providing productive, profitable and satisfying employment. The latter must depend partly on existing culture, modern education and oil company policies, and on the possibility of 'natural' economic development or of more exotic activity like space research, organized humanitarianism, military conquest or permanent holidays abroad. But this constitutes the core – and ethical – problem of gigantic oil revenues in tiny communities, and it lies outside the present treatment.

(4) educational and training policy and the quality of consulting education whether adapted to policies under previous heads, whether designed to implement information or develop processes of thought, whether doctrinaire or pragmatic, and whether, in its political aspects, related to the local situation;

(5) policy towards foreign economic enterprise and towards the immigration, naturalization and general treatment of foreigners;

(6) policy towards labour organization and other sectional associations;

(7) policy towards the old and new culture and the creation of a homogeneous society;

(8) recruitment, training and organizational policy for the state machine and security forces;

(9) foreign policy;

(10) ruler's policy towards his family and, in particular, to their share of oil revenues, perpetuation in the senior offices of state, ostentation, and treatment of the public.

Two other types of policy must also be considered. The first of these are policies adopted by the oil companies. Oil companies are sensitive to their social obligations and the need to isolate themselves from politics; it is not always clear whether they recognize their industrial activity as implicitly political in the highest degree, in that its consequences are certain to terminate existing regimes and may well result in prolonged political instability or chaos. Their policy towards the training of nationals, labour organization, employment of national importers and contractors or stimulating the emergence of such a class, and the location of headquarters may ultimately prove as crucial for the political development of a country as their production and concession policies. In particular, a wise and confident Ruler, with eventual democracy in mind, might do well – were it possible – to forgo financial gain and to insist on oil operations which rested on labour rather than automation.

In the second place, the attitudes of foreign representatives and advisers are also significant, influencing, as they may, the policies of the rulers themselves. Official foreign representatives are frequently men of insight and analytical capacity; they are, however, confronted with strongminded, idiosyncratic rulers, who have unique and self-conscious expertise on traditional society and politics, no clear conception of the more or less objective forces of social change, and a marked dislike for the political development of Kuwait. When rulers are faced with a modern challenge they may conceivably react with acumen; to induce them to act long before the need is apparent requires a personal relationship and authority which cannot, perhaps, be guaranteed at all, and certainly not by the rigidity and short tenure of official appointment, brilliant though its outcome sometimes is. The policy of foreign states may demand, moreover, that rulers should be thrust into the maelstrom of material, social and even political change without ensuring that the prerequisites of stability are simultaneously laid down. Here the responsibility is usually recognized by official foreign representatives, even if it is difficult to discharge; but where purely economic advisers are introduced the responsibility may not even be recognized. Their functions, the economic advisers may argue, are economic, not political; if the country can be presented with a modern facade and employ its revenues for the state and public, it would be impertinent to obtrude political considerations which might taint the economic plan itself in the eyes of an experienced and still autocratic ruler. To this argument, if it were permissible to defile social science with ethics, the reply might suggest itself: If you are not in a position to advise him on modern politics, you have no business to advise him on modern economics.

In conclusion, the factors we have been reviewing may be predictable in a given principality within a given space of time, but can hardly be generalized for the whole area or for an unspecified period. It is not too difficult to suppose, as we have done, that some rulers might retain the power to decide at what point and to what form the regime should change; but we cannot necessarily suppose that any one form of regime would operate stably and efficiently throughout the area, nor make significant predictions except from the detailed dispositions of individual states, nor perhaps hope to make any very systematic prediction at all for a state which has hardly started on the course of development. Certain generalities might, however, be permitted. The spontaneous emergence of mobilization regimes is unlikely, with their requisite of a united, dedicated, case-hardened and widely accepted ideological party, and if such a regime were imposed by military force or diplomacy, the absence of the same requisites would hardly permit it to survive. The more probable alternatives may be stated simply. First – and this paper has striven to show that this is not inconceivable – there might be a more or less stable advance, first to a workable mixed regime with democratic forms, directed by a modernizing ruler or some other gifted leader or group of leaders,[58] and eventually to a workable reconciliation system and ultimate democracy; at every change of authorities or regime there would, of course, be the possibility of breakdown. In the second place, a country might fall into a development trap, embodied in the perpetuation of an ineffective mixed regime in its many subtypes, from self-seeking parliamentary oligarchy to soldiers playing the adult statesman. Such a regime can always, for a few months, support some group of incompetents; but it can never concentrate or perpetuate enough authority and ability for an advance to a new level, and it prevents society itself from developing the requisites for advance. In any case, the outcome begins to take form at the moment an oil agreement is signed, and it is determined more precisely with every subsequent decision. The ruler who affixed his signature to such a contract should pray for divine protection and for far-sighted and not too compliant advisers; otherwise, like the assassin leader, he may have lost this world and the next.

[58] Leadership for a post-shaikhly regime has been dealt with implicitly rather than in detail. Here, too, oil companies might unconsciously play a formative part.

PART III

SOCIOLOGY AND CULTURE

IO

SOME SOCIAL ASPECTS OF THE TRUCIAL STATES

P. A. LIENHARDT

THE POSITION OF WOMEN IN THE SOCIETY OF THE TRUCIAL COAST

In the Trucial Coast of Oman, external forms present immediate and striking evidence of the extreme social difference between women and men. Women, whether young or old, appear in public as little as can be managed. When they do appear, they wear masks and veils and their black outer clothing stretches down to their feet. In the coastal villages, if a woman sees a strange man approaching in the street, it is proper for her to turn to the wall until he has passed. If she has the opportunity, she may hurry away down a side street to avoid him completely. In this part of Arabia, as in other Middle Eastern countries, traditional houses are designed so as to provide a maximum of privacy for the women of the family. The rooms are built around a courtyard on to which the windows face, the houses presenting only blind walls to the street. Immediately inside the doorway which opens from the street into the courtyard of a house, one usually finds a curtain wall, so that even when the door is opened people cannot see in. Such external forms as these are connected with a whole complex of attitudes towards women and of beliefs about their proper status, how they should behave and how they should be treated. Taken together, these matters form an important part of the local value system and play their part in determining the social forms observed in Trucial Coast society even in circumstances from which women are absent.

The wealth that is now coming into the Trucial States cannot help but produce profound changes in the society, and there can be no doubt that one of the things that is likely to change most is the status of women. There are two obvious reasons for expecting this. One is that wealth opens up communications and in so doing it not only provides opportunities for people to gain some knowledge, however superficial, of other societies and to compare their own society with these, but it actually forces them to do so. Of course, for technological reasons, such comparisons are going on increasingly throughout the world in any case, but one may expect wealth to add considerably to the speed of the process in this particular instance. Secondly, the sudden development of education for both boys and girls encourages them to reject an old way of life and develop something new.

The purpose of this paper, however, is not to discuss change, which in any case is at its very beginnings, but to give some account of the traditional position of women in Trucial Coast society. One cannot, after all, notice change, let alone assess or analyse it, without first having considered its point, or points, of departure. And though the segregation of women from men not closely related to them is one of things that must at once meet the eye of any visitor to the towns and villages of the Trucial Coast, this segregation makes it difficult for a visitor to gain any precise knowledge of the women's position. Apart from its being difficult for a man to talk to women there, it is not even proper for him to ask very much about them, particularly to ask in any detail about specific cases. Things are not quite so bad as suggested by the Kuwaiti historian Yusuf ibn ᶜIsa al-Qinaᶜi, who says that a traditional Kuwaiti, mentioning a woman in the course of telling a story to his friend, would say, *Akramak Allah*, an apologetic expression he would not use 'if he were mentioning an insect'. But gathering information is a slow process, and in the earlier stages one can easily be misled, particularly in assessing the extent of male dominance. In the Trucial Coast, as in numerous other places, men are not as dominant in society as they claim to be. The difficulty here lies in gathering other information with which to compare the men's generalizations.

People in the Trucial Coast regard women as being inferior to men in an absolute sense. They hold this to be a fact established by the divine dispensation and made clear in religion. This, rather than heavier responsibility, is held to be why the Koran lays down as a general principle that a woman inherits half of what is inherited by a man when the two are in equivalent positions relative to a deceased person. In law, the evidence of a man as a witness is equal to the evidence of two women, a circumstance which suggests a certain absolute standard of comparison. The Koran itself states quite clearly that men have pre-eminence over women. When they speak of women in general, men in the Trucial Coast will often say that women are prone to temptation and need to be kept in check by men if they are not to go astray. And the views of some of the more old-fashioned people can be extreme. I have several times been told quite seriously that it was a good thing to teach girls to read, so that they could read the Koran and devotional books, but a bad thing to teach them to write, because they might be tempted to write letters to young men. In the past, however, it was most unusual for women to be literate at all. One of the things often mentioned to illustrate the remarkable progressive-mindedness of Shaikh Mani^c, the Dubai shaikh who tried to bring into being a reform movement in opposition to Shaikh Sa^cid ibn Maktum, the father of the present ruler, some thirty years ago, is that he taught his daughter to read and write.

The local picture of the ideal good woman is that she should be modest and shy and should stay at home as much as possible. She should avoid contact with men other than those who are closely related to her. Moreover, she should not mix too widely with women outside the family circle, since some of them may be immoral and may lead her into difficulties. She should look after her husband and children and manage the household economically. If her husband is happy at home, he will not spend so much time wasting his money outside the house. Among the poorer people it is thought that a woman ought to sew at home to earn a little extra money in order to buy extra things for her children.

Many women are very devout, and they may shame some of the men into keeping up with religious observances. On the two main feasts of the year, when the prayers are performed in the open air, the women appear in public and form up into ranks a little distance behind the ranks of the men in order to join in the prayers and listen to the sermon. But mortuary ceremonies stress the distinction between the sexes. A woman is *haram*, forbidden, to strangers in death as in life. Whereas it is a meritorious act for any man to help to carry the bier of a dead man, a woman's bier is carried only by men closely related to her. The body of a man is wrapped in a single shroud, but a woman's body is wrapped in two and a curtain is spread over the grave so that onlookers cannot see the body being laid out there.

There can be no doubt of the inferior status of women in the society of the Trucial Coast, and the seclusion in which women are expected to live is one of the results of their subordination. Their place is, very definitely, in the home, and they have no place in the market or in the public meeting. But of course the 'home' in question is not that of a tiny elementary family, but of a wider family group. And this family group is one upon which many of the affairs of the Trucial Coast, social, economic and even political, turn. In relation to families, the very limitation of a woman's scope can be regarded from another point of view as a specialization, and the fact of the seclusion of women can be seen to exclude men from a range of contacts which women have among themselves. The public role of men and the private role of women in the society are symbiotic in a sense far beyond simple conjugality.

The seclusion in which women are expected to live places them under considerable economic disabilities. Most women would find it very hard to support themselves independently of men. If a woman is particularly enterprising, and if the men of her family permit it, she can open a little shop in her house, selling goods entirely to other women from round about. But most shopping, even for household goods and supplies, is done by men. Given the necessary business acumen, richer women with inherited capital can speculate on property values and invest in merchant voyaging and smuggling. In order to do so they need to have men acting on their behalf, agents through whom they can deal with other men. (I am afraid I do not know enough of such situations to be able to tell how easy or difficult it is for them to get honest treatment or to check the actual profits made out of their money in some of these transactions.) Without any capital at all, there is no respectable way for a woman to earn money except by sewing and perhaps selling a few eggs and a little milk from the chickens and goats in the yard. Employment for wages, even as a domestic servant, is out of the question because of the imperative need to avoid men of other households. In the past, slave women did domestic work, but here it was perfectly legal and respectable for their masters to have sexual relations with them if they so wished. It is said that in the 1930s and 1940s when many slaves were emancipated because they were no longer profitable and their owners could no longer afford to keep them, many slave women found they could turn only to prostitution to earn a living. On the other hand, neighbours in Ras al-Khaimah told me of two slave women living together in great poverty who had remained so modest that they had never been into the market there.

The economic disabilities of women, which follow from their seclusion, have a marked effect on family relationship, particularly when a husband can divorce his wife at will and then has no further responsibility to support her. So long as a divorced woman has a son the weakness of her position can become, paradoxically, a strength, giving her such a strong claim over the son in terms of helplessness that the claims of the father in terms of authority cannot compete with it. This is one of the points where one can see a clear discrepancy between some generalized local values and other values which are applied to particular cases. In general, authority and responsibility are associated with the father and the paternal line. Perhaps one remark made in passing in the course of a conversation about religion suggests ways in which people think of the paternal line better than does many a more general formulation: a young man who was telling me that any sensible person ought to be a Muslim said, 'What is the good of being a Christian and obeying God without obeying his Prophet Muhammad? It is just like obeying your father without obeying your father's brother'. And in one sense the lives of agnates are con-

sidered to be interchangeable. The blood feud
unlikely, in the towns of the Trucial Coast,
agnates to the fourth or fifth generation are he
for any killing committed by any of them. On
say that it is not important who a man's moth
his father is. A proverbial local expression has i
foot', which is explained by another expressi
man's attitude to divorcing his wife: 'I have l
will get some more'. Nevertheless, a man whe
serious risk of alienating his sons, particularly among the poorer people.
The practical need of the mother weights the moral obligation on her side.

at leisure, satisfied' woma gre

A man can divorce his wife at will, and even on the spur of the moment,
simply by pronouncing the appropriate formula. When this happens, the
divorced wife must veil her face immediately in front of her husband,
pack up her belongings and return to her father's house. Her father or,
if he is dead, her brother is expected to look after her until she is married
again. For an older woman the situation can be a very difficult one. It
may be hard for her to marry again, and she may find herself treated as a
nuisance in her brother's house. So long as her father is alive a woman is
usually secure, but in her brother's house, where her presence may make
demands on very limited sleeping accommodation and a slender income,
tension often arises between the woman and her sister-in-law. For the
social reasons I have mentioned already, there is nothing a poor woman
can do for herself in these circumstances, and so if she has a son he is
under a strong obligation to look after her. If his father divorces his
mother, a son is thought to be obliged to look after the mother, who
formed his body out of her blood and her milk. He is expected to leave
his father's house and set up a house of his own where his mother can
live with him. If the son is too young to do this at the time of the divorce,
then he should do so as soon as he is old enough. Only if the mother
marries again does the obligation lapse.

The position of a woman who wishes to obtain a divorce from her
husband in the Trucial Coast is, in practice, rather stronger than in some
other traditional Islamic societies. Perhaps this should be attributed to
the influence of bedouin society as compared with the influence of peasant
life. Though a woman can only divorce her husband in exceptional
circumstances, her family acting on her behalf before a court, it is possible
for her to leave him, and if she does so there is no social pressure to
oblige her family to send her back. Social pressure works the other way,
impelling the husband towards divorcing her. A husband who tries to
hang on to his wife against her wishes lays himself open to ridicule and
contempt. When, as often happens, a man divorces in haste and repents

he tries to get his wife back by what is called 'making her
, which means giving her money or property. The more a
n is able to get out of her husband in these circumstances, the
ater is her future security likely to be. Women are expected to keep
their own assets. Even among the poor, it is not usual for a wife to
confuse her money with her husband's. The woman who is in charge of
the housekeeping for a poor family will have her husband's money
entrusted to her and he will ask for it when he wants it. But if she has
any money of her own she keeps it separately.

In spite of the inferior status of women in the society of the Trucial
Coast, here as elsewhere, the true basis of marriage is thought to lie in
the love and mutual comfort which a husband and wife give to each other.
But in formal terms the marital bond here, being easily dissoluble, is
weaker than in some other societies. The bond of a woman with her natal
family is correspondingly stronger. When a woman marries, her husband
takes over responsibility for her from her father, but if she is divorced
the responsibility reverts to her own agnates. In law it is held that a
husband has a right to forbid his wife to visit even her father except if he
is mortally ill. In practice it is much more common to find fathers inter-
vening between their daughters and their sons-in-law, trying to protect
the daughters' interests and promote their wellbeing. A complaint brought
before the ruler of Ras al-Khaimah will illustrate the way these questions
arise among the poor. (As far as they can, richer people try to settle their
disputes among themselves and keep the rulers out of their affairs.) In
this instance, a father complained that his daughter was not being properly
treated. Her husband and his brother, who was also married, had a house
with only one room and a yard. At night the two married couples slept in
the same room. The complainant thought this improper and suggested
that his daughter and her husband should go and live in a hut that his
daughter's brother owned some distance away from the house. The husband protested that if they were obliged to do this he and his brother
would be put to the expense of maintaining two separate households,
whereas it was much cheaper and better for them to share the housekeeping. He said that if they were not allowed to share the room for
sleeping it would be better for him and his wife to go and sleep in the
hut at nights and live in the house in the daytime. In any case, his brother
was shortly going to work in Kuwait and later he was going there himself.
Having found that there was no date fixed for the departure of either
brother, the ruler said that the present sleeping arrangements were dis-
graceful and could not be allowed to continue. On the other hand, the
hut was too far away for the complainant's daughter and her husband to
go and sleep there every night. He thought it unnecessary for the brothers

to divide their housekeeping, and so told them that they must dismantle the hut and re-erect it in the yard of the house. He then granted a further request from the complainant that his daughter should be permitted to live with her parents whilst her husband was away in Kuwait.

Such a case as this illustrates how the local ideology stresses the agnatic bonds of men rather than those of women, but it shows also how the latter can undermine the former. Powerful men can often draw daughters' husbands, and even more their daughters' sons, into their own orbit. Even when women are transferred in marriage to the keeping of another family, as social persons they carry the social group of their own family with them into their married life. It is significant that if a wife is unfaithful to her husband, so long as he divorces her as soon as he finds out, the situation carries much less shame for him than it does for her father, her paternal uncles and her brothers. If she is to be punished – and sometimes she may be killed – it is for her own family to punish her. In this society where the premise of divorce is a part of the idea of marriage, it is only in a limited way that a woman's social person is transferred to her husband and his family on marriage, since the transfer is, at most, no more final and absolute than the marriage itself.

The contrast in social circumstances between men and women implies certain contrasts in inclination and will. This is particularly the case where moving from place to place is in question. Here, as far as men are concerned, the seafaring and bedouin traditions associated with the old ways of livelihood open to the people of the Trucial States lead to attitudes markedly different from those of a peasantry, more particularly a peasantry in countries where cultivable land is scarce. Seafarers, like bedouin, can move from place to place without great financial loss, and it has been common for people in the Trucial Coast to move in order to avoid oppression or to seek greater profit. Sometimes they have moved in quite large groups, like the group of Al Bu Falasah and Rumaithat who set up the present government of Dubai in 1833. But many more have moved singly and in small groups, as they still do. For women, however, movement has very different implications from those it has for men. Given a social circle restricted to the women of related families and their friends, a woman who goes to live in a foreign place with her husband loses much of her company and the emotional security it provides, and if her husband treats her badly she has nowhere to turn for help. Hence women are on a whole unwilling to move away from their fathers' families. Conversely, a man moving into a new place is likely to marry a local wife. By doing so, he integrates himself into a particular group of the community he joins. Hence, as far as geographical movement is concerned, the influence of women is towards stability and integration in two senses, on the one hand restraining men from moving and on the other, if they do move, helping to integrate them into their communities of adoption.

For the same reasons of security as make it uncommon for women to move away from their natal families, Arab parents in the Trucial Coast prefer in general to give their daughters in marriage to men who are related to them already. In discussing the matter, people do not usually express any strong preference for the marriage of paternal first cousins – that famous Arab marriage – and speak with enthusiasm of the son of the father's sister or the son of a brother or sister of the mother. Even affinity, once established, is a cause for promoting further marriage ties. People say that when they are related to some other family already they know much better how their daughter is likely to be treated if she marries into it. In such marriages there is a further idea of holding families together and, among richer people, of preserving the family property and the family reputation. 'What falls from the moustache drops into the beard.' It is thought shameful for a girl to marry her social inferior, but if she marries amongst those who are kin already the question of inferiority does not arise. People speak of high social position in terms of two criteria, origins – of being of pure Arab stock – and wealth. Neither of these without the other is enough to establish a man in high position. Though purity of stock is the more strongly stressed of the two, when a family has been wealthy for some generations there seems to be less doubt raised about its purity than there might be otherwise. Whilst these criteria set the pattern of new marriage alliances, the reaffirmation of old marriage ties by the making of new ones on the same lines steadies down the process of social mobility. Hence the pattern of marriages is an element in the stability of the social classes.

Here, although I have been asked to write about social questions, I must touch briefly on history and politics before I can continue with any discussion about women in relation to the class system of the Trucial States. To judge from what one is constantly told when one inquires into history and politics from local people, anyone who judges the Trucial Coast from its days of poverty in the thirty-year interregnum between the collapse of the pearl fishing industry and the new wealth of oil could be seriously misled by appearances. The traditional system of social hierarchy in the Trucial States was founded on occupations and fortunes which, in those impoverished times, had wasted away. In the traditional system, as it was described to me over and over again when I was doing research in the Trucial States – and this would go equally well for Kuwait – the more important and wealthy families in the towns were those that managed the pearl-fishing industry and the dhow trade. These were thought to be the truly honourable occupations, and success in them required not only the management of capital but also the management of men, often in large numbers. Both industries ran on profit sharing and debt, and each family of pearl merchants and boat owners had a number, and sometimes a great number, of families of pearl fishers and seamen working for it, depending often on its patronage whether financial or political and usually relying on loans to keep going until the next season came round. The prestige of such leading families increased their control over people and their control over people increased their prestige. Their dependants were potential fighting men, and in addition many of the leading families regularly entertained bedouin supporters. When I was doing research in the Trucial States, people often spoke of the importance of such families in the past and of how they had become impoverished when the pearling industry collapsed, losing not only their livelihood but also their capital, since most of that was loaned out in debts which could not be recovered. There were many complaints that British representatives in the Trucial States, whose decisions were influential, attached far too much importance to the shaikhs relative to other families and thereby increased their power over what it had been before.

In the times of poverty the leading Arab families found it difficult to engage successfully in other sorts of trade, and the external distinctions of wealth largely disappeared, but one of the things that marked family and personal status, the inclusiveness and corresponding exclusiveness of marriage between families, could not disappear with the same speed as did economic prosperity and economic differentiation. Long-term relationships of family with family through the giving of women in marriage – family matters only hesitantly discussed with strangers – would seem to have survived to a considerable extent, and such marriages express something surviving from the old class system. Through women, family is still excluded from family, however familiarly the men of these families mix with each other and however little they seem to be distinguishable in wealth. The broad, public society of the men is quite a different thing from the smaller and more private societies of the women and the houses. It seems quite possible that the former leading families still retain a network of influences to allow them to return to high positions.

I think therefore that it would be a great mistake to suppose, even in a place like Abu Dhabi which was hit particularly hard by the collapse of pearl fishing and which until recently had a ruler who, whatever his virtues, could not bring himself to spend money or even to allow other people to make it, that all the people were an undifferentiated proletariat attached to a little aristocracy of shaikhs – though there are shaikhs who might like it to be so and to convince other people that it is indeed so.

(It is said that towards the end of his reign when his mother's brother died Shaikh Shakhbut of Abu Dhabi discouraged the merchants from closing the market as a gesture of respect on the grounds that he was 'not a shaikh', even though he was shaikh of the Qubaisat section of the Bani Yas and had he not been so he would not have been able to prevent the murder of one of Shaikh Shakhbut's own brothers in 1927.) On the other hand it is quite clear that even in the traditional system the shaikhs always had a kind of authority which went far beyond simple leadership. They were much more than *primi inter pares*. Though Shaikh Maniᶜ of Dubai, whom I mentioned earlier as being leader of a reform movement, made his living as a pearl merchant, it was not in that character that he tried to take over the government of Dubai in 1939. He was also a leading member of the ruling family of Dubai, being the son of a former ruler.

The shaikhs in the Trucial States rule as individuals and as families, and the balance in power between the individual ruler and the other shaikhs of his family can vary a great deal with individual characters and circumstances at particular times. Invariably, within any ruling family, there exist rivalry, personal and political tension and some sort of balance of power. These are not matters which can be discussed here in detail, but they have a considerable bearing on the marriages which members of any particular ruling family make, and also on the position of women born or married into ruling families *vis-à-vis* the families as wholes and the public in general. Here some women achieve remarkable influence and power. Since shaikhs, great and small, are political personages, their marriages have a much clearer political dimension than the marriages of other people. As we have seen, marriages within any family are thought to be a way of holding the family together. In the case of a ruling family, the marriages of shaikhs' daughters to other shaikhs' sons are a matter of trying to hold together a dominant political group, and often such marriages also represent efforts to maintain or improve the position of political personages within that group. It is not the tradition to give daughters of a ruling family in marriage outside the family, even to members of other ruling families, and some daughters of shaikhs have had to stay spinsters although this is very much against what Islam recommends. It would be possible to give numerous examples of marriages which have not had the desired effect of reconciliation within ruling families. One nephew of a ruler, whose uncle gave him his daughter in marriage, is said to have remarked, 'He has married his daughter to me. Does he expect me to spend all my time in bed now?' and later the nephew rose against his uncle and drove him from power. But such marriages certainly have a complicating effect on political affairs. In the case mentioned, the wife stayed with her husband and if her son becomes the next ruler, which seems likely, he will be under strong moral pressure to bring his maternal cousins back to the state.

When shaikhs marry the daughters of men other than shaikhs, they tend to seek wives on lines which will increase their support within the community. As well as marrying women from leading families among the settled people, they also marry bedouin women. The manners of bedouin women are rather different from those of the towns and villages. Though they do not mix with men not related to them in public gatherings, bedouin women do not cultivate the extreme shyness of women of the settled communities. They will readily meet and speak to strangers, and no one suggests that their way of behaving is dishonourable or shows any lack of becoming modesty. It should be remembered that at most times in the desert bedouin women are moving about with their kin, separated from strangers not by walls but by distance. Moreover, as far as the limits of the tribe, the honour of any bedouin woman is to some extent the concern of all the men.

The marriage of shaikhs with bedouin women may be one of the reasons why the women of shaikhly families in general seem to lead a rather less secluded life than most others. Another reason, probably, is that the houses of important shaikhs are filled with bedouin guards who take social access to the women of the family for granted. When they are women of strong character, the senior women of ruling families can play an important part in affairs. Though women of the community can, and sometimes do, approach shaikhs directly in case of need, it is much easier for them to go and explain their difficulties to the wives or mothers of the shaikhs, and these shaikhly ladies may in turn help to explain their petitioners' difficulties to the shaikhs or else take action on their own account. The shaikhahs also entertain important women of the community socially, and it is to be presumed that thereby they, like other women, learn a good deal about the internal affairs of other families and pass the information on to their husbands and kinsmen.

One remarkable woman of the Trucial Coast, Shaikhah Hussah bint al-Murr, the mother of the present ruler of Dubai and wife of his predecessor, went far beyond this. Shaikhah Hussah came so far out into open public affairs as to hold her own *majlis* (public meeting), not for women but for men, sitting receiving visitors, as people said, like a shaikh, and when her husband was ruler it is said that more men visited her *majlis* than visited his. This remarkable lady was an outstanding figure both in politics and in business. In politics she played a leading part in opposing Shaikh Mani⁶ (one of whose daughters was married to her younger son) and his supporters when they introduced the idea of a consultative assembly and other policies in Dubai in 1939 and 1940. The political struggle led to

ıd the subsequent tricking and expulsion of the reformist party.
lucation, street cleaning and the like, had to wait for another
ırs. In the course of the civil war, her husband Shaikh Saᶜid ibn
educed himself to penury. His wife restored the family fortunes
by property development, trade, and, one gathers, that profitable but
risky enterprise of Dubai, smuggling with Persia and India.

The holding of a public majlis for men by a woman was unusual even
for the wife of a ruler, but it is an extreme example of the potential
importance of leading women in public affairs. On the whole, however,
if women approach public affairs they do so from private positions. In
public, women are separated from men and the men mix widely in the
public circle of the market. The women, on the other hand, mix in a
large number of smaller groups, more exclusive than the society of men
and consisting largely of closer and more distant kin, affines and other
women who are friends of the women of the family. The concerns of
these two kinds of group are rather different, not merely because of the
natural difference in concerns of the two sexes, but also because of the
convention whereby men consider it improper to discuss in any detail
family affairs which concern women excepting with other members of
the family. But families are one of the basic groupings of the society in
its economic and political, as well as its moral aspects. Here, in some
senses, the range of women is greater than that of men, and it is the
very seclusion of women and impropriety of discussing them in male
company that makes this so. Women in general are a necessary part of
the network of communications which provides information for their
menfolk, and at the head of the social hierarchy are some of the women
of the ruling families who form a focus for the smaller groupings of
women and a bridge between their concerns and the public concerns of
men.

I I

MEASURING THE CHANGING FAMILY CONSUMPTION PATTERNS OF ARAMCO'S SAUDI ARAB EMPLOYEES – 1962 AND 1968

THOMAS W. SHEA

I. INTRODUCTION

In 1962 and again in 1968, the Economics Department of Aramco carried out comprehensive household expenditure surveys of a stratified random sample of its Saudi employees for the purpose of preparing and maintaining an up-to-date consumer price index. The surveys measure actual spendings patterns of Saudi households of different sizes and with different levels of income. The indices show how price changes affect levels of living. This is an interim report, because both the analysis of the expenditure study and the preparation of the revised 1968 Saudi consumer price index are still in process.

These sample surveys contain information on family composition, housing characteristics, and expenditure patterns of Aramco employees and their dependants, representing a universe of about 84,000 persons – about 20 per cent of the population of Saudi Arabia's Eastern Province. This universe is not typical of the Eastern Province population, however. It is, in fact, an elite, because Aramco salaries and benefits are higher on the average than those paid by other major employers in the area for comparable jobs. Aramco benefits are of types which significantly influence expenditure patterns. For example, all Saudi employees of Aramco receive free medical care for themselves and their dependants. Aramco's Home Ownership Plan makes it possible for Saudi employees to buy houses on easy payment plans which also incorporate an approximately 20 per cent subsidy. Free transportation is provided from most residential areas to places of work. Aramco's commissaries sell certain food items at subsidized prices. These benefits are generally not offered by other employers.

However, Aramco, as a major employer is a leader in establishing both compensation norms and living standards in the Eastern Province as well as elsewhere in Saudi Arabia. Aramco-trained Saudi skilled and technical workers are moving in rising numbers to other employment. On the one hand, Aramco's operations have entered a phase requiring a smaller number of employees than was true in past years; on the other, there has in the past few years been a rapid increase in employment opportunities outside Aramco. Saudi Arabia is, in fact, experiencing an acute labour shortage which must to a great extent be filled by foreigners. In this skilled labour market, former Aramco employees are the principal Saudi competitors against foreigners. Increasingly, therefore, the incomes and expenditure patterns of Aramco's Saudi employees are becoming representative of Saudi skilled workers in the Eastern Province as a whole, and so long as comparisons are made only in terms of broad expenditure categories, the Aramco data may be regarded as broadly representative of Saudi Arab urban workers as a whole.

Moreover, breakdowns of Aramco household expenditures into expenditure and income classes provide useful measures of the probable expenditure patterns of the country's urban residents of Saudi nationality in similar income groups. The Aramco survey may also prove to be a helpful model in the design and conduct of similar studies elsewhere in the country.

II. METHOD

A. Sample Design

The 1962 Saudi Employee Household Expenditure Survey was designed to update a price index prepared five years earlier. It was felt that since then there had been changes in living and expenditure patterns so far reaching as to justify revising the old index.

The 1962 survey was based on a proportionate random sample stratified by job grade (or salary code) and by place of work (Table I). The Economics Department calculated, after extensive pre-tests (which, incidentally, took far longer to carry out than did the rest of the survey) that the limited time span and manpower available for this work would permit us to handle about 250 acceptable and complete interviews, or about $2\frac{1}{2}$ per cent of the Saudi work force, which then totalled over 10,000 people. The number of employees in job grades 29 and above were so few that most of the sample cells in these grades would have been vacant, or would have had no more than a single member in a proportionate sample. It was therefore decided to include employees in job grades 22–28 only. This secured coverage of 98 per cent of the Saudi work force.

The same stratification format was used in 1968 as in 1962, except that job grade 22, having since been abolished, was excluded, and grades 29 and 30 were added. This extended the universe to include all Saudi nonprofessional employees, comprising 98 per cent of the total Saudi work force when the sample was drawn in December 1967, or over 9,600 people. It was decided to reduce substantially the sample error over that of a straight proportionate sample by weighting each cell (job grade within district) by the standard error of the total household expenditures in the cell computed from the 1962 survey results. This led to a considerably larger number of employees in the higher job grades being included in the sample than strict proportional representation would dictate, and a smaller number being included from the lower grades, because total expenditures were more uniform in size in the lower than in the higher grades. Tables I and II show the distribution of the 1962 and 1968 surveys by grade within district. In processing the 1968 data, the original weights were re-applied to each cell as multipliers before making basic computations in order that the survey results would faithfully represent the universe from which they were drawn.

The same sample selection procedure was used in each survey. A list of twenty two-digit numbers was first selected from a table of random numbers. Lists of employees the last two digits of whose badge numbers corresponded with each of the two-digit numbers on the list was obtained from the Accounting Organization, and to ensure randomization within each of the twenty lists, employees in each list were arrayed by month and day of vacation date. Employees on each list were then grouped by grade within district. The number of employees in each cell of this sample fund was at least double the size of the sample, in order to allow for rejects. Quotas for each cell including replacements for rejects or no shows, were filled *seriatim* from the twenty lists.

Employees whose families lived outside of the Eastern Province and employees who were unable or unwilling to supply adequate information on family expenditures were excluded. Ability of respondents to supply comprehensive and detailed information was evaluated by interviewers on the basis of responses to eight questions on respondents' roles in shopping and in planning family expenditures.

Of 281 interviews completed in 1962, twenty-eight were rejected because of ambiguity of responses and internal inconsistencies. In 1968, the number of rejects was much larger – ninety-nine – mainly because the standards of interview acceptability were set at a much higher level than in 1962.

B. *Questionnaire Design*

The questionnaires used in these surveys were initially designed with reference to that used by the US Department of Labor in their 1960–1 Survey of Consumer Expenditures, but we incorporated additions, deletions, and emendations suggested by Aramco Saudi employees well-informed about the consumer spending habits of their colleagues. These questionnaires as first designed were then pre-tested on eight employees selected in such a way as to represent as wide a range of grade, household organization, and expenditure as possible. The 1962 questionnaire contained, in addition to questions about family size, composition, and shopping habits, entries for about 350 goods and services; the 1968 questionnaire followed closely the 1962 questionnaire, the main difference being that the number of commodity entries was dropped from 350 to less than 200.

Because climatic variations in the Eastern Province are marked, and because many commodities are available only seasonally, the Economics Department decided that coverage of a full year's expenditures should be attempted. Achieving this objective involved many procedural difficulties. The largest number of interviewers employed at one time was seven, and most of the time only four were available. None had prior background in consumer expenditure survey work, whereas administering a questionnaire designed to cover an entire year's expenditure imposed unusually heavy demands on the interviewer. The alternative of using self-administered questionnaires was rejected on the grounds that this procedure is frequently ineffective even with educated persons accustomed to questionnaires. Finally, pressure of other work limited the amount of time the Economics Department's professional staff could devote to supervising the data collection and processing phase of this assignment to a single three- or four-month period.

The defect of using a questionnaire covering an entire year is obvious: a respondent's memory of outlays which are varied and frequent, as most expenditures on food are, tends to become blurred very quickly. US Bureau of Labor Statistics experts believe that between two weeks and a month is about the maximum period of effective recall of such purchases. People tend to forget the details even of large purchases made nine or ten months ago. Memory of large numbers of incidental expenditures which are individually insignificant but collectively quite large is usually faulty and may cause major distortions.

The offsetting advantages, however, were impressive and decisive. There was virtually no observable employee hostility to the interviews. Only one employee refused interviews in 1962 and only two in 1968. Saudi employees tend to have fewer outside distractions diverting their attention from family affairs than do Westerners. Saudi households appear to be closely knit, and far more of employees' free time appears to be devoted to family finances than is true among Westerners. Moreover, there is, especially in the lower income groups, little room for flexibility in expenditure patterns and employees, who typically are responsible for the support of very large households, are obliged to supervise household expenditures closely, in order to avoid financial disaster. Last but not least, Saudi husbands do most of the family shopping.

In designing the questionnaires, close attention was paid to the importance of minimizing the amount of writing done by the interviewer, and maximizing the attention given to frequency and timing of purchases. In the sections dealing with actual expenditures on specific items, provisions were made for recording answers in highly abbreviated forms, using a glossary of shorthand terms prepared by the project directors. In the sections dealing with food purchases, for example, separate columns were reserved for frequency of purchase (into which entries such as 'W' for weekly purchases, '2M' for bi-monthly purchases, were put), number of months during the year when purchased, number of units bought each time, value per unit, and total amount spent at given time intervals. In this way, interviewers could easily record statements about purchases made at widely different intervals. Ample space was left at the end of each expenditure category (such as fresh fruits, meats, canned goods) to enable the interviewer to enter commodities which were bought by the respondents but were not included in the questionnaire list.

C. *Interview Procedures*

In the 1962 survey, six Saudi interviewers were obtained on temporary loan from other departments of the Company, of whom four were personnel counsellors from the Industrial Relations Organization. In addition, a retired Saudi personnel counsellor was employed as interview supervisor. Although none of the interviewers had previous experience in consumer expenditure surveys, the insight and *savoir faire* they brought with them from their regular jobs was readily adaptable to consumer survey work. Their close familiarity with local consumption habits, their insight into workers' attitudes, and behaviour patterns, and their experience in dealing tactfully with employees more than compensated for their lack of formal training in survey work of this type and made them far preferable to the team of experienced interviewers we first intended to bring in from Beirut.

Because in 1968 we were unable to obtain on loan the interviewers we used in the 1962 survey, the interviews of the second survey were carried out by Dr Ramsey Madany of the Economics Department, co-director of the survey, and by three employees of the Economics Department who had extensive experience with the processing of the 1962 survey questionnaires and/or comprehensive knowledge of consumer economics in the Eastern Province.

In both surveys, a two week training period was set up to familiarize interviewers with the questionnaire forms and the system of abbreviations used; to indoctrinate them in sound interview techniques; and to give them practice.

It was decided that only employees, not their family members, should be interviewed and that the interviews should be conducted away from the employees' homes. The general practice of *purdah* among Saudis in the Eastern Province effectively precluded strangers visiting Saudi employees' homes, particularly if their object was to conduct family expenditure surveys. But in any event, the time involved in locating employees at their homes would have been excessive. The interviews were therefore conducted in rooms set aside for the purpose in each of the Company's three districts.

Individual interview forms were carefully checked and hand tabulated as soon as possible after the completion of the interviews – usually the same day or the day after. This enabled a detailed evaluation to be made of the internal consistency of responses and was thus an effective device for continuing appraisal of interviewers' performance while the interview results were still fresh in their minds.

The time required for interviews and preparing of the approximately 250 interview reports used in each survey for machine processing was about four months in 1962 and about seven months in 1968. In 1968, much more extensive use of machine processing was possible than in 1962.

D. *Definition of Terms*
The following definitions were used in the survey:

Household: All persons who live in the same or adjoining dwellings, whose financial affairs are managed jointly, and who usually eat together. In the case of employees with two wives who live separately, both households are treated as a single one if the husband manages the finances of both. The term 'family' as used in this report is equivalent to household.

Expenditure Categories:
Housing: Includes all expenditures on the quarters in which employee's household resides, including land purchase and rental, together with expenditures on home repairs, structural additions, painting and all other expenditures involving maintenance or improvement of land and/or buildings.

Foodstuffs: Includes all types of food expenditure for human use, including payments to restaurants.

Clothing: Includes all types of adults' and children's clothing together with cloth purchases, and the cost of tailoring or stitching. Also included are watches, jewellery and haberdashery.

Furniture and Durable Goods: Includes rugs, bedding, kitchen utensils, and all types of house furniture, together with automobiles, motorcycles, bicycles, radios, televisions, fans, refrigerators, sewing machines, and similar items.

Household Expenses: Includes house cleaners and cleaning equipment; incidental items of household use such as matches and napkins; utilities such as electricity, running water, LPG, ice, and fuels, exclusive of fuels for motor vehicles.

Transportation: Includes bus fares, taxi fares, and auto fuel and maintenance. In 1962 it also included travel to locations outside the Eastern Province.

Miscellaneous: Includes outlays on personal care items; tobacco; entertainment and education; services, equipment repair other than autos; and the wages of household servants.

III. SURVEY RESULTS

A. *Summary*

I will first discuss the size and composition of family household units, then the physical characteristics of the houses they live in as measured by two indicators – construction material of house and presence or absence of utilities (electricity and running water). I will say a few words about the commuter status of employees (i.e., whether employees live at home during the work week, or in Company facilities), because this affects family consumption patterns.

I will then move on to a discussion of the relationship between employee income and expenditures in the different salary groups, as revealed by the 1968 survey.

The bulk of the remainder of my paper will be devoted to a comparison of expenditure patterns in the 1962 and 1968 survey by household, and on a *per capita* basis in money terms, then in real terms – i.e. corrected for price changes since 1962.

Briefly, this survey shows that the family expenditure of Aramco's Saudi Arab employees rose by nearly 50 per cent between 1962 and 1968, but that much of this increase was absorbed by an increase in the average size of family and by rising prices. The increase in real *per capita* expenditures was over 18 per cent in six years, or nearly 3 per cent per year. The most striking change in consumption patterns in the six-year period was a doubling of real *per capita* outlays on furniture, durable goods, and household expenses. This increase is associated with a more than 100 per cent increase in the proportion of employees with electricity and running water in their houses.

Average expenditures for employees in each Aramco salary grade during 1968 were lower than incomes, although many individuals spent more than they earned. Employees whose expenditures exceeded their incomes appear mainly to have been employees who made large outlays during the year on house improvements and on durable goods.

B. *Size and Composition of Households, 1962 and 1968*

Saudi families in the Eastern Province are large by European standards. Not only do they typically include large numbers of children, but many have parents and other relatives living together. Families are also growing quite rapidly in size. In 1962 the average family of an Aramco Saudi employee had 7.7 members. By 1968, it had grown to 8·7 members – a rise of 13 per cent in nearly six years, or roughly 2 per cent per year. There has been a comparable rise also in the number of dependants per worker. Table III shows changes in the average household size and composition between the period of the two surveys. It is apparent from the table that it is the increase in the number of children per household which is the most pronounced. The number of children per family rose from 4·2 to 5·5 in nearly six years – a rise of about 4½ per cent per annum. The rise in the number of children per working adult was at almost the same rate – 4·3 per cent.

Table IV shows the distribution of Aramco Saudi employees by size of family in 1962 and 1968. The model family size has risen from between 7 and 8 in 1962 to between 9 and 10 in 1968. Families with less than 7 members fell from 38 per cent of the total in 1962 to only 27 per cent in 1968. In 1968 the largest family in the survey had 43 members – 5 working adults, 8 adult dependents, and 30 children. They lived in two adjoining houses, but took their meals together and shared income and expenses as a single consumption unit.

The proportion of respondents having 2 or more wives was about the same in each survey – 10 per cent. Between 96 and 97 per cent of those with multiple wives had two wives only; the remaining 3 to 4 per cent had three wives. About a third of employees with multiple wives maintained separate residences for their other wives.

C. *Location of Household Residence and Commuter Status of Employees, 1962 and 1968*

The families of the interviewed employees lived at varying distances from Aramco's three major installations of Dhahran, Abqaiq, and Ras Tanurah. More than half lived in scattered communities situated in two oases,

Qatif and al-Hasa, which are about 120 km. apart. The Qatif oasis, with an area of 21 sq. km. is located on a littoral about 30 km. by road from the Aramco refinery at Ras Tanurah and has one major city, Qatif, with a population of about 14,000. The al-Hasa oasis with an area of 80 sq. km. is 84 km. south of the major Aramco producing centre at Abqaiq, and has two major towns, Hofuf and Mubarraz (with populations estimated at 60,000 and 30,000 respectively). Slightly more than a fifth of the employee families lived in two communities adjacent to the Company's main refining and producing areas, which were originally developed by Aramco's Home Ownership Division to cope with a severe housing problem caused by the total absence of any residential facilities near these installations at the time they were established. Just under 20 per cent of the employees live in the two large commercial centres of Dammam (a port city of 40,000 persons, 18 km. from the Aramco headquarters at Dhahran) and al-Khubar (a trading centre of about 27,000 (including ancillary towns) situated 12 km. from Dhahran). Most of the employees living in al-Khubar and Dammam have houses in two residential areas developed by the Aramco Home Ownership Program. A small proportion of employees live on the Island of Tarut, lying just off the Qatif Oasis and connected to the mainland since 1964 by a causeway. The remaining 1 per cent of employees live in various scattered towns and villages. There has been some drift of employees from the Qatif and al-Hasa oases to the Company town sites in the past six years, but the overall distribution of employee residence has remained almost the same (Table V).

There has in the past six years been an increase in the proportion of employees living with their families during the work week. Partly this is a result of the institution by Aramco in 1965 of a cash travel allowance, partly it is due to an increase in the proportion of families with cars (16 per cent in 1968 compared with 10 per cent in 1962), and partly it is the result of the construction since 1962 of improved roads to villages within the oases. In particular, the building of the causeway from Tarut Island to the mainland has been accompanied by a rise in the proportion of daily commuters from zero to 100 per cent (Table VI).

The rise in the proportion of employees living with their families during the week was of major importance in facilitating the conduct of this survey, as it was associated with more comprehensive knowledge of family expenditure habits by successful respondents than was true of the 1962 survey.[1]

---

[1] The large proportion of employees whose households live in the Company town sites, but who themselves live in Company quarters or elsewhere during the week (26 per cent) is presumably explained by inter-district transfers, and by the inclusion in the survey of employees who work on exploration crews and drilling rig crews.

D. *Home Ownership Status and Physical Characteristics of Homes*

The proportion of employees who owned or are in the process of acquiring full title to their homes rose slightly – from 85 to 87 per cent. This figure is probably an underestimate, however, because many employees rent the houses they build under the Company's home loan plan to outsiders and live in cheaper rented quarters. The survey collected information on the home ownership status of the actual place of family residence only (Table VII).

The proportion of families living in rented parts of houses, or in apartments has risen slightly, whereas the proportion of families living in tents, cane and reed huts, and other temporary quarters has fallen from 2 per cent to nothing.

The proportion of employees living in cement block or stone houses, types of construction material which in the Eastern Province today are virtually always accompanied by such improvements as tiled floors, indoor plumbing, and cooking ranges, rose from 71 per cent of total houses to 84 per cent. Most of the remainder of employees lived in huts of mud brick construction, the traditional construction material chiefly used in settled areas before Aramco began its operations (Table VIII).

There has been a spectacular increase in the proportion of employees' houses with electricity and running water from 36 per cent in 1962 to 81 per cent in 1968 (Table IX). In the interim period, electric power lines were extended to Tarut Island, and to many communities in the Qatif and al-Hasa oases which were hitherto without power. Although roughly 18 per cent of the employee households still do not have electricity, all but about 2 per cent have running water. Municipal drinking water, sewage, and drainage projects began after the time-period covered by the 1962 survey, and almost all areas where Aramco employees now live have water and sewage lines.

E. *Levels of Income and Expenditure, 1968*

Significant numbers of Aramco Saudi non-professional employee households have more than one source of income. As Table X shows, 14 per cent of the households derived income from more than one wage earner, of which roughly half have additional workers employed by Aramco and half have additional workers employed elsewhere. Three fourths of the households with multiple wage earners have two workers, and the remainder have three or more workers. The largest household, with 43 members, had five workers.

Of the 86 per cent of households with only one worker, about three fourths or 6,316 employees, derived their income solely from employment with Aramco. Thus Aramco earnings were the sole source of income for only about two-thirds of the work force.

The supplemental non-wage earnings reported by about a fourth of the single-earner households consisted mainly of rental income. Many Aramco employees rent or lease all or portions of the homes they have acquired under the Home Ownership Program, and draw from these properties rentals ranging typically from £100 to £300 per year. In addition to supplementary sources of income, many families have small plots under cultivation from which they obtain dates and vegetables; a small number of others have flocks. However, only the income contributed by multiple wage earners adds significant amounts to the Aramco salaries earned by the respondents to the survey.

No attempts were made in the interviews to collect information on supplementary sources of income, because it was the unanimous opinion of a large number of staff members who are well informed about Saudi employee attitudes that such enquiries would have generated mistrust and jeopardized the collection of information on expenditures, which was the primary survey objective.

As the purpose of both surveys was to record family outlays in the Eastern Province on consumer goods and services, including residential housing and durable goods for family use, many types of expenditure have been excluded from consideration. Expenditures not recorded include remittances to relatives living apart from the family unit, expenditures on travel outside the Eastern Province, purchases of corporate stock or of real property for investment purposes, purchases of livestock and feed, acquisition and maintenance of vehicles other than automobiles, motorcycles, and bicycles, payment of specific debt service charges, and purchase of gold in forms other than jewellery.

The information for this section was gathered by comparing incomes with expenditures of single earner households only i.e., for the first two groups listed in Table X. Income and expenditure have been grouped by Aramco pay grade. Included in income is Aramco base salary for the year 1968, plus overtime and allowances, for each employee.

Table XI shows that the average expenditures for all grades were below actual Aramco gross earnings in 1968. The distribution of expenditures is irregular, with expenditures ranging between a low of 70 per cent of incomes in grade 28 to a high of 96 per cent of incomes in grade 27.

An analysis of the dispersion of expenditures within grade shows a range which is exceptionally wide compared with income distribution within grade. Table XII shows the range of family expenditure in single-earner households compared with income ranges. In some grades, expenditure highs were multiples of three to four times expenditure lows. In no case, however, were Aramco earnings highs as much as twice earnings lows.

Table XIII shows the proportions of single-earner households whose expenditures exceeded their gross Aramco earnings by designated amounts. The expenditures of the majority of households in each job grade under-ran income. The expenditures of 70 per cent or more of the households in each grade except 23 were either below earnings, or did not exceed earnings by as much as 10 per cent. In no grade did more than 16 per cent of the single-earner households spend amounts in excess of their earnings by 20 per cent or more. The results of a debt survey undertaken in 1965 indicated that overspenders financed their outlays mainly by withdrawals from their Aramco thrift plan deposits and by credit arrangements with local merchants.

The major destabilizing factor affecting the level of average expenditures by job grade appears to be the great variation in the range of outlays on housing and durable goods. A preliminary study indicates that overspenders generally spent very large proportions of their total outlays on durable goods and housing, whereas underspenders spent little or nothing on housing and durable goods.

But more than offsetting the large outlays by some employees on consumer durables and housing is the tendency for consumer expenditures in the Eastern Province to be held in check by the absence of local entertainment and cultural facilities. In the Eastern Province outside of Aramco facilities, for example, there are no cinemas, theatres, family-type coffee houses or restaurants, bars, or music halls, and no public parks offering organized amusement facilities. The commercial centres of cities have a stern, utilitarian atmosphere which keeps consumer traffic at the minimum necessary to buy household needs. In addition consumer outlays on books, records, or educational facilities in the Eastern Province are very low. Important reasons for the dearth of entertainment facilities include both government regulations severely limiting the scope of public entertainment and the strongly puritanical Wahhabi religious and social mores which prevail among the Eastern Province populace, as well as in Saudi Arabia generally.

One explanation for the shift of the expenditure curve at grade 28 is possibly the fact that employees in higher grades tend to make larger outlays on travel outside the Eastern Province (excluded from the 1968 survey) than do lower grade employees. Employees in grade 28 and above have, on the whole, been more exposed than have others to an environmental perspective transcending the limits of life inside the home. Owing to the absence of entertainment or cultural outlets in the Eastern Province, many employees search for them abroad.

It appears likely also that investment outlays (omitted from both surveys) are proportionately higher among higher-grade employees. Many buy land and houses for investment purposes; some buy interests in construction, or trucking firms, or in the numerous contracting firms supplying maintenance services to Eastern Province municipalities, to the Dhahran International Airport, or to large business enterprises. For the most part superior education and work experience offers employees in grades 28 and above far wider investment horizons than are open to employees in the lower grades.

It is also possible that one by-product of the wider range of education and the greater diversity of interests among higher grade employees is a decreased concern with the details of family financing. As reading, travel, and efforts at job improvement make successively larger inroads into workers' free time, these interests tend to displace attention formerly given to the details of consumer expenditures. Moreover, there is also a greater tendency to leave shopping to wives and other non-working adults in the family. As a result it is probable that respondents in higher grades have a bias toward under-reporting of expenditures caused by forgetting.

F. *Household Expenditures, Per Capita Money Expenditures and Per Capita Real Expenditures, 1962 and 1968*

The purpose of this section is to show the effect which changes in prices, real incomes, and the size of families have had on the overall pattern of outlays on major expenditure categories.

Table XIV shows the changes in household expenditures on seven major expenditure categories between 1962 and 1968. The most striking increase is in expenditures on furniture and durables and in household expenses. These increases reflect the greater scope for outlays on home appliances and the rising cost of household operations brought about by the almost universal availability of electricity and running water, which in 1962 were available to only a minority of employees. The decrease in transportation reflects the exclusion of travel expenditures outside the Eastern Province from the 1968 survey.

Despite the substantial rise in outlays on most categories, there has been little change between 1962 and 1968 in the proportionate division of outlays among the seven major categories. Food continues to account for about half of consumer outlays, and housing is second, or about 16 per cent. Proportionate outlays have increased for furniture and durable goods from 7 per cent of total expenditures to 10 per cent. Other changes have been minor.

Table XV shows the change which has taken place between 1962 and

1968 in *per capita* money outlays as well as in *per capita* outlays expressed in terms of 1962 prices. Because the growth in the average size of family eroded the effect of the rise in money expenditures, the actual increase in *per capita* money expenditures was only 30 per cent, or substantially below the 47 per cent increase in money outlays per household. But prices also rose during the same period (Tables XVI and XVII), and because the price rises were unevenly distributed by expenditure class, the level of expenditures on each class expressed in constant, or 1962, prices is some-what different from the levels stated in terms of current price levels. When consumer outlays in 1968 are expressed in terms of 1962 prices, furniture and durables together with household expenses remain the categories with the most impressive expenditure increases – real expenditure on them doubled. Real outlays on clothing increased moderately (by 30 per cent). But real outlays on housing, food, and miscellaneous items (mainly services, tobacco, and personal care items) increased only slightly over the six-year period. Overall real *per capita* expenditures rose by more than 18 per cent, between 1962 and 1968, or nearly 3 per cent per year.

G. *Food Expenditures, 1962–1968*

Table XVIII shows average annual outlays per household on seven food sub-categories in 1962 and 1968. Table XIX shows average *per capita* outlays expressed in current (1968) prices, and also in 1962 prices.

It should be borne in mind that household expenditure surveys of 1962 and 1968 measured only money transactions, not total real consumption. In expenditure categories other than durable goods and housing, money payments may be safely assumed to equal real consumption levels over a one-year period. In the case of durable goods and housing, money outlays may diverge widely from actual consumption as measured by use, as for example when cash is paid for a new automobile. However, there is no universally agreed-upon method for measuring depreciation, and it may be reasonably be assumed that in the survey as a whole, instances in which cash payments are reported probably offset instances in which expenditures upon durable goods still in use were made at some time prior to the survey.

In the case of food expenditures, however, the fact that only money transactions have been recorded understates real food consumption levels. Many families derive foods such as vegetables, dates, and other fruit either from their own property, or from relatives. Some families also raise sheep, goats, and chickens, or obtain meat from relatives with animals.

Money outlays on foodstuffs rose by 41 per cent between 1962 and 1968, with the rise being fairly evenly distributed among most of the eight food categories. However, outlays on fruits and vegetables rose by

65 per cent, whereas restaurant expenditures, and outlays on canned and bottled goods increased by only 24 per cent and 28 per cent respectively.

There has been a shift away from food grains and bakery products, and an increase in proportionate outlays on fresh fruits and vegetables since 1962, but other changes are minor. Foodgrains and bakery products, fresh fruits and vegetables, and meat and seafood each accounted for about 20 per cent of food expenditures in 1968. Canned and bottled items account for 13 per cent of 1968 outlays, and other food items (mainly sugar, tea, coffee, and cardamom) accounted for 10 per cent of 1968 outlays.

The increase in *per capita* money expenditures on food was only 24 per cent, compared with the 41 per cent increase for households as a whole, and when corrections are made for price changes since 1962, the increase is much smaller – only 6 per cent, or just under 1 per cent per year (Table XIX). The only food categories in which there were significant increases in real expenditures were fresh fruits and vegetables, which rose by 20 per cent, and food grains and bakery products, which rose by 13 per cent. Real expenditures on oils and fats declined by 8 per cent from the 1962 level, and real restaurant expenditures decreased by 1 per cent.

What foods do these money expenditures buy in real terms? In Table XX the 1968 prices of the more popular food items are listed by major food categories, together with average monthly *per capita* expenditure figures in Saudi Riyals for each food category as revealed by the 1968 survey. This table is included as background information from which the reader can form for himself a picture of the ability of the average Aramco Saudi employee family member to buy various combinations of food.

Table XXI shows the calorie content of one illustrative combination of foodstuffs purchasable by the typical family member in 1968. It may be assumed that the variety of food categories included provides adequate amounts of vitamins and other nutrients. It is evident that average *per capita* expenditures are ample to sustain a balanced diet with a calorific content substantially above the minimum necessary to maintain health. It should, of course, be noted that the *per capita* figures used here are calculated simply by dividing average household expenditures by the average size of household, and that they therefore make no distinctions between children and adults.

IV. SUPPLEMENTARY ANALYSES

In addition to the topics discussed here, machine runs have been prepared showing expenditures on the seven major categories and the seven food sub-categories discussed here, on both a household and a *per capita* basis by job grade, size of family, and place of residence.

The most striking fact these tables point up is the pronounced effect family size has on expenditure patterns. *Per capita* outlays on most expenditure categories drop sharply as family-size increases; proportionate outlays on food increase significantly, and on housing decrease. Percentage changes in other expenditures, however, are not closely associated with family size.

An additional set of tables which may prove to be the most important of all to economists is now being prepared. These tables will show household and *per capita* outlays on major expenditure categories and on food sub-categories in 1968 by amount of total expenditure. Eleven annual expenditure categories are being used, ranging from SR 3,000 (£278) to SR 38,000 (£3,519), with all intervals except the lowest and highest spaced SR 2,000 apart. These tables should make possible the measurement of income elasticities for major consumption categories. Although taken from a section of the Saudi population which is in many ways atypical of the population as a whole, the study will be the first of its kind which has been undertaken in depth within Saudi Arabia. Pending the appearance of additional studies of this nature it will be a useful analytical tool in national income estimates now being prepared by the Saudi Arabian Government and Aramco's Economics Department.

NOTES ON TABLES

1. Value figures were converted from Saudi riyals to UK pounds at the exchange rate of 10·80 riyals per pound. In the case of tables showing percentage of change in expenditures between 1962 and 1968, the percentage figures were calculated from the original riyal values. Rounding of riyal values to pound values has introduced minor discrepancies, as a result of which, figures showing percentage of change do not always accord with their pound values.

2. Percentage totals may not add to 100·0 because of rounding.

TABLE I – *Stratification of Sample by Grade and District, 1962*

Grade	Number of employees in sample			Total
	Dhahran	Ras Tanurah	Abqaiq	
22	12	8	7	27
23	11	12	8	31
24	25	17	19	61
25	26	15	18	59
26	22	13	16	51
27	7	5	5	17
28	3	2	2	7
Total	106	72	75	253

TABLE II – *Stratification of Sample by Grade and District, 1968*

Grade*	Number of employees in sample			Total
	Dhahran	Ras Tanurah	Abqaiq	
23	9	4	2	15
24	9	16	7	32
25	21	18	19	58
26	16	18	18	52
27	7	5	10	22
28	17	12	5	34
29	6	5	4	15
30	6	2	6	14
Total	91	80	71	242

*Grade 22 abolished

TABLE III – *Aramco Saudi Employees: Household Size and Composition and Dependent–Earner Ratios 1962 and 1968*

	Members/household 1962	1968	Household members/worker 1962	1968
1. Average household size	7·7	8·7	6·8	7·8
2. Number of children*	4·2	5·5	3·7	4·8
3. Number of dependent adults	2·3	2·1	2·0	1·8
4. Number of working adults	1·2	1·2	1·0	1·0
5. Child/adult dependency ratio†	1·8	2·6	1·9	2·7

*Under 18 yrs.
†Line 2, line 3
Note: Lines 2–4 may not add to line 1 in each column because of rounding

TABLE IV – *Aramco Saudi Employees, by Household Size, 1962 and 1968*

Household size	1962 Estimated no. of employees	%	1968 Estimated no. of employees	%
2–4	1,228	11.5	920	9·6
5–6	2,795	26·1	1,696	17·6
7–8	3,176	29·6	2,019	21·0
9–10	2,117	19·7	2,674	27·8
11–13	1,059	9·9	1,657	17·2
14–20	339	3·2	543	5·6
over 20	0	0	106	1·2
Total	10,714	100·0	9,615	100·0

TABLE V – *Aramco Saudi Employees: Location of Household Residence, 1962 and 1968*

Location of household residence	1962 Estimated no. of employees	%	1968 Estimated no. of employees	%	Distance from nearest Aramco facility (km.)
Qatif Oasis	3,473	32·4	2,790	28·9	31
Al-Hasa Oasis	2,710	25·3	2,332	24·2	84
Company town sites	1,736	16·2	2,429	21·8	1
Dammam	974	9·1	896	11·4	18
Khubar	1,101	10·3	691	8·8	12
Tarut	466	4·3	340	3·5	39
Other	254	2·4	137	1·4	–
Total	10,714	100·0	9,615	100·0	

TABLE VI – *Proportion of Employees Living with Households during Work Week, by Place of Family Residence, 1962 and 1968*

Place of family residence	1962	1968	Distance from nearest co. facil. (km.)*
Dammam	87·0	100·0	18
Tarut	0·0	100·0	39
Qatif Oasis	59·8	88·0	31
Khubar	88·5	86·9	12
Company town sites	85·3	74·2	1
Al Hasa Oasis (Hofuf)	1·6	24·3	84
Total	52·4	69·8	

*Qatif and Al Hasa Oases extend over large areas. The distances shown here are from the main gate of the nearest of the three Aramco installations to the centre of Qatif town and Hofuf town respectively.

TABLE VII – *Aramco Saudi Employees' Home Ownership Status, 1962 and 1968*

	1962		1968	
	No. of employees	%	No. of employees	%
Owned house	9,147	85·3	8,352	86·8
Rented house	1,228	11·5	790	8·2
Rented part of house	85	·8	405	4·2
Rented apartment	–	–	68	·7
Other (tent, makeshift quarters)	254	2·4	–	–
Total	10,714	100·0	9,615	100·0

TABLE VIII – *Aramco Saudi Employees: Construction Material of House, 1962 and 1968*

	1962		1968	
Type of material	No. of employees	%	No. of employees	%
Cement block or stone	7,580	70·8	8,107	84·3
Mud brick	1,609	15·0	879	9·1
Barasti	551	5·1	328	3·4
Tent	127	1·2	–	–
Furush	85	·8	168	1·7
Company portable	42	·4	–	–
Other (mostly wood)	720	6·7	133	1·5
Total	10,714	100·0	9,615	100·0

TABLE IX – *Aramco Saudi Employees: Number and Proportion of Homes with Utilities, 1962 and 1968*

	1962		1968	
	No. of employees	%	No. of employees	%
Electricity and running water	3,855	36·0	7,802	81·2
Running water, no electricity	5,082	47·4	1,594	16·6
Electricity, no running water	84	·8	41	·4
No electricity, no running water	1,693	15·8	178	1·8
Total	10,714	100·0	9,615	100·0

TABLE X – *Aramco Saudi Employees' Sources of Income, 1968*

	No. of employees	%
1. Aramco earnings of respondent only	6,316	65·7
2. Line 1 plus respondent's other earnings	1,926	20·0
3. Lines 1 or 2 plus Aramco earnings only of other household members	423	4·4
4. Lines 1 or 2 plus other earnings only of other household members	696	7·2
5. Lines 1 or 2 plus Aramco and other earnings of other household members	254	2·6
Total	9,615	100·0

Note: Lines 1 and 2 include households with one full-time worker
Lines 3, 4 and 5 include households with more than one full-time worker

TABLE XI – *Aramco Saudi Employees Single-Earner Households: Average Gross Aramco Earnings and Expenditures by Job Grade, 1968 (U.K. £/Year)*

Job Grade	Average gross Aramco earnings	Expenditures	Earnings less expenditures	Expend. as % of earnings
23	805·53	755·44	50·09	93·8
24	954·79	739·98	214·81	77·5
25	1,126·63	1,045·62	81·01	92·8
26	1,324·04	1,132·65	191·39	85·5
27	1,599·31	1,539·96	59·35	96·3
28	1,904·20	1,333·76	570·44	70·0
29	2,262·07	1,779·39	482·68	78·7
30	2,444·65	2,076·42	368·23	85·4

TABLE XII – *Aramco Saudi Employees Single-Earner Households: Range of Household Expenditures and Gross Aramco Earnings by Job Grade, 1968 (U.K. £/Year)*

Job Grade	Range of family expend.		Range of gross Aramco earnings	
23	460·64	1,343·76	750·44	858·22
24	339·80	1,797·17	819·61	1,094·97
25	583·50	2,207·99	867·47	1,325·70
26	478·60	1,799·49	1,032·28	1,899·58
27	733·77	2,809·64	1,276·07	2,151·14
28	703·31	2,298·45	1,565·79	2,365·40
29	904·97	3,180·74	1,789·30	2,769·74
30	1,362·18	2,724·46	1,850·60	2,897·51

TABLE XIII – *Proportionate Distribution of Single Earners, by Grade, whose Expenditures Exceed their Incomes by Designated Percentages, 1968*

		Expenditure > income by %			
Grade	Expenditure < = Income	·01– 9·99	10·00 19·99	20·00 and over	Total
23	70·0	0	20·0	10·0	100·0
24	89·8	3·4	0	6·8	100·0
25	64·7	9·8	9·8	15·7	100·0
26	72·1	9·3	9·3	9·3	100·0
27	65·0	10·0	10·0	15·0	100·0
28	85·7	10·7	0	3·6	100·0
29	71·4	0	14·3	14·3	100·0
30	61·5	15·4	23·1	0	100·0
Total	100·0	100·0	100·0	100·0	

TABLE XIV – *Aramco Saudi Employees: Average Absolute and Proportionate Household Expenditures on Major Categories, 1962 and 1968 (U.K. £/Year)*

	1962	%	1968	%	% Change 1968 over 1962
Housing	130·6	16·5	194·9	16·7	+49·2
Food	407·4	51·4	574·9	49·4	+41·1
Clothing	67·5	8·5	98·8	8·5	+46·4
Household expenses	45·4	5·7	85·4	7·3	+88·2
Furniture and durables	56·4	7·1	121·8	10·5	+116·1
Transportation	29·3	3·7	25·8	2·2	−11·7*
Miscellaneous†	55·5	7·0	63·2	5·4	+14·0
Total	792·1	100·0	1164·8	100·0	+47·1

* Expenses incurred for travel outside the Eastern Province excluded in 1968 survey
† Mainly personal-care items, tobacco, entertainment, education, and medical services outside Aramco. (Aramco supplies free medical care and supplies to its Saudi employees and their families)

TABLE XV – *Aramco Saudi Employees: Average Per Capita Expenditure on Major Categories, 1962 and 1968, in 1962 Prices (U.K. £/Year)*

	1962	1968	% Change in money expenditure	1968 Expenditure in 1962 price	% Change in real expenditure
Housing	17·0	22·4	+31·5	17·1	+·5
Food	53·3	66·0	+24·2	56·5	+6·1
Clothing	8·8	11·4	+29·5	11·5	+30·5
Furniture and durables	7·4	14·0	+88·8	15·3	+106·3
Household expenses	5·9	9·8	+65·6	11·6	+95·3
Transportation	3·8	2·9	−22·0*	2·9	−22·0
Miscellaneous†	7·2	7·3	+1·3	7·3	+1·3
Total	103·4	133·8	+29·5	122·2	+18·4

* Expenses incurred for travel outside the Eastern Province excluded in 1968 survey
† Mainly personal care items, tobacco, entertainment, education and medical services

TABLE XVI – *1968 Price Levels of Major Expenditure Categories, 1961/2* = *100*

Housing	130·7
Food	116·9
Clothing	98·9
Furniture and durables	91·4
Household expenses	84·6
Transportation	101·2
Miscellaneous	99·6
Total	109·4

Note: Base year = 2nd quarter 1961 to end of 1st quarter 1962
Current year = 2nd half 1967 to end of 1st half 1968

TABLE XVII – *1968 Price Levels of Food Expenditure Categories, 1961/2* = *100*

Oils and fats	135·5
Food grains and bakery products	108·8
Fruits and vegetables	120·7
Meat and seafood	119·9
Canned and bottled goods	109·6
Other foods	117·3
Restaurants	114·6
Total	116·9

Note: Base year = 2nd quarter 1961 to end of 1st quarter 1962
Current year = 2nd half 1967 to end of 1st half 1968

TABLE XVIII – *Aramco Saudi Employees: Average Absolute and Pro-portionate Household Expenditure, Major Food Categories, 1962 and 1968 (U.K. £/Year)*

	1962	1968	% Increase	% of total food 1962	% of total food 1968
Oils and fats	33·8	47·5	+40·5	8·3	8·3
Food grains and baked prod.	84·0	116·5	+38·7	20·6	20·2
Fresh fruits and vegetables	67·5	111·5	+65·2	16·6	19·4
Meat and seafood	80·8	114·2	+41·4	19·8	19·9
Canned and bottled items	57·4	73·5	+28·1	14·1	12·8
Frozen foods ⎱	48·1	8·9 ⎱	+39·6	11·8	1·6 ⎰
Other food items* ⎰		58·3 ⎰			10·1 ⎰
Restaurants	35·8	44·5	+24·3	8·8	7·8
Total	407·4	574·9	+41·1	100·0	100·0

*Mainly sugar, coffee, tea and cardamom

TABLE XIX – *Aramco Saudi Employees: Average Per Capita Expenditures on Major Food Categories, 1962 and 1968 in 1962 Prices (U.K. £/Year)*

Food Categories	1962	1968	% Change in money exp'diture	1968 exp'diture in 1962 price	% Change in real exp'diture
Oils and fats	4·4	5·5	+22·9	4·1	−8·3
Food grains and baked prod.	10·9	13·4	+22·9	12·3	+12·7
Fresh fruits and vegetables	8·8	12·8	+45·3	10·6	+20·0
Meats and seafoods	10·6	13·1	+24·6	10·9	+3·5
Canned and bottled items	7·5	8·4	+12·3	7·7	+2·5
Other food items*	6·3	7·7	+22·1	6·6	+4·4
Restaurants	4·7	5·1	+7·8	4·3	−0·8
Total	53·3	66·0	+24·2	56·5	+6·1

*Mainly sugar, coffee, tea and cardamom

TABLE XX – *Foodstuffs Obtainable with Average Monthly Per Capita Expenditure on Food Categories, 1968 (In Saudi Riyals)**

Selected foodstuffs in each category	Unit price 1967/8	Amount available *per capita* per month
1. *Oils and Fats*		4·91
Cooking oil (2¼ pint can)	3·44	
Vegetable fat (5 lb. can)	5·13	
Butter (1 lb.)	3·01	
2. *Food Grains*		8·01
Flour (1 kg. bag)	·88	
Rice (1 kg.)	1·30	
3. *Bakery Products*		4·04
Arab bread (8 pieces)	1·00	

TABLE XX *cont.*

Selected foodstuffs in each category	Unit price 196/78	Amount available *per capita* per month
4. *Fruits*		6·73
Bananas (1 kg.)	2·00	
Dates, khalas (21 kg.)	19·50	
Oranges (1 kg.)	1·63	
5. *Vegetables*		4·80
Eggplant (1 kg.)	1·44	
Onions (1 kg.)	1·00	
Potatoes (1 kg.)	1·06	
Tomatoes (1 kg.)	2·13	
6. *Meat and Fish*		11·82
Fish, hamoor (1 kg.)	2·63	
Lamb (1 kg.)	6·00	
7. *Canned Goods*		7·60
Powdered Milk (1 lb. can)	2·25	
Tomato juice (Doz. 5 oz. cans)	4·88	
8. *Other Foods*		6·95
Eggs (dozen)	3·00	
Coffee (1 kg.)	5·75	
Sugar (1 lb.)	2·50	

*10·80 Saudi riyals = £1·00

TABLE XXI – *Calorie Content of One Alternate Combination of Foodstuffs Purchasable in Saudi Arabia with Average Daily Per Capita Outlays on Major Food Categories (In Saudi Riyals)*

	Representative item	Price per kilo	Average Exp'diture /day	Amount buyable day (100kg.)	Calories** per 100 gm.	Calories/ day
Oils and fats	Veg. fat	2·24	·16	·71	879	624
Foodgrains and bak. prod.	Rice	1·30	·40	3·08	360	1109
Fruits	Dates (dried)	·92	·22	2·39	255	609
Vegetables	Tomatoes	2·13	·16	·75	19	14
Meat and seafood	Lamb	6·00	·39	·65	241	157
Canned goods	Dried milk	4·96	·25	·50	506	253
Other	Sugar	5·51	·23	·42	387	162
						2928

*Average for 1967/8
**Food Composition Tables, FAO, Rome, 1954, Table 1
Note: 10·80 Saudi riyals = £1·00

12

EDUCATION AND THE PRESS
IN SOUTH ARABIA

ALI MUHAMMAD LUQMAN

EDUCATION IN SOUTHERN YEMEN

On the eve of Independence Day, 30 November 1967, the Federation of South Arabia was renamed 'The People's Republic of Southern Yemen'. The new Republic comprises the ex-British Crown Colony of Aden, and both the Western and Eastern Aden Protectorates together with the islands of Kamaran, Perim, Kuria Muria and Socotra.

Administrative Reorganization

Prior to independence, the Republic consisted of more than twenty sultanates and shaikhdoms with traditional and hereditary rulers. The Federation was an attempt to fuse a great number of those separate states together and remove the barriers among them. The new administration, however, saw fit to reduce the administrative units to six only and re-grouped states or parts thereof into six large governorates. Aden with all the islands and part of the old State of Lahej forms the First Governorate. Old Hadhramaut is the Fifth and the Mahrah, excluding Socotra, is the Sixth. The other odd seventeen states now make the Second, Third and Fourth Governorates. Each Governorate has a Governor with his own administration set-up exercising municipal and local administrative authority.

The population is estimated at between $1\frac{1}{2}$ and 2 millions. However, with the exception of Aden, no properly organized census has ever been carried out in the other parts of the territory.

Education – Historical Background

Education in Southern Yemen is on two different systems. In Aden and what was known as the Federation of South Arabia, the syllabuses were uniform following the pattern developed in Aden over the last five decades. In the eastern parts, the Hadhramaut, the new schools followed the Sudanese curriculum.

Attempts are now being made to revise both systems with a view to setting up a common one for all and which will be in line with systems adopted in other Arab countries.

The visit of H.R.H. the Duke of Connaught to Aden in 1920 marked the first agitation by the Aden people for better educational facilities.[1] But no attempts were made to provide them until 1925 when Mr Lory, the Director of Public Instruction in Poona, India, was deputed to prepare a report on education in Aden. He recommended free primary education with a view to producing clerks for Government service.

Education in the ex-colony of Aden was administered by the Director of Education appointed by the Governor. An educational advisory committee comprising representatives of the various communities sat from time to time to advise on matters of general policy or any other subject that might be referred to them.

In the colony budgets, provisions for education exclusive of capital works within the period April 1937 to March 1943, was as follows:

1937–8   Rs. 93,900 = £7,043 (5.64 per cent of total estimated expenditure).

1942–3   Rs. 122,580 = £9,194 (3.55 per cent of total estimated expenditure).[2]

The primary school course covered the first four years of regular full school education. No infant or kindergarten classes were provided. The lower secondary course covered three years post primary and led to the next four year course of higher secondary.

In his brochure *Is This a Scrap of Paper?* Junius, an anonymous publisher, wrote 'No candidate has been sent up for the Matriculation Examination of any University in eighty-four years. Let alone success'.

After Aden had been withdrawn from the Bombay Administration in 1937 and transferred to the charge of the Colonial Office, education improved slightly at the secondary level and pupils started to prepare for the Cambridge School Certificate Examination. A new Director of Education was appointed and a system of financial aid to existing schools was introduced.[3]

The Protectorate

Prior to 1937 the Western Aden Protectorate, now Governorates 2, 3 and 4, had only a traditional form of education, limited to Koranic schools in villages.

By the end of 1943 three such schools were subsidized and the Aden Protectorate College for the Sons of Chiefs was opened in Aden to be closed down in 1952 as uneconomical.[4] Those pupils who remained were

[1] Junius, *Is this a Scrap of Paper* (Bombay), p. 54
[2] *Report of the Education Department, Aden 1937-43*, p. 10.
[3] A. M. Luqman, *A Study of Aden Public Mind*, 1947.
[4] *Ministry of Education Report, Jan.-Dec. 1965.*

placed at Aden schools to complete their education or were sent on scholarship to the Sudan.

In 1965 the situation changed and a new educational system emerged. Full-time education at all levels was provided for about 44,000 pupils exclusive of teacher trainees. Evening and part-time classes were organized and children began their schooling between the ages of 7 and 8.

Assuming direct responsibility for education in Aden after the merger in 1963, the Federal Ministry of Education provided for full universal primary and intermediate education for all Aden boys and girls who sought it. Places at secondary schools were provided for 50 per cent of the boys and 42 per cent of the girls who competed for them at an annual entrance examination. Evening classes provided co-education for the first time in the history of South Yemen for about 400 boys and 40 girls who failed to get places at the day classes of the secondary schools.

In the states other than Aden, with a population estimated at 330,000, there were 16,635 children in primary schools and 1,772 in the intermediate schools.

The policy was to provide school places for 40 per cent of the primary school leavers but only 25 per cent of those who leave intermediate schools gain entry to the Lahej Secondary School and the People's College at the People's City known as Ittihad city, capital of the ex-Federation Government.

Girls' education was provided in the states in fourteen primary and three intermediate schools.

Cost of Education

Total estimated expenditure was £1,605,760, as follows:

Office of the Minister and HQ	£185,108
States' Education	£596,112
Aden Education	£924,540

It is estimated that 53.5 per cent of the total expenditure was met by subsidies in the form of C.D. & W. Funds, Overseas Aid Schemes and British Technical Assistance grants to South Yemeni scholars in the United Kingdom.

Average cost per pupil was estimated as follows:

Type of School	Aden	Federal States
Primary	£26 approx.	£14·15
Intermediate	£41	£100·00
Secondary	£117	£518·10

The need for boarding facilities, expatriate staff and inducement allowances in Federal States explain the high cost of education there *pro rata* as compared with costs in Aden itself.

Besides instruction in the basic three Rs, religious knowledge instruction, handicraft, etc., spoken English is introduced in the fourth primary year. The medium of instruction in both primary and intermediate schools has always been Arabic but at the secondary-school level everything was taught in English because all courses and syllabi were geared to overseas examinations in English, G.C.E., R.S.A. or the like.

There are three maintained boys' secondary schools and two girls' secondary schools in Aden and two in the states. In addition, there are eight other grant-aided or independent secondary schools managed and maintained by missionaries, societies and other national bodies. With the exception of one independent school which follows the Iraqi syllabus, all are required to adopt the Government system and regulations. The end product is either the London University G.C.E. Examination or the Cambridge Joint School Certificate Examination. Technical education is provided at the only Technical Institute in Aden which has its associations with the Royal Society of Arts and the City & Guilds of London.

It is believed that opportunities for secondary education in Aden were greater than those in some developing countries with far greater financial resources such as Kuwait, Libya and Ethiopia. At Aden College, pupils follow an academic course leading up to the Cambridge School Certificate. Provision was available for a limited number of boys to continue their higher studies for a further two years to Advanced Level. In 1965 there were 35 boys following varied A-Level courses with financial assistance from the Government in the form of bursaries.

The Government Boys' Secondary School which began as a secondary modern school for second-string pupils has been changed to a comprehensive school catering for certain zones of Aden and offering an academic course leading up to School Certificate Examinations as well. The first lot of pupils presenting themselves for such examinations appeared in December 1965.

The Junior Secondary School, opened in 1962, provides a two-year course for children of lower academic ability. Successful pupils are offered a two-year clerical training course at the Technical Institute where they are prepared for the R.S.A. examinations.

The two Girls' Secondary Schools in Aden follow the same courses leading to the Cambridge School Certificate Examination. Between them they provide about 42 per cent of the accommodation for intermediate school leavers.

States' Secondary Schools

The People's City College which was opened in 1962 has facilities for 280 boarders and the Hautah Secondary School which was started in 1965 can accommodate about half that number. Both offer a grammar-school course culminating in the Cambridge School Certificate Examination.

Technical Education

The Technical Institute which was opened in 1952 has succeeded in producing almost all the senior craftsmen, technicians and technologists working in Aden today in spite of its chequered career and the public prejudice and aversion for technical education introduced formally for the first time in the area.

At present the Institute offers a four-year course leading to the G.C.E. (Building and Engineering) Examination organized by the Associated Board. In addition there are at the Institute facilities for vocational training (clerical), classes for indentured apprentices, O.N.D. courses in at least three trades and possibilities for any technical courses as required by government or industry.

Teacher Training

There are two Teacher Training Colleges in Aden, one for men and another for women. A new Centre at the People's City was opened to train primary school teachers for the schools of the other states.

The two Aden colleges offer a two-year course for trainees intended for primary and intermediate schools as well as a one-year course for in-service trainees. The courses consist of academic studies and professional training together with practical teaching spells in selected schools under supervision.

Post-Secondary Education

There is no university or university college in Southern Yemen for such would have been both premature and uneconomical. However, promising pupils who managed to obtain the necessary matriculation requirements and thus became eligible for admission into either British or Middle East universities were given every encouragement and awarded scholarships to read whatever subjects they chose without compulsion or even the faintest promise to return and serve the Government.

In April 1963 the Government approved the setting up of two boards to deal with overseas studies, the Overseas Training Board under the chairmanship of the Public Service Commission which concerned itself with the training of serving members of the Civil Service, and the

Overseas Scholarship Board under the chairmanship of the Minister of Education to select suitable candidates from outside the Civil Service for higher studies abroad.

In 1965 there were 61 students pursuing courses of advanced studies overseas, 48 of whom were in the United Kingdom, 12 in Lebanon and 1 in the United Arab Republic.

The Eastern Governorates

In the Fifth and Sixth Governorates, the ex-Qaiti–Kathiri sultanates and the Mahrah, the educational systems and policies differed. Primary education was introduced in 1938 when Shaikh al-Qaddal Saᶜid al-Qaddal was recruited from the Sudanese Ministry of Education to start education on modern lines. The new system naturally followed the Sudanese syllabi. In the first 20 years 28 boys' schools and 6 girls' schools for a total of 4,300 pupils were built. Later, more schools were built and by 1963–4 there was a total of 55 boys' and 11 girls' schools shown on official returns and catering for 9,000 pupils.

Following the Sudanese system closely, the education policy was:

1. to prepare children for public life through knowledge of Arabic, arithmetic, religion, etc.;
2. to prepare the child to be able to face life's problems morally through school activities;
3. to offer opportunities to children to join intermediate schools.

Certain aspects of the Sudanese curriculum had to be altered in order to suit the Hadhramis. For instance, the Shafiᶜi sect was taught in religious knowledge in place of the Maliki. Local measurement units and Hadhrami history were substituted for their Sudanese counterparts. However, the Mukalla new secondary school, opened in 1962, prepares pupils for the Sudanese School Certificate Examination.

Intermediate schools were started in the Fifth Governorate in 1941. By 1958–9 there were 3 boys' schools and by 1963–4 the number rose to 9 while the first girls' intermediate school was opened at al-Ahqaf valley.

While intermediate education in Aden and the Federal states was for three years, here it was a four-year course following the Sudanese pattern. This extra year had a tremendous effect on the quality of the pupils turned out by Hadhrami schools who were to compete more favourably with Aden boys at Aden College which reserved a certain number of places for Hadhrami boys at the beginning of each academic year.

The Qaiti budget was £1,427,228 out of which £288,151 or about 27 per cent was allocated for education for the year 1966–7. C.D. & W. funds contributed £79,276 in 1963–4, £112,090 in 1964–5 and £192,350 in 1965–6. The Charitable Association, a semi-official body paid £7,050, £8,350 and £8,200 respectively.

By 1965–6, there were 112 primary schools, 17 intermediate and 2½ secondary schools (this half being the Qaiti share in the Seiyun Secondary School shared between the two states) and three teacher training centres. There are no secondary schools for girls yet.

Hadhrami scholars proceed to the Sudan, UAR, Syria, Iraq, Lebanon, UK and the USA for higher studies.

The Kathiri sultanate depended entirely on British aid and the customs duty. In 1965–66, the sultanate paid £20,152 and C.D. & W. Funds contributed £60,348 for educational services. The sultanate has a system of free education throughout the three stages. There are 30 primary and 4 intermediate schools. The first girls' intermediate school was started in 1965. It also has a secondary school whose first batch of boys will be sitting for the Sudan School Certificate Examination in 1969.

The Sixth Governorate, the Mahrah, has primary schools only.

The Future

'The People's Republic of Southern Yemen is in a financial predicament,' declared the Ministry of Economy, Commerce and Planning in *The Problems Facing the Emergent State of the People's Republic of South Yemen*, published by the Ministry of Culture and National Guidance in Aden in 1968. The brochure continues, 'The general economic situation and its previous dependence on the British presence make sufficient remedial action by the Government almost impossible in the immediate future. This is specially so since the Government finance itself was based on British aid, and the problem is greater when the military takes a big share of Government expenditure, while the rest is not sufficient for the simple administrative machinery and the rudimentary social services. If aid for the budget is not continued, at least, at the same rate then the situation will be serious especially when as is shown the taxable income is being depressed. However greatly the taxation potential is mobilized, the budgetary deficit will still be considerable. .... All this, of course, limits the Government actions in the field of development and in correcting remedial policies to reorientate the economy to the present conditions and the hard economic facts.'

The following 1967/8 figures are officially given in this respect:

Total actual expenditure	£25,168,117
Military expenditure	£13,893,458
Actual local revenue	£4,803,700
British aid	£20,364,417

Dwelling briefly on the limited social services available, the Ministry writes on education:

'In the educational services, the schools available at the various levels of education are as follows:

Primary   227 schools
Intermediate   37 schools
Secondary   11 schools

But despite all the shortcomings, the National Government is more than anxious to meet the growing educational needs of the population by introducing better and adequate services and facilities as part of the general government policy of reconstruction and development. International assistance towards this end, would, of course, be highly appreciated.'

In view of the new situation, the Government in the field of education reduced the expenditure as follows:

Estimates 1967–8		*Estimates 1/4/68 to 30/6/68*
Office of the Minister and HQ	£205,115	£27,457
States' Education	£890,305	£170,810
First Governorate	£1,141,755	£203,515
Antiquities	£15,675	£2,498

To plan for the future, a conference on education was held in Aden from 12/6/68 to 27/6/68 to discuss ways and means of introducing the new system of the Arab Cultural Charter. Primary education will, thus, cover six years, the intermediate will cover three years and the secondary three years. Pupils will be presented in their twelfth year for the examination of the Cairo School Certificate.

As far as grants in aid are concerned, the conference recommended that aid for secondary schools should be as follows:

1   (a) 80 per cent of salaries
or (b) Pupils' expenses in a government school,
or (c) whichever is the less provided:

(i) that aided schools follow government syllabuses,

(ii) that any expansion in the teaching of languages and science should have the approval and consent of the Ministry of Education,

and (iii) that primary and intermediate classes in such schools should come under the direct supervision of the Ministry of Education.

2   (i) The Principals and their Assistants must be from among the sons of the Republic;

(ii) Expatriates are only to be recruited when and where necessary;

(iii) Schools must follow government syllabuses;

(iv) Supervision by the Ministry is essential.

Among the recommendations of the technical committee of the conference was the introduction of French, German, Russian, Italian and Spanish in addition to English which should continue to be taught for eight years beginning from the fifth year primary at the rate of nine periods of 35 minutes a week per class. Girls' technical education throughout the Republic should include domestic science, arts, agriculture and other technical subjects.

It was recommended that the existing Technical Institute should provide places for the following:

Description	Present No. of Places	Recommended No. of Places
G.C.E. technical	60	60
General education	nil	30
Building trade	nil	20
Machine shop	35	20
Carpentry	nil	20
Industrial	nil	20
Motor vehicle mechanic	nil	20
Electrical fitting	5	20
Welding	nil	20
Commercial boys	51	20
Commercial girls	26	nil
Professional	60	nil

The Financial Committee forecast the following figures for the future:

School	No. of Schools	Boys	Girls	Teachers
Primary (B)	416	65,138	—	2,031
Primary (G)	61	—	16,079	483
Inter. (B)	44	9,042	—	315
Inter. (G)	13	—	2,402	100
Secondary (B)	9	1,626	—	101
Secondary (G)	2	—	638	36

The Press in Southern Yemen

It was only in 1853 that the first printing machine was brought to Aden. The British Administration of the ex-colony of Aden, in that year, ordered a small printing machine as part of the 'hard labour' in the prison of Aden. Some inmates were sent to Bombay to train as compositors and printers. On their return, they were made to train other inmates in order that they might serve their sentences more fruitfully.

Twenty-four years later Cowasjee Dinshaw and Bros, a Parsee firm in Aden, imported a printing machine with English, Gujarati and Arabic types to print all Government stationery locally. In 1889 a Jewish family, Howard & Bros, established their press with English, Arabic and Hebrew types. In 1925 the Roman Catholic Mission in Aden and Pallonjee Dinshaw, another Parsee firm in Aden, started their printing presses.

In the thirties Arabic printing expanded as new printing concerns were started to meet the growing demands of Arab merchants and traders. The most important Arabic printing establishment was Fatat al-Jazirah, opened by the late Muhammad ᶜAli Luqman, an Arab advocate, in 1940. It was the first Arabic printing press to add publishing to its other activities in South Yemen. A number of dailies and weeklies in Arabic and English together with books and pamphlets on various subjects were printed for local and overseas markets.

Prior to Fatat al-Jazirah, local Arabic newspapers were unknown while English weeklies had been published in the area since 1900, when Captain W. Beale, the then Political Resident, edited and published the *Aden Weekly Gazette* in eight pages of English. The *Gazette* published news, literary articles and poems. On Beale's transfer from Aden, Murray of the Aden Coal Company continued to publish the *Gazette* until financial difficulties forced its closure.

Captain Beale returned to Aden as Colonel Beale in 1915 and on 14 April of the same year he published the *Aden Focus*, which was printed for him by Howard & Bros Press, Aden. By May 1917, the paper's balance sheet showed eight rupees credit only and so it had to disappear too.

The Forces in Aden had their own papers and both the *Star* and the

Echo were circulated within camp but civilians had a chance to read them too.

In 1932 the Government of Aden started publishing the *Aden Gazette* and the *Aden Protectorate Gazette.*

Arabic Newspapers

Any reference to newspapers in Southern Yemen must be restricted to Aden only as there were no papers published elsewhere in the territory. And only in 1940 did the British Government agree to license the publication of an Arabic newspaper. That was *Fatat al-Jazirah* which first appeared as an eight-page weekly.

Introducing the first issue of his *Fatat al-Jazirah*, the late M. ᶜA. Luqman wrote in January 1940:

'In the name of God the Compassionate, the Merciful, I decided to publish this newspaper in order to serve this country and its people by disseminating Arabic culture in an attempt to march with the civilized world in the fields of education, agriculture, industry, trade, science and technology.'

The paper appeared in time of war with Hitler's victorious armies spreading terror east and west. News had therefore to be carefully sifted and edited to avoid the censor. Apart from news and news stories, the paper published feature articles, short stories, human interest accounts, interviews, sports, interpretative reporting and the Woman's page. The editors and patrons of the paper were responsible for establishing several cultural, social and political associations such as Mukhaiyam Abi al-Taiyib, the Aden Cultural Council and the Poor Boys' Relief Fund.

Newspaper work, however, proved to be a difficult task in South Yemen. Between 1940 and 1952, fourteen weeklies and dailies had to close down after a transitory existence. Business, although exciting, was not paying. In an environment like that of Southern Yemen, conservative and uneventful, a journalist found it difficult to obtain anything of news value for publication. Men preferred their old way of life and sought no change. Officials capitalized on this passive attitude and the Government found it more convenient to keep the public uninformed. The press and Registration of Books Ordinance of July 3, 1939, governed all publications. The first Arabic newspaper was also governed by 'any other law for the time-being in force'. Such was the text of the licence granted for the publication of *Fatat al-Jazirah.*

The Press Ordinance declared:

'It shall not be lawful for any person to print, publish, edit or assist in the printing or editing of any newspaper within the colony unless the printing and publication of such newspaper or periodical shall be authorized by a licence in writing for the purpose granted by the Governor and signed by the Chief Secretary, which licence, the Governor may, at his discretion, grant, refuse or revoke.

'Every such licence shall, unless revoked, continue in force for a period of twelve months.'

Apart from all other laws governing the press then, it was also governed by a policy that aimed at keeping the place peaceful. The Court followed the Indian Civil and Penal Codes. A defamation case was heard in public. Consequently, an insulted man, though innocent, preferred to bear the insult bitterly to save himself the trouble of wider circulation of it through the court.

Freedom of the press was also influenced by national traditions and religious customs. It was very difficult for a newspaper man to attempt a wholesale reform of time-honoured customs, such as the veil system. To advocate the emancipation of women was to attempt the impossible and subject one's self not only to ridicule but to danger. Amir Ahmad Fadl al-cAbdali of Lahej once published a short poem on music. Both he and the publisher earned the people's anger. Some even applied to the Government to interfere and stop the publication of the paper.

As soon as the war was over, newspapers of varied political affiliations appeared like mushrooms; but many of them had to close down because of financial loss. Circulation was limited – not more than five hundred copies for the most successful one – and printing expensive. By 1956, the labour movement was born. The ATUC started their own paper and what was then called 'political parties' began to take shape. Every 'political party' had an organ to propagate their aims. Arab nationalism was incensed by the Anglo-French-Israeli war against Egypt. The local Arabic press reacted against this unjustifiable attack furiously. From then onwards, nationalistic writings replaced all newspaper technique until the day of Independence, 30 November 1967.

Political differences, however, brought about libellous and seditious writings. But the Court heard only two cases of this sort throughout the history of the Press. Few newspapers had their licences withdrawn or suspended for such reasons. In 1948, after the abortive coup in Yemen, when Imam Yahya ibn Muhammad Hamid al-Din was assassinated, the first violence against the press was recorded. That was the beginning of a series of violent attacks against the local press by arson, explosives and murder threats. At one time, three dailies and two weeklies were either burnt down or blown up with explosives in 1965 and 1966. Editors' cars were also set on fire.

Type-setting was by hand until two dailies, the *Fatat al-Jazirah* and *al-Aiyam*, introduced lino-type machines in 1965, but no change in the form, size or material of the publications was made. All dailies had a standard form of 16 x 12 in. four pages with printed size of 14 x 10 in. with five columns of 11 ems per page.

By 1967 there were twenty-four newspapers and magazines. Twenty further applications were under consideration. Six were dailies, *al-Akhbar, Fatat al-Jazirah, al-Aiyam, al-Yaqzah, al-ᶜUmmal* and *al-Tariq.* The rest were weeklies and monthlies.

Southern Yemen had two English weeklies prior to independence, the *Recorder* and the *Aden Chronicle.* They were owned, edited and published by local Arabs. The *Recorder,* however, had to close down long before independence for financial reasons. But *Fatat al-Jazirah's* sister, the *Aden Chronicle,* continued to appear until the withdrawal of its licence in the first week of December 1967. The *Dhow,* an English weekly, was published by the Forces and the B.P. Refinery have their own house magazine. A weekly Urdu paper was published by an Indian Adeni and a small Gujarati magazine was also in circulation. English papers had a wider circulation than that of the Arabic ones. At one time the *Aden Chronicle* reached the peak of 3,000 copies per week. Advertisers preferred to advertise in the English weeklies, besides Reuters' daily news bulletin which is still in circulation.

Of the Arabic weeklies, *Saut al-Janub* was the official mouthpiece of the Federation of South Arabia, published by the Ministry of Information and National Guidance. Articles on the progress and development of the Federation appeared in *Saut al-Janub* constantly. The paper was for distribution throughout the states.

In 1966 it became apparent that the British forces would evacuate the base in Aden and South Yemen was to become the fourteenth Arab independent State in the Arab League. The armed struggle was coming to a successful end. Leaflets by revolutionary organizations took up the role of the newspapers, which were still governed by Aden Laws and Federal enactments. They were usually cyclostyled handouts distributed daily, sometimes, twice a day. Each party or organization used them to present their views and spread their activities. Newspapers co-operated and reproduced the leaflets to give them wider circulation as part of their contribution to the revolutionary cause.

In the Fifth Governorate, the Hadhramaut, specifically in Mukalla, there were three Arabic weeklies, *al-Taliᶜah, al-Rai' al-ᶜamm* and *al-Jamahir.* Two had party affiliations. One had a bomb thrown into its premises and so disappeared. The other two had to close down after a demonstration during which violence took place.

Soon after independence all newspaper licences were withdrawn. An official announcement banning all newspapers urged the editors and publishers to reapply for fresh licences. Some did apply but no licence has yet been issued. Three semi-official papers are in circulation in the People's Republic of Southern Yemen today in addition to a bi-monthly army magazine. The daily *14th October* and the weekly *al-Thauri* (The Revolutionary) publish all Government decrees, orders, and notices with interpretative articles on current affairs, socialism and Government policy matters. In Mukalla, *al-Shararah* (The Spark) is published on the same lines. Both *al-Thauri* in the first Governorate and *al-Shararah* in the fifth were on occasions suspended for policy reasons.

The Arab Army have their own *al-Jundi* (The Soldier) with army news, pictures, military and religious feature articles.

The Southern Yemen press, despite all the difficulties that it had to encounter, has made a considerable contribution towards the progress of this part of the world in the fields of education, social welfare, labour and industrial relations and above all freedom from foreign rule. In twenty-eight years, the local press played a major role in liberating the Yemen from autocracy, in emancipating women and introducing democratic and constitutional patterns of government in South Arabia.

PART IV

ECONOMICS

13

OIL AND STATE IN ARABIA

EDITH PENROSE

There are undoubtedly few, if any, aspects of the political, social or economic life in Arabia that are today entirely untouched directly or indirectly by the development of the region's oil resources. And since the organization and activities of governments are themselves responsive in some degree to changes taking place among their peoples, a full examination of the relation between oil and state in Arabia would not only require an extensive historical treatment of topics about which much is already well known but would also inevitably lead us into a discussion of most aspects of Arabian life. Education, including study abroad, greatly improved communications, including radio and even television, travel and wider contacts with foreigners, have all been instrumental in changing attitudes and aspirations among the population, and all have directly or indirectly been made possible on an increasing scale through the availability of oil revenues. The organization of the state in the established oil-exporting countries has been radically changed, the position of the religious authorities significantly undermined, and the personal power of ruling families eroded. Doubtless such changes would have come about eventually in any case, but they have certainly been hastened by the development of oil, which necessarily opened the countries with accelerating rapidity to influences from elsewhere, and especially from the industrialized Western world.

Oil was discovered in Bahrain in 1932 and exports began in 1934. Revenues, which were around $9,000 in 1933, exceeded $1m. by 1940 and $10m. by 1954. Last year they were estimated at around $20m. The next discoveries in Arabia were made in 1938 in Kuwait and Saudi Arabia, although their rapid development, and especially that of Kuwait, had to await the end of the war. Kuwait's revenues in 1948 were only $12m.; by 1958 they exceeded $350m. and in 1967 they reached $700m. Between 1950 and 1960 Saudi Arabia's revenues rose from around $50m. to over $330m., and by 1968 approached $1000m. Part of Kuwaiti and Saudi revenues come from the Neutral Zone, where oil was discovered in 1953. Oil was found in Qatar in 1939 but exports did not start until ten years later, the wells having been plugged and the installations stripped during the war. Revenues rose from only $1m. in 1950 to over $100m. in

1967. Oil exports started from Abu Dhabi in 1962 and revenues exceeded $100m by 1967. The country is now the world's twelfth-largest oil producer and there is more to come, for new fields are still being discovered and new concessions granted. The Fatih field in Dubai was discovered in 1966 and exports are about to begin. Production also began in the Sultanate of Oman in 1967 and when exports are established payments are estimated to reach between $50m. and $100m. by the end of 1969.

The influence of oil makes itself felt in many ways: through the direct effect of the productive operations of the oil companies; through the direct receipt of foreign exchange revenues by governments or rulers who must needs deal with them; through the ways in which these receipts are spent; through the relations with oil companies and other foreign interests of countries producing (or hoping to produce) oil; through the changes in the international political relations of oil (or potential oil) countries both within the Arab world and with countries outside it, which follow from the enhanced economic significance with which oil endows its possessors; or through the entry into oil operations by the governments themselves. Because of the pervasive influence of oil directly on the role and structure of the state and indirectly through social and economic changes, any discussion in a paper of this length must be highly selective. I propose, therefore, to confine myself to an analysis of the significance for the role of government of a few of the peculiar characteristics of the organization of the oil industry in the Middle East. I shall conclude with a brief discussion of the entry into the oil industry of the state itself through national oil companies.

There are three important characteristics of the oil industry in the Middle East which are of especial importance for an understanding of the relation between oil and state: (a) receipts from the export of oil do not naturally accrue to indigenous exporters, as is the case for most export commodities in the non-communist world, but come directly to the government; (b) the exploration for and the production of crude oil has been traditionally conducted under a system of concessions to foreign companies; (c) the most important companies producing crude oil are wholly-owned affiliates of internationally integrated firms and in consequence most crude oil is produced for use within the integrated framework of the major firms and is not sold in an open market.

Because of the first characteristic, the effect of export receipts on economic activity was in the first instance dependent on the way the government chose to spend the money, and this in turn necessarily gave the government a dominant role in the economy whether or not it was adequately prepared for such a role or even wished to assume it. The second necessitated a special type of negotiation between companies and governments, the outcome of which gave the companies an extraordinary degree of control over the countries' resources and was largely responsible for the prolonged nearly complete domination by a very few companies over Middle East oil resources. The third made the exporting countries dependent on the companies for markets and made necessary an arbitrary formula for the valuation of the oil produced.

Dominance of Government Revenues
Production for export, like any other productive activity within a country, uses domestic resources, including labour, and thus creates employment and domestic incomes. This is a primary, direct effect of production itself, the importance of which depends upon the amount of resources used. By and large the oil industry does not use a great deal of labour in relation to the value of its output, and it imports most of its other inputs. Of course, where the domestic population, and especially the supply of skilled labour, is small, even oil production may absorb a large proportion of the available workers. When the export industry is in foreign hands, the expenditures of the foreign companies will also bring foreign exchange to the country since the companies must acquire the domestic currency for their domestic expenditures by purchasing it with foreign exchange, or else expend foreign currency, gold, or other acceptable coins or metals directly. The sale of output abroad gives rise to foreign exchange receipts, but the effect of these receipts on the economy depends on how they are spent, and this in turn will differ according to who receives the sales proceeds.

If they are received by domestic exporters – which might be termed the 'normal case' – then it could be expected that much of the proceeds would be exchanged by them for domestic money which they would then spend on consumption or further investment. This would induce further employment and create more income, to the extent that the money was not directly spent for additional imports. If the exporters are foreigners, they too may retain some of their receipts for further investment in the country, but a further part – if not all – of the money may be retained abroad and contribute nothing to the domestic economy. If the government taxes foreign exporters, then most of the proceeds from exports may accrue to the domestic economy only through the tax receipts of the governments. This would put the government in the position of having to spend money if the export receipts were to have any effect on the economy at all.

In Arabia, governments and rulers have received revenues from oil companies in many forms – concession rents, fees, royalties and income taxes, but by far the most important form for those countries in which export production has been established is the income tax. The expenditures of the oil companies in the several countries are a further contribution to their foreign exchange receipts, but because of the amounts of money involved the direct impact of oil on the economy comes primarily through government expenditures. Sooner or later the pressing need to spend its money reasonably (or to get it into the hands of private individuals other than royal relatives and court favourites) has forced the governments into extensive reorganization (sometimes after a change of rulers), and to create financial institutions, budgets and methods of administration which could deal with the many problems involved, not the least of which have sometimes arisen because of the arrival on the scene of hordes of foreign businessmen, contractors, freelancers or even government representatives, all pressing their own proposals for the expenditure of government funds.

When oil was discovered in Bahrain, Qatar and Kuwait they were all British protectorates and the expenditure of the oil revenues, together with the changes in the organization of the government, were powerfully influenced by British guidance and advice. From the time when oil revenues started in Bahrain in the early 1930s, only one-third of them went to the shaikh for his personal and family affairs; half of the rest were devoted to meeting current government expenses and to the financing of development projects, and half were reserved for investment abroad against future needs. Government services of all kinds increased rapidly and the appropriate government agencies had to be created to provide them. Oil revenues levelled off in the late 1950s while population continued to increase. The shaikh has apparently not been willing to respond so readily as he had earlier to British advice, with the result that appropriate adjustments have not been made to declining *per capita* oil revenues.

In Qatar, on the other hand, oil revenues have continued to increase. As in Bahrain, only a third of the revenues were allocated to the shaikh, the rest being reserved for public expenditure of one kind or another and for investment abroad.[1]

In Kuwait the history of the administrative and governmental adaptation to the expenditure of the oil revenues is a history of the gradual transformation of a system of direct and personal family rule to a con-

---

[1] It should be recognized, however, that much of the money expended for 'public purposes' will inevitably become diverted to private hands without any apparent productive *quid pro quo*. Moreover, a third of oil revenues easily made multimillionaires of the rulers and their families.

stitutional one in which administration is, in principle at least, in the hands of civil servants, properly organized in government departments headed by ministers responsible to an elected national assembly. Since the very idea of a civil service is completely alien to traditional culture, the transformation is by no means complete. Nevertheless, given the fact that less than a generation has passed since oil revenues have been available on a really large scale, Kuwait has moved with great speed in the acquisition of the attributes of a modern state, and the organization and administration of the Kuwait Fund for Arab Economic Development is almost a model of its kind.

On the other hand, very large revenues accruing to the Government gives it almost unlimited ability to employ people, and since employment in the 'civil service', unlike employment in industry or agriculture, requires almost no complementary productive inputs and men often can easily be employed even where there is no 'job' to fill, government employment tends to burgeon beyond all bounds, with personal influence the key to getting a post, especially in an economy so very heavily dependent on expenditures by government. The World Bank Mission to Kuwait reported that in 1953 nearly 10 per cent of the *population* (not labour force) was in the civil service. Nearly a third of these were illiterate and many had private jobs as well, there being no clear distinction between public duty and private interest. There has, of course, been considerable advance in this respect over the last fifteen years, but the problem still remains.

When oil exports began Saudi Arabia was neither a British protectorate with effective foreign advisers nor did she have a ruler who had much understanding, or even wish to understand, how oil revenues might be used to benefit his country. In the early years of oil exports, therefore, not only were the revenues received by the King to a very considerable extent spent in non-productive ways, but in spite of a flow of revenues reaching over $300 million in 1955 – a thirty-fold increase in ten years – the King had actually to borrow money. The country got into severe financial difficulties; the free market rate of the riyal fell by about half, inflation set in and consumer goods became in short supply. An extensive governmental and financial reorganization was required and under the leadership of Prince Faisal as Prime Minister, was taken in hand. Although budgets of a kind were published as early as 1947/8, it took roughly ten years before a reasonably sound system of financial management could effectively be imposed. The government had been too unprepared, technically and psychologically, to cope with the expenditure of so much money so quickly, but by the 1960s the problem of using oil revenues had been largely responsible for the establishment of modern administrative and financial institutions and for the emergence of an outlook on the country which gave a high priority to economic development.

Abu Dhabi, coming much later into oil money, and with the benefit again, of strong foreign advisers seems (again after a change of rulers), likely to be in a position to handle its funds with greater sophistication, as probably will Dubai whose people have had a longer contact with the outside world than have those from the more inward-looking Arabian states, such as Muscat and Oman. Here there will apparently be a somewhat more severe struggle between a conservative ruler suspicious of all things new and the forces of modernity which will press with growing insidiousness on the society.

The Concession System

An oil concession is an agreement between one or more oil companies and the government within whose borders the relevant territories lie. Except in the United States, underground oil is everywhere the property of the State and can be exploited by private companies only with the express permission of the government. The early concession agreements in Arabia, as in the rest of the Middle East, gave a single concessionaire exclusive rights over the exploitation of oil resources in a very large proportion of the territory of the country for a very long period of time in return for a variety of stated payments to the government. The result was the establishment of a highly monopolistic control over the exploitation of the region's oil resources.

All of the production of Arabia came under the control of a very few international companies whose territorial rights covered much larger areas than they could effectively exploit.[1] This, combined with the apparent profitability of oil operations, led to demands for extensive changes in existing concession terms after the Second World War. Such demands gained added strength from the much more favourable terms that the governments had been able to obtain for the new concessions granted in

[1] The early history of the concessions has been set forth in several authoritative publications which discuss the influence of political factors, including the rivalry between Britain and the United States, as well as of economic factors, such as the inability or unwillingness of any but the large and well-financed companies to undertake the risk and expense of exploration and development. The ownership of oil in Arabia is closely bound up with the economic position of the parent companies, including their access to markets. See especially George Lenczowski, *Oil and State in the Middle East*, Cornell Univ. Press 1960; S. H. Longrigg, *Oil in the Middle East* (Oxford Univ. Press, 2nd edn, 1961); the United States Federal Trade Commission, *The International Petroleum Cartel* (Washington, D.C., 1951). All of the oil of Saudi Arabia, Qatar, Bahrain and Kuwait (with the exception of the Neutral Zone) was owned in unequal shares by eight international companies, seven of which produced 85 per cent of the output of the world outside North America, China and the Soviet bloc in 1950 and also controlled nearly three-quarters of refinery throughput and probably a similar proportion of marketing.

the 1950s and 1960s. The abundance of low-cost oil, together with the price policies of the major companies, attracted many newcomers to the Middle East, and competition for concessions among companies other than the established 'majors' who had traditionally dominated the field, immensely enhanced the bargaining position of governments. Indeed, some of the new agreements are more in the nature of contractual than concessionary relationships and it is possible to see them as pointing the way from 'concessions to contracts',[1] thus radically changing the nature of the relationship between oil companies and governments.

The major demands of governments have been for changes in financial terms in order to give governments a greater share in revenues, for relinquishment by the companies of unexploited areas held under exclusive concession thus enabling governments to offer concessions to other companies, and for equity participation for the government in the companies producing oil. We shall discuss each of these in turn.

Originally the oil companies were exempt from all taxes under their concession agreements but paid to the government a royalty of four gold shillings per ton of oil produced. With the great expansion of production after the war the governments were pressing for an increased share of the profits attributed to crude oil, and in 1950 Aramco in Saudi Arabia led the way by agreeing to pay the Saudi King 50 per cent of its profits in the form of an income tax.[2] Other governments soon obtained the same terms and oil revenues jumped, partly because of the tax itself, but partly also because the '50-50' arrangements made it necessary to determine and announce a price for crude oil, which was higher than the price that had previously been attributed to crude oil by some, if not all, of the companies. The governments of the producing countries granted the companies a substantial marketing allowance for tax purposes, but this was later gradually eliminated.

The next important financial changes occurred after the formation of the Organization of Petroleum Exporting Countries in 1960, for OPEC was responsible for a virtual freezing of the 'tax prices' of crude oil – the so-called posted prices – which meant that the companies were no

[1] This is the title of a paper presented to the fifth Arab Petroleum Congress (Cairo, 1965) by the Organization of Petroleum Exporting Countries.
[2] It should be noted that the tax cost Aramco nothing since the sum paid the Saudi Government could be deducted from the company's liability under the U.S. income tax laws. In other words, the payment was at the expense of the U.S. Treasury and the arrangement was accepted by the Treasury. At this time the United States government was particularly concerned to strengthen the position of the U.S. oil companies in the Middle East. In 1948 also there had been a substantial increase in royalty payments in terms of dollars when Saudi Arabia and Iraq insisted that payments should be based on the free market price of gold in the Middle East rather than the price of $35 an ounce fixed by the U.S. and British governments.

longer free to lower these prices at will.[1] For the first time the governments obtained partial control over the prices attributed to their crude oil. OPEC was also instrumental in forcing the companies to 'expense' royalties – that is, to treat the $12\frac{1}{2}$ per cent royalty they paid on crude as a cost instead of as part of the tax on profits paid to the governments. Again oil revenues per ton of oil produced rose substantially, although the full effect of eliminating royalty expensing is being spread over a number of years in view of the weak position of crude and product markets since 1964 when the expensing agreement was made.

The original concession agreement in Saudi Arabia made provision for relinquishment at the discretion of Aramco of areas it did not exploit, but it was not until 1948 that the company agreed on a programme of relinquishment. In most of the agreements with the newcomers taking up concessions in the late 1950s and early 1960s, provision was made for relinquishment according to a predetermined timetable, and other concessionaires voluntarily accepted the principle. By 1963 Aramco had relinquished about 75 per cent of its original concession area; the Qatar Petroleum Company's concession area has been cut by about one-third; KOC has given up about half of its original concession; and even in Abu Dhabi, the ruler has already been able to offer relinquished territory for new bidding. The fact that major companies can no longer indefinitely keep unexploited areas out of the hands of possible rivals has further weakened their monopoly over oil resources.

A number of Middle Eastern governments, but in particular Saudi Arabia, have strongly pressed their major concessionaires to admit the government as a full partner in the companies producing crude oil. This has been consistently refused, but the new concession agreements with non-major companies provide for equity participation. The move towards partnership with the state oil companies was led by French, Italian and Japanese companies as a means of facilitating the expansion of their Middle East oil interests. Although the established major oil companies had in one way or another been forced to improve the terms on which they operated in the 1950s, they were adamant in maintaining the '50-50' principle in the division of profits as well as their 100 per cent ownership of their producing affiliates.[2] In bidding for new concessions, the French,

[1] When product prices fall the value of crude oil is reduced, and in such circumstances the companies would normally reduce posted prices for crude. In fact oil prices had been falling for ten years up to June 1967 but the companies have been required to pay 'income taxes' to the governments of the producing countries on a posted price unchanged since 1960.
[2] Under the San Remo Agreement of 1920 Iraq had been promised a 20 per cent equity share in the oil company to be formed in Mesopotamia, but she was later persuaded to give it up in return for a royalty. The problem posed for the major integrated companies by the demand of governments for partnership is discussed below.

Italian and Japanese showed little hesitation in breaching both principles. Moreover, the governments have also pressed for the right to participate in 'downstream' operations – that is, in refining and marketing – and to have a share of the profits attributed to these stages of the industry. Again, the major companies have, by and large, insisted that this was impossible.

The first concessions in the Arab Middle East providing for equity participation and violating the '50-50' principle were made by the Japanese in 1957 and 1958 in the agreements signed with Saudi Arabia and Kuwait for offshore rights in the Neutral Zone.[1] Subsequently Saudi Arabia led the way in forcing the pace of such agreements and continually improving their terms. In 1965 Petromin, the Saudi Government-owned company, and Auxirap, a company backed by the French government, formed a partnership for the exploitation of an area in the Red Sea zone of Saudi Arabia which had been relinquished by Aramco. The agreement provided for a 40 per cent share-holding but equal voting rights for Petromin, for the extension of Petromin's activities into refining and marketing, and for taxation at existing rates. In effect, the government was to receive some 80 per cent of the profits made on crude exports under this arrangement. Even more favourable agreements, providing for partnership, downstream integration, and a higher take for the government, were signed at the end of 1967, one between Petromin and ENI (the Italian Company) and one with American independents.

Although Saudi Arabia has pushed most vigorously in the new agreements, both Kuwait and Abu Dhabi have made similar arrangements with newcomers. In 1968 the Kuwait National Assembly ratified an oil agreement between the Kuwait National Oil Company and Hispanoil, a Spanish group sponsored by the Spanish government. Under the agreement the joint company was guaranteed a 25 per cent share of the Spanish market for fifteen years. Abu Dhabi also signed an agreement with Maruzen Oil Company of Japan in December 1967 with very favourable financial and participation terms.

As stated above, however, no progress whatsoever has been made in obtaining equity participation in the concessions of the major companies – Aramco, KOC, and the IPC group which also owns the Qatar Petroleum Company. The heart of this problem lies in the significance for integrated companies of the acceptance of non-integrated partners in the production of their raw material.

---

[1] The first such agreement in the Middle East was made in Iran in 1957 with the Italian state company.

The Problem of Partnership with Governments

The important companies that produce oil in Arabia are all wholly-owned affiliates of internationally integrated oil companies. Their output accrues to their parent companies, each of whom is entitled to a share in output proportional to its equity ownership in the affiliate. Thus they are not independent producers themselves exporting to world markets at world prices and free to make independent contracts for their crude and to export to whatever markets would gain them the highest prices. They are subsidiaries, producing oil in accordance with the international plans of their owners. As already noted, the parent companies taken together dominate the international petroleum industry at all levels and for the most part the oil they produce in their Arabian affiliates is produced for use in their own refineries or is sold among themselves on special terms.

Although the governments want to engage in integrated oil operations through their national oil companies, they are not yet in a position to use a partner's share of crude oil from the major concessions. Nor do they seek partnership merely to obtain greater revenues. The oil minister of Saudi Arabia stated very firmly last year that Saudi Arabia's long-term plan was to *control* all oil operations. And it is the possibility that increased control by a non-integrated governmental partner will result in pressures to increase output that creates the biggest problem for the oil companies. Merely to permit the government partner to take a partner's share of crude oil would not be a serious obstacle; the possible greater cost to the companies could be looked upon as part of the continuous process of bargaining over revenues, which the companies do not expect to cease in any case; but control that enabled the governments to press for increased output which the companies would be expected to dispose of is another matter, for it would involve serious pressure to increase market sales and hence to cut prices. The problem is manageable for crude-producing affiliates that supply only a small part of the parent company's crude requirements, but even a small percentage increase in the output of one of the major affiliates would create very large amounts of oil to be disposed of.

In principle, the governments of the crude producing countries recognize the underlying problem and are fully aware that an increase in free market sales carries with it the likelihood of a deterioration not only in crude prices but in product prices as well. In principle, therefore, a government should be prepared, in demanding partnership, to agree that it would not press for increased output which would force greater market sales. The Saudi Oil Minister has, for example, made it clear that the Saudi Government, which has been opposing OPEC's attempts to establish quotas to control the output of each country's oil, would change its policy and support such measures if product prices fell to the point at which the maintenance of posted prices for crude oil became untenable.[1]

The difficulty is, however, that no individual government is in a position to appraise the overall circumstances of the parents of its major concessionaires and thus to take an active part in the determination of the international distribution of their supplies of crude oil. In these circumstances, co-operation by an individual government partner in policies designed to regulate output of the producing company in accordance with the outlets provided by the integrated operations of the other owners, and by their established contracts and the market sales which were considered possible at ruling prices without intensifying competition in product markets, would in practice imply government consent to a kind of prorationing operated by the companies.[2] But this is precisely what many of the governments object to in the present situation; as we have seen one of the reasons behind the demand for equity participation is the desire of governments to have some control over, or influence on, offtake. Clearly, the only alternative would be for the governments as a group, perhaps through OPEC to join with the companies as a group in an effective cartel to plan the amount and distribution of oil supplies. There is as yet no evidence that this would work.

Although it seems, on the face of it, to be eminently reasonable that the governments of the oil-exporting countries should be able to become partners in the exploitation of their own oil if they are willing to pay for

[1] Referring to Saudi Arabia's latest oil agreements, in a seminar in Beirut in June 1967, the Minister pointed out that taxes and royalties in these agreements were based on posted prices, but that there was also a provision requiring the foreign partner to market Petromin's share of crude oil production at an agreed realized price, for the determination of which a formula had been set out. He added, 'However, if it turns out that the realized price for sales to third parties is below what we are prepared to accept, we are entitled to institute a reduction in the overall production from the venture as a whole. In other words we are prepared to cut back output rather than allow the price to fall below a certain level. And the motive for this lies in our recognition of the fact that any cut-price marginal sales can have a damaging effect on the whole price structure.' Quoted in *Middle East Economic Survey*, vol. xi, no. 32 (June 7, 1968), p. 3.

[2] Although the level of offtake in any one country is under the control of the oil companies, they are subject to political pressures from the governments. Iran, for example, has used its political bargaining power very effectively to gain increases in production. One of the problems in establishing production quotas arises from the fact that a number of countries are dissatisfied with their *share* of the market, and since market shares can only add up to 100 per cent, an increase in the share of some (including new producers such as Abu Dhabi) must reduce the share of others. In spite of the Saudi Minister's statement above, he has also made it clear that his government would act to safeguard its own interest if the oil companies succumbed to the pressure of other governments at the expense of Saudi production.

an ownership share, it can now be seen that such a change could have far-reaching consequences for the organization of the international companies, who might well prefer to withdraw from ownership of their major sources of crude oil and become contractors to governments. This the Saudi Oil Minister has set himself firmly against for fear that it might cause a drastic reduction in oil prices. The oil companies may offer a compromise in the form of arrangements which give the appearance of partnership without granting the government partner any share of control over offtake. In my view, this would only be a stop-gap measure and merely postpone the fundamental issue; it would be unlikely to last until the end of the concession period, which is not until 1999 for Aramco and 2026 for the Kuwait Oil Company.

The governments are not putting all their hopes of entering the oil industry on the prospect of obtaining an equity interest in their major concessions. In addition to the partnership arrangements made with their new concessionaires, most of them have established national oil companies, which we shall now briefly discuss.

National Oil Companies
The two important national oil companies in Arabia are the Kuwait National Oil Company and the General Petroleum and Minerals Organization (Petromin) of Saudi Arabia. KNPC was established in 1960 with a 60 per cent government and a 40 per cent local private ownership. Petromin was created in 1962 as a public corporation wholly owned by the Saudi government.

Both companies intend to build up an international oil business, which will be in some degree integrated, in co-operation with foreign enterprises as well as on their own initiative. KNPC has completed the construction of an advanced export refinery and has set up an international marketing department with headquarters in London. A Danish subsidiary of the company has completed a terminal in Copenhagen and is already storing oil products. Supply contracts have been accepted in several parts of the world. As noted above KNPC has joined with Hispanoil in a joint enterprise (Kuwait Spanish Petroleum Company) owned 51 per cent by KNPC, to operate the concession obtained from the government. KNPC also does all the local marketing of products in Kuwait.

Similarly, Petromin has lost no time in entering the petroleum industry. In addition to local marketing, which is the first activity usually reserved to a national company, Petromin has a 75 per cent interest in a refinery in Jiddah and a 71 per cent interest in a lube oil blending plant to be set up also in Jiddah. The company is gaining experience in exploration through its joint ventures with the French, Italians and others under the new agreements discussed above. It has also set up service companies for drilling and geophysical surveys, which work on contract for oil companies. In the international field, Petromin is planning to undertake refining and distribution enterprises outside Saudi Arabia, has sold oil to Rumania under a barter agreement, and is setting up a tanker company.

Petromin has not confined itself to petroleum operations proper but is attempting to advance the industrialization of Saudi Arabia, building on her mineral resources. A large urea plant owned 51 per cent by Petromin is under construction using natural gas as the raw material; sulphur production is another major project of the company; a steel rolling mill in Jiddah – the first stage in an iron and steel manufacturing programme – went into operation in 1967, and further stages are being planned. Provision is made for a joint petrochemical venture in the new oil agreement with the Italian companies. Most of these ventures depend in some degree on foreign co-operation and usually involve joint companies with a 51 per cent ownership for Petromin.

In addition to the national oil companies, a new Arab Organization has been created which is in some respects a kind of international Arab oil company. The Organization of Arab Petroleum Exporting Countries was established in 1967 on the initiative of Saudi Arabia, with Kuwait, Libya and Saudi Arabia as founders. It has two types of function. One is to establish co-operation among the members and promote their interests. The other is more interesting. It is to 'utilize the common resources and potentialities of members in establishing joint ventures in various phases of the oil industry such as may be undertaken by all the members or those of them that may be interested in such ventures' (Art. 2. e). The organization is a juridical entity and can operate as a commercial organization. It could therefore make direct arrangements with consuming agencies on behalf of its members if this were desired. It is not designed to displace OPEC, but to supplement it for the member Arab states. Only an Arab state for which oil constitutes 'the principal and basic source of its national income', is eligible for membership. Egypt is thereby excluded, as is Algeria, since in neither case is oil the principal source of national income. Whether OAPEC will become an important organization in the Arab oil world remains to be seen.

Conclusion

We have discussed the more important changes during the past twenty years in the direct relations between the governments of the oil-exporting countries of Arabia and their foreign concessionaires, and we have examined the evolution of the role of governments in the oil business itself. Starting as little more than a collector of royalties, the governments of the larger exporters are now actively engaged in almost all aspects of the industry and in addition bargain with their concessionaires on equal terms. Great changes have taken place in the general political circumstances of the world as a whole, including the emergence in Arabian oil of important countries, such as Japan, France and Italy, who were willing to take an independent line in oil matters, as well as changes within the Middle East itself, including changes in the competence and aspirations of governments. These changes have placed the governments in a very different position today than they were when the original concessions were negotiated. The very need to spend oil revenues with a reasonable degree of efficiency, forced extensive administrative reorganizations in the structure of the state and sometimes extensive political changes as well.

There are many aspects of oil and state in Arabia that we have not discussed. To mention only a few: the role of oil in boundary disputes and the progress made in the fixing of boundaries that would have been unimportant in the absence of the possibilities of oil; the settling of off-shore rights, in particular the disputes over the Persian Gulf between Iran and Saudi Arabia; the interstate economic co-operation that has taken place, including the Kuwait Fund for Arab Economic Development.

The most important issue in the relation between companies and governments in the coming few years will centre around the question of equity partnership for the governments of the oil-producing countries. In Arabia this will involve primarily Kuwait and Saudi Arabia, for the other governments are not in a position to enter the industry. Saudi Arabia has taken the lead in pressing demands for partnership. What type of compromise, if any, can be achieved on this issue will depend partly on what happens to the markets for oil and products. If, for some reason or other, the rate of supply is kept under reasonable control (recently the dispute of the companies with Iraq as well as other political events in the area have helped to ease the so-called oil surplus) and prices do not come under severe pressure, the companies may be able to work out acceptable arrangements which would last until the governments began to feel the desire for a more effective control than such arrangements would be likely to give. If, however, the prices of crude oil and products resume their downward trend, the companies will feel less able to offer more to the governments and may prefer to withdraw from the ownership of their crude-oil production. Such a move would fundamentally change the role of the governments of the producing countries in the international oil industry, and would certainly raise more urgently than ever the question of the establishment of a governmental producers' cartel.

While these more sophisticated disputes go on, the face of the Trucial Coast will rapidly change as the expenditure of oil revenues accelerates in Abu Dhabi, Dubai and Oman and as exploration (with its attendant fees to governments) continues in the lesser shaikhdoms.

14

PROBLEMS AND PROSPECTS OF
DEVELOPMENT IN THE
ARABIAN PENINSULA

INTRODUCTION

The Arabian Peninsula has an area of about 1·2 million square miles but only some 11·5 million inhabitants – roughly ten persons to the square mile.[1] In absolute terms this makes the Peninsula one of the least-populated regions in the world. However, as we will have occasion to indicate further on, the population is not sparse if account is taken of the scarcity of water, the niggardliness of nature except for oil, the low level of economic performance, and the narrow base of development.

Were it not for oil, there would have been very little of interest to write about from the standpoint of a philistine economist. An economic survey would then have probably described the Peninsula as being underdeveloped with a backward population, with an extremely low income per head in spite of small variations between one country and another.

Thanks to the spectacular development of the oil industry in Saudi Arabia, Kuwait, Bahrain, Qatar, Abu Dhabi and Muscat-Oman, the region now has very striking contrasts. It can claim the highest and the second highest income per head in the world, in Abu Dhabi and Kuwait respectively, and one of the lowest incomes in parts of the People's Republic of Southern Yemen. It can claim a very high level of techno-logical development in the oil industry and an abysmal level in most sectors in non-oil-producing parts of the same country. And, in certain localities where oil has been found in abundance, one comes across the startling contrast of resource development alongside backwardness of population. The problems and the prospects of development, which will occupy us in the rest of this paper, are not unrelated to the facts under-lying these contrasts and to their implications.

I. PROBLEMS OF DEVELOPMENT

Table I records some of the known basic economic facts of the various political units of the Peninsula. Some of the figures are no better than estimates or intelligent guesses; nevertheless the table can serve as background to discussion.

1. No doubt the discovery of rich oil reserves has drastically changed the economic map of the oil-rich countries. Yet one can still make generalizations which apply to the whole region, particularly to the population. The social impact of the expenditure of oil revenue, while noticeable in Kuwait and Saudi Arabia, is yet much less noticeable than the physical impact. Consequently, one can safely say that the most widely observable social characteristic of the region as a whole is traditionalism and tribalism. Social organization, loyalties and values – even in a society as sophisticated by Arabian standards as Kuwait, the large urban centres of Saudi Arabia, or Dubai – still betray the clear underlying streaks of traditionalism and tribalism.

Because of the bias in his training, the economist will tend to underestimate the likely richness of the cultural heritage of a tribal society. Nevertheless, with this professional hazard in mind, and taking into account the economically-positive value of certain characteristics of tribal organization and heritage, we can still safely say that on balance tribalism is a serious problem across the course of development in Arabia. Furthermore, tribalism need not, and indeed must not, be sought only among the 20–25 per cent of the population still in a nomadic state; for tribalism dies hard even in old established urban centres.

Long-standing mercantile activities, education, industrialization, travel, entry and residence of tens of thousands of more advanced Arabs, Europeans, Americans, and of other nationals, and the new and expanded range of jobs in the oil-producing countries have begun, though in varying degrees, to erode the tribal structure and values of Kuwait, Saudia Arabia, Bahrain, Qatar and Dubai, and to a lesser extent Abu Dhabi and Oman. Farther south, the Yemen, which in the late Emile Bustani's words was in 1962 dashing headlong into the fifteenth century, has been forced as a result of the five-year association with the Egyptian army to jump a couple of centuries, though it has not quite reached the late eighteenth century yet, the landmark of the Industrial Revolution. Yet farther south, Aden's status as a British colony gave it something more than a battle cry and some income: it brought it into that degree of contact with the outside world and introduced to it advanced and varied economic activities which together largely destroyed the inherent tribal structure of the community.

2. But education still only touches a small proportion of the children of school age in all parts of the region except Kuwait, Bahrain and Qatar, as Table 2 shows. Not only has formal education not been diffused on a

wide front, but the diffusion of skills is also extremely limited, whether these skills are acquired in training institutions or through on-the-job training. Of course, in saying this we have in mind only the nationals of the various parts of the Arabian Peninsula.[2] But even if the tens of thousands of expatriates are taken into account, the availability of skills would still be very meagre – and largely restricted to the oil sector and its ancillary activities – except in the case of Kuwait.

3. Closely related to education and skills is the degree of acceptance of new ways of doing things, of new technology. This degree is very low, and this is all the truer the further one gets from trading centres and from the oil sector. Perhaps dramatic tales of the resistance of traditional communities to such 'innovations' as the telephone, electricity, or the radio, and the condemnation of these innovations as the work of the devil, are already recollections of the past, if they were ever true.[3] But whether the tales are apocryphal or not, it remains true that the treatment of the fruits of modern technology – the radio, the car, the air-conditioner, to name only a few instances – is anything but conducive to the extraction of maximum and longest service. One glaring illustration of the non-familiarity with modern technology is the low level of repair and main-tenance, even the relative non-concern with these. And, of course, the region is still very far from the stage of making modern gadgetry and from broad acceptance of technological change.

4. Sanitary and health conditions have come a long way in the past two decades, but they still constitute an impediment to physical perform-ance to be contended with. The relevant statistics are only adequate for Kuwait, which has moved furthest in health services. Between 1949 and 1967, the number of doctors in government service rose from 4 to 547. In addition, there are 135 doctors in private practice and private hospitals. This makes a ratio of one doctor per 690 inhabitants, one of the best in the world. The number of dentists rose from zero to 43 between the two reference years, of pharmacists from one to 70, of qualified nurses from 7 to 827. The number of hospital beds has reached a total of 3,684, of which about 90 per cent are in government hospitals.[4] Next to Kuwait, but far behind, lie Saudi Arabia, Bahrain, and Qatar in the provision of health services. Abu Dhabi, though rich for over five years now, has only just begun to put an adequate part of its financial resources into social services, under the rulership of Shaikh Zayid ibn Sultan.

5. Understandably, the public administration of the various political units in the Peninsula is still backward, again except for Kuwait which has taken large strides towards modernization, the former Aden Colony, and lastly Saudi Arabia. The defects of public administration are com-posite; they include a low level of education and of specialization, par-

ticularism, and the weakness of administrative tradition. Even in Kuwait, the country with the largest reservoir of skills to draw upon, the civil service suffers from serious shortcomings. The welfare philosophy of the state has resulted in the accumulation of a huge civil service – a total of over 75,000 in a population of 468,000. A fraction of this number, well chosen from among the total, could handle the task of administration more efficiently, and of course, at lower cost. The educational status of the civil service can be seen in Table 3, where the low level of education of officials, particularly the Kuwaitis among them, is evident.

6. Budget-making is a major function of an administration. Budgets in the modern sense are a very recent phenomenon in the Peninsula. In most instances the ruler combined in his person the authority to spend public funds and to collect them. The distinction between the ruler's private purse, which used to be the repository of revenue, and the public treasury in the proper sense was largely unknown. This explains the fabulous riches accumulated by the ruling families of the oil-rich states or shaikh-doms, and the misspending of huge public funds for the private ends of certain members of ruling families. As recently as 1958 this latter practice was to be seen in Saudi Arabia, where the country had accumulated foreign debts reportedly as enormous as the whole oil revenue of 1958 – some $310 million. The cause of indebtness was the irresponsible building and equipping of a complex of palaces which it would have been impossible to justify and to finance under proper budgetary control. One can safely say that King (then Prince) Faisal's assumption of effective control over finances marked the beginning of proper budgeting and budget control in Saudi Arabia.

Elsewhere in less generously endowed parts of the Peninsula the implications of the budgetary situation just described were not very serious, because the revenues were very small. For instance, according to a recent survey, '. . . if Abu Dhabi and Dubai are excluded, the combined total revenues of the other five (Trucial) States is little more than £250,000'.[5]

7. One other related aspect of serious implication for development is the smallness of the middle class whose contribution to development it will be idle to deny. The elements pertaining to this class are still a mere nucleus: merchants in the urban centres, entrepreneurs, better educated and enlightened civil servants, members of free professions. Only the first group is of some numerical substance in the cities, but this group is not generally renowned for development-mindedness and public-spiritedness. The leavening effect of the intelligentsia is still hardly noticeable, except in Kuwait. Most of the activist political awareness in the region takes the form of protest, mainly in the ranks of labour. And, in most

instances except in and around Aden, the driving force is expatriate Arab elements.

Closely related to this point is the fact that pressure groups in the region, outside the burgeoning labour movement, do not take the more modern form of parties and parliamentary blocks. But what is more significant, the pressure transmitted is only marginally development orientated.

8. The last point to discuss in relation to population is the sparseness of population as an impediment to development in the oil-rich parts of the Peninsula. This might sound paradoxical. But it is here argued that the population map as we know it explains the underdevelopment in part when superimposed on the resources maps. Social and economic over-head capital becomes very costly when the beneficiaries are few and the technical minimum size of investment in infrastructure is large. Granted that there is a minimum list of facilities and services that have to be provided by government, the cost per unit of population is necessarily very high when the land is vast and the population small and widely scattered.

9. Reference has already been made to the meagreness of resources, apart from oil in the eastern side of the Peninsula. This creates a secondary category of problems: the narrowness of the agricultural base. If Saudi Arabia, Muscat-Oman, the People's Republic of Southern Yemen, and Yemen are left aside for the moment, it can safely be said that in Kuwait, Bahrain, Qatar and the Trucial States agricultural land is negligible: it constitutes less than one-fourth of 1 per cent of total area. By 'agricultural land' we mean here arable land and land under permanent crops, permanent meadows and pastures, and forested land, as these terms are defined in the F A O *Production Yearbook*.[6]

The area of arable land and land under permanent crops in Kuwait is unofficially reported as 10 sq. km. out of a total land area of over 15,000 sq. km. There are no permanent meadows and pastures, no forests. Saudi Arabia, according to the same F A O source, has 373,000 hectares of arable land and land under permanent crops and 1·7 million hectares of forested land out of a total area of 225·3 million hectares of land area. Here again the area of arable land and forests is negligible, constituting together just under 1 per cent of total land area. It ought to be admitted, however, that Saudi Arabia has a vast amount of rough grazing land, somewhat over one-third of the total area. No information is available on the area of arable land in Yemen, but forested land is unofficially estimated at 1,500 sq. km. out of a total land area of 195,000 sq. km. It is generally believed by knowledgeable travellers that Yemen has the largest ratio of arable land in the Peninsula, but then the Yemen is a relatively small country, constituting less than 7 per cent of the Peninsula. In the People's Republic of Southern Yemen arable land and land under permanent crops amounts to about 1 per cent of total land area, while forested land constitutes about 9 per cent. Rough grazing land is just over one-third of total land area.

These statistics are indeed depressing, given present technology and established cost-return relationships pertaining to desalination of sea water and its use in irrigation. They are superimposed on the absence of notable rivers and a rainfall that averages some four inches annually. It is obvious that agriculture, which is the normal backbone of economics the world over, is a very small sector in the Peninsula. The pockets of agriculture here and there, in oases in Trucial Oman or Muscat-Oman and in Saudi Arabia, as well as in large patches in the south-western part of the Peninsula, do not constitute a large enough exception to our generalization to warrant serious modification of it. (However, the discovery of huge reservoirs of underground water in Saudi Arabia, and the implications of this event, are an aspect of the prospects of development which will be discussed further down.)

10. The drastic limitation of arable land under permanent crops has meant a heavy dependence by the inhabitants of the Peninsula on the importation of agricultural commodities – foodstuffs and raw materials alike.[7] This dependence is lowest in Saudi Arabia, Yemen and the People's Republic of Southern Yemen. In Kuwait it is almost complete because of the very high standard of living, which has meant a departure from simple life and from the consumption of a narrow range of foodstuffs. But apart from Kuwait, where the substantial oil revenues have left their mark on the level of living of the masses, consumption of foodstuffs is low, even in oil-producing countries. According to one FAO study, the calorie intake as per cent of requirements in Saudi Arabia was 83 in 1962, as against 100 for the United Arab Republic and Lebanon, 98 for Syria, 95 for Iraq, 93 for Sudan, and 92 for Jordan. Saudi Arabia ranks lowest among the Arab countries covered in the study for the consumption of pulses and nuts, and lowest except for the Sudan and UAR in the consumption of fruits and vegetables. It ranks among the better fed with regard to meat, fish, and eggs (after Lebanon, Sudan, and Iraq), but among the less well-fed with regard to milk (with only UAR and Jordan worse off).[8]

11. No large industrial sector exists; the service sectors are largely restricted to personal services and trade; and infrastructure still ranges from very poor to inadequate, except in Kuwait and to a lesser extent Saudi Arabia. The latter country is moving fast toward the correction of this deficiency, and the oil-rich shaikhdoms are doing likewise, but at a slower pace. Obviously, owing to the small size of these shaikhdoms and

the large oil revenue per inhabitant, the task of building social and economic overhead will be relatively easy, given wise leadership and the continued ease of using expatriate skills for the purpose. However, the convenience of small scale in this instance ought not to lead us to the belief that the process will be smooth when the shaikhdoms concerned try to develop manufacturing industry and service sectors like banking, transport and communications, hotel-keeping and the like. There will be many bottlenecks in the realms of manpower, work traditions and values, organization, public administration and markets.

12. What we are saying adds up to one global problem: the narrowness of the base of the oil economies.[9] This narrowness drastically limits the range of products and makes the economies, outside the oil sector, largely importing-consuming economies. This can easily be seen from a comparison of commodity imports and exports for the two countries for which adequate information is available. In Kuwait, exports other than oil amounted to KD 13 million in 1967, while imports reached KD 212 million.[10] Saudi Arabia had SR 1,693 million of imports in 1964–5, against SR 278 million of exports (excluding petroleum).[11] The inclusion of invisibles makes the picture even less favourable for Kuwait and Saudi Arabia alike.

13. The narrowness of the economic base of oil-producing countries in the Peninsula has serious implications for the future, given the extreme shortage of water, the scarcity of arable land, and the primitiveness of the skills, institutions, and forms of organization essential to industrial development. To begin with, the high income achieved is not the product of the performance of the society and its productive forces; the oil sector is an island of advanced technology and organization and intensive capital investment, in a sea of underdevelopment and backwardness. All depends on oil except in Saudi Arabia. And while it is true that the oil-rich country can adopt policies that will ensure the flow of oil exports and the inflow of oil revenues for a few decades more at least, it is also true that the prospects of the distant future depend on the ability of the country to use the oil revenues in developing other productive sectors, so that there will be other large income-producing activities than oil in the future. A look at the steep rise in imports in Kuwait in recent years, and at the large size of the budget – particularly the salaries and wages section in it – is enough to illustrate what we have in mind. This is that the economy of Kuwait – and other small shaikhdoms may follow in the same footsteps – is not building up alternative productive sectors fast enough and large enough to assure the country of a steady flow of income if oil revenues were in the future to decline owing to a radical shift in the use of energy sources in the world.

The case of Saudi Arabia is similar in nature, though this country has not gone as far as Kuwait in diverting resources to consumption. Furthermore, an examination of the imports of Saudi Arabia since the early sixties will show that there has been a clear emphasis on development revealed in the steady shift in the composition of imports towards capital goods, raw materials and intermediate goods. In fairness, it ought also to be emphasized that Saudi Arabia has a wider potential base for development outside the oil sector, with underground water, some arable land, several minerals capable of commercial extraction and use, and a large enough population to constitute a decent-sized market.

14. Yet one other serious implication of the oil economy in the Peninsula is the development of the welfare state. It is undoubtedly understandable why the oil-rich countries should provide basic services – education, health and sanitation, housing, water, power – free or at subsidized prices in a desire to make the population benefit from the oil revenue. Yet there is another side to this coin of social mindedness. There is increasing emphasis on distribution to the point that the link between production and distribution is only dimly seen by the work force. Kuwait is the prize illustration of this tendency. The Kuwaitis show very little interest in the manual and mental skills needed for the running of the modern economy. They rely on the expatriates to do the various jobs required, from surgery to accounting to drilling to carpentry to hairdressing to lorry-driving. The occupational distribution of Kuwaitis and non-Kuwaitis shows a total of 1,263 Kuwaiti professionals to 11,672 non-Kuwaiti, 754 to 2,887 farmers and fishermen for the two groups respectively, 191 to 862 miners and quarrymen, 5,709 to 12,353 transport workmen, 5,423 to 12,353 craftsmen.[12] In fact, while non-Kuwaitis constituted some 51 per cent of total population in 1965, their share of the working population was 78 per cent.[13] An examination of the educational distribution of the civil service suggests that most of the important critical functions are performed by expatriates. (See Table 3 for this distribution.)

15. There is strong evidence here, and in other indicators, of heavy dependence by the oil-rich countries on expatriates. This is understandable at an early stage of development. But the seriousness of the situation lies in the fact that in the small oil shaikhdoms the tendency is strong to leave the uninteresting tasks and the positions that involve the actual running of government and business in the hands of expatriates, while retaining the positions of status and authority. If the basic services can be obtained free or at low, subsidized prices, and if generous welfare payments are made to the unemployed, and if jobs are created in large numbers in the civil service merely in order to provide employment, then why should the nationals undertake to learn plumbing or carpentry or typing?

Such an attitude would be unobjectionable were the governments of these shaikhdoms liberal in their naturalization policy. However, they guard the right of citizenship most jealously, much though they need expatriate skills. Here lies a contradiction that promises to be a serious impediment to development: the slow acquisition of skills by nationals, the dependence on expatriate skills, the non-acceptance of expatriates into citizenry. Under the circumstances, an element of precariousness continuously underlies the development work of the country.

16. The last cluster of problems to be discussed relates to the political fragmentation of the units of the eastern Peninsula. The total population of the eleven units concerned – Kuwait, Bahrain, Qatar, Abu Dhabi, Dubai, Sharjah, ᶜAjman, Umm al-Qaiwain, Ras al-Khaimah, Fujairah, and Muscat and Oman – is about 1,330,000 inhabitants. Surely this is too small a population for 11 political units? The same way that there are economies of large scale, there are diseconomies of small scale, in the field of public administration, infrastructure, supervision of works and in markets. Indeed, without losing sight of the dictates of the right of self-determination, one can make a strong case for the pressurizing of the seven units constituting Trucial Oman, and preferably all eleven except Kuwait, to form themselves into one political unit.

On purely economic and social grounds, one could go further and argue that the present situation is wasteful of resources and morally objectionable. It is extremely difficult to justify the stupendous riches that good fortune makes available to minuscule small populations while brother Arabs in Yemen, Southern Yemen, or even Saudi Arabia are so capital-hungry. The objection is all the stronger because the fabulous wealth of the few is almost certainly going to lead to soft, unproductive lives, corruption, and the amassing of huge personal fortunes that cannot be justified even economically, lying in some distant safe or distant investment as they would certainly be.

II. PROSPECTS OF DEVELOPMENT

1. An evaluation of the prospects of development in the Arabian Peninsula ought to be dynamic in nature and to take into account not only the 'natural' or obvious areas where there is *prima facie* a good case for resource development, but also those areas where change in technology, the discovery of new resources, the development of man-power in terms of education and technical skills, and change in organization can lead to new resource combinations, the production of new products, and generally improvement in economic performance.

2. The satisfaction of the conditions just enumerated has gone furthest

in Kuwait and Saudi Arabia, whose development effort will be discussed in some detail further down. Elsewhere in the Peninsula the situation is different, although precise information is not available for most parts to justify firm judgment. Information is scantiest for the Yemen and the People's Republic of Southern Yemen, as well as for the non-oil-producing shaikdoms. Bahrain, Qatar and Dubai (although the last-named has no oil revenues at the present) have registered relatively noticeable progress in the provision of social and economic overheads and in some areas of private business. Abu Dhabi, which is endowed with a large oil fortune, was very slow in using its oil revenue for development purposes. The development budget for 1965 amounted to £165,000 while oil revenue was £10·75 million for the same year.[14]

In Kuwait and Saudi Arabia an impressive effort has been exerted to develop the economy and diversify the sources of the national product. Kuwait's serious development effort started earlier than Saudi Arabia's, in the early 'fifties as against 1960, largely because there was an earlier commitment to development in Kuwait. In both countries there is today a development-orientated leadership with energy and vision, set on the task of widening the base of the economy. The two countries are extending and consolidating the social and economic infrastructure essential for the emergence and growth of directly-productive projects. This is not the right place for a discussion of all the development efforts undertaken in Kuwait and Saudi Arabia.[15] Instead, emphasis will be on the prospects and the rationale underlying the evaluation of these prospects.

3. Saudi Arabia is better endowed than Kuwait with development potential outside oil, natural gas and their derivatives. The country currently exploits, or is in the process of arranging to exploit, its deposits of granite, limestone, gypsum, marble, salt, gold, silver, copper, zinc, lead, titanium, iron, silicon and borite.[16] Other natural resources include fish and shrimp, which already form the base of an established fishing, refrigeration and canning industry. In addition to all this, Saudi Arabia has pushed agriculture to the limits of available water and arable land, although much room for expansion exists, as we shall see presently.

The basis for optimism with regard to Saudi Arabia's development prospects is the commitment of the government to development, the energetic extension of the infrastructure, the building of critically important institutions both inside conventional ministries and as autonomous organizations (the General Petroleum and Minerals Organization – Petromin – is the leading illustration), the diffusion of education and technical skills, the search in all sectors for development openings through far-reaching and thorough surveys, and the country's greater fortune in the availability of arable land, underground water and rich mineral deposits.

Efforts in the agricultural sector include the exploration for underground water in large parts of the country – efforts that have met with unexpected and spectacular success; the development of artesian wells already in existence; the building of dams to avoid seepage and wastage of flood waters; general irrigation work; agricultural survey of most of the country by competent foreign firms; the setting up of centres for social welfare to serve the countryside; the setting up of experimentation stations, extension service centres and machine stations; the development of the livestock of the country; settlement of nomads, involving the distribution of portable pumps and of forage-crop seeds and vegetable seeds, the purchase and storage of hay and cereals for distribution during bad seasons, the building of dirt dikes across the wadis, the drilling of deep-water wells near pasture areas and housing schemes in several large projects; the establishment of an agricultural training centre for Saudi youth; and experimentation for the selection of plants and trees most suitable for soil and humidity conditions prevailing.

The country is making proper use of its oil and natural gas resources as power, directly and in the generation of electric power. The abundance of these sources of energy constitutes a promotive factor for industry, though the cost of electricity is believed to be still high. Although the growth path of electricity generation is rising, the power available is still not sufficient to satisfy potential, expanded demand.

In the field of industry other than oil there is noticeable growth, but greater potential. The number of industrial establishments rose from 5 with a total capital of SR 42 million in 1954, to 67 with a capital of SR 211 million in 1964. The private sector has put up factories for cement, gypsum, detergent, tanning and leather products, date processing and packing, dairy products, shrimp and fish canning, macaroni and biscuits, textile and wearing apparel, wood, flour milling, metal furniture, aluminium household utensils, paper products, brick making, marble, alabaster and paint. The public sector, via Petromin, is developing minerals, particularly an integrated steel industry. Several other projects are being developed which represent a total investment by the government of SR 300 million, apart from investment by foreign firms which are invited to participate in joint ventures.

The invitation of foreign managerial and technical skills, as well as capital, through the instrumentality of the joint venture shared between Petromin and the foreign firm is a matter of energetic policy. So far the arrangement has proved useful and of great promise. Its long-term value depends on the ability of the Saudis to acquire as many of the skills and as much of the organizational and managerial expertise involved as possible. The Petroleum and Mineral College at Dhahran, the technical schools elsewhere, and the students specializing abroad constitute a reservoir of young men which should be drawn upon in the running of existing establishments, and later the setting up of new, complex industrial establishments.

Lastly there is the oil industry. The oil sector is developing fast inasmuch as the production of crude petroleum is concerned. But in addition, there are refineries for local needs and export purposes. Projects are underway or already complete for the production of chemical fertilizers, synthetic resins, polyvinyl chloride, plastic products and sulphuric acid. Here again these projects are joint ventures, with the initial entrepreneurial function performed by Petromin, and the financing, management, and production and sales functions undertaken jointly. Much more could be said with respect to the development of petrochemicals, but it is not intended to turn this part of the paper into a descriptive survey of the efforts of Petromin and the government.[17]

4. Much the same thing can be said of Kuwait with regard to the commitment of government to development and the energetic efforts put into the expansion and consolidation of social and economic infrastructure; the building of institutions geared to the growth effort, such as industrial estates, experimental stations, an institute of tests and measurements and development financing agencies; and the education and training of manpower. However, Kuwait's natural endowment is much more limited than that of Saudi Arabia – except for oil and natural gas.

Thus arable land is extremely scanty, and underground water much less in evidence. But the search for water continues, and experimentation in the selection of plants appropriate to soil and humidity conditions is active. Settlement schemes for nomads and semi-nomads are of generous and substantial size.

Kuwait has gone further than Saudi Arabia, relatively speaking, in the use of oil and natural gas as sources of power, directly or in the generation of electricity, for domestic use, industrial use and desalination of sea water. Thus Kuwait is better prepared to meet potential demand for power.

As in Saudi Arabia, the joint venture is popular. However, in Kuwait more than in Saudi Arabia the mixed sector involving the participation of government and the public has come into prominence. Most large projects fall into this sector.

Among the leading projects already completed in Kuwait are the establishment of a fishing company for fish and shrimp canning and processing, the acquisition and operation of a tanker fleet, the establishment of factories for the production of brick, cement, asbestos products, compressed wood, prefabricated houses, flour mills, soft drinks, and dairy and other food products.

Industrial activities in the oil sector, apart from refining, include the production or preparation for the production of chemical fertilizers, sulphuric acid, caustic soda, synthetic resins, polyvinyl chloride, and plastic products. Here again, the projects fall in the mixed sector and involve co-operation with foreign firms in financing and selling arrangements.

5. The prospects for development seem brightest in Saudi Arabia, although the small oil-rich shaikhdoms produce the statistical illusion that they are much better off because of their very high income per head. Here arises an almost philosophical question as to what one expects of the economy and of life in general. Purely in terms of income per head, Abu Dhabi and Kuwait are at a higher level of development than even the United States of America. But surely one's definition of development ought to be much wider and much more meaningful than the arithmetic average of income would suggest. Furthermore, if very little development can be brought about outside the oil sector, and the development of the oil sector itself owes much of its reality to foreign capital, foreign technology and foreign management, of what lasting value is the achievement in terms of income per head?

Assuming the flow and lucrativeness of oil for many more years, what will the oil-producing countries be able to achieve while their fortune continues? No doubt they will build all the roads, schools, hospitals, cinemas, garages, and shops needed, and they will buy all the gadgets and durable household goods they have a fancy for. But unless there is some productive activity in which the population at large is engaged, this population will turn into a massive group of consumers and rentiers, and will lose the valuable habit of working for a living. This will probably be the fate of all the oil-producing units of the Peninsula except Saudi Arabia, which has a broader economic base to begin with.

6. Here lies a grave danger and a major challenge for the oil-rich shaikhdoms. The danger is obvious. The challenge needs some elaboration.

It is here maintained that the political situation as it now exists in the north-eastern side of the Peninsula – specifically with regard to the separateness of Bahrain, Qatar, the units of the Trucial Coast and Muscat and Oman – is quite absurd. And it is a situation that threatens to continue now that there is a large material stake in separateness. As we suggested in the section on Problems of Development, the fortunes that will be accumulated in the shaikhdoms will be fabulous and beyond the conceivable need of the populations and more so of the individuals within. It is only because human greed stops the marginal utility of money ever becoming zero that oil-rich shaikhs, contractors, and merchants continue to amass fortunes. From a strictly economic standpoint, these fortunes fructify away from the shaikhdoms and from the Arab world as a whole, thus contributing only to the accumulation of compound interest which, itself, also remains abroad.

We submit that, to maximize the prospects of development in the Peninsula the resources of the oil-rich shaikhdoms should be reallocated. Ideally, these shaikhdoms should enter into some form of association with Saudi Arabia. The combined oil revenue of the shaikhdoms (always excluding Kuwait) plus Saudi Arabia's amounted to $1,100 million in 1967. The combined population amounts to some 4,860,000 assuming the Saudis to number some 4 million. The use of the total revenue for the development of the whole region will make much better economic sense, given Saudi Arabia's potential in agricultural and mineral wealth.

7. Human nature being what it is and the attachment to self-determination being what it is, we doubt that the optimal solution will be accepted by the shaikhdoms. Alternatively, therefore, we suggest the creation of an effective federation of the ten political units concerned and the allocation of oil revenues on rational economic grounds within the whole federation. It is here presumed that there will also be population movements in response to economic pulls and pressures. It ought to be admitted that this solution will only reduce the vast inequalities between the haves and the have-nots in oil, but it will still leave a total oil revenue (at 1967 rates) of $260 million in the hands of 860,000 inhabitants. This is not affluence, but a great advance on Saudi Arabia's oil revenue per head. And Saudi Arabia is not doing poorly.

8. If the shaikhdoms fail to form an effective federation and insist on remaining separate political entities, then the most one could hope for would be for the oil-rich shaikhdoms to be public-spirited like Kuwait and to form a development fund for helping first the non-oil shaikhdoms, and then Yemen and Southern Yemen. There is already a modest flow of aid to the 'poor relations', but the volume must become larger if it is to be of significance for development. Kuwait herself can be relied upon to continue the help it has been rendering for a number of years and even to expand it. The Arab League fund will be a third source of aid. But all these arrangements are in fact second best, to be accepted only if the more radical solutions are turned down.

9. But whatever solution is adopted, all the oil-rich shaikhdoms, including Kuwait, ought to make the largest investment in manpower consistent with other demands on finances. Given the frugality of natural endowments outside the oil sector, man is the only 'resource' that can be developed substantially. The objective in these shaikhdoms should be the creation of a new sector, the 'man-and-money' sector, involving the high-level training of thousands of young men and women. Investment

opportunities should then be sought in Asia and Africa, and men plus funds should strike out together. The contribution of the shaikhdoms can then become financial as well as managerial and technical. To think of the Peninsula as providing high-level skills may sound fanciful today, but it is probably the soundest direction that development could take in the long run.

10. It is a cheering aspect of the prospects of development in the Peninsula to note the acceleration of investment for development work, both in infrastructure and in directly-productive projects. There is no information on hand relative to this point, except for Kuwait and Saudi Arabia, and only for investment by the public sector in these two countries.

In Saudi Arabia, development outlays have risen to some 38 per cent of total government outlays in 1967 (from 7 per cent in 1960), while in Kuwait the share of development expenditure was about one-third of the total budget.

It ought, however, to be pointed out that allocations are invariably far beyond the capacity of government machinery to utilize. On the average actual expenditure rarely rises beyond 50 per cent of allocations. The causes must be sought in the defects and weaknesses of the civil service, the inadequacy of technical and economic studies for development projects, and the general slowness of the flow of the various inputs that are to be combined in the investment process.

11. Lastly, the prospects of development, whatever they are, call for proper planning. The belief in many quarters that the abundance of capital in the oil-rich parts of the Peninsula makes planning unnecessary is a fallacy of serious implications. For, while it is true that capital is no bottleneck here, there are other suffocating bottlenecks whose existence requires the proper use of resources. Indeed, almost all other resources are in short supply, human and material. The desired image of the future ought to be defined, the objectives and quantitative targets determined, the priorities established and the development strategy formulated. The problems and obstacles to development are enormous. the prospects restricted, and therefore the course of development ought of necessity to be carefully charted and designed for maximum benefit to result.

NOTES

1. Estimates of area in different sources do not diverge widely. However, population figures, particularly for Saudi Arabia and Yemen, the two most populous countries, vary within a very wide range. The former's population, for instance, was at one time, early in the sixties, estimated

by an authoritative but private agency at 3·25 million but by the Saudi authorities at 6 million. Asfour's study for the Economic Research Institute at the American University of Beirut (see later) independently estimated the population at 3·2 million, using an approach different from the ones used in the other estimates. Yemen's population, according to the 3rd edition of the RIIA's *The Middle East*, is 'certainly 4 and perhaps as much as 8 million strong' (p. 73). But, in the words of a recent publication, 'according to reliable estimates the total population numbers approximately 3,500,000 to 4,000,000'. (Manfred W. Wenner, *Modern Yemen 1918–1966*, p. 29.) The population and area figures for the whole Arabian Peninsula as quoted in the text, and as in Table 1 below, are collated from different sources. Cross-checks were made in the following references:

(a) K. G. Fenelon, *The Trucial States: A Brief Economic Survey* (Khayat, Beirut, 1967), Table IX, p. 83;
(b) Arabian American Oil Company, *Aramco Handbook: Oil and the Middle East* (Dhahran, Saudi Arabia, 1968), p. 175;
(c) General Union of Chambers of Commerce, Industry, and Agriculture for Arab Countries, *Economic Development in Arab Countries 1950–1965* (Beirut, 1967), pp. 71 and 72. (In Arabic.);
(d) Royal Institute of International Affairs, *The Middle East, A Political and Economic Survey*, 3rd edn, Oxford University Press 1958, pp. 73, 94, 102, 106, 113, 122, 131, 138, 141, and 142; and
(e) Manfred W. Wenner, *Modern Yemen 1918–1966* (The Johns Hopkins University Press, Baltimore, 1967), p. 29.

2. For the educational pattern in Kuwait, see Kuwait Planning Board, *Statistical Yearbook 1968*, Section Three, 'Education'. The highlights of educational activity in the whole Peninsula can be seen in Table 2. In Saudi Arabia, 'approximately 10 per cent of the Saudi labour force had (in 1962) completed primary education'. See United Nations, United Nations Economic and Social Office in Beirut, *Studies on Selected Development Problems in Various Countries in the Middle East, 1968* (New York, 1968), p. 25.

3. See *Aramco Handbook*, p. 184, for a reference to this point.

4. Kuwait, Planning Board, *Statistical Yearbook 1968*, data collated from Tables 2, 3, 5, 6, and 7 in Section Four, 'Health Statistics'.

5. Fenelon, *op. cit.*, p. 25.

6. Food and Agriculture Organization, *Production Yearbook 1967*, vol. xxi (Rome 1968), pp. 5 and 6 for data on land relating to Kuwait, Saudi Arabia, Yemen, and People's Republic of Southern Yemen. For data relating to the other parts of the Peninsula, see Fenelon, Table IX, p. 83.

7. For details of the composition of international trade, see Food and Agriculture Organization, *Trade Yearbook 1967*, vol. xxi, (Rome, 1968). See also the statistical yearbooks and trade statistics of Kuwait and Saudi Arabia; the General Union of Chambers of Commerce, Industry, and Agriculture, *op. cit.*, as well as the half-yearly issues of the *Arab Economic Report* published by the General Union beginning with December 1962.

8. Food and Agriculture Organization, *Indicative World Plan for Agricultural Development 1965–1985 – Near East*, Sub-regional Study no. 1, vol. i, text (provisional), (Rome, 1966), Table 3, p. 35, Table 4, p. 36, Table 5, p. 37, and Tables 6 and 7, p. 40.

9. Industry in Kuwait represented 3·6 per cent of Gross Domestic Product for 1966–7, while agriculture and fishing represented 0·5 per cent, building and construction 4·7 per cent, trade 8 per cent, government 5·8 per cent, gas, electricity and water 2·3 per cent, transport, communication, and storage 2·8 per cent, other services 11·3 per cent (including rents and real estate, finance, entertainment, health and education in the private sector, hotels and restaurants, and personal services), and oil 61·1 per cent. See Planning Board, *First 5-Year Plan of Economic and Social Development 1967/68–1971/72*, (Kuwait, undated), p. 35. (In Arabic.), In Saudi Arabia, revenue from oil (including local expenditure by Aramco) was estimated to represent 41 per cent of Gross National Product. No estimates for the other sectors exist. See Edmond Y. Asfour, *Saudi Arabia: Long-Term Projections of Supply of and Demand for Agricultural Products*, (Economic Research Institute, American University of Beirut, 1965), p. 46.

10. Kuwait, Planning Board, *Statistical Abstract 1968*, Tables 3 and 4 of Section Eleven, 'Foreign Trade'.

11. *Economic Development in Arab Countries 1950–1965*, p. 115.

12. Kuwait, *Statistical Abstract 1968*, Table 5 in Section Two, 'Population and Vital Statistics'.

13. Kuwait, Planning Board, *First 5-Year Plan of Economic and Social Development*, calculated from Table 9, p. 44.

14. The information included is collated from the following sources:
   (a) Publications of the General Union of Arab Chambers of Commerce, Industry, and Agriculture in the Arab Countries cited above;
   (b) UN, UNESOB, *Studies on Selected Development Problems in Various Countries in the Middle East*, (New York, 1967);
   (c) UN, UNESOB, *Studies on Selected Development Problems in Various Countries in the Middle East, 1968*, (New York, 1968);
   (d) United Nations, *Industrial Development in the Arab Countries*, (New York, 1967);

(e) United Nations, *Report of the Symposium on Industrial Development in Arab Countries*, (New York, 1967);

(f) International Bank for Reconstruction and Development, *The Economic Development of Kuwait*, (The Johns Hopkins University Press, Baltimore, 1965);

(g) Kuwait, Planning Board, *First 5-Year Plan* . . . , cited above;

(h) *Aramco Handbook* . . . , cited above;

(i) Ahmad Fu'ad Khalifah, *Agricultural Extension in the Arab Countries: A Comparative Study* (Centre for Community Development in the Arab World, Sirs al-Laiyan, UAR, 1967) (in Arabic); and

(j) Food and Agriculture Organization, *Land Policy in the Near East* (Rome, 1967), published for the Government of Libya by FAO and compiled by Mohammed Riad El-Ghonemy of FAO.

16. UN, UNESOB, *Studies on Development Problems in Various Countries in the Middle East, 1968*, p. 25.

17. The past development and the prospects of the oil industry are left out of this account, although the oil sector is by far the most significant factor in the economic life of the Peninsula. The exclusion is due to the fact that this sector ought to receive separate treatment in a paper all by itself. Suffice it to indicate here that the oil-producing parts of the Peninsula produced some 312 million tons of crude oil in 1967 and earned some $1,812 million in direct revenue to governments. The implications of so large a revenue need no emphasis.

TABLE I – General Information on the Arabian Peninsula

	Kuwait	Bahrain	Qatar	Abu Dhabi	Dubai	Sharjah	ʿAjman	Umm al-Qaiwain	Ras al-Khaimah	Fujairah	Muscat and Oman	Saudi Arabia	Yemen	P.R. of South Yemen
Area (ooo sq. miles)	6·2	0·2	0·4	26	1·5	0·1	0·1	0·3	0·6	0·4	82	927	74	112
Population (ooo)	468	143	45	25	60	15	2·5	3	12	3·5	550	4,000	5,000	1,100
Gross National Product 1967 ($ m.)	1,890	n.a.[1]	n.a.	n.a.	n.a.	n.a.	n.a.	n.a.	n.a.	n.a.	n.a.	1,575	n.a.	n.a.
Oil Revenue 1967 ($ m.)	710	25	102	116	—[2]	—	—	—	—	—	16·3	843	—	—
Oil reserves 1967 (bn barrels)	76·7	0·4	3·7	15·0	—	—	—	—	—	—	2·5	83·7	—	—
Oil production 1967 (ooo b/d)	2,501	70	324	384	—	—	—	—	—	—	150[3]	2,806	—	—
Receipts, current account, balance of payments, 1967–8 ($ m.)	1,093·1[4]	n.a.	n.a.	n.a.	n.a.	n.a.	n.a.	n.a.	n.a.	n.a.	n.a.	1,744[7]	n.a.	n.a.
Payments, current account, balance of payments, 1967–8 ($ m.)	679·0[4]	n.a.	n.a.	n.a.	n.a.	n.a.	n.a.	n.a.	n.a.	n.a.	n.a.	n.a.	n.a.	n.a.
Commodity imports 1967–8 ($ m.)	613·2[5]	n.a.	n.a.	n.a.	n.a.	n.a.	n.a.	n.a.	n.a.	n.a.	n.a.	1,675[8]	n.a.	n.a.
Commodity exports 1967–8 ($ m.)	37·2[6]	n.a.	n.a.	n.a.	n.a.	n.a.	n.a.	n.a.	n.a.	n.a.	n.a.	608[9]	n.a.	n.a.
Government, budget-expenditure 1966–7 ($ m.)	694·7	n.a.	n.a.	n.a.	n.a.	n.a.	n.a.	n.a.	n.a.	n.a.	158[10]	992	n.a.	n.a.
Development allocations in budget, 1966–7 ($ m.)	199·6	n.a.	n.a.	n.a.	n.a.	n.a.	n.a.	n.a.	n.a.	n.a.	n.a.	382	n.a.	n.a.

Notes:

1 n.a. indicates 'not available'.

2 — indicates zero or not established.

3 Oil production (and therefore revenue) in Muscat and Oman began only in August 1967.

4 Receipts include only Government's share of oil revenue (i.e. not export value of crude petroleum). Consequently payments do not include share of companies in profits of crude sales.

5 Imports f.o.b.

6 Commodity exports exclude crude petroleum.

7 Receipts include total oil exports.

8 Payments include the net earnings of oil companies transferred abroad.

9 Imports c.i.f.

10 Total commodity exports of $1,567 m. less exports of crude petroleum of $1,409 m. The balance $158 m. includes the value of refined products exported.

Sources:

a Area and population (except for Yemen and P.R. of Southern Yemen, and for Saudi Arabia's population) from K. G. Fenelon, *The Trucial States: A Brief Economic Survey*, Appendix B p. 79 and Appendix E Table IX p. 83. For Yemen: area from RIIA, *The Middle East*, 1958 edition, p. 94. Population, *ibid*, with adjustment to bring figure to the mid-sixties. For P.R. of Southern Yemen: area, *ibid*, p. 102. Population: *ibid*, pp. 106 and 113 plus adjustments.

b Gross national product: Kuwait, Planning Board, *First 5-Year Plan for Economic and Social Development*; revised edition; in Arabic; p. 37, plus adjustment for 1967. Saudi Arabia – Edmond Y. Asfour, *Saudi Arabia, Long-Term Projections of Supply of and Demand for Agricultural Products*, 1965, p. 135, plus adjustments.

c Oil revenues 1967: The Middle East Research and Publishing Centre, Beirut, *Middle East Economic Survey*, vol. xi, no. 50, 11 Oct. 1968, Table 1.

d Oil reserves 1967: Aramco, *Aramco Handbook 1967*, p. 99. Figure for Bahrain obtained from MERPC.

e Oil production 1967: *Aramco Handbook 1967*, p. 94.

f Balance of payments: Kuwait unpublished report by Kuwait Institute of Economic and Social Planning in the Middle East, 1969. Saudi Arabia – S.A. Monetary Agency, *Annual Report 1386–87* (1967), p. 23.

g Commodity imports and exports: Kuwait-Kuwait Institute unpublished report. Saudi Arabia – SAMA Report.

h Budget (including development) allocations: Kuwait – The Economist Intelligence Unit, *Middle East Oil and the Arabian Peninsula*, 1967 Annual Supplement, p. 47. Saudi Arabia – SAMA Report, pp. 5 and 26.

TABLE 2 – *Education Statistics for Six Countries in the Arabian Peninsula*

	Kuwait[a]	Bahrain[b]	Qatar[c]	Saudi[d] Arabia	Yemen[e]	P.R. of[f] Southern Yemen
Elem. education (incl. kindergarten)						
No. of teachers – male	1,344	1,213	643	9,931	1,487	1,042
– female	1,645	754			27	276
No. of students – boys	36,511	27,494	11,740	213,354	65,583	28,420
– girls	28,909	17,898			3,556	7,562
Preparatory education (intermediate)						
No. of teachers – male	1,086	—	83	1,618	76	226
– female	901	—			—	98
No. of students – boys	19,107	—	1,222	22,442	1,426	5,781
– girls	14,110	—			—	2,236
Secondary education						
No. of teachers – male	470	—	37	125	42	76
– female	282	—			—	33
No. of students – boys	5,706	—	338	3,428	433	1,425
– girls	3,085	—			—	780
Religious studies in schools						
No. of teachers	36	—	17	274	69	—
No. of students	278	—	116	4,378	991	—
Technical education (incl. Commerce, Agriculture, etc.)						
No. of teachers	334	—	34	385	1	24
No. of students	1,931	—	233	1,718	25	232

Teachers' institutions (all levels)

No. of teachers – male	154	—	10	204	5	19
– female	143	—	⎰	⎰	—	8
No. of students – male	1,134	—	57	3,438	90	134
– female	1,250	—	⎰	⎰	—	91
Adult education						
No. of schools	—	—	—	508	—	—
No. of teachers	—	—	—	1,548	—	—
No. of students	—	—	—	37,698	—	—
College education						
No. of teachers	n.a.	—	—	286	—	—
No. of students	886	—	—	1,893	—	—
Total no. of students (all levels, private and government institutions)	127,957	45,392	13,706	303,040	72,084	46,661
Students as % of population	27·4	31·7	30·5	7·6	1·4	4·2

Sources and Notes:

a Kuwait, Planning Board, *Statistical Abstract 1968*, Section Three, 'Education'. Data in Table are for 1967–8 and cover government schools only, as the enrolment in private schools is given only in total and not broken down by cycle of schooling. The private schools had 15,050 pupils in the year in question, or 13·4 per cent of total school enrolment. It is worth noting that girls represent 42·5 per cent of all pupils in government schools, and 46·7 per cent in the University of Kuwait. Kuwaiti teachers represent 10·6 per cent of all teachers in government schools. No breakdown is given for teachers in private schools. The size of the faculty of the University is likewise not given.

b Bahrain, Directorate of Education, *Education in Bahrain*, 1968. (In Arabic.) Data cover government education only for 1967–8. The first boys' school was opened in 1919; the first girls' school in 1928. The high ratio of students to population mostly reflects the energetic and continuous effort to expand education. In part it also arises from the likely underestimation of the population figure quoted in Table 1 above. The population was probably 183,000 in 1967–8.

c Qatar, Ministry of Education, *Report on Educational Developments 1966–1967*, July 1967. Data cover government schools for 1966–7. The position in 1967–8 was as follows:

Schools – all levels: 50 male,   35 female
Teachers – all levels: 596 male,   325 female
Students – all levels: 8,685 male,   5,651 female

The first girls' school was opened in 1955. The same comments apply here as in the case of Bahrain with regard to the high ratio of school enrolment to population. Qatar's population in 1966–7 was probably 55,000.

d Saudi Arabia, Ministry of Education, Directorate of Statistics and Research, *General Education Statistics for 1386–1387, 1966–7*. (In Arabic.) Data cover 1966–7 for government institutions. Female education in government and private institutions. Female education in government and private schools for 1966–7 is summarized below:

	Government	Private
No. of schools, all levels	233	33
No. of teachers, all levels	3,239	383
No. of students: Elementary	67,903	4,681
Intermediate	1,252	954
Secondary	129	365
Teachers' institutes	1,718	—
Technical institutes	158	—
Pre-college	—	2,488

(The government had no budget for girls' education before 1960.)

See General Directorate of Girls' Schools, Directorate of Statistics, *Statistical Directory of Saudi Girls' Education During Seven Years, 1380/1–1386/7*.
Private institutions include 6 schools, 121 teachers and 755 pupils in technical training, and 65 schools, 556 teachers, and 10,565 pupils in regular schooling.
There are altogether 5,809 students in night schools, the number of teachers is not stated in the source (*General Education Statistics 1386–1387*).
All university students are male.

e Yemen Republic, Ministry of Education, *Report for 1965–1966*. (In Arabic.) Data in table cover government and private schools, but the latter have 3·5 per cent only of the total number of students.
Bursaries abroad numbered 778 in 1965–6, about 40 per cent of whom were in UAR.

f People's Republic of Southern Yemen, Ministry of Education, *General Report 1967/1968*, data collected from various tables, and cover government institutions. Private institutions are of minor significance.

TABLE 3 – *Kuwait Government Officials According to Nationality and Educational Status in 1964*

Nationality	College or University		Secondary		Intermediate		Less than Intermediate		Literate		Illiterate		Total
	No.	%	No.	%	No.	%	No.	%	No.	%	No.	%	
Kuwaiti	180	1·6	366	3·2	895	8·0	979	8·7	5,943	52·7	2,911	25·8	11,274
Non-Kuwaiti	1,700	15·9	4,370	40·6	2,085	19·3	950	8·8	1,599	15·1	95	0·1	10,799
Total	1,880	8·5	4,736	21·5	2,980	13·5	1,929	8·7	7,542	34·2	3,006	13·6	22,073

Source: Kuwait, Planning Board, *Statistical Abstract 1964*, Table 36, p. 44

Note: Total number on government payroll (except army) was 60,820 in 1964, divided as follows (as in Table 37 pp. 42 and 43):

Officials:
    Kuwaiti   11,274
    Non-Kuwaiti 10,799
                 22,073

Employees:
    Kuwaiti   5,422
    Non-Kuwaiti 8,849
                 14,271

Labourers:
    Kuwaiti   4,296
    Non-Kuwaiti 20,180
                 24,476

Total all levels:
    Kuwaiti   20,982
    Non-Kuwaiti 39,838
                 60,820

INDEX